ADEN INSURGENCY

ADEN INSURGENCY

THE SAVAGE WAR IN YEMEN
1962-67

by

Jonathan Walker

Pen & Sword
MILITARY

First published in Great Britain in 2005 by
Spellmount Ltd

Reprinted in 2014 and 2018 by
Pen & Sword MILITARY
An imprint of
Pen & Sword Books Ltd
47 Church Street
Barnsley, South Yorkshire
S70 2AS

The right of Jonathan Walker to be identified as the Author of this work has been
asserted by him in accordance with the Copyright, Designs and Patents Act 1988.

A CIP catalogue record for this book is available from the British Library

Printed and bound in in Great Britain by CPI UK

Pen & Sword Books Limited incorporates the imprints of Atlas, Archaeology,
Aviation, Discovery, Family History, Fiction, History, Maritime, Military, Military
Classics, Politics, Select, Transport, True Crime, Air World, Frontline Publishing, Leo
Cooper, Remember When, Seaforth Publishing, The Praetorian Press, Wharncliffe
Local History, Wharncliffe Transport, Wharncliffe True Crime and White Owl.

For a complete list of Pen & Sword titles please contact
PEN & SWORD BOOKS LIMITED
47 Church Street, Barnsley, South Yorkshire, S70 2AS, England
E-mail: enquiries@pen-and-sword.co.ok
Website: www.pen-and-sword.co.uk

Contents

List of Maps		ix
Acknowledgements		xi
Oral Testimonies		xv
Introduction		xvii
I	The Kingdom of Sheba (Saba)	1
II	Federation	21
III	Empire Revived	41
IV	Operation 'Nutcracker'	71
V	The Radfan Campaign	93
VI	'Semper Occultus'	117
VII	Hearts and Minds	141
VIII	Hill Forts and Hunters	165
IX	Street Fighting	181
X	Front Page	201
XI	Panic in Whitehall	219
XII	Mutiny	239
XIII	Who's to Pay the Piper?	259
XIV	Epilogue	285
Appendix:	Tribes and States of South Arabia	301
Glossary of Terms and Abbreviations		303
Bibliography		307
Index		319

For my late father
Sir Gervas Walker

List of Maps

1   Aden – Staging Post for the Empire, 1945   3

2   States of South Arabia   23

3   The Middle East, 1962   43

4   Yemen: Situation September 1964   51

5   Dhala and The Radfan   75

6   Radfan Operations, 30 April–27 June 1964   95

7   Aden State   133

8   Aden and Khormaksar   143

9   Crater, 20 June 1967   246

10 Argylls' Entry into Crater, 3–4 July 1967   267

Acknowledgements

One of the rewarding aspects of researching a part of Britain's 'End of Empire' story is discovering the rich pool of personal experiences that can still be related first-hand. Many of the central participants, as well as those who played lesser parts in the South Arabian episode, have kindly recounted their experiences for this book. I would like to thank those I have listed at the end of my acknowledgements, for giving me a greater understanding of the life of British servicemen, officials and civilians during the Aden Insurgency.

I am especially indebted to Glencairn Balfour-Paul, who retains an encyclopaedic knowledge of the Middle East, for his hospitality and for imparting his knowledge of Britain's withdrawal from her Arab dependencies. My thanks also to another expert Arabist, Stephen Day, whose knowledge of the myriad tribes and terrain of South Arabia is unsurpassed. Ronald Bailey, another ex-ambassador from the Arab World, gave me valuable insights into the colourful pre-revolution Yemen.

General Sir John Waters and General Sir Richard Lawson pointed me towards useful sources and I am grateful for the benefit of their extensive knowledge. During his lifetime, I enjoyed many spirited discussions about South Arabia with Major-General John Cubbon and, although he left no papers, his son Robin has kindly provided background details. Major-General W B 'Sandy' Thomas did chronicle his role in the early years and has generously allowed me to quote from his records. Similarly, my appreciation for hospitality and advice from Brigadier Sir Louis Hargroves, who imbued me with tales of soldiering in the Radfan and left me in no doubt as to the ferocity of the enemy. Brigadier David Baines gave me much valuable advice and encouragement as well as important information on the 'horse gunners', while Lieutenant-Colonel John Jago helped me trace RHA veterans.

Curators and Archivists in Regimental Museums were generous with their limited time and resources, none more so than Colonel T Vines of The Prince of Wales's Own Regiment of Yorkshire. Colonel Dick Sidwell RM was, as ever, a most helpful source of information on the activities of the Royal Marines Corps. 'Four Five' Commando, Royal Marines were the longest serving unit in South Arabia and I am indebted to Colonel Robin McGarel Groves, a former Commanding Officer, for his assistance and recollections of operations.

The Rev. Robin Laird kindly helped with contacts and sources and convinced me – as if it was ever in doubt – that Army Padres have always provided invaluable support to soldiers in the front line as well as in reserve; that was certainly true in Aden and I am grateful for help given by The Office of the Deputy Assistant Chaplain-General.

My research was made easier by the help of Kate O'Brien at the Liddell Hart Centre for Military Archives, King's College, London. Hannah Watkins offered similar support at the British Empire & Commonwealth Museum, Bristol, and I am also grateful to Gill Spence and the staff of Sidmouth Library who supplied me with an endless stream of printed books on the Arabian Peninsula and insurgency warfare. My thanks also to Murray Graham for his help with the early story of Aden. His knowledge of BP's important role in this region brought me into contact with the BP Archive at the University of Warwick – an invaluable and often overlooked source. Peter Housego, the BP Archive Manager, was most helpful in granting permission to quote from their extensive records. My investigations into the Yemen civil war, as well as the Aden Insurgency were greatly assisted by records held in the Arab World Documentation Unit, University of Exeter. The Assistant Librarian, Ahmed Abu-Zayed, and his colleague Bobby Coles were most helpful in allowing me access to this splendid resource centre for research into all aspects of the Gulf region and Arab World.

I am indebted to Simon Tidswell for his knowledge on RAF sources and to those veterans, Chris Golds and David Malin of 43(F) Squadron, who described in vivid terms the exhilaration of flying one of the great classic aircraft. Mike Rudd of the Hunter Flying Club at Exeter Airport made time between Air Shows to demonstrate the mechanics and armaments of the Hawker Hunter, while Bob Douglas was generous in helping me with information on 84 Squadron as well as allowing me access to his extraordinary collection of regional maps.

Bryan Curryer was most helpful with police links, and through Joe Tildesley and the National Association of Retired Police Officers (NARPO) I was able to reach many ex-policemen and ex-servicemen who had served in Aden.

Ann Cuthbert coloured in my previously rather black and white views of civilian life in Aden. Her acute and amusing anecdotes brought light relief and balance to a story dominated by military operations. Barbara Binns provided very welcome material on medical services, and I am most grateful to Jasper Humphreys, Joe and Lindsay Roderick, Dr David Hall, Robin Knight-Bruce and Linda Kellett, all of whom gave me valuable support. The prolific author, David Foot, offered wise counsel as well as

ACKNOWLEDGEMENTS

encouragement, and I am also grateful to his fellow 'Pickwickian', Major Roddy Mellotte, for his sorties into the more discreet corridors of the Foreign Office.

Although the insurgency took place nearly forty years ago, the loss of a young son is never repaired: I am therefore indebted to Bill Rose and Pamela Davis for their frank and moving discussions with me concerning the loss of their sons, and for making their papers available.

I am grateful to the following for allowing me to examine or quote from archive material within their collections: The Trustees of the Liddell Hart Centre for Military Archives; The Arab World Documentation Unit, University of Exeter; British Petroleum Limited; The Trustees of the British Empire & Commonwealth Museum, Bristol. While Crown copyright still subsists in material held in the National Archives, Kew, London, since 1999 permission to publish extracts is not required in the case of documents unpublished at the time they were deposited.

For allowing permission for the reproduction of photographs, my thanks to the Trustees of the Photographic Archive, Imperial War Museum; Brigadier David Baines; Colonel David Smiley; Robin Cubbon; Pamela Davis; Terry Cheek; Bill Rose and Geoff Richards.

I acknowledge permission to quote passages from the following; to Macmillan Publishers Ltd for *At the End of the Day* by Harold Macmillan, and *One of the Originals* (Pan Books) by Johnny Cooper; Palgrave Macmillan for *Studies in International Security* (Chatto & Windus); David Higham Associates Ltd for *The Uneven Road* (John Murray) by R A B Hamilton; Susan Mitchell for *Having Been a Soldier* (Hamish Hamilton) by Lieutenant-Colonel Colin Mitchell; The Middle East Research and Information Project, Washington USA for *MERIP Reports*; The Royal United Services Institute for *RUSI Journal*; Spellmount Ltd for *The Royal Tank Regiment* by George Forty and *Soldier On! The Testament of a Tom* by Joe Starling; Robin Lunt for *The Barren Rocks of Aden* (Herbert Jenkins) by James Lunt; The Random House Group Ltd for *Open Secret: The Autobiography of the Former Director-General of MI5* (Hutchinson) by Stella Rimington; Ted Thomas for *Front Line* (Jonathan Cape) by Clare Hollingworth; Rt Rev. Michael Mann for *The Regimental History of 1st The Queen's Dragoon Guards*; HarperCollins Publishers Ltd for *Looking for Trouble* by General Sir Peter de la Billière; Colonel David Smiley for *Arabian Assignment* (Leo Cooper); Galago Publishing Ltd, SA for *See You in November: The Story of an SAS Assassin* by Peter Stiff. Every effort has been made to trace and obtain permission from copyright holders of material quoted or illustrations reproduced.

Regimental journals and magazines are a rich source of contemporary experiences and I wish to thank The Prince of Wales's Own Regiment of Yorkshire, The Royal Regiment of Artillery and The Queen's Lancashire Regiment for permission to quote extracts from their publications.

I would also like to thank Rear Admiral Nick Wilkinson, Secretary of the 'D' Notices Committee for his assistance and those in Whitehall and Cheltenham who read drafts of the typescript. Similarly I would like to thank Major-General David Thomson, Major Alastair Campbell and the Regimental Headquarters of the Argyll and Sutherland Highlanders for their constructive help and for the Trustees' permission to reproduce Peter Archer's painting, 'Argylls' Entry into Crater'. My appreciation also, to the Commanding Officer, 1st Regiment Royal Horse Artillery, for permission to use 'Action in South Arabia' by David Cobley. I should add that the views expressed are my own and none of the persons or establishments mentioned can be held responsible for any mistakes or omissions.

My appreciation also to my publisher Jamie Wilson and editor David Grant for their constructive help and advice.

Finally, my thanks to my wife Gill and my family for their unstinting help and support.

Jonathan Walker
2004

Oral Testimonies

I would like to thank the following who generously contributed their personal experiences of the Aden Insurgency or the events in Yemen 1962–7. Their rank or position at that time is shown in brackets:

Baines, Brigadier David, MBE (CO, 1 RHA)

Bailey, Ronald, CMG (HM Chargé d'Affaires, Taiz, Yemen 1960–2)

Beard, Nicholas (2nd Lieutenant, 60 Squadron, RCT)

Binns, Barbara (Ex-nurse)

Buchanan, Jim (Trooper, 45 Commando RM)

Carroll, Rev. Dr Robert (L/Cpl 1 Lancashire Regiment & Medical Orderly)

Cheek, Terry (L/Cpl, 1 Somerset and Cornwall Light Infantry)

Collings, Mervyn (Corporal, RAF Provost & Security Services)

Collings, Mary (Service wife)

Crook, Brigadier Paul, CBE, DSO, MA (Security Operations Advisor to High Commissioner)

Cubbon, Major-General John, CB, CBE (dec'd 1997), (GOC, MELF)

Cuthbert, Ann (Wife of Derek Cuthbert, Senior Plant Engineer, BP Ltd)

Day, Stephen, CMG (Assistant High Commissioner)

Douglas, Robert (Air Signaller, 84 Squadron)

Emson, Brigadier James, CBE (ADC to GOC MELF)

Fairholme, Bill (Aden Special Branch)

Fincher, Terry (Photo-journalist)

Finn, Jim (Acting Corporal, RAF Police)

Forde, Martin (Sergeant Pilot, 1st The Queen's Dragoon Guards)

Golds, Chris, AFC (Flight Lieutenant/Squadron Leader, 43(F) Squadron)

Graham, Murray (Executive, BP)

Hargroves, Brigadier Sir Louis, CBE, DL (Brigadier, 'Radforce' and Aden Brigade)

Hudson, Colonel Leslie, OBE, RM (Captain, Staff 24 Brigade)

Jones, Gareth (Acting Corporal, RAF Police)

Keeling, Major-General Andrew, RM (Mortar Officer, 45 Commando)

Lambe, Shaun (Lieutenant, 1 RHA)

Lawson, General Sir Richard, KCB, DSO, OBE (Chief of Staff, South Arabian Army)

Littlewood, Dr Mark (Medical Officer, BP Hospital)

Malcolm, John (Executive, Shell Oil)

Malin, David, DFC (Flight Lieutenant/Flight Commander, 43(F) Squadron)

Mallard, Brigadier John, TD (Commandant, Federal National Guard)

McGarel-Groves, Colonel Robin, OBE, RM (CO, 45 Commando)

Mogridge, Major Michael (dec'd 2004) Captain, 1 The Staffordshire Regiment)

Mort, Simon (2nd Lieutenant, 9th/12th Lancers)

Oates, Sir Thomas, CMG, OBE (Deputy High Commissioner, 1963–7)

Lady Prendergast (widow of Sir John, Director of Intelligence)

Ranft, Peter (Marine, 45 Commando RM)

Richards, Geoffrey (Superintendent Translator)

Roe, Rev. Robin, MC (Chaplain, 1 Lancashire Regiment)

Rudd, Michael (Chief Technician, RAF)

Russell, Charles (Corporal, 1st The Queen's Dragoon Guards)

Smiley, Colonel David, LVO, MC**, OBE (Military Advisor to Imam of Yemen)

Smith, Major Christopher RM (Adjutant, 45 Commando)

Tillotson, Major-General Michael, CB, CBE (Major, 1 Prince of Wales's Own Regiment of Yorkshire)

Thomson, Major-General David, CB, CBE, MC (Lieutenant, Intelligence Officer, 1 Argyll and Sutherland Highlanders)

Tower, Major-General Philip, CB, DSO, MBE (GOC, MELF)

Other confidential sources – retired members of Army, Air Force, Police and Civil Intelligence units.

Introduction

There is an unusual memorial to the fallen at Downside School in Somerset. In addition to a stone monument, there is a gallery of photographic portraits. As you pass along the gallery, bright, sepia toned subalterns from the Great War stare down. Apprehensive faces from the Second World War follow, and then those few from the small wars at the end of Empire. Until recently, there was no portrait for one boy who was killed in Aden.

As part of a project to update the war memorial, Major Roddy Mellotte sought to rectify the missing picture of Derek Rose. Further investigations produced a portrait and also a picture of Rose's funeral. His flag draped coffin was given a burial at sea from HMS *Appleton*, off the coast of Aden. Yet, Derek Rose was not a military man. Major Mellotte was intrigued and probed the Ministry of Defence to confirm Rose's exact rank or position, for inclusion in the memorial. The Ministry offered a number of vague job titles within the Foreign Office, but it was only after persistent requests that they finally admitted he had been a member of the Information Research Department (IRD). Rose's father Bill, who had spent the last war working on the 'Ultra' decoding operation, always had his suspicions that his son was working in the intelligence field but never felt it right to question his diplomatic cover. Now it was confirmed. Derek Rose had indeed been part of a secret war in South Arabia.

Denstone College War Memorial bears the name of another Aden casualty, but his rank and service in that bitter war was clear. Second Lieutenant John Davis was a regular soldier with the 1st Battalion, Royal Northumberland Fusiliers and he, like Rose, was killed at the end of the Aden Insurgency in 1967. Both brave young men met particularly brutal deaths in controversial circumstances. They were killed with many others in a savage war that often belied the term 'low intensity conflict', for it was a war that went beyond the shabby back streets and confines of the old Crown Colony of Aden. The fight was also contested in the wadis and mountains of the Radfan region to the north, and among the hill forts of the old Aden Protectorates – those wild and remote tribal areas of South Arabia, where British Advisory Treaties were notionally in force.

The insurgency in South Arabia started with agitation from nationalist and tribal elements but was soon fuelled by external forces. Aden may have lost its rationale when India became independent, but it soon found another role as the Cold War developed and Russia attempted to extend her influence in the Middle East.[1] Egypt, despite the anti-communist stance of her President, Gamel Abdul Nasser, was fast becoming a conduit for Russian arms and was susceptible to financial leverage. In 1962 Nasser attempted to create a client state in Yemen, the ancient kingdom to the north, in the hope of extending his influence throughout the Arabian Peninsula and gaining the ultimate prize of Saudi oil. As part of this strategy, Britain would have to be forcibly expelled from South Arabia. The 1962 republican coup in Yemen was followed by years of civil war, during which the British engaged in clandestine operations in support of the royalist cause – after the 1956 Suez fiasco, overt action against Arab countries was out of the question.

Historians often treat the Yemen Civil War as a separate conflict to the war in South Arabia. Yet Nasser's sponsorship of the revolution in Yemen gave heart to the radicals in the south and from 1962 onwards they felt that a united Yemen, comprising the northern and southern regions and without British influence, was a real possibility. Fear of this threat affected British military planners, and their operations in South Arabia were often allied to the need to keep supply lines open to the royalists in Yemen. The involvement of Egypt and Russia thus elevated the conflict beyond a regional squabble to the chess board of the Cold War. Consequently, although the official 'State of Emergency' was declared on 10 December 1963, this study covers the insurgency from 1962 to 1967 when British troops finally withdrew.

This account of the military operations spans both conventional mountain warfare in the hinterland, and internal security duties in and around Aden State – two very different deployments. As the security situation deteriorated, conflicts in command emerged, especially over the handling of the later Crater operations.[2] It was also a time when the British Army found its role was changing. Troops arriving in South Arabia found they were expected to be both soldier and policeman, a role which years in the British Army of the Rhine had barely prepared them for. Tensions arose among some regimental officers and their men who felt that their job of soldiering was compromised by 'blue warning cards' and 'no-go' areas. Consequently, a study of military operations cannot be complete without consideration of the political constraints placed upon senior Commanders. For decades the Royal Air Force was the instrument of British policy in the region and its contribution during the years of the insurgency cannot be overstated. The Intelligence Services played a similarly vital role, both inside and outside South Arabia, but their problems and vulnerability in the face of a ruthless enemy had a serious effect on the outcome of the conflict. But the bloody climax of the insurgency and the speed of the Federation's collapse surprised everyone except the hardened cynics.

When Lieutenant-Colonel (later Sir Julian) Paget wrote a study of the military operations in Aden and South Arabia, *Last Post: Aden 1964–1967* in 1969, the conflict was a recent controversy and the Cold War was very much alive. Although the book was dedicated to the men who fought there, it was a semi-official history of the conflict.[3] Over forty years later, issues surrounding the insurgency are still contentious but the passage of time has allowed more subjective views to evolve. Also, under the 'thirty-year rule', many previously confidential records have now been placed into the public archives. While these records have provided the bulk of the primary sources for this study, they have been treated with caution. Such placements are still made selectively by government, and many files have been heavily weeded and are still subject to recall.[4] Nevertheless, the official papers on Aden and South Arabia released since 1997 give a clearer picture of the motives and constraints behind the military operations. The 1993 White Paper on Open Government, launched after an initiative by William Waldegrave and Douglas Hurd, also fostered a new openness over certain intelligence matters.[5] While the Secret Intelligence Service (SIS), popularly known as MI6, still do not release files into the public domain, those files released by the Secret Service (MI5), Joint Intelligence Committee (JIC)[6] and Defence Intelligence Staff (DIS) enable the mechanics of the 'secret war' to be pieced together.

Oral testimony supplements this written evidence and colours the personalities, and although some of the Commanders and their men have since died, it seems an opportune time to record the opinions of those surviving participants.

The British Army had an impossible task. However, against a background of shifting loyalties, and political ineptitude, the battalions, many of whom would lose their identities in the forthcoming amalgamations, proved remarkably resilient. They adapted to the new way of campaigning, fighting alongside photo-journalists and television cameras. The tactics to combat urban guerrilla warfare, already experienced in Palestine and Cyprus, were honed in the streets of Crater. But in the end, it was alleged that South Arabia was the only insurgency war that the British Army ever lost. If they were not defeated in the field, what went so terribly wrong?

NOTES

1   One of the main preoccupations of British Foreign Policy in the Middle East was the fear of Russian expansion in the Arabian Peninsula. See Joint Intelligence Committee, 'Likely Developments in the Arabian Peninsula', 4

December 1957, CAB 158/30, National Archives (formerly Public Record Office), Kew, London (hereafter NA).

2   Crater was the main commercial district of the Colony of Aden. Situated within the bowl of an extinct volcano, this Arab township became the scene of an Armed Police mutiny in June 1967.

3   Lieutenant-Colonel Julian Paget was CO Coldstream Guards and Head of the Security Secretariat in Aden during 1965. He has had a wealth of first-hand experience in insurgency situations and has written widely on the subject.

4   Many files within the PREM series, NA, placed in the public domain during the 1990s, were recalled as recently as 2001–3, with papers and sections retained under Section 3 (4), Public Record Act 1958. Some selected records relating to South Arabia will remain secret for a further thirty years.

5   Richard J Aldrich, 'Grow Your Own: Cold War Intelligence and History Supermarkets', *Intelligence and National Security* (Spring 2002) pp. 135–52. This issue contains papers from a research conference held in 2001 at the National Archives, Kew, London, 'The Missing Dimension? British Intelligence in the 20th Century'. Additional papers submitted by Sir Stephen Lander (DG MI5) and Gill Bennett on the declassification policies of UK Intelligence Agencies.

6   The JIC comprises the heads of the four intelligence agencies, the chairman and deputy of the Assessments Staff, the head of the Permanent Under-Secretary's Department, FCO, and the Co-ordinator of Intelligence and Security.

After decades of dictatorships in the Middle East, the dynamics of the region are changing. Fired by a desire for democracy, popular revolutions have taken place in Tunisia, Libya and Egypt, though the outcomes are still uncertain. Syria and Iraq are currently consumed by civil war and the threat from forces of the Islamic State. In Yemen, there are constant threats to the government from rebel tribes and southern separatists. In all these countries the internet and mobile phones have spread ideas far wider than the reach of Nasser's transistor radios in the 1960s.

However, the wave of unrest is unlikely to break evenly across the Arab world. The conditions inside Yemen still remain hostile to change. The harsh geography of the country still restricts the reach of central government and the forces of separatism remain strong. Tribalism and blood feuds are constituents of daily life, alongside grinding poverty. Nonetheless, the focus will remain on Yemen, for not only is it strategically placed, but increasingly it has become a control centre for Al-Qaeda operations, notwithstanding the death of Osama bin-Laden in 2011.

Before she left southern Yemen in 1967, Britain was ridiculed for attempting to impose a very limited form of democracy on an intensely tribal and sectarian country. Despite the omens, it is to be hoped that new progressive forces within Yemen will fare better in the years ahead.

October 2014

CHAPTER I

The Kingdom of Sheba (Saba)

To the British servicemen and women who served in South Arabia in the 1960s, the abiding memory is the heat. Intense, searing and unrelenting, it hit you as soon as the aircraft doors were opened after touchdown at Aden's Khormaksar airport. Other memories are of the squalid townships, the baboons and the vast forbidding mountains. There are also the memories of friends, and the bonds that were forged under fire; flashbacks of street patrols and ambushes; the assassinations and indiscriminate killings; the comrades who still lie in Silent Valley Cemetery.

However, the story of the bitter conflict in South Arabia, or the 'Aden Insurgency' as it became known, goes far beyond these images. Geographically, the war ranged wider than the old colony and military base of Aden and enveloped the south-west of the Arabian Peninsula. This included the wild and remote interior, known as the Protectorate,[1] and also the adjacent kingdom of Yemen. Yet in popular histories, the whole area is often described as Aden, which as one historian has pointed out, is rather like referring to England as London.[2]

Apart from strategic and commercial necessities, the British had always held an emotional attachment to the region. The spell of 'Arabia Felix', as the Romans called the land, was indeed seductive: for despite the harsh wastes of the Rub' al Khali (Empty Quarter), the coastal areas and mountains had a startling beauty.[3] It was also an area of great antiquity and historical importance, and the coastal regions had claim to strong biblical connections. Allegedly, Yemen was once ruled by a monarch descended from Noah, and it also formed part of the kingdom of Saba (Sheba), which was ruled by the Queen of Sheba, a figure who has continued to fascinate artists and romantics through the ages.[4] However, it was the hope of commercial and strategic gain rather than the quest for exploration or archaeology that first brought the British to Aden and South Arabia.

The area was once part of the ancient incense route. Myrrh and frankincense trees grew wild in Yemen, as well as in southern Oman, but as these trees were impossible to cultivate elsewhere, the funereal incense obtained from them became a valuable source of revenue. Caravans

1

bringing spices from the East travelled through Yemen, collecting the incense, before heading north to the great Mediterranean markets.[5]

Later, during the 16th century, the Ottomans vied with the Portuguese for control of the region. However, the following century saw traditional local power bases reassert themselves. In the northern region of Yemen, the religious leader, or Imam, of the Zaydi sect, who had exerted local control since the 10th century, became the main power broker, while the south was ruled by numerous tribal fiefdoms headed by sheikhs. Serious British trade contact with South Arabia started in 1618, with the great coffee boom, and the East India Company set up a trading post at Mokha, on the Red Sea, to export the commodity. Although coffee originated in Yemen, by 1770 competition from the plantations in the West Indies forced coffee prices down and the Red Sea area became an economic backwater. However, with the rise of British power and influence in India, the small settlement of Aden and its hinterland took on a strategic importance as a halfway base. Furthermore, in 1798 Napoleon Bonaparte captured Egypt, which threatened British influence in the Red Sea, and consequently her sea route to India. The French were soon ejected from Egypt, but British military planners still feared for their return, as the French continued to influence Muhammad Ali, a future ruler of Egypt, who by 1833 had extended his control to cover Sudan and the greater part of Yemen.[6]

Because India was the jewel of the Empire, it became of prime importance for Britain to protect Indian maritime routes. Until the advent of steam navigation in the mid 19th century, the journey around the Cape took five months, but the new steamships could reduce the journey to two months by using the Mediterranean and Red Sea. However, that was dependent on the provision of a coaling station on the South Arabian coast. There was little doubt as to who should be responsible for the station: it lay closest to Bombay, on India's west coast. Bombay, like the other two 'Presidencies', or regional governments of India, had its own sphere of Imperial control and although subservient to London, it could still act on its own initiative. Consequently, the Bombay Presidency commissioned Commander Stafford Haines, a surveyor in the Indian Navy, to identify a suitable site for the station. Haines selected the small peninsula of Aden, on the south-west coast of Arabia. With its safe harbour, it was an ideal location, but as it was still formally under the control of the nearby Sultan of Lahej, Haines needed a pretext to occupy the settlement. In 1838 a large Indian sailing ship, the *Duria Dowlet*, was plundered by the townspeople of Aden. This provided an excuse and soon the British enforced a blockade. A series of skirmishes between Arabs and British troops followed and in January 1839 a force, consisting of the Bombay Regiment and 24th Regiment Bombay Native Infantry, stormed the town and captured it, for the loss of only fifteen men. Aden

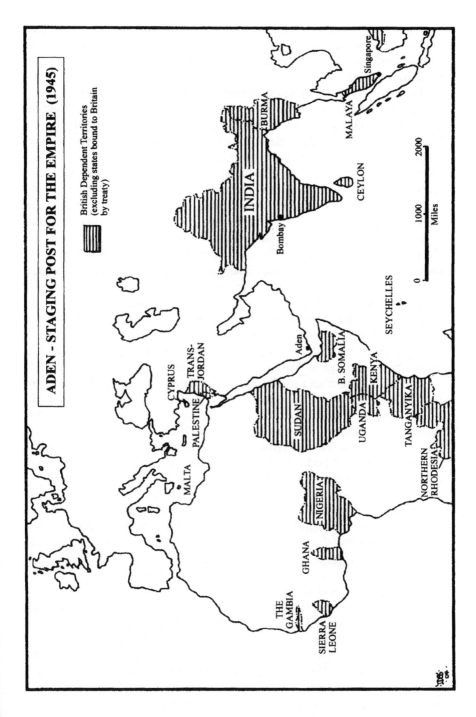

ADEN - STAGING POST FOR THE EMPIRE (1945)

British Dependent Territories
(excluding states bound to Britain
by treaty)

3

was the first acquisition of Queen Victoria's reign and would remain part of the Empire for the next 128 years. It was also unique in that it became Britain's only Arab colony and a colony in which there was only limited white settlement.[7]

The Aden that Haines knew covers an area of approximately twenty square miles and lies 100 miles to the east of the entrance to the Red Sea. There are two large bays on either side, dominated by Jebel Shamsan, a towering mountain that rises to over 1,700 feet and whose only inhabitants are crows and baboons. On the eastern side of the peninsula lies the old town that was developed as the main commercial centre, built within the bowl of an extinct volcano, and aptly named Crater. On the western side, the township of Ma'alla adjoins Steamer Point and the port. Three miles to the west is the promontory of Little Aden, which, together with a strip of mainland, combined with Haines's Aden to form the Crown Colony of Aden, officially created in 1937. The colony only measured a total of seventy-five square miles compared to the surrounding hinterland, which became known as the Protectorate, which covered over 112,000 square miles. This interior was nearly the size of England and Scotland and ran 700 miles along the coast of South Arabia.

Despite Haines's commercial aspirations, Aden was essentially a strategic prize for Britain. Like the later seizure of Cyprus in 1878 and occupation of Egypt in 1882, it maintained the lines of communication with India.[8] It was also a useful stepping-off base for military expeditions into Africa, such as the Bombay Expeditionary Force, commanded by Sir Robert Napier, which defeated the Abyssinians at Magdala in 1868.[9] Sixteen years later, the British were formally in control of British Somaliland, in the 'horn of Africa', and when combined with the island of Perim, which they had occupied to combat French designs, gave them control of the entrance to the Red Sea.

The opening of the Suez Canal in 1869 ushered in a new era of prosperity for Aden. In order to protect her new acquisition, Britain sought to extend her influence to the hinterland of South Arabia, as a buffer against the Turks who had reoccupied Yemen in 1871. Sheikh Othman, a small settlement about ten miles inland from Aden town, was soon acquired, while in the interior, a series of 'Protective treaties' were signed with 'whoever appeared to be the main leader, of what appeared to be the dominant tribe, in any given area'.[10] The tribal leaders in the Protectorate attempted to keep roads and passes open, in return for stipends paid in Maria Theresa *thalers* (dollars) or rifles and ammunition.[11] This seemed to keep a limited sense of order in the ill-defined border territory between Yemen and the Protectorate, allowing the Aden garrison of 1,500 men to remain within the town walls. It was a principle that was successfully repeated elsewhere in the Empire. Through treaties with the British, Indian principalities and the sultanates of Malaya enjoyed an independence from the Crown, which meant they could continue as native monarchs.[12]

Meanwhile, Britain was able to extend her domination over two-thirds of the coastal region of the Arabian Peninsula, or *al-Jazira* as it was known to the Arabs. This lasted until the outbreak of the Great War in 1914. However, while the competing armies on the Western Front swiftly dug in and formed static trench lines, the war in South Arabia knew no front line. In fact, it was chaotic and control over British deployments was poor, resulting in a less than distinguished campaign.

In November 1914 the 29th Indian Brigade, en route through the Red Sea to Egypt, was diverted, in order to attack Turkish positions at the entrance to the Red Sea. Light damage was done to Turkish forts, but unfortunately the action enraged the Turks and their host in Yemen, Imam Yahya.[13] As a consequence, the Aden authorities, who had never sanctioned the action, were soon greeted by some 5,000 Turks crossing into Dhala, in the Aden hinterland, and threatening Aden itself. On 3 July 1915 the Turks defeated the forces of the loyal Sultan of Lahej, but were then confronted by the 1,000-strong Aden Movable Column. This column comprised mainly Indian units and artillery but also included 400 men from the 1st Brecknockshires, the Territorial Battalion of the South Wales Borderers. This unit of volunteers had already suffered four deaths from sickness in several months of garrison duty in Aden, and they now succumbed to the intense heat. As they marched the nineteen miles to Lahej to meet the Turks, over 300 of the Territorials fell out through exhaustion, leaving the rest to stall the enemy advance from a small defensive position in Lahej. It was a hopeless task, made even worse for the Welshmen by the desertion of their local bearers, who made off with the water and ammunition.[14]

Every one of the seven Ford motor cars that Aden possessed were hastily requisitioned, packed with ice, and sent out to the desert to relieve the troops. But the cars became stuck in the sand. Reinforcements were then sent up from Aden and were greeted by their ally, the Sultan of Lahej, who rode towards them to warn them of enemy dispositions. He was mistaken for a Turk and promptly shot dead. The survivors fell back through Sheikh Othman, and left it open to the advancing Turkish Army, who were no doubt delighted to find it contained a number of legendary brothels. It was fortunate for the hapless Resident (Governor) of Aden, Brigadier-General Charles Price, that there was enough British naval firepower offshore to dissuade the Turks from assaulting the town of Aden; for he had placed all his guns facing out to sea. Panic soon set in when Turkish scouting parties ventured onto the isthmus in front of the town. The famous alarm, 'The Turks are on the golf course', was swiftly cabled to London. Despite the comic appeal of the Turks failing to understand golfing etiquette, there was enough concern in London for the able General Sir George Younghusband to be dispatched from Egypt, with a relief force, to stabilise the British front line.[15]

The opposing armies maintained their approximate positions throughout the rest of the war. Due to manpower shortages on other fronts, the British Government refused to supply further reinforcements to retake the Aden hinterland. Remembering the disaster in Lahej in 1915, Younghusband was reluctant to risk an offensive with his limited resources, so had to content himself with attempts to subvert the Imam in his Yemen territory. Meanwhile, Younghusband's forces were re-formed into two new brigades. The old Movable Column became the Aden Infantry Brigade and the units under the direct command of the General Officer Commanding (GOC), were now known as the Aden Field Force. From September 1917 to February 1918 they were engaged in a series of skirmishes in which they lost over 300 men, but thereafter, losses were minimal until November 1918 when 176 men died as a result of the flu pandemic.[16]

The end of the war saw the collapse of the Ottoman Empire and the final withdrawal of the Turkish army from Yemen. Imam Yahya immediately attempted to reassert his authority and to lay permanent claim to those parts of the Aden hinterland captured by the Turks in 1915. In fact, he did not recognise any part of the tenuous border between Yemen and the Protectorate and throughout the early 1920s he managed to control large tribal areas of the border region. British diplomacy, which went hand in hand with buying tribal loyalty with bribes and rifles, failed to keep Imam Yahya in check. He was an autocratic and belligerent ruler, but a man who brought prosperity, and by Yemeni standards, some semblance of order to a wild country. Captain R A B Hamilton, a legendary political officer and Commander of the Aden Protectorate Levies (APL), described the Imam as 'a short stout man, with a beard trimmed to a "fisherman's fringe", and possessing a harsh voice'. However, Yahya was also a skilful operator and an adept handler of tribal feuds and intrigues. To gain the upper hand, the British were in need of a more novel strategy.[17]

By 1926 the financial burden caused the London Government to seriously consider abandoning their claim to all but the immediate hinterland around Aden.[18] However, the sight of Imam Yahya dallying with not only Russian, but more worryingly, Italian diplomats, caused the British to think again. Progressive officials such as Sir Bernard Reilly, started to push British policy towards expansion rather than contraction in the Protectorate. But it was the advent of air power which really brought about this change of heart.[19] Development of the aeroplane rapidly accelerated during The Great War and its role had expanded from reconnaissance to fighter and bomber operations. So, by the early 1920s, it was possible for Britain to exert authority over parts of the Empire, largely by air control, without resorting to full-scale occupation on the ground.

This had the appeal of reducing defence expenditure while at the same time giving a very visible display of power to those who might oppose the British writ. In 1920 air control was successfully applied in British Somaliland, and during the following year, in the mandated territory of Mesopotamia (Iraq), the Royal Air Force took over control from an expensive army garrison.[20]

Aden and the Protectorate were similar territories to Iraq, with large featureless deserts and arid mountain ranges. Consequently, the success in Somaliland and Iraq and the prospect of more financial savings encouraged the experiment of air control to be repeated. In 1927 the Air Ministry assumed responsibility for the defence of South Arabia, initially using No. 8 Squadron as its active arm. Captain R A B Hamilton, described a typical bombing operation carried out in retaliation for a tribal murder on the roads:

> The Air Staff would work in the closest contact with the political officer. It was my task, equipped with a portable wireless set, to camp as close to the scene of operations as I considered possible, so as to facilitate the surrender of the tribe and to reduce the extent of the operations to a minimum. Two, and one-day warnings were dropped on the tribe, followed by an hour's warning before the first attack, so that women and children could be taken to a place of safety and every effort was made to inflict losses in property rather than lives.[21]

This concept of 'proscription' bombing meant that once the leaflets had been dropped, all humans and livestock were legitimate targets within the proscribed area, but care was taken to exclude women and children. In addition, the RAF would occasionally have to bomb or strafe rebel tribesmen, and while this was straightforward while they were at arm's length and in open terrain, it was too late if the enemy had advanced too close to friendly forces. Consequently, the RAF had to receive early warning of rebel movements. This required good intelligence, and could only be achieved by putting more political officers out into the field, together with an increase in scouts and military patrols.[22] This increased activity in the mountains of the Protectorate resulted in the construction of a large number of landing strips to cope with the increase in air traffic. These, in turn, needed guarding.

The Aden garrison, which consisted of one British and one Indian battalion, was clearly insufficient for the job. There was little desire to build up the force to division strength, so the Aden Protectorate Levies (APL) was formed to recruit suitable local Arabs from the tribal areas.[23] They had British officers and were trained according to British military methods, to defend the Protectorate. Tribesmen, who had spent years robbing and killing each other, were now recruited in return for regular pay and a smart uniform. Other local forces which were raised before the Second World War, such as the Government Guards (frontier) and the Tribal Guards (sheikh's personal retinue), were very much irregulars, but few needed instructions on how to fire a rifle.

To many Britons, thirsty for tales of adventure and daring, the APL and the desert world became part of the romantic legend of South Arabia. The region had much to recommend it, especially as it contained one of the last unexplored areas on earth. The Rub' al Khali, which spanned the borders of Saudi Arabia and the Protectorate, was the world's largest sand desert and it was reputed to contain the ruins of the lost city of Ubar. The quest for this discovery led to a host of British explorers and adventurers travelling across the Empty Quarter. In the 1930s Bertram Thomas and St John Philby crossed the wastes, and later in 1948 Wilfred Thesiger, a Special Air Service (SAS) veteran of the Western Desert, travelled with *Bedu* across the 400 miles of waterless desert.[24] The neighbouring kingdom of Yemen attracted other inquisitive men, like the Hon. Aubrey Herbert, who on arrival was greeted by the sight of an old criminal who had been fettered to the ground for forty years. Hugh Scott, the celebrated entomologist, recorded similar eccentricities when he arrived in Yemen in 1938, seeing the elderly Imam being carted to prayers in a massive four-wheeled carriage, accompanied by dancing bodyguards wielding huge umbrellas.

However, the 'spell of Arabia' did not captivate everyone. R A B Hamilton, who, as the Master of Belhaven later wrote about his experiences as a political officer, described this spell as 'a sickness of the imagination'.[25] Neither did the Hadhramaut region to the east impress the writer Vita Sackville-West, who described it as 'a salty hell'. But it did prove irresistible to several other doughty female adventurers. The writer and traveller Freya Stark made two celebrated journeys, clad in breeches and floppy hat and transported by either camel or donkey, the latter being steadier for taking photographs. Doreen Ingrams, wife of Harold Ingrams, the political officer, made similar explorations and produced a remarkable survey of local life and customs.[26]

During the 1930s there were moves to make the Bombay Government, and eventually the whole Government of India, autonomous. Aden, which in 1932 had come under the control of the Central Government of India, would be an awkward accessory to a federal India and administratively it made sense for Aden and the hinterland to be transferred to direct control by Britain. Consequently, in 1937 the settlement of Aden (comprising the Aden peninsula, Sheikh Othman and Little Aden) became a Crown Colony, with its own Governor.[27] At the same time, the hinterland, which, unlike Aden Colony, had always suffered from a lack of a development policy, was formally divided into a Western Aden Protectorate (WAP) with a 'British Agent' and an Eastern Aden

Protectorate (EAP) with its own 'Resident Advisor'. The Colonial Office now controlled both Protectorates, and it was hoped that increased investment would follow. The infrastructure in the Protectorates was in a dire state, with the Chief Commissioner, Lieutenant-Colonel (later Sir Bernard) Reilly, admitting that even the roads in Yemen were in a better state than in the Protectorates.[28]

South Arabia was largely untouched by the Second World War. In Yemen, Imam Yahya announced that he had been courted by Hitler and received presents from him, but turned down a treaty with Germany and maintained a policy of neutrality. However, he did make overtures to the Italians, who posed a threat to the British in South Arabia from their base across the Red Sea in Ethiopia. In the event, the British shot down the odd Italian plane, and there was the occasional Italian bombardment of Steamer Point, but as always it was the internal tribal disruption in South Arabia that occupied the local forces.[29] These forces were bolstered by the formation of the Hadhrami Bedouin League (HBL), just before the outbreak of war. Established to offer an academic, as well as military education, the HBL drew its recruits from the most influential families of the Hadhramaut region in the EAP, to act as a security force for the British Resident Advisor.[30]

By the end of the war in 1945, Aden and the Protectorates found them-selves host to numerous military and aviation formations. The RAF exercised control of Aden and the Protectorates from HQ British Forces, at Steamer Point. This was one of six subordinate HQs that came under the overall control of Middle East Command, based in Cairo. The main operational centre for Aden was at Khormaksar airfield, four miles from Aden town, where 621 Squadron (Wellingtons) was initially based.[31]

Virtually all infantry battalions then serving in South Arabia were from the Indian Army. But illustrious names such as the Punjab Regiment and the Hyderabad Lancers would soon be a distant memory, for within two years of the end of the war India was independent. As a consequence, vast numbers of Indians would no longer contribute to Empire defence and therefore the need for conscription, or National Service as it became known, would have to continue long after the Second World War had ended. Britain was still a great power, but in the words of Lord Alanbrooke, 'the loss of India will leave a great gap in the jigsaw puzzle of Empire defence'.[32]

One of the important remaining pieces of that jigsaw was of course Aden. For despite a barren treasury after the huge demands of the war, Britain still sought to preserve her pre-eminence in the Arab world: Aden was the gateway to the Red Sea; Egypt was now the barrier to Soviet expansion in Africa, and the Suez Canal remained Britain's jugular vein. In addition, the reconstruction of post-war Britain would need Middle Eastern oil.[33]

9

As the British Mandate in Palestine ended in 1948, the Arab world vented its anger against Britain who it incorrectly alleged had sided with the Jews. There was widespread rioting in Baghdad and other Arab capitals; and in Aden, Jews were attacked in Crater and Sheikh Othman. Even in times of peace, the Arab population of Aden had resented the Jewish residents, whose small population was further reduced by mass emigration to the new state of Israel. So severe was the rioting in Aden, that two British battalions had to be moved down from Egypt to help maintain the declared State of Emergency. The same year, there was turmoil in Yemen, but the cause was radically different.

On the morning of 17 February 1948 the 80-year-old Imam Yahya was assassinated. However, his heir, Ahmed, moved swiftly to claim the Imamate, and within a month Ahmed had despatched thirty of his father's conspirators, by employing a large grinning slave to behead them in public in the great square at Hajjah.[34]

The new Imam Ahmed started his reign by blaming Britain for his father's death, and claiming that dissident groups, such as 'The Free Yemeni' movement, were sponsored by the British administration in Aden. To enforce his message, he ignored the 1934 Sana'a Treaty and contested the border region. But Britain, too, exacerbated the old contest by allowing an oil exploration party to test for oil in the disputed and sensitive border area of Shabwa.[35] However, the border incursions by Yemeni tribesmen continued, and throughout 1949 and 1950 No. 8 Squadron RAF was occupied in bombing rebellious tribesmen and demolishing illegally built Yemen forts within the Protectorates.[36] The squadron flew several operational sorties with its new Brigand B1 light bomber, firing 60lb rocket projectiles (RPs) against forts at Naqd Marqad and Wadi Hatib. Even though it only had an establishment of eight Brigands, No. 8 Squadron was the sole operational unit covering Aden, the Persian Gulf and East Africa. While there were three supporting communications units, it was combat planes that were distinctly lacking, and both pilots and logistical support became severely stretched.[37] Most flying activity was in support of ground operations, which usually involved the APL, but from 1948 until 1957 the Levies ceased to be under the control of the Army and came under the RAF. The Air Force found themselves increasingly involved in ground operations, with units such as No. 10 Squadron manning as well as maintaining their Ferret Mark II armoured cars.[38]

Meanwhile, outside the Arabian Peninsula, the proclamation of the People's Republic of China in 1949, followed by the outbreak of the Korean War in 1950, concentrated the mind of the United States on the communist threat to the Far East. It was anticipated that if American and British forces were drawn towards the Chinese threat, then the Soviets would launch an attack on Western Europe. For the years leading up to

Suez in 1956, the Americans were pre-occupied with these twin threats and largely left the Middle East alone. Britain continued to exert considerable influence in the Middle East but, in common with all colonial powers, Britain's interests were being increasingly challenged in the early 1950s by local nationalist unrest. While Britain became occupied with the Mau Mau campaign in Kenya, these 'winds of change' were blowing towards South Arabia, where two crucial events would have a profound effect on Britain's position.[39]

When the 'Free Officers' movement, led by Gamal Abdel Nasser, ousted King Farouk in 1952, it encouraged nationalist sentiments throughout the Arab world. The British Government was already in conflict with Farouk over his abrogation of the 1936 Anglo–Egyptian Treaty, and Nasser soon made his nationalist intentions clear, with the export of his revolution high on his agenda.[40] As part of this policy, young Arab students from other countries, including Yemen, were to be educated in Cairo on government scholarships. One of these students was Abdul Aziz Addali, who later became a Yemeni Government Minister. He recalled the heady atmosphere in Cairo:

> I think we started to recognise the huge difference between our country and what we saw outside our country. It was in Egypt that we learned about the 1948 coup against the Imam. The Yemeni students in Cairo discussed its failure, and how to rescue our country from such backwardness. We were pushed to think in new directions by the fact that our education was not through official channels because we had fled the country. We started contact with students from other countries. We started knowing much about the outside world. Then we organised ourselves, taking the example of the other students. We immediately gravitated to political activities. I came back frequently to my village in the North [Yemen] and to Aden, and those visits were more than to say hello. We were trying to contact people about revolution.[41]

In the same way that many of the nationalist leaders in Algeria and South-East Asia cultivated their radical ideologies in the Parisian lycées, so many Cairo educated Yemenis developed plans for revolt in their homeland. It was reported that there were over 300 Yemeni children in Egyptian secondary schools, and 100 Yemeni students at Cairo University. The contacts that were made by these students, especially those developed with the Egyptian Intelligence Service, would come to fruition in the 1960s.[42] This process was aided from the early 1950s by a steady stream of nationalist and radical literature, emanating from Egypt, which found its way into Aden and the Protectorates.

Another tool of the Egyptian revolution was the infamous Cairo Radio.

At a time when transistor radios were becoming widely available, even to poor Yemeni tribesmen, 'The Voice of the Arabs' was an extremely effective propaganda weapon.

Meanwhile, the other event of the early 1950s that was crucial to developments in South Arabia, was the installation of the British Petroleum (BP) refinery. Even before the loss of its Anglo–Iranian operation, due to Musaddeq's nationalisation in 1951, BP decided to build another refinery to supply oil to the markets, and for shipping between Africa and India. A site was selected at Little Aden, across the bay from Crater, but it required a huge civil engineering commitment to construct a strong breakwater, reclaim 200 acres of land, and dredge a deep-water channel. When the refinery was finally completed in 1954, it boasted a staff of 250 British and 1,500 Arab and Indian workers. Although in later years this workforce would be halved, the refinery was still the largest industry in the area and required mostly skilled and semi-skilled labour. Most of this labour came in from Yemen and was consequently open to political manipulation from the Yemen authorities. This unionised labour force became the biggest social problem for the government in Aden through-out the decade. The refinery also generated local 'white-collar' businesses such as banks, insurance companies and wharf offices, all of which attracted young men from elsewhere, susceptible to radical ideas. The irony was that BP's arrival in Aden heralded great opportunities for the colony, but much of the organised labour it attracted would one day play a part in the nationalist revolt.[43]

While Aden had its role to play in refining and transporting oil, the Arabian Peninsula as a whole offered Britain access to oil deposits that she desperately needed in order to rebuild her economy after the Second World War. Oil production in the Gulf had grown at an extraordinary rate, from 15 million tons in 1938 to 157 million tons in 1955 and the region provided Britain with over half her oil requirements. While there was the possibility of oil deposits in the Eastern Aden Protectorate, enough to interest the Arabian American Oil Company (ARAMCO), Britain's real prize was Kuwait.[44]

Whenever oil was on the agenda, relations between America and Saudi Arabia on one side, and Britain and her acolytes in the Arabian Peninsula, on the other side, rapidly deteriorated: for as long as Saudi Arabia had been a poor country, her ruler Ibn Saud was content to leave British influence unchallenged. However, the discovery of oil changed that, and Ibn Saud's successors, Saud and Feisal, with the backing of both the American government and ARAMCO, sought to reduce Britain's influence in the Arabian Peninsula. In 1956 Saudi Arabia broke off diplomatic relations with Britain, ostensibly because of Suez, but the real reason was a dispute over a suspected oil deposit near the Buraimi Oasis.[45] The Buraimi dispute was a small incident, but it became a running sore, especially as it followed on from earlier ARAMCO incursions into the British EAP. America was determined to strengthen her grip on oil concessions in the peninsula and vitriol continued to pour out of the State Department in Washington. In front of British diplomats, the Secretary of State, John Foster Dulles would grip the arms of his office chair, until the whites of his knuckles showed, and roundly condemn 'British aggression'.[46]

Suez had exposed the widening gap between the United States and Britain over the issue of influence in the Middle East. The US had traditionally played a neutralist and 'honest broker' role between the British and Arab nations, but Palestine had caused a temporary rift in 1948, and the growing vocal Jewish lobby in America, coupled with an ever-growing dependence on imported oil, caused the United States to see the Middle East as an important region that was worth wresting from Britain. Although the Jewish lobby stopped the US supplying arms directly to Egypt, the American State Department continued to court Nasser.[47] Foster Dulles saw Nasser as a better deterrent to the communist threat in the Middle East than any British inspired pacts, and through the American Embassy in Cairo told Nasser as much. The American Central Intelligence Agency (CIA), controlled by Foster Dulles' brother Alan, had established contact with Nasser, even before his coup in 1952, and now the Cairo CIA station chief, James Eichelberger, encouraged further links with Nasser. Even the American Ambassador in Cairo, Jefferson Caffery, was 'malevolently anti-British', and the American Government was soon supplying wheat and oil to Egypt, allowing Nasser to fund future external military adventures.[48] Overall, US policies during Suez were more damaging to British interests than those of Nasser, as Miles Copeland, a senior CIA officer, observed:

> If he [Nasser] had to be 'anti' anything (and he did, in accordance with the principle that it's easier to rally followers against something than for something); we preferred that it be 'imperialism' rather than Israel.[49]

American pressure over Suez was resented by sections of the British Government, who hated Nasser with a passion. Anthony Eden, the Prime Minister at the time of the crisis, felt that Nasser was a threat to world peace, with 'his thumb on our windpipe'. Furthermore, Eden was determined to 'knock Nasser off his perch' and wished it known that he wanted Nasser 'destroyed', though the British Ambassador in Cairo, Humphrey Trevelyan, was alarmed at the extreme measures being discussed in Whitehall.[50] The French Government of Guy Mollet had a similar fear and loathing of Nasser, whom they regarded as one of the external forces behind the Algerian rebellion. But in the end, it was as much American pressure, as world opinion, that neutered 'Operation Musketeer' at Suez. Foster Dulles made sure that with 15% of Britain's currency reserves lost and no oil from the Middle East, Britain had little room to deal. Dulles informed Eden that unless he capitulated, the US would not support sterling and it would surely collapse. So, faced with a British cabinet revolt, Eden capitulated. It was clear that in any future developments in the Middle East, it would be the US rather than Britain that dictated the outcome.[51]

Because of the withdrawal of British forces from Palestine in 1948 and more recently from Suez, and with bases in Cyprus under threat, British defence policy was redefined in the 1957 Defence White Paper. This document, which was the brainchild of the Minister of Defence, Duncan Sandys, based future defence policy on the deterrent value of nuclear weapons. It was envisaged that by 1962, the manpower of the three services could be reduced from 690,000 (of whom over 50% were national servicemen) to a regular force of 375,000. This meant that the Army would have to cut seventeen battalions from an existing establishment of twenty cavalry regiments and sixty-four single battalion infantry regiments. Another requirement was the phasing out of National Service by 1 January 1960. Britain's dwindling world influence would depend on military bases in the East of Africa and the area East of Suez, and although it was envisaged that independence would be granted eventually to Kenya, Uganda and Tanganyika, it was expected that these East African British bases would last for at least another decade.[52] Colin Campbell, a Deputy Commissioner in the Department of Development in Uganda, recalled the atmosphere at the time:

> Making comments about political developments was starting to get difficult, but Africans were gradually being promoted and integrated into the Civil Service and Government offices. During the 1950s, the outlook seemed stable and with a country rich in minerals, coffee and cotton, we all thought the colonial relationship, together with the British military presence, would carry on for much longer than it did.[53]

It was anticipated that Britain's international commitments would be met by constructing a central military strategic reserve, from which mobile units could be airlifted to any flashpoint in the world. While a carrier group based in the Indian Ocean would be reinforced from the air by forces based on the British mainland, an Amphibious Warfare Squadron would operate from Aden. However, it soon became clear to Service Chiefs that Britain did not possess sufficient RAF transport aircraft to airlift a central reserve, and so the reserve became dispersed over the remaining worldwide bases. This more flexible defence strategy meant that bases such as Aden and Kenya would actually have to be expanded, and investment was increased accordingly. [54]

The Macmillan Government meanwhile, was determined to consolidate and even extend British influence in the region, at a time when the Empire was in retreat. Without doubt, part of the reason for this reversal of the trend was a desire by some in the British Government to recapture ground in the Arab world, in retaliation for the recent humiliation by Nasser. But Nasser's nationalisation of the Suez Canal had further emboldened Arab nationalists, and British influence with Arab rulers was starting to ebb away. General Glubb, Britain's advisor to the Kingdom of Jordan, was dismissed that same year, and in 1958 the pro-British rulers in Iraq were ousted. An army coup, led by Brigadier Abdul Kassim, destroyed the Iraqi Hashemite Monarchy, killing the young King, the Crown Prince and Nuri al-Said, the Prime Minister and steadfast friend of Britain. Indiscriminate lynching of foreigners followed, and the British Embassy was burnt and looted.[55] It now looked as if Iraq would fall into Nasser's embrace, as his concept of a pan-Arab nation was taking shape.

Britain's fear of Nasser's regional ambition was well founded. 1958 had seen his creation of the socialist United Arab Republic, joining Egypt, Syria and the Kingdom of Yemen. The union envisaged a single army, foreign policy, education system and currency but none of this materialised. Syria had joined because its powerful Socialist Arab Ba'ath Party had been fearful of Communist influence in the country and hoped that Nasser would provide a bulwark against it. Meanwhile, in Yemen, it was Imam Ahmed's heir, Prince Mohammed al-Badr, who brought about the extraordinary link between Nasser and Yemen. Ever mindful of his future succession, he had courted the Egyptians as backers in his bid to remove the British from South Arabia. And although he was aware of Nasser's plots against the monarchies of Jordan and Saudi Arabia, he saw the union as an insurance policy against his own kingdom's demise. For his part, Nasser believed that it would be easier to remove kings who worked with him than against him.[56]

As al-Badr had already established good contacts with Socialist and Communist countries, it was a short step for Yemen to fall into Nasser's embrace. Between 1956 and 1958, al-Badr made visits to Eastern Europe, Russia and China, which resulted in Russian arms shipments to Yemen, including thirty aircraft, thirty T34 tanks and 100 field guns, together with Russian pilots, mechanics and advisors. The Russians soon made useful contacts with Yemeni officers, which was vital preparation for the time when Russia and Egypt were ready to sponsor a revolution against the Imam. In addition to Egyptian educated Yemenis, the revolution would be further bolstered by over 300 Yemeni students sent to Czechoslovakia and other Communist Bloc countries, ostensibly to train as engineers, but who would return as revolutionaries.[57] Imam Ahmad was wisely suspicious of Russian motives, but his son was intent on increasing foreign influence in their country, and when the Imam went to Italy for medical treatment in 1959, al-Badr allowed in a flood of Egyptian advisors, including a military mission.[58]

While making overtures to the new revolutionary regime in Iraq, Nasser set about destabilising their neighbour and British ally, King Hussein of Jordan. Nasser coordinated Egyptian and Syrian Intelligence in a bid to assist Jordanian opposition groups in a bombing campaign, which was followed by more overt efforts to topple Hussein.[59]

Meanwhile, there were British successes in the region. The festering rebellion in Oman's interior was quashed, when the Sultan's Army, under the command of Lieutenant-Colonel David Smiley, successfully beat back Saudi backed rebel forces. The Trucial Omani Scouts were ably assisted by the Life Guards, REME and Royal Signals, as well as aerial support from Aden based Shackleton bombers. Slow progress was made during 1958, but in January 1959 22 Regiment Special Air Service (22 SAS), in a spectacular assault, finally drove the rebels from their stronghold of Jebel Akhdar. Despite the successes, these operations showed that air power was no longer the paramount method of controlling tribal rebellions. Ground troops, well acclimatised and with air support, were deemed to be the way forward.[60]

NOTES

1   At this stage the hinterland was technically one Protectorate. It was only later that it was formally divided into a Western and Eastern part.
2   Paul Dresch discusses the complex geography and nomenclature of the region in his preface to *A History of Modern Yemen*, CUP, 2000.
3   In writing a foreword to Bertram Thomas's *Arabia Felix*, T E Lawrence confirmed his passion for this wild and remote area. He was thrilled when Thomas eventually explored it by foot and camel in the late 1920s. See Bertram Thomas, *Arabia Felix*, Jonathan Cape, 1938.
4   The British Museum mounted an exhibition in 2002, 'Queen of Sheba – Treasures from ancient Yemen'. For a guide to this exhibition and the history of Yemen, see *Yemen – In the Land of the Queen of Sheba*, Pallas Athene, 2002.
5   Caroline Singer, 'Arabia Felix, Land of Fragrance', in *Yemen – In the Land of the Queen of Sheba*, op. cit., pp. 45-7.
6   From the advent of Britain's informal empire in the Middle East, the concept grew that it was 'a realm held in trust'. This contrasted with the French model which assumed perpetual control; for the French threat, see Z H Kour, *The History of Aden 1839–72*, Frank Cass, 1981, pp. 4–5, and Robin Bidwell, *The Two Yemens*, Longman, 1983, p. 28.
7   The story of Haines and the early government of Aden, as well as his eventual demise, is well documented. He published articles in contemporary issues of the *Journal of the Royal Geographical Society* and his extensive correspondence and reports are preserved in the R20 series of the Oriental & India Office Collections (IOR), administered by the British Library. See also published works, particularly Gordon Waterfield, *Sultans of Aden (With an Envoi by*

Stephen Day), Stacey, 2002; R J Gavin, *Aden under British Rule 1839–1967*, C Hurst, 1975; Robert Stookey, *South Yemen – A Marxist Republic in Arabia*, Croom Helm, 1982. Stookey was the American representative in Yemen.

8   By 1897, when Queen Victoria celebrated her Diamond Jubilee, over two million Britons lay buried in India. Large numbers of them had served the Bombay Presidency (the poorest of the three Indian Presidencies), which administered Aden until 1932. The Central Government of India then took over for five years before passing control to the Colonial Office in 1937. See CO 725/83/7, NA.

9   In a bizarre twist, the defeated Emperor Theodore shot himself through the mouth with a pistol originally presented to him by Queen Victoria.

10   Protective Treaties were later replaced by Advisory Treaties, which were more highly prized by Tribal leaders; Glencairn Balfour-Paul to Author, 17 February 2004.

11   The Maria Theresa silver dollar was introduced into the Middle East by Napoleon in 1798. It was initially minted in Austria and latterly in Britain and Bombay. Production lasted until 1960 but usage, particularly in Yemen, continued for some time after. It had a high silver content and because there were no notes in the currency, large heavy bags had to be used to carry them.

12   A typical Protectorates' Tribal Treaty is reproduced in Appendix I, David Holden, *Farewell to Arabia*, Faber & Faber, 1966.

13   After invading Yemen, the Turks offered Imam Yahya the position of spiritual leader if he surrendered his temporal authority.

14   An incomplete draft of 'A Military History of Aden' by Harry Cockerill, *qv.*, covers the period up until The Great War. While a detailed examination of this period is outside the brief of this study, the draft provides many useful sources, especially on the Victorian Army in Aden. I am indebted to Murray Graham and Colonel Robin McGarel-Groves for making this available. For the Brecknockshires, see Ray Westlake, 'Remembering the Great War at St. Mary's Parish Church, Brecon', *Stand To!*, April 2003.

15   The golf course was poor. Any golfer miss-hitting the ball would have raised a cloud of dust rather than divots. Following the Turkish invasion, Governor Price was sacked. See Sir Tom Hickinbotham, *Aden*, Constable, 1958, p. 15.

16   'Medical Services during the Operations in the Aden Protectorate', in Major-General Macpherson et al, *History of the Great War based on Official Documents: Medical Services*, HMSO, 1921. See also Bidwell, *Two Yemens*, op. cit. pp. 60–5.

17   David Smiley, *Arabian Assignment*, Leo Cooper, 1975, p. 106. Also, R A B Hamilton (as The Master of Belhaven), *The Kingdom of Melchior: Adventure in South West Arabia*, John Murray, 1949, p. 56.

18   CIGS Memo, 7 Dec. 1927, CAB 24/188, NA.

19   'Air Power and Expansion', in Gavin, op. cit. 277–317. For a detailed analysis of expansion of empire in the Protectorates against a background of imperial retreat, see Dr Spencer Mawby, 'Britain's Last Imperial Frontier: The Aden Protectorates 1952–59', *Journal of Imperial and Commonwealth History* 29/2, May 2001.

20   Captain D W Parsons, 'British Air Control: A Model for the Application of Air Power in Low-Intensity Conflict' in *Aerospace Power Journal*, Summer 1994, p. 4.

21   R A B Hamilton (as Lord Belhaven), *The Uneven Road*, John Murray, 1955.

22   The number of political officers grew from two in 1934 to twelve in 1941. For a good analysis of proscription bombing, see Dr Spencer Mawby, 'From Tribal Rebellions to Revolution', in Article 5 *Electronic Journal of International History*, p. 15. www.history.ac.uk/ejournal.

23 The APL operated until November 1961, when they were incorporated into the Federal Regular Army (FRA). For a detailed history of the APL, see Frank Edwards, *The Gaysh: A History of the Aden Protectorate Levies 1927–61 and the Federal Regular Army of South Arabia 1961–67*, Helion, 2003. Also Cliff Lord and David Birtles, *The Armed Forces of Aden 1839–1967*, Helion, 2000.

24 Recently, the explorer Sir Ranulph Fiennes took up the challenge of finding the lost city of Ubar. Despite his efforts, it remains elusive. See Ranulph Fiennes, *Atlantis of the Sands – The Search for the Lost City of Ubar*, Bloomsbury, 1992. For Philby and Thesiger, see Peter Brent, *Far Arabia*, Weidenfeld & Nicolson, 1977, pp. 201–26. Thesiger crossed the Empty Quarter twice and also visited the Hadhramaut. It was only in 1966 that he entered Yemen. See Wilfred Thesiger, *Arabian Sands*, Longman, 1959.

25 R A B Hamilton (as The Master of Belhaven), *Melchior*, op. cit.

26 Robin Bidwell, *Travellers in Arabia*, Hamlyn, 1976, pp. 174–5. For Stark, see *Freya Stark – A Biography*, Hodder & Stoughton, 1993, pp. 79–92. Doreen Ingrams managed to travel with the HBL's first camel patrol in 1943, a distance of over 500 miles. Both women subsequently received Royal Geographical Society Gold Medals for their survey work.

27 Glencairn Balfour-Paul to Author, 31 January 2003. Also *Aden and South Arabia*, R.5671/66, Central Office of Information, London 1966, p. 7.

28 Minutes of Imperial Defence Committee, CO 725/52/9, NA.

29 For the Italian occupation and its effects on neighbouring states, see Angelo Del Boca (P Cummins, translator), *Ethiopian War 1935–41*, University of Chicago Press, 1989. Italian influence in Yemen continued after the war with a number of their doctors practising in Taiz and Sana'a.

30 A Clark Hutchinson, 'The Hadhrami Beduin Legion' in *Journal of the Royal Central Asian Society*, Vol. LVII, 1950.

31 With a lighter bombing role envisaged for the Protectorates, 114 Squadron soon replaced 621 Squadron. It used the more up to date Mosquito VI in place of Bostons.

32 Quoted in Philip Darby, *British Defence Policy East of Suez 1947–68*, OUP, 1973, p. 11. For the causes and effect of Indian independence, see P J Cain and A G Hopkins, *British Imperialism: Crisis and Deconstruction 1914–1990*, Longman, 1993, pp. 196–200.

33 Glen Balfour-Paul, *The End of Empire in the Middle East*, CUP, 1991, p. 9.

34 There are several accounts of Imam Yahya's murder. See Dana Adams Schmidt, *Yemen: The Unknown War*, Bodley Head, 1968, pp. 37–9. Also Hickinbotham, op. cit. pp. 71–5, and R W Stookey, *Yemen: The Politics of the Yemen Arab Republic*, Westview Press, 1978, pp. 213–22. Seven of Yahya's sons died violently.

35 The party were entitled to be in the region as concessionaires, but it was hardly tactful. Tom Little, *South Arabia: Arena of Conflict*, Praeger, 1968, p. 39. For details on the Free Yemeni Movement, see B R Pridham (ed.), *Contemporary Yemen: Politics and Historical Background*, Croom Helm, 1984, pp. 34–45.

36 Most of these bombing raids took place within the Protectorates. Any reprisals into Yemen had to be authorised by the Governor of Aden after sanction by both the Colonial and Foreign Secretaries. See CAB 128/27 and CAB 129/69, NA.

37 Most pilots found that the Brigand was not as manoeuvrable as its predecessor, the Tempest VI.

38 For the rationale behind the setting up of local forces, see Memorandum PM Office, 19 October 1955, PM/55/142, PREM 11/1582, NA. For a review of

security forces in Aden during this period, see Air Chief Marshal Sir Denis Barnett Papers, Liddell Hart Centre for Military Archives, King's College, London (hereafter LHCMA). See also Lord and Birtles, op. cit., p. 22.

39   Sir William Jackson, *Britain's Triumph and Decline in the Middle East*, Brassey's, 1996, pp. 118–19.

40   For a detailed account of the July 1952 Revolution, see Anwar el-Sadat, *In Search of Identity*, Collins 1978, pp. 94–115. After the Egyptian coup, Nasser moved to oust his more senior confederate, Neguib, and made himself virtual dictator. He swiftly suppressed his most potent opposition, the Moslem Brotherhood, and in 1954 he crushed the communists. The revolutionary rhetoric that came from his government followed an Arab National Socialist line rather than a Marxist position. For the early Nasser years, see Tom Little, *Modern Egypt*, Ernest Benn, 1967, pp. 143–59.

41   Abdul Addali, quoted in *Middle East Research & Information Project* (hereafter MERIP), Washington DC, No. 15, March 1973, p. 4, Yem 3., Arab World Documentation Unit, Exeter University (hereafter AWDU).

42   The policy of sending Yemenis to be educated in Egypt was started by Imam Yahya in 1947. He believed this would introduce a small, educated elite that he could control. See Ali Rahmy, *The Egyptian Policy in the Arab World: Intervention in Yemen 1962–1967*, University Press of America, 1983, pp. 74–5, 81.

43   Report 78/85/81, File 78082, BP Archive, University of Warwick (hereafter UW); see also MERIP, op. cit. p. 4., and Henry Longhurst, *Adventure in Oil*, Sidgwick & Jackson, 1959, pp. 248–55.

44   Sir William Luce, 'Britain's Withdrawal from The Middle East and Persian Gulf', in *RUSI Journal*, March 1969. In the EAP, commercially viable oil deposits were not exploited until 1984, Mawby, 'From Tribal Rebellions', op. cit., p. 2.

45   This oasis, consisting of nine villages, lay in the poorly defined border area between Abu Dhabi, Oman and Saudi Arabia, an area where the American oil conglomerate, ARAMCO, was prospecting for oil. The Saudis, with American encouragement, sent troops in to occupy the oasis. However, as two bordering British acolytes, Abu Dhabi and the Sultan of Muscat, claimed the area, Britain organised a company of the Trucial Oman Scouts to force out the Saudis in 1955. See Glen Balfour-Paul, op. cit., p. 114–15. Also Ritchie Ovendale, *Britain, the United States and the Transfer of Power in the Middle East, 1945–1962*, LUP, 1996, p. 125. Also Holden, op. cit., pp. 201–13, and Jonathan Bloch & Patrick Fitzgerald, *British Intelligence and Covert Action: Africa, Middle East and Europe since 1945*, Junction Books, 1983, p. 134. As late as 1960, ARAMCO were still viewing British action as 'illegal'; See Roy Lebkicher, *Aramco Handbook*, Aramco, 1960.

46   American Secretary of State, John Foster Dulles, quoted in Fred Halliday, *Arabia Without Sultans*, Saqi Books, 2002, p. 281. For the Buraimi dispute see Jane Priestland (ed.), *Buraimi Dispute Contemporary Documents 1950–61* Vol 1–10, Archive Editions, 1992. Also Anthony Verrier, *Through the Looking Glass: British Foreign Policy in an Age of Illusions*, WW Norton, 1983, pp. 180–2.

47   Nasser was a CIA protégé in the early 1950s.

48   Sadat, op. cit., p. 154. For Eichelberger, see Richard Aldrich, *The Hidden Hand – Britain, America and Cold War Secret Intelligence*, John Murray, 2001, pp. 476–7. For Caffery, see Verrier, op. cit., pp. 85–6, 123.

49   Miles Copeland, *The Game Player*, Aurum Press, 1989, p. 198.

50   Quoted by Anthony Nutting in Nigel West, *The Friends: Britain's Post-War Secret Intelligence Operations*, Weidenfeld & Nicolson, 1988, pp. 107–8. Also

Aldrich, op. cit., p. 480. Humphrey (as Sir Humphrey) Trevelyan later became High Commissioner for Aden.

51 Jackson, op. cit., pp. 132–9. Also Keith Kyle, *Suez*, Weidenfeld & Nicolson, 1991, pp. 555–60.

52 Sandys' proposals encountered a rough ride with Service Chiefs. See Sir Ewen Broadbent, *The Military and Government*, Macmillan, 1988, pp. 20–3. Also General Sir William Jackson and Field Marshal Lord Bramall, *The Chiefs*, Brassey's, 1992, p. 319, and Keith Wilson (ed.), *Imperialism and Nationalism in the Middle East*, Mansell, 1983, pp. 150–2.

53 Colin Campbell to Author, 11 February 2003.

54 Independence came to the East African countries remarkably quickly; Tanganyika on 31 December 1961; Uganda on 9 October 1962; Kenya on 12 December 1963. The speed of the retreat from Empire surprised many, including those in the Treasury who had invested heavily just prior to independence. See Darby, op. cit. pp. 203–8 and Gillian King, *Imperial Outpost – Aden: Its Place in British Strategic Policy*, OUP, 1964, pp. 8–10. Also Field Marshal Lord Carver, *The Seven Ages of the British Army*, Weidenfeld & Nicolson, 1984, p. 272.

55 For a detailed account of the Iraqi revolution, see Humphrey Trevelyan, *The Middle East in Revolution*, Macmillan, 1970, pp. 133–205.

56 Al-Badr also established diplomatic relations with the People's Republic of China. See Tom Little, *Modern Egypt*, op. cit., pp. 201–2. Also Rahmy, op. cit., pp. 59–60.

57 Most of these armaments lay rusting in fields and parks, because Imam Ahmed forbade their use. See Edgar O'Balance, *The War in the Yemen*, Faber & Faber, 1971, pp. 55–6, and Stephen Page, *The USSR and Arabia*, Central Asian Research Centre 1971, p. 38; also Tom Little, *South Arabia*, op. cit., p. 51. For students, see Peter Somerville-Large, *Tribes and Tribulations*, Robert Hale, 1967.

58 Minutes of Joint Intelligence Committee (JIC), 4 December 1957, 57/125, CAB 158/30, NA. The minutes concede that Arab governments might wish to remain independent, but there is a critical point at which Communist aid requires a payback. For the military mission, see Rahmy, op. cit., p. 60. Also Page, op. cit., p. 48.

59 Andrew Rathmell, *The Secret War in the Middle East: The Covert Struggle for Syria 1949–1961*, I B Taurus, 1995, pp. 149–53; For background to the Ba'ath Party, see Tareq Ismael, *The Arab Left*, Syracuse University Press, 1976, pp. 20–51.

60 22 SAS were first transferred from Malaya to Oman in November 1958. Smiley, op. cit. pp. 59–88. See also General Sir Peter de la Billière, *Looking for Trouble: SAS to Gulf Command*, HarperCollins, 1994. Also Darby, op. cit., pp. 128–33.

CHAPTER II
Federation

The origins of the idea of Federation went back to 1950 when the Political Agent and Advisor to the WAP, Kennedy (later Sir Kennedy) Trevaskis, drafted a plan for the Governor, Sir Tom Hickinbotham. The concept involved the Eastern and Western Protectorates, which had always maintained their own identities, continuing as separate federal areas that would be ruled by the historic tribal chiefs. It was hoped that an elected assembly would eventually replace this Council of Rulers. As Britain's position in the Middle East was being increasingly challenged, the point of the plan was to show to the Arab world that local leaders could still maintain their autonomy under a British protective cloak, while the federal authorities would not involve themselves in the internal affairs of each member state. Broadly, these states would be created out of the existing tribal areas, the idea being to reduce and streamline the large number of tribal treaties currently in existence with Britain.[1]

While Hickinbotham's original attempt to graft a Federation together in 1954 had failed, by 1959 circumstances were more conducive. The tribal rulers were faced with both the threat of internal subversion, and externally, from Nasser's creation of the UAR and his designs on the Arabian Peninsula. Federation was also attractive to tribal leaders who feared the constant muscle flexing of the Sultans of Lahej.

The idea of Federation coincided with Britain's renewed and energetic interest in the hinterland of South Arabia. It was a reversal of the trend of British retreat in the Arab world, which was propelled by Nasser and the evacuation of Suez and the Canal Zone. Donal McCarthy, Counsellor and later Political Advisor to the C-in-C, Middle East Command, explained the reasons for this about-turn:

> We knew that decolonisation was imminent. We did not want to leave fragmentation. It represented a poor Colonial legacy. The more sophisticated realised that worthwhile investment could only be attracted if the unit were larger than any individual state. Finally, there was the enthusiasm of highly intelligent, but limited and nineteenth century-type individuals, like Trevaskis.[2]

To assist this expansion, it was decided that better communications between the tribal areas might add cohesion to the Protectorates. Although successive British governments had always been lethargic about development in the hinterland, some new roads were built during the 1950s to open up the old tribal boundaries. But in a land where extortion was a time-honoured tradition, development funds were attractive for other reasons, as Lieutenant-Colonel (later Major-General) Sandy Thomas, Commander of the 4th Battalion Aden Protectorate Levies observed:

> We watch the frontier, throw back the small raiding parties, watch for dissidents who return with Yemeni arms and training . . . meanwhile the sheikhs are gathering in their new impressive parliament building, to see how talking can possibly help them. They are aware that by doing all this, vast sums of money will come their way. Apart from the generous salaries they will receive, they well know that 5 out of every 10 shillings spent by the English on road construction, wells, irrigation projects etc. will inevitably find their way into some of the tribal coffers.[3]

Finally, after a delegation of tribal rulers had met in London, six states from the WAP set up a 'Federation of Arab Amirates of the South' and in February 1959 they signed a Treaty with Britain. The Treaty, signed by the new Governor of Aden, Sir William Luce and the states of Beihan, Audhali, Fadhli, Lower Yafa, Dhala and Upper Aulaqi, was one of friendship and mutual co-operation with Britain.[4] The rulers were obliged to accept Britain's 'advice' only after they had expressed their views, but the continuance of the British military base in Aden was sacrosanct. Importantly, Britain recognised the Federation's 'desire to develop ultimately into an economically and politically independent state', but the word 'independence' was deliberately absent from the agreement.[5] At this stage, the Prime Minister, Harold Macmillan, became nervous of upsetting the status quo and made sure that his Colonial Secretary, Alan Lennox-Boyd, skirted around the issue. Macmillan was adamant, stating: 'We must get rid of this horrible word "independence". What we want is a word like "home rule". The thing to do is to think of the Arabic for "home rule" and then work backwards from it.'[6]

Six months later, and with a new, able sultan, Lahej joined the Federation, which thus brought in the largest and most influential state outside Aden. By the end of 1962 the addition of Dathina, 'Aqrabi, Lower Aulaqi, and Wahidi, brought the Federation up to eleven states.[7] There remained the four states of the EAP, which were consumed with rivalry and although they continued their loose association with Britain, none, except the state of Wahidi, ever joined the Federation. The EAP, which

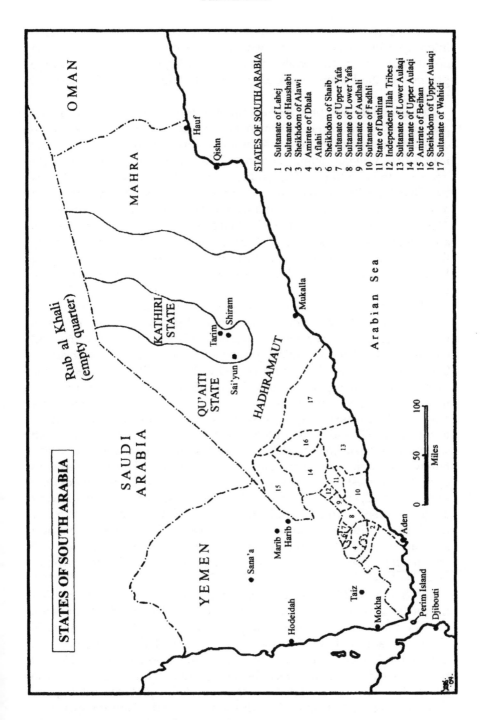

STATES OF SOUTH ARABIA

STATES OF SOUTH ARABIA

1 Sultanate of Lahej
2 Sultanate of Haushabi
3 Sheikhdom of Alawi
4 Amirate of Dhala
5 Aflahi
6 Sheikhdom of Shaib
7 Sultanate of Upper Yafa
8 Sultanate of Lower Yafa
9 Sultanate of Audhali
10 Sultanate of Fadhli
11 State of Dathina
12 Independent Illah Tribes
13 Sultanate of Lower Aulaqi
14 Sultanate of Upper Aulaqi
15 Amirate of Beihan
16 Sheikhdom of Upper Aulaqi
17 Sultanate of Wahidi

23

was twice the size of its Western counterpart, was 98% barren land, intersected by occasional fertile wadis. However, there was the prospect of oil exploration, and while this hope was kept alive there was little prospect of the Eastern rulers joining a Federation and sharing their oil revenues.

However, the concept of the Federation was an affront to Imam Ahmed and his Zaydhi followers in Yemen. His power base was the Shia branch of Islam, but his adherents were in a minority within his kingdom. He feared that a Shafei (Sunni) dominated Federation on his border might appeal to the two thirds of his country who followed the more orthodox branch of the faith. Consequently, throughout the 1950s Ahmed instigated as much turmoil as possible amongst the tribes of the future Federation. This came to a head during 1954–5 when a series of tribal revolts in Beihan and Dhala severed important British communications and seriously threatened trade within the WAP. With the Egyptian Army supplying Russian arms to Yemen, Ahmed was well placed to inflame this tribal unrest.

While the hinterland was the scene of constant tribal ferment, there was also unrest in Aden Colony. The better-educated sons of the Adeni merchant class were becoming impatient with the old conservative and consensus based local political groups such as the 'Aden Association'. Some were radicalised by improved education facilities in Aden, while others learnt their politics abroad; but all wanted a faster route to independence and a future that was not reliant on Britain. Some were attracted to nationalist groups such as the 'South Arabian League', founded in 1950 and based in the Sultanates of Lahej and Fadhli, which surrounded Aden Colony. This movement was dominated by the al-Jifri family and supported by the Sultan Ali al-Karim of Lahej who saw an opportunity to establish a new power base. Traditionally, because of their wealth and adjacent position to Aden, the sultans of Lahej had always assumed a central role in South Arabia. Though it was not endorsed by tribal custom, this pre-eminence was enhanced by Britain, largely because she had originally acquired Aden from the Sultan of Lahej. Now the Sultan felt his position threatened as the British gave equal weight to other tribal leaders.[8]

The South Arabian League was significant because it was the first nationalist group to draw support from both Aden and the hinterland, and the movement vigorously supported tribal rebellions like those in Upper Aulaqi. In June 1958 the Commandant of the Lahej State had defected to Yemen, taking with him army units and equipment. He was soon followed by Qahtan al-Sha'abi, the agricultural officer for Lahej, who absconded with state funds.[9] To compound the problem, intelligence reports indicated that Sultan Ali, who had come under Nasser's spell, was about to take his state of Lahej out of the WAP and join Nasser's UAR.

Such a serious potential threat to the forthcoming Federation demanded swift action from the British, and in 1958 the al-Jifri brothers were expelled and the Sultan of Lahej was deposed.[10] But other nationalist groups within the Arab world, like the burgeoning Arab Nationalist Movement (ANM), were spawning radical factions that found their way into the increasingly vocal Aden Trade Union Congress (ATUC), which drew support from the refinery and port workers.

The first trade unions in the Colony were established in 1953 and grew rapidly, gaining the majority of their members from among the Yemeni immigrant workers. Ironically, in the early years it had been a feature of British policy to encourage trade unionism in the Colony, but the franchise in Aden was narrow and only extended to about 10% of the population.[11] The ATUC was formed in 1955 and soon agitated for the extension of this franchise to include Yemenis, many of whom would only be resident in Aden for several years while they earned enough money before returning to live comfortably in their native villages. At the same time, intimidation of those who could vote in local elections in Aden resulted in low turnouts – in one case, a paltry 27%.[12]

With funding and encouragement from Yemen, the ATUC grew rapidly, producing a credible leader in Abdullah al-Asnag. He was a personable man and with his comfortable physique, he seemed to many a nationalist with whom Britain could do business. He certainly impressed the Opposition Labour Party in Britain, who saw him as an earnest trade union leader with an agenda of workers' rights. But he was a wily operator who could quickly change his persona from amiable negotiator to revolutionary firebrand. In the opinion of Kennedy Trevaskis, al-Asnag was a classic 'Jekyl and Hyde' figure.[13]

An important part of the South Arabian economy was the Aden Port Trust, which was subject to control by the British High Commission. A total of twenty-four ships could be moored at the buoy berths in the harbour together with a further thirteen at pipeline berths, and there was still room for another eleven working ships. By 1960, with the facility of BP's oil harbour across the bay at Little Aden, Aden Port became the largest oil bunkering port in the world, handling over 5,000 ships a year. It was also a Free Port with customs duty that only applied on alcohol, tobacco, scent and qat.[14] Consequently, industrial unrest had huge economic as well as social implications and when strikes occurred at the Port in 1959 and 1960, much of the maritime business was lost to the strike-free port of Djibouti, in French Somaliland, in the horn of Africa.[15]

The ATUC leader, al-Asnag, cultivated his links with the British Labour Party and TUC, no doubt anticipating the day when they would be in power at Westminster. In June 1962 two Labour MPs, George Thomson and Bob Edwards, went out to Aden as guests of the ATUC and addressed a crowd of Yemeni workers.[16] As it was al-Asnag's intention to thwart the impending merger of Aden Colony with the Federation, a general strike followed the visit of the MPs. Shortly afterwards a political arm to the ATUC was also set up under the title of the People's Socialist Party (PSP). Containing many of the same leaders as the ATUC, the brief of the PSP was to cause labour unrest that would in turn provoke a government crackdown. This would then be heralded as the act of an 'oppressive oligarchy'; more moderate locals would be drawn in and the cycle of unrest would continue. Both the ATUC and PSP became increasingly open about their willingness to subordinate jobs in Aden Port and the BP Oil Refinery to a wider nationalist ambition.[17]

The Federation started out with the proper trappings of a state. A federal capital was set up, called al-Ittihad ('union'), just inside the Aden Colony boundary and mid-way between the Khormaksar/Sheikh Othman built-up area and Little Aden. The administration had control of its own Federal National Guard, which was responsible for 'the main-tenance of internal security within the Federation'. This was a local gendarmerie force formed by the merger of the old Government Guards and Tribal Guards and was split into two units: Federal National Guard 1 (FNG I) comprised Arabs raised from all over the Federation and was centrally controlled from headquarters in Aden, while Federal National Guard 2 (FNG 2) tended to come from individual states and be influenced by local rulers.[18]

The four rifle battalions of the Aden Protectorate Levies (APL), which had been under British control, were taken over by the Federation on 30 November 1961 after a colourful parade and RAF flypast. The BBC and *The Daily Telegraph* reported that it was the finest parade ever seen in Arabia. The new force was known as the Federal Regular Army (FRA) and at its formation it numbered about 4,250 officers and men. The objectives of the FRA were 'the defence of the Federation frontiers, to support the Federal Guard and to assist the civil power in maintaining law and order among the tribes'.[19] However, as the FRA still included nearly 300 British servicemen, it was hoped to 'Arabise' the force as soon as possible.[20]

The inherent problem that faced the Federation was that it was largely alien to those who governed it. Warrior-like tribal leaders were not the best material for consensus politics or even the debating chamber, usually preferring to settle disputes with the rifle or sword. If they were based in al-Ittihad, they were also out of personal contact with their tribes and as plotting and feuding were regular features of the hinterland, power bases could easily be lost. Also, the new administration, which initially com-prised the hereditary rulers, failed to satisfy demands from the moderate nationalists for a wholly elected government.[21]

The population of the Federation could not have been more different. The cosmopolitan, politically aware Adenis were a stark contrast to the tribesmen from the hinterland, who could have belonged to another age.[22]

Brigadier (later Major-General) James Lunt, Commander of the FRA, described his encounter with a man in the wild territory of Audhali:

> From navel to crown he was painted indigo blue. His hair, vermin-ridden and lank, had been trimmed below his ears into a rough bob and was kept out of his eyes by a strip of dirty cloth. The only attempt at adornment was a pair of silver amulets, one fastened above the right elbow and the other below the left knee with pieces of twine. Crude sandals fashioned from goatskin protected his horny feet from snake and scorpion and the shaker thorns, and his body was scarred from old bullet and knife wounds. An ancient musket lay beside him, bound with strips of copper wire. He smelt so rankly of unwashed body, goat and sesame oil that I had to adjust my position upwind.[23]

Lunt's tribesman may have seemed medieval, but he would have been more likely to carry a rifle than a musket. For by the beginning of the century, Martini-Henri and Remington rifles had largely replaced the old flintlocks, enabling tribesmen to kill each other more frequently and thereby extend the number of blood feuds. Illegal rifles poured into the isolated mountains of South Arabia through Red Sea ports, but there was no central authority to stop the traffic.[24] Britain's writ did not extend over this wild interior and apart from projects such as the cotton schemes in Abyan and Lahej, little attempt was made to either invest in the area or exploit the few raw materials available. Even in the Colony of Aden, apart from a few entrepreneurs, there was little European settlement, a situation that was unusual among British possessions.

However, despite this paucity of material aid, the British Government (HMG) was still determined to keep the sultans 'on-side'. If the old and largely successful policy of tribal treaties broke down, RAF proscription bombing could still coerce rebellious tribes. But a more enduring domination meant winning 'hearts and minds'. By the late 1950s more political officers were required to go out and live among the tribes, with the prospect of bringing British money and limited development aid. Stephen Day, a young modern languages scholar, recalled his bizarre recruitment interview at the Colonial Office:

> I attended the interview at a red-bricked office in Whitehall. The kindly, silver-haired official commended me for choosing an honourable career. Turning pink, stretching and gazing intently out of the window, he asked whether I had experienced any 'funny business' at school. 'No, Sir,' I replied with equal embarrassment. 'Oh good, I am so pleased,' he spluttered. 'I do apologise but one has to ask that sort of thing these days.' Cleared of any association with Burgess and Maclean, I was passed for service in the Western Aden

Protectorate as an Advisor to the assortment of sultans, sheikhs and tribal despots. There was no training for the job, perhaps because there was no one with even a passing knowledge of the place, to offer instruction. It was assumed that a decent British education and a half-decent degree at Oxford or Cambridge would fit one to advise on how to govern a chunk of Arabia. Language might be a problem, so a ten-week course in colloquial Adeni Arabic had been arranged at the school of Oriental and African Studies. However, the Home Office had denied a work permit to the Adeni recruited to give practical lessons, with the result that the thinnest veneer of Arabic was passed on.

Three volunteers had been found that year, a record crop. Equipped with sound boots, rifle, shotgun, camp-kit and a small book on hints for health in tropical climates, we set sail from Liverpool into a dying sunset.[25]

Stephen Day and his colleagues were deposited without much ceremony in the Protectorates to make what they could of tribal lore. And if there was one common thread running through South Arabia, it was tribalism. This described a complex network of social, clan or kinship connections that thrived in the hinterland, and in the Hadhramaut region alone there were estimated to be 1,400 different tribal units. Nonetheless, not all the inhabitants of the Protectorates belonged to a tribe.[26] The minority who were non-tribesman and therefore landless, could if they chose stay in the hinterland, become tenants or live under 'tribal protection'. These non-tribesmen played an increasingly important role in nationalist agitation. Many moved into Aden and found common cause with trade union activists or nationalist militants seeking enfranchisement.[27]

For all the apparent rigidity of this tribal system, rulers could be unseated surprisingly easily and there were practically no cases of popular uprisings if a ruler was deposed.[28] This encouraged the British to attempt to manipulate the succession of sheikhs and sultans, and with the creation of the Federation they rewarded and promoted those sheikhs who were tactically important to Aden. This upset the natural balance of tribal hegemony.[29] Furthermore, the creation of the Federation gave some tribes the excuse to take up arms against the British if a rival tribe was the state representative at al-Ittihad.

Another important element of tribal attitudes was the value of 'face', for to lose a fight to a humbler or inferior combatant was the greatest humiliation for a warrior. Worse still, a tribesman's womenfolk might pour scorn on him. Honour was the key concept. Therefore, to be defeated by RAF bombing sorties was no disgrace as they were considered an enemy whose firepower was unassailable.[30]

Tribal feuding was usually caused by the theft of scarce resources. The major livelihood was often the exacting of tolls from caravans, and although some did subsist by agriculture, others felt it unworthy of their warrior destiny. The conventions that regulated tribal behaviour meant that it was the responsibility of a tribe to avenge a wrong done to any member. These feuds often resulted in set-piece battles between armed tribesmen, which seemed to an observer strangely choreographed. They were good marksmen but the casualty rate from blood feuds had increased dramatically during the 20th century due to the introduction of precision rifles.[31]

The tribe was generally the principal unit, being a military and political, as well as social group and could field up to several thousand armed fighters. The tribe was split into clans; the clans into sections and each section contained a number of families. Within the tribe, the members looked to a chief (sheikh), who acted as a judge or mediator to settle inter-tribal disputes. With the exception of the Sultan of Lahej, these chiefs were elected by tribal elders from among the members of a recognised ruling family.[32] Lieutenant-Colonel Sandy Thomas, recalled a typical sheikh:

Sheikh Husein bin Hushein is an old rogue but a great favourite of mine. Less than a year ago he was fighting against us, and over some cinnamon tea in his house, he told me, his eyes twinkling, that he often lay on the hilltops with his men and watched the Levy patrols go by through the sights of his rifle. He is a short, stockily built man of perhaps fifty (although age is hard to judge here; they seem to die mostly before fifty). He sports an untidy and never-too-clean goatee beard, and dresses like his followers in loose garments and futah, clasped by an embroidered cartridge belt containing some two hundred rounds. In the centre of his ample belly, is a really beautifully wrought silver *jambiya*, with its ivory handle studded with deeply inlaid pure gold. He comes in to see me in my office in the fort quite often, bringing wild honey – the old rogue is always on the scrounge, for a vehicle to take him somewhere, but one just cannot help liking him. He is a feudal lord, with the power of life and death at his very whim. He says he likes me, and therefore he will co-operate with the Government and there is more in this than our masters in Aden are aware of. The Arab pins his loyalty and obedience (such as it is) to the person, rather than to anything nebulous such as a government or parliament.[33]

The tribes of the south were 85% settled. They did share a common culture with the northern tribes in that some from the south chewed *qat*, the mildly narcotic leaf, and wore similar clothes including the *futa* or coloured kilt together with the *jambiya* ornamental dagger. The blade of this dagger, which was a symbol of South Arabia, was slightly curved and rested in a sheath that curved tightly round. It was usually only sharpened at the tip but could still gouge out an eye.

It took about two hours to fly across the old Western Aden Protectorate (WAP), a land where wealth was usually retained within ruling families by the power of elders to arrange marriages and fix bride prices. Girls were usually married by the time they were 14 years old, to boys who were barely 16. Despite the short childhood, boys soon learnt to be warriors, or at least to look the part when confronted by British army officers:

> A colourful figure, complete with flashing silver *jambiya* and cartridge belt, appeared on a black pony and turned his horse at me, at a canter, and raised his rifle high in the air. It was the sense of a warrior attacking that he hoped to convey. He pulled up alongside the Landrover and we exchanged the usual courteous Arab greetings. When they take your hand, the Arab hillsman grasps the wrist rather than the fingers, and he raises it slightly towards his face, at the same time making a kissing sound with his lips followed by a sharp and audible intake of breath.[34]

The Eastern Aden Protectorate (EAP) had a separate social ethos and considered itself part of the older, historical Yemen. The Hadhramaut, which had prospered from the old incense trail, also produced an industrious émigré population, who built up communities in Indonesia and Singapore. They in turn sent money back to their homeland, which funded the construction of extraordinary eight-storey houses in towns like Seiyyun and Tarim.[35] Despite the sporadic wealth in the region, the population of the EAP were mostly illiterate. They lived in the four states of Wahidi, Qu'aiti, Kathiri and Mahra, which also included the island of Socotra, lying 220 miles off the Arabian coast. Qu'aiti was by far the largest state with a population of 250,000 and contained the important coastal town of Mukalla and to underline its historical importance, its ruler was granted the title 'His Highness' by the British, together with the right to an eleven-gun salute. Islam played a central role in the Hadhramaut region, and even 'Sharia' (Islamic) Law was applied, but it had less influence in the new states of the Federation, where justice was more likely to be meted out by a panel of tribal elders.[36]

It was in this arcane and unforgiving world of South Arabia that the RAF had mounted bombing sorties and ground reconnaissance missions using local forces. In 1957 they had relinquished control of military operations and handed over the Army, who successfully engaged rebels during frontier clashes with Yemen in 1959–62.[37] However, the local nature of military command in the Gulf region was changing as the idea of a Strategic Reserve gained favour with military planners in London. This strategy involved maintaining regional Reserves as well as Reserves in Britain, which could be flown at a moment's notice to any trouble spot. The instability of the Middle East persuaded the planners to base part of this Reserve 'beyond the barrier' of Suez, firstly in Kenya and then in Aden. Furthermore, if the Aden base was enlarged, it would provide a vital link with Singapore, Britain's bastion in the Far East. For since Malaya's independence in 1957, Britain had guaranteed her independence, largely because of the continuing threat from Indonesia, in return for unfettered access to the UK military base in Singapore. This policy was endorsed by the British Colonial Secretary, who stated, 'our military base at Aden is a vital stepping-stone on the way to Singapore'. [38]

On 1 March 1961 Middle East Command (MEC) Headquarters were established in Aden with the New Zealander, Air Marshal (later Air Chief Marshal Sir Charles) Elworthy, as Commander-in-Chief. Several years earlier it was decided that British forces in Arabia should be controlled from London rather than the base in Cyprus. To this end, a unified Command was set up to administer British land and air forces in Arabia, together with control of naval forces in the Persian Gulf. This was an innovation in military thinking as MEC was the first attempt at a unified or joint services command since the Second World War.[39]

Although MEC was based in Aden, its land forces operational arm, 24 Brigade, remained geographically separated. Because of the instability in Kenya, HQ 24 Brigade, together with some of its units, remained in Kenya, while companies from its battalions were spread across South Arabia and the Gulf. After Kenya became independent, HQ 24 Brigade redeployed to Aden between March and December 1964, while its remaining units returned to Britain. To coincide with this build up in the military establishment, the British Government embarked on a massive military building project in Little Aden, the settlement surrounding the BP refinery across the bay from Aden town. It was the largest project of its kind ever undertaken in South Arabia and provided secure housing for over 2,500 troops together with 1,000 women and children.[40]

Meanwhile, the Headquarters of the air arm, Air Forces Middle East (AFME), was established at Steamer Point, Aden, while its operational base was situated at the nearby Khormaksar Airfield, one of the RAF's largest stations. In 1961 it had at its disposal Squadron Nos 8 and 208, equipped with a total of thirty-two new higher specification Hawker Hunter FGA Mk 9 fighter-bomber and four Meteors.[41] This was the first aircraft based in Aden to break the sound barrier and there were initially strict controls on supersonic operation.[42] The attack aircraft were supported in transport, reconnaissance and supply by Squadron Nos 37 (Shackleton), 78 (Twin Pioneer CC Mk 1), 84 (Beverley C Mk 1) and 233 (Valetta C Mk 1). For strategic support in the event of a wider conventional war in the Middle East, the RAF relied on the Vulcan B1/1A bomber, operating out of RAF Waddington on the British mainland.

Steamer Point was also the base for the Headquarters of Army Command, known as Middle East Land Forces (MELF),[43] as well as the Naval arm, controlled by Flag Officer Middle East (FOME), which moved there in 1963. It was vital that this unified command was in place by the early 1960s as throughout this period, the 'high table' of British intelligence, the Joint Intelligence Committee, saw the Middle East as one of the tripwires for a nuclear conflict with the Soviet Union.[44]

Between 1960 and 1962 military activity was quieter within the Federated states and those remaining states of the old WAP and EAP, but it was not without incident. Patrols in the hinterland behind Aden were subject to sporadic ambushes, while on 19 July 1961 a bitter fight took place in the EAP when a rebel tribe attacked a post occupied by the Hadhrami Bedouin League. The HBL suffered fifty casualties, including sixteen killed, and retribution by the RAF was swift and decisive. Using a Shackleton, with Hunters, Meteors and Twin Pioneers, the RAF soon quelled the unrest but the attack showed how quickly trouble could break out.

In April 1960 45 Commando, Royal Marines ('Four Five'), under the command of Lieutenant-Colonel Billy Barton, arrived in Little Aden and leased the 'old camp' from BP. They soon created a second home 'up country' at Dhala Camp, near the Radfan mountains, but surprisingly it was in Kuwait, rather than Aden, that they met their first serious challenge.

Kuwait had been under British 'protection' since 1899, though there was no formal operational British base in the country. In the face of rising nationalism, it was decided to release Kuwait from her formal ties and grant her sovereign independence in June 1961, retaining a defence treaty with Britain. However, that treaty was put to the test as soon as independence was granted when General Kassim's regime in Iraq threatened to invade Kuwait. To deter Iraq, a British military force, including Four Five Commando, swiftly moved to Kuwait, a move that proved a great morale boost to other British troops in the Middle East. Lieutenant-Colonel Sandy Thomas, in temporary command of the whole APL Force in South Arabia, noted:

> It was pleasing to see the smooth efficiency of the whole operation, the great planes coming in from England and Africa and moving no less than two brigade groups complete in the matter of a few days. There is no doubt that the operation was highly successful, and all our friends in the Middle and Near East and also our enemies, were vastly impressed at the speed we could come to the aid of a friend. For once it was not 'too little, too late'.[45]

However positive it looked on the ground, the crisis highlighted severe shortcomings in the new defence strategy of redeployment from mainland

Britain, and caused a rethink in the numbers of troops retained in bases like Aden. HMS *Bulwark*, which was at Karachi, Pakistan, and several days steaming from the Persian Gulf, had landed 42 Commando RM in Kuwait. Four Five Commando, airlifted from their base at Little Aden, soon joined them. While Four Five's operations in South Arabia had acclimatised its men, this did not apply to any troops airlifted direct from the United Kingdom, who suddenly had to face temperatures in excess of 120°F. With high humidity and sandstorms, it was estimated that some 10% of troops were out of action for the first five days because of heat exhaustion.[46] In the event, the Iraqi threat never materialised, but it showed the difficulties of implementing Britain's new defence doctrine. Apart from the cost (over £1 million in 1961), rapid deployment placed great reliance on air support, which in turn required Arab countries to allow access to their air space. However, the value of the 'Commando Carrier' strategy was confirmed and the aircraft carriers HMS *Bulwark* and HMS *Albion* would continue to carry a Commando together with its support units that could be rapidly and flexibly deployed anywhere in the world.[47]

Until December 1963, when the British 24 Brigade became permanently based in Aden, local South Arabian forces bore the brunt of controlling the region. However, armour, in the shape of Ferret scout cars and Saladin armoured cars was provided by 9th/12th Royal Lancers. They divided their squadrons between Little Aden and up-country, but it was the mountains, according to Troop Leader, 2nd Lieutenant Simon Mort that provided the best soldiering:

> The first of my up-country missions was to Dhala, an immensely beautiful place with rugged mountains and a variety of crops. In these mountain stations we lived in a way that must have been similar to that enjoyed by the British and Indian armies on the North West Frontier. Our time was spent in setting up OPs or in escort patrols. These were comparable to cavalry duties on the Frontier, although our part had a more 20th century facet in travelling at the front of the Landrovers so that the Ferrets would take the force of any mine. Mines were always a hazard and Dummy mines found in the sand tracks had to be poked by mine-prodders or (safer, as they were longer) wireless aerials. Arab FRA soldiers frequently got blown up by mines on their way home for leave.[48]

In addition to this armour, a British field artillery battery had always supported the Aden Protectorate Levies and their 1961 reincarnation, the FRA. However, in September 1960 the first battery of Horse Gunners arrived – C Battery, 3rd Regiment Royal Horse Artillery (3 RHA).[49]

As a standard mobile unit, 24 Brigade was part of Britain's Strategic

Reserve and its HQ was based in Kenya, together with the core of its battalions. Its sphere of operations covered not only Kenya and the Federation of South Arabia but also the oil-rich dependencies of the Persian Gulf. Elements of the Brigade rotated between Kenya and South Arabia, and at the time of the Kuwait Crisis, the 11th Hussars, 3rd Carabiniers (Prince of Wales's Dragoon Guards) and Four Five Commando were stationed in Aden. Armoured support was supplied in the form of Centurion tanks, Ferret Scouts and Saladin armoured cars.[50] When Kenya eventually became independent in December 1963, 24 Brigade joined Middle East Command (MEC) in Aden.

The advance party of Four Five Commando, under Major Dai Morgan, arrived in Aden in March 1960 and this was the beginning of the Commando's unbroken service in Aden that lasted until withdrawal in 1967. Four Five, which had been formed in 1943, soon set up a base camp in Little Aden in huts leased from the BP refinery, while a second camp was established 'up-country' at Dhala. The 'Dhala Convoy', which involved reinforcing the garrison every fortnight, became a well-known experience among the Marines. It took ten hours from Aden to Dhala, travelling up rock-strewn tracks, through deep gorges and ravines, and risking the possibility of sniper attacks or ambushes from dissident tribesmen. Four Five even proved they could attempt this eighty-mile trek on foot when E Troop, accompanied by their old friend Harry Cockerill, completed the exhausting march in three days.[51] Life for the Marines at Dhala Camp was a mix of patrolling, weapons training and fitness exercises. Apart from rebellious tribesmen, the other local hazard was the baboon population, as 18 year-old Marine Peter Ranft discovered:

> The baboons were everywhere and they'd often throw rocks at us, but you kept out of their way because they could give you a nasty bite. One day, a baboon took a close interest in the latrines. They were very basic six-seaters, with a large hole underneath. When the earth closet reached capacity, it was normally filled in, but in this case, before another hole could be dug, the baboon dived into the mess and came out covered in muck with lavatory paper all over him. He then proceeded to charge into the bivouacs, one tent after another, and he smelt to high heaven. In the heat of the day the smell was so bad, we had to shoot him.[52]

There were differences between the organisation of Army and Marine units. While the disposition of Army units was in companies, comprising some 120 men, rather than full battalions, by the time Four Five Commando came up to full strength in 1962, it consisted of 650 all ranks. The old formation of five Rifle Troops had been dispensed with in favour of three Companies (X-Ray, Yankee and Zulu), each commanded by a

Captain or Major. In addition, the Commando contained a Support Company and HQ Company as well as a Recce Troop. The Rifle Companies were in turn split into smaller Rifle Troops, similar in size to an army platoon.[53] The small size of the Marine Corps enabled a system of 'trickle drafting' to be employed whereby individual Marines, in groups of fifty, would arrive and depart each month, rather than whole Companies. This ensured that unlike regular infantry battalions who came out *en bloc*, Four Five always had a core of experienced Arabian hands.[54] South Arabia soon became a regular training ground for Four Five, and few Marines from the unit missed the experience. It looked as if the arrangement would continue for many years, as the 1962 Defence White paper marked out Aden (together with the UK and Singapore), as one of the three points of global military deployment.[55]

Meanwhile, the Federation was gaining strength. On 26 September 1962 the Aden Legislative Council narrowly approved the merging of Aden Colony with the Federation. The decision to merge had come about principally because Duncan Sandys, who had recently taken over as Colonial Secretary, stated that it was Britain's intention to lead South-West Arabia 'as soon as practicable to sovereign independence'. There was the caveat that Britain would retain her base in Aden and, indeed, the Macmillan Government felt that retention of the base would only be viable if concessions were made to nationalist sentiment.[56]

However, the grafting on of the Crown Colony of Aden (which became the State of Aden) to the other states of the Federation was never going to be easy. The marriage was formalised four months later, in January 1963, but from its conception the Federation of South Arabia comprised two disparate hierarchies. On the one hand, the hinterland produced hereditary rulers from a sparse population of farmers and herdsmen who were predominantly from the Sunni (orthodox) branch of Islam. With strong tribal ties, they inhabited a land that was tough and inaccessible and had never been a British Colony. On the other hand, Aden Colony had a legislative council, made up of a largely elected body, albeit from a small franchise out of a population of 230,000. Arabs from Aden and the Protectorates made up the bulk of the Federal population, together with some 20,000 Indians and 15,000 Somalis, but by far the most volatile element of the mix were the 60,000 immigrants from Yemen, most of whom were adherents of the Shia religion. Aden had not only a cosmopolitan trading class, but also a port and oil refinery employing an organised and politicised workforce. [57] At its core was the military base, and according to Donal McCarthy, the main reason for the Federation's existence:

> The merger of Aden in the Federation was seen as arranging a *cordon sanitaire* for the base ... which proved more like a chastity belt: uncomfortable but not proof against impregnation.[58]

Despite the difficulties, there was great enthusiasm for the Federation among senior Colonial Office men. Sir Charles Johnston, who was Governor during the years 1960 to 1963, was a leading proponent. He observed that 'whatever the administrative distinctions inside Arabia – Colony, Federation, Protectorate, Islands – it was quite essential for us to have a single view of the whole area'.[59] Yet this was the nub of the problem. Britain had fallen into the trap of trying to apply a logical solution, in the shape of the Federation, to a region that defied conformity. Although the British had a capable ally in the shape of Hassan Ali Bayoumi, Aden's Chief Minister who did more than anyone to try and make the Federation work, barely four months after Aden joined the Federation, Bayoumi was dead from a heart attack. Britain had lost another Nuri al-Said, and with him, a chance of reconciliation in South Arabia.[60]

Harold Macmillan privately feared that the Federation had shaky foundations. Following a Cabinet meeting, he wrote in his diary:

A long and very important discussion about Aden Colony and the Protectorates. Two schemes will be prepared for us to consider. The real problem is how to use the influence and power of the sultans to help us keep the Colony and its essential defence facilities.[61]

The power of the sultans was already under attack. Since 1959 Nationalists, in the shape of the South Arabian League, had attempted to take the issue of decolonisation to the United Nations. In August 1962 they finally managed to include the issue in the Agenda of the General Assembly of the UN. Britain's role and influence in South Arabia was now open to international scrutiny.[62]

NOTES

1   The origins and development of the Federation of South Arabia has been examined in detail by many published sources including the architect of federation, Kennedy Trevaskis, *Shades of Amber: A South Arabian episode*, Hutchinson, 1968; For Hickinbotham's account see *Aden*, Constable, 1958; also Tom Little, *South Arabia* op. cit; Glen Balfour-Paul, *The End of Empire*, op. cit., and Robin Bidwell, *Two Yemens*, op. cit. An authoritative account by Peter Hinchcliffe, ex political officer and acting Assistant High Commissioner, is in preparation.
2   Donal McCarthy to Sir Richard Beaumont, 20 November 1967, FCO 8/41, NA.
3   Major-General W B 'Sandy' Thomas CB, DSO, MC*, ED Silver Star USA, Chronicle 1961–2, p. 5, I am grateful to Major-General Thomas for permission to quote from his chronicle, a copy of which is held in papers belonging to Brigadier David Baines.
4   'Bill' Luce, an intelligent and perceptive Arabist, possessed an unsurpassed knowledge of the Middle East. Colonel David Smiley to Author, 16

September 2003. Not all the federated states were enthusiastic, for example Fadhli, which viewed the concept with great suspicion.

5   Central Office of Information, *Aden and South Arabia*, R.5671/66, p.10, AWDU. The concept of Federation was already successfully applied to Rhodesia & Nyasaland (1953) and was being prepared for Malaysia in 1963; see Karl Pieragostini, *Britain, Aden and South Arabia: Abandoning Empire*, Macmillan, 1991, pp. 40–1.

6   Macmillan memo, 28 June 1958, PREM 11/2616/46, NA.

7   Aden joined the Federation in 1963, together with the Sheikhdom of Sha'ib and the Haushabi Sultanate. By 1965, with the addition of Upper Aulaqi, 'Alawi and Muflahi, the number of states finally rose to seventeen.

8   Stephen Day to Author, 3 March 2004.

9   Al-Sha'abi would eventually rise to prominence as leader of the National Liberation Front (NLF).

10   The al-Jifri brothers moved to Cairo and then to Saudi Arabia, which subsequently backed the South Arabian League, see Stookey, op. cit., pp. 53–4. For the movement's own account of its activities, see *South Arabian League Publications 1967*, Yem 3a, AWDU.

11   Sir Tom Hickinbotham (Governor, 1951–6), who had been Manager of the Aden Port Trust, actively encouraged trade unions in Aden.

12   Recorded in the January 1959 elections to the Aden Legislative Council. See King, op. cit., p. 50.

13   *Aden 1963/64*, Research and Information Commission, Netherlands, Yem 3a, AWDU; see also David Ledger, *Shifting Sands: The British in South Arabia*, Peninsular, 1983, pp. 37-9.

14   *BP Visitors' Guide to Aden*, BP Archives, UW. *Qat* is a mildly narcotic leaf. In Yemen, *qat* chewing takes place during early afternoon to late evening. The leaves are chewed in a bunch, the juice swallowed and the masticated leaves spat out. Copious amounts of water are taken with the *qat*. Where once only certain tribes in the south chewed the leaf, today its use is widespread. Stephen Day to Author, 3 March 2004.

15   The members of the General and Port Workers Union were particularly susceptible to strong union leaders. Most of the 3,000 Sea Coolies and Hammels came from the hinterland where the rule of tribal leaders was unquestioned.

16   In the 1964 Labour Government George Thomson became Minister of State for Foreign Affairs.

17   The published output from both the ATUC and the PSP was prolific; see for example ATUC, 'A Curtain Raiser to Repression by British Colonialism against Workers of Aden and their Families', Dar el-Hana Press, Cairo, 1963, Yem 3a, AWDU. For the background to the nationalist groups, see Tareq Ismael, *The Arab Left*, Syracuse University Press, 1976 and Helen Lackner, 'The Rise of the National Liberation Front', in Pridham op. cit., pp. 46–61; also Little, *South Arabia* op. cit., pp. 45–56 and Bidwell, *Two Yemens*, op. cit., pp. 100–3.

18   The FNG also fulfilled the role of supporting local political officers; see 'Report on Ministry and Force HQ, Federation of South Arabia', June 1964, DEFE 13/570, NA.

19   Ibid.

20   By 1965, all four battalions of the FRA were commanded by Arabs; see Thomas Chronicle, op. cit., pp. 12–13.

21   Attempts at more democratic reform were made in July 1964 with the publication of the *Federation of South Arabia Conference Report*, involving the

reshaping of the Constitution; see *Conference Report by Secretary of State for the Colonies*, Cmnd. 2414, HMSO 1964, AWDU.

22 Some of the young tribal rulers were educated at British public schools, but this merely served to distance them even further from their tribesmen.

23 James Lunt, *The Barren Rocks of Aden*, Herbert Jenkins, 1966, p. 115. The book takes its name from the famous old bagpipe tune, composed by a member of the 78th Highlanders while based in Aden.

24 Helen Lackner, *PDR Yemen*, op. cit., p. 12. Even today, there are an estimated 60 million firearms in circulation for a population of 20 million. Every type of firearm is available for sale in Sana'a. A revolver costs £30 and an automatic rifle fetches £200.

25 Stephen Day to Author, 4 October 2001. After seven years as a political officer and advisor, he became Assistant High Commissioner for the Federation. His later distinguished diplomatic career included appointments as Ambassador to Qatar and Tunisia.

26 Tareq Y Ismael and Jacqueline S Ismael, *PDR Yemen: Politics, Economics and Society*, Frances Pinter, 1986, p. 6.

27 Sir Kennedy Trevaskis to *New Statesman*, 5 May 1967.

28 Gavin, op. cit., note 70, p. 441.

29 One central flaw of the Federation was that the British assumed there was an order of precedence among the tribal rulers. Influence from Bombay ensured that the rulers were seen more as Indian Princes than tribal mediators. Stephen Day to Author, 3 March 2004.

30 Bidwell, op. cit., pp. 86–7; also Stephen Day to Author, 26 March 2002. The RAF did suffer casualties. In July 1958 Flight Lieutenant Foster of 8 Squadron was attacking a Yemeni field gun position near the border when a hostile 12.7mm anti-aircraft gun fired on him. He was hit but managed to crash his plane into the enemy field gun.

31 The image of tribes being essentially violent is not supported by all studies; see Shelagh Weir, 'Are Yemeni tribes disorderly, violent and against states?' in Yemen Conference 1998, op. cit.; for fragmentary nature of tribes, see Glen Balfour-Paul, op. cit., pp. 55–6.

32 Probably the best account of the social organisation of the tribes in the Protectorates is contained in a lecture by R A B Hamilton (Belhaven) to the Royal Central Asian Society, see CO 725/84/14, NA; see also *Journal of the Royal Central Asian Society*, Vol. 30, 1942, pp. 142–57.

33 Thomas Chronicle, op. cit., pp. 11–12.

34 Ibid, p. 17.

35 Jim Ellis, Oral Testimony # 810, British Empire & Commonwealth Museum, Bristol (BECM); also Doreen Ingrams, *A Survey of Social and Economic Conditions in the Aden Protectorate*, 1946, and Halliday, op. cit., pp. 166–9.

36 For a detailed examination of tribal justice, see Husan al-Hubaishi, 'Litigation and Arbitration in Yemen' in Conference Papers, 'Yemen: The Challenge of Social and Economic Development in the Era of Democracy', 1998, AWDU.

37 For a detailed analysis of operations during this period, see Spencer Mawby, 'From Tribal Rebellions to Revolution', in *Electronic Journal of International History*, Article 5, www.ihrinfo.ac.uk.

38 House of Commons Debate, 13 November 1962, quoted in King, op. cit., p. 33. See also Air Commodore J R Gordon-Finlayson, 'Defence Problems of Aden' in *Brassey's Annual 1957*, pp. 220–33.

39 The original 1957 plan also included British Somaliland, but on 1 July 1960 it was granted independence; see Darby, op. cit., p. 125.

40 Shortly before leaving Kenya, over £3m was spent on improved facilities for 24 Brigade; see Darby op. cit., pp. 210, 279–80.

41 No. 8 Squadron was formerly known as No. 114 Squadron and had recently been in operation against the Mau Mau in Kenya. No. 208 Squadron was originally created as an RNAS Squadron in 1916. In March 1963 43(F) Squadron was added to the establishment at Khormaksar.

42 Because of the threat posed by the revolutionary Iraqi regime to Kuwait, these two squadrons alternated between Bahrain and Aden.

43 MELF were available for use anywhere in the Persian Gulf. The Kuwait Crisis in 1961 saw 45 Commando airlifted from Aden to Kuwait. On all Royal Marine issues, Four Five still deferred to its 3rd Commando Brigade HQ in Singapore.

44 The JIC illustrated this scenario in 'The Likelihood of War with the Soviet Union up to 1966'. See Peter Hennessy, *The Secret State: Whitehall and the Cold War*, Allen Lane/Penguin, 2002, p. 38.

45 Thomas Chronicle, op. cit., p. 37.

46 While the Ministry of Defence and the subsequent Official History (Air Historical Branch) contradicted these figures, a controlled experiment in Aden proved that material losses should always be expected from heat exhaustion among new troops in desert conditions. For MOD statement, see *The Times*, 23 July 1962. For Official History, see Air Chief Marshal Sir David Lee, *Flight from the Middle East*, HMSO, 1980, pp. 182–3; Also King, op. cit. pp. 15–16; Balfour-Paul, op. cit., p. 119.

47 For the details of the 'Commando Carriers', see James Ladd, *By Sea, By Land: The Royal Marines 1919–1997*, HarperCollins, 1998, pp. 288–305.

48 The 9th/12th Lancers were formed in 1960 from an amalgamation of the 9th Queen's Royal Lancers and 12th Royal Lancers (Prince of Wales's). They served in South Arabia from September 1962 to April 1963. Simon Mort to Author, 15 March 2004.

49 Previous units included 33 Parachute Light Battery (PLB), 41 PLB and from 1958–60, 14 Field Regiment.

50 The 11th Hussars (Prince Albert's Own) were originally raised as Dragoons in 1715 and later redesignated 11th Hussars in 1921. The term 'hussar' historically referred to light cavalry used for reconnaissance. The 3rd Carabiniers (Prince of Wales's Dragoon Guards) were formed in 1922. The term 'dragoon' referred to mounted soldiers, trained to fight on foot.

51 The march was code-named 'Operation Barbara'. Harry Cockerill was a legendary figure in South Arabia. A wartime SAS veteran, he later worked for BP. After a number of adventures near the Yemen border, his employment with BP ended. He provided useful information on the region to both Intelligence and Special Forces.

52 Peter Ranft to Author, 10 June 2003.

53 Colonel R J McGarel Groves (CO Four Five, 1964–6) to Author, 14 September 2001.

54 However, there was always a cadre of raw recruits. The Army, with its large formations, had to employ 'Arms Plotting'; Major-General David Thomson to Author, 16 April 2004.

55 The 1963 Malaysia Defence Agreement further reinforced this.

56 Philip Murphy, *Alan Lennox-Boyd: A Biography*, I B Taurus, 1999, p.194; also Glen Balfour-Paul op. cit., pp. 78–9.

57 *Arabia: when Britain goes*, Fabian Research Series 259, Fabian Society 1967, AWDU; also *Census Report 1955*, Government Press, Aden, pp. 10–13, AWDU.

58 Donal McCarthy to Sir Richard Beaumont, 20 November 1967, FCO 8/41, NA.
59 Charles Johnston, *The View from Steamer Point*, Collins 1964, p. 83.
60 'Confidential Political Situation Report', Brigadier Sir Louis Hargroves Papers.
61 Harold Macmillan, *At the End of the Day*, Macmillan 1973, p. 265.
62 *South Arabian League Publications*, op. cit., AWDU.

CHAPTER III
Empire Revived

It was the custom in the British Legation in Taiz, Yemen's second city, for telegrams from London to arrive late at night. One night in January 1962 the doorbell rang and Ronald Bailey, the Chargé d'Affaires, sleepily opened the door. Expecting to receive a missive from the Foreign Office, he was horrified as a crazed Arab charged in and lunged at him with a knife, stabbing him repeatedly in the chest and neck. Outside, the night watchman was writhing on the ground with similar knife wounds. Bailey's wife, Joan, on hearing the commotion, came out of their bedroom in her nightdress and with split second timing, leapt against the assailant and pushed him down the stairs where he fell on his own knife. The attacker then staggered off into the night, leaving Joan Bailey to tend to her husband and the night watchman until help arrived.[1]

The unprovoked attack on the Chargé d'Affaires was an example of the random violence that occurred in this region and the risks encountered by European diplomats. The assailant was eventually arrested but at his trial gave no indication as to why he had attacked Ronald Bailey, only complaining that 'Mrs Bailey had not behaved like a lady'. The convicted man served his sentence in a ball and chain, for penitence was a very public affair, and although dungeons were available, large prisons didn't exist in Taiz: many of those who fell foul of the Imam's laws, like the Director General of Civil Aviation, found that they had to go to the office carrying a ball and chain. For such a harsh land it was surprising that execution was not the preferred sentence for murder – beheading was reserved for those who attempted to kill the Imam. However, when a beheading was called for, it was a public spectacle to be photographed and the pictures displayed as a warning to others. The practice of cutting off the hands or feet of felons, which had existed under Ahmed's father's rule, was no longer as prevalent, but the removal of tongues still held a certain appeal.[2]

The British presence in this isolated, almost medieval, country was a recent development. Communications with Yemen had always been dealt with through the offices of the British Embassy in Cairo, but in 1951 Imam Ahmed eventually allowed the creation of a British Legation in the

41

southern city of Taiz.[3] Despite the cross-border aggravation that the Imamate caused the British, contact was still desirable; as long as the feudal monarchy survived, there was little incentive for Arab nationalists in South Arabia to agitate for unity between Yemen and South Arabia.[4]

At the time that the British Legation opened, the only other legation in Taiz belonged to the Italians. However, in 1958, both the Russians and the Chinese were allowed representation in return for financial aid for capital projects, and in a balancing gesture, the Imam allowed the United States to establish a legation the following year in return for the supply of American wheat together with the provision of engineers to help with road building.[5] This was sorely needed, for there were few roads to connect the 74,000 square miles of mountainous terrain, but with a population of only four million there was not a large pool of labour for capital projects. Although the land could be harsh and arid, Yemen had the highest rainfall in the Arabian Peninsula and the highlands in the interior remained fertile and green, yet lacked any agricultural development.[6]

As this extraordinary kingdom slowly edged out of its isolation, it had an unsettling effect on the British position in South Arabia. Imam Ahmed, who had always been a master at playing off one foreign power against another, was losing his grip and his country was becoming too dependent on aid from the Communist Bloc. Soviet aid meant that the Red Sea port of Hodeidah was expanded in 1961, though the Soviet press, including *Pravda*, were quick to pronounce that the intention was only to relieve Yemen from exporting goods through Aden.[7] However, it was clear that a Red Sea naval base would prove extremely useful to the Soviet fleet. The Joint Intelligence Committee, responsible for analysing intelligence from the different British agencies, warned:

> If the Soviet leaders are able to avoid the dangers of overplaying their hand, they will achieve their ends by allowing Arab Nationalism to lead itself into a position of economic and military dependence, which takes the Arabs beyond the point of no return.[8]

Fears about Soviet designs on South Arabia were confirmed by the stream of rhetoric coming from Moscow Radio and other official organs denouncing the British presence with its military base, oil refinery and port. For the Soviet Union viewed the Middle East, including Yemen, not only from the perspective of its global rivalry with the US, but also from the position of a near neighbour. The Middle East region was adjacent to the Soviets' southern border, and power shifts in this part of the Arab world were significant for her regional security.[9]

One man who watched the development of Hodeidah port with great interest was Colonel Abdullah Sallal. The son of a blacksmith and

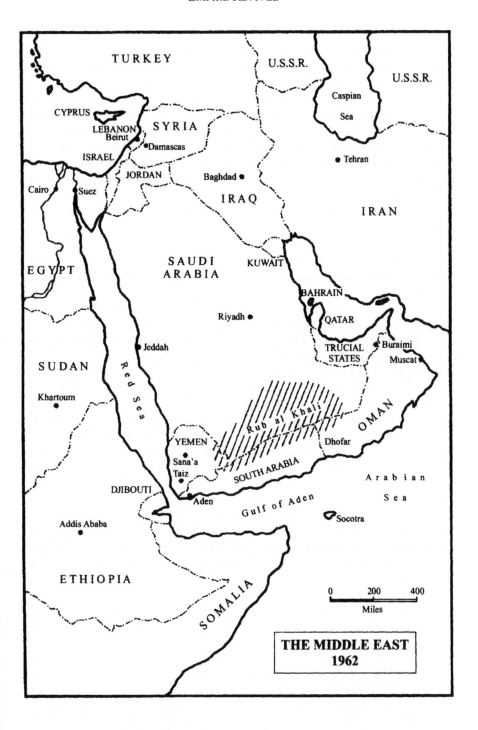

THE MIDDLE EAST
1962

charcoal-seller, he was originally one of a group of young Yemeni officer cadets sent to be educated in Iraq in 1936. He returned to Yemen in 1939 and was promptly arrested for subversive activities. Later that year, he was released and went back into the Yemeni Army where he persisted in subversive activity. By 1948 he was back in prison, this time for seven years, and spent much of his sentence reading books on the French Revolution and conspiring with other nationalists. He was eventually released at the request of the Imam's heir, Crown Prince al-Badr, who was flirting with Arab socialism and unwisely took Sallal into his confidence. Sallal was given back his army commission and in 1959 al-Badr sent him to Hodeidah as the port's harbour-master. It was a fatal mistake, for it enabled Sallal close access to Soviet and Egyptian advisors at the port.[10]

Imam Ahmed had always played a delicate balancing game with the superpowers. While al-Badr, with his socialist leanings, naively accepted Russian and Chinese aid and arms, the Imam wanted to take a more neutral international stance. He was happy to accept modern weapons, to which his army was often totally unsuited, in order to offload his old arms onto rebellious tribes across the border in the Protectorates. But by the end of 1961 the number of Russian and Chinese advisors had escalated to 1,100, and his meagre treasury was creaking under the strain.[11]

Meanwhile Moscow was becoming unhappy with Imam Ahmad. He was not quite the ally they had envisaged, and when he attempted to redress the political balance by accepting American aid in 1961, his position became untenable. Furthermore, his personal health and state of sanity was also causing alarm in Moscow. He was known to be a morphine addict, and reports were circulating of him hallucinating in a special chamber filled with spinning coloured lights and toys.[12] Robert McGregor, a former official at the British Legation, recalled that meeting the Imam was certainly a daunting experience as the diminutive figure, with his large darting eyes and broken teeth, emitted short rasping noises. Other lurid stories circulated, some of doubtful origin, which told of Imam Ahmed tying cord around his neck to make his eyes bulge out in order to frighten his subjects.[13] However, Ronald Bailey remembered only an artful despot:

> There were no cinemas in the country, but the Imam did own a film projector, and knowing that he was a Liverpool fan, I sent him films of football matches. In my estimation Imam Ahmed was not mad. Perhaps terrifying to those who crossed him, but he was also very shrewd, unlike his son al-Badr. By his policy of isolation, Yemen may have remained a backward country, but during Ahmed's reign, it was largely free of outside interference. He may have antagonised the British but he kept all the world powers at arms length.[14]

Imam Ahmed could never maintain his country's isolation and neither could he keep his internal enemies at bay. He had fought off rebellions in the past and eliminated many of the older generation of contenders after an abortive coup in 1955. But new enemies were surfacing all the time. He antagonised the tribes in the north by beheading one of their senior leaders, while in the towns Yemeni merchants, who had suffered under punitive taxation, wanted to throw off the Imam's restrictions on trade and gain access to world markets. But it was the army that would organise any coup and there were growing numbers of young army officers, many of whom were educated in Egypt, who wanted a Nasserite state. For his part, Nasser wanted to be rid of the Imamate and a revolutionary government in Yemen would de-stabilise not only the British in South Arabia but also the Kingdom of Saudi Arabia with its prize of oil. Furthermore, if Yemen was under Egyptian control, Nasser could dominate the Red Sea from the Suez Canal down to the Bab-el-Mandab Strait.[15]

In March 1961 there was an attempt to assassinate Imam Ahmed when he was opening a hospital in Hodeidah. Four of his bodyguards were killed but Ahmed survived, albeit with bullets still in his body. However, one of the would-be assassins eventually sought refuge in the nearby harbour-master's office. The harbour-master was none other than Sallal and the frail Imam soon had him removed for complicity. Incredibly, al-Badr refused to accept the link and, seduced by Sallal's enlightened ideas, promoted him to be Commander of his personal bodyguard. Under al-Badr's patronage Colonel Sallal was appointed Commandant of the Army Academy, bringing him once again into contact with Egyptian Intelligence officers.[16]

The rise of Nasserite Arab nationalism was not unstoppable and in October 1961 the United Arab Republic started to collapse. It had been unravelling almost from the time that it was created. The Ba'ath Party in Syria had resented the domination of Nasser's Intelligence Services and especially the presence in Damascus of Nasser's Viceroy, Major-General Abdul Amer. Amer had presided over the dismantling of the Syrian Ba'ath party structure and this loss of independence by the Ba'ath was deeply resented.[17] They struck back at Nasser by organising a military coup in Syria in September 1961 and a month later, Syria withdrew from the UAR. Meanwhile in Yemen, the Imam had become restless with the growing Nasserite influence in his country and started to criticise the UAR. He had read out a poem over Sana'a Radio, attacking socialism and Nasser in particular. An incandescent Nasser replied in December 1961 by formally expelling Yemen from the UAR and calling for the Imam's overthrow.[18]

Imam Ahmed was now over 70 years old, a good age in Yemeni terms, and spent his final months fending off further plots and assassination attempts. He ultimately surprised everyone by dying in his bed on 19

September 1962. The following day, the *ulema,* comprising the religious leaders of the kingdom, elected al-Badr as the new Imam, but his short rule was abruptly halted during the night of 26 September 1962.

At his Basha'ir Palace in Sana'a, al-Badr closed a meeting of his cabinet, attended by Sallal, at 10.30pm and made his way to his private quarters on the third floor. Outside the palace, a number of tanks rumbled into the main square and pointed their guns towards the building.[19] A loud hailer announced a coup and the Imamate Guard were called upon to surrender al-Badr. Inside the palace, a guard suddenly tried to shoot the Imam but others intervened, and as the would-be assassin was wrestled to the floor, shells slammed into the building. The rebel tanks and armoured cars kept up a bombardment, but al-Badr managed to scuttle down the tiny staircases and out through a side door before the cordon could be tightened around him.[20] Meanwhile, rebel troops soon captured the radio station and key government buildings, announcing al-Badr's death and the creation of the Yemen Arab Republic (YAR) under the leadership of the recently self-promoted Brigadier-General Sallal.[21]

The struggle in Sana'a was short. Most officers soon went over to the revolutionaries, but although most of the ranks had been locked in their barracks during the coup, some who supported the Imam put up a bloody resistance and over eighty were slaughtered.[22] To consolidate his power Sallal ordered the customary executions of the old regime, despatching seventy-five key royalists including fifteen members of the Imam's family together with scores of advisors and governors, whose bodies were left in the streets of Sana'a to be eaten by dogs. As al-Badr escaped north-west to Hajjah to rally support, Sallal confiscated his estates and implemented immediate reforms, including the abolition of slavery.[23]

Meanwhile, the British received sparse intelligence about these events in Yemen. As it was a foreign territory, the Secret Intelligence Service (SIS), more commonly known as MI6, covered any developments. They maintained a base in Aden, which as a Crown Colony was notionally the preserve of the Security Service (MI5), but as in Malaya and Singapore, it was a Crown Colony that still supported an SIS base, in this case the section known as P17.[24] Hubert O'Bryan-Tear, the SIS officer who ran the section, had substantial experience of special operations having served in the SOE sponsored unit, 'The Jedburghs' during the Second World War and later in post-war SIS operations in the Ukraine.[25] But regional support for O'Bryan-Tear (known universally as 'OBT') was limited. Since 1956 there had been no formal SIS representation in Egypt and relations with Saudi Arabia had yet to be normalised following the break after Suez. Despite the many rumours of plots circulating in Sana'a and Taiz, little was picked up by the British about Egyptian intentions and any intelligence that did emanate from British sources seemed to come via the Americans.[26] Bizarrely, it was Abdul Wahad, the Egyptian Chargé d'Affaires in Taiz, who knew and certainly connived in some of the plots surrounding the Yemen coup, yet warned al-Badr of his imminent danger.

As soon as the rebels had secured Sana'a, revolutionary cells took control of Taiz, Hajjah and the port of Hodeidah. However, in the months that followed the coup, a royalist revival took place among the tribes in the north of Yemen. To measure the strength of this recovery, the Governor of Aden, Sir Charles Johnston, had to look beyond his normal meagre sources of intelligence. He confirmed that reports from the *Le Figaro* correspondent, Patrick Chauvel, together with a photographer from *Paris Match*, were his only objective sources. Other journalists such as Dana Adams Schmidt of the *New York Times* and James Mossman of the BBC's 'Panorama' were expected to supplement information from the royalist lines.[27]

But there was another 'journalist' that SIS relied upon for information from the Yemen. Kim Philby, the SIS officer, had arrived in Beirut in 1956 after being publicly exonerated of spying by the Prime Minister, Harold Macmillan. He was despatched to Lebanon as the Middle East correspondent for *The Observer* and *The Economist* and by 1962 was regularly reporting to his old friend and colleague, Nicholas Elliott, the SIS chief of station in Beirut.[28] In his role as journalist, Philby travelled to Aden, the Hadhramaut and Yemen, regaling colleagues with tales of old Arabia that he had gleaned from his famous father, the legendary explorer St John Philby.[29] Just after the September revolution in Yemen, Kim Philby filed his whimsical copy for *The Observer*:

> The oddest feature of the situation is Australian recognition of the revolutionary government. There is speculation whether this foreshadows Australians chewing *qat* or Yemenis playing cricket.[30]

Philby's last main journalistic assignment took him to Yemen in November 1962. The trip had been arranged by the Saudis, to introduce Philby and a number of other journalists to Imam al-Badr and to witness the royalist military progress. After staying in Saudi Arabia, they were taken into Yemen where they met a confident and buoyant Imam and even witnessed some fighting, but according to a colleague, Eric Downton, Philby was 'listless and his reporting, lacklustre'. Downton later surmised that:

> He [Philby] must have seen and heard a great deal in Yemen and in the Saudi palaces, of interest to Soviet intelligence. It would be fascinating to be able to compare the reports he wrote on his Yemen excursion, for MI6 in London and the KGB in Moscow.[31]

Eric Downton, a foreign correspondent for Reuters, was with a group of reporters who were the first to interview the stocky 45-year-old President Sallal:

> The President looked very tired, his face drawn and covered by a growth of stubby beard. He wore a peaked service cap and an untidy khaki uniform. The revolution had already succeeded, he claimed, his government was in control, and there would be close cooperation with the Egyptian President Nasser. Without Nasser's help, he acknowledged the revolution could not have succeeded. I asked if he really believed that Imam al-Badr was dead. He was convinced the Imam had died during the fighting and that his body was somewhere under the great piles of rubble in the palace courtyard.[32]

Reaction to the coup in Yemen was predictably swift among the nationalists in South Arabia. On 28 September 1962 the PSP organised a demonstration in Aden in support of the YAR and called for the unification of Yemen and South Arabia. In a foretaste of what was to come, rioting erupted during which five agitators were shot and one killed. Across the bay from Aden the charged atmosphere was also felt in Little Aden, the base of 45 Commando and also the site of the BP refinery. Ann Cuthbert, whose husband Derek was the refinery's senior plant engineer, lived with her family nearby in quarters at Marine Drive. Writing to her parents, she sensed the change in mood:

> Internal relations here seem to be slipping. A great many Yemenis have resigned from unskilled jobs in the refinery. Most of the houseboys have gone back – we gather to claim their plot in the Imam's land. The BP Club boys have resigned en bloc. The General Manager's boys are all Yemenis as is Ismail, our houseboy. Some 'Nationals' have started to tell people hastily, 'your house will be my house soon' and there's uncertainty everywhere. Aden harbour and the seas all around are full of RN ships on manoeuvres. These have also been going on in the desert and around us ever since the trouble started.[33]

The revolution in Yemen came at a time of escalating international tension over the Cuban Missile Crisis and both the West and Eastern Blocs were preoccupied. Nonetheless, Khrushchev's Politburo, busy installing missiles in Cuba, was the first to recognise the new YAR regime and sounded a warning that 'any act of aggression against Yemen would be considered an act of aggression against the USSR'. But in countries where the Soviet Union had not carefully prepared the revolution herself, she was cautious of direct military involvement. As Anwar Sadat, a member of Nasser's Presidential Council, later confirmed, 'the Russians made a practice of letting us [the Egyptians] fight their battles for them, as happened in Yemen and elsewhere'.[34] Meanwhile, the Chinese, who had accepted invitations to provide aid for road building in Yemen, were consumed with their own border war with India.

In Britain, all attention was directed to the Cuban Missile Crisis, which came to a head on 27 October with a standoff between President Kennedy and Premier Khrushchev. Harold Macmillan authorised the RAF's nuclear Vulcan Bombers to be on fifteen minutes readiness at the end of their runways.[35] Even so, he was deeply worried by events in the Yemen, noting in his diary, 'during the month of October, in spite of more immediate dangers elsewhere, I felt gravely concerned about our position in Aden. We agreed to prepare defensive measures in case Aden or the Protectorates were openly attacked'.[36]

While Sallal occupied the post of President of the YAR, another more influential conspirator quietly slipped into Yemen from Egypt. Dr Abdurrahman al-Baidani was chairman of the Egyptian-sponsored Free Yemenis, a nationalist group based in Cairo and Aden. Al-Baidani was personally well connected to the Egyptian regime having married the sister of Anwar Sadat, Nasser's colleague and the future Egyptian president.[37] He was a German trained economist and, despite having an Indian father and Egyptian mother, had always promoted himself as a Yemeni nationalist. It was no coincidence that the very week that he was installed as Sallal's deputy, a troopship docked at Hodeidah bringing the first Egyptian *Saaqah* (Special Forces) to 'defend the revolution' and to provide a personal bodyguard for Sallal. Meanwhile Egyptian paratroops landed to help defend key installations.[38] David Ormsby-Gore, the British Ambassador in Washington was in no doubt that the coup was sponsored by Egypt. Writing to Lord Home, the British Foreign Secretary, he complained, 'it was sickening to have to listen to Egyptian complaints about interference from outside into the affairs of the Yemen. We all knew that the revolt had been, to a considerable extent, engineered by Nasser'.[39]

Al-Baidani was a consummate political operator and invaluable to a raw and inexperienced YAR cabinet who had to resort to Egyptian blueprints on how to run a government. One of his first briefs was to convince the British in South Arabia that they had nothing to fear from the new republic and that they should recognise it without delay. There was opposition to this from some in the British Conservative Government, but there were voices in support of recognition, especially from officials in the Arabian Department of the Foreign Office and the diplomatic community. Christopher Gandy, who was Ronald Bailey's successor in Taiz, was a strong supporter of recognition.[40] While he doubtless knew that the Legation would have to close if the British refused to recognise the YAR, he felt that recognition would keep the heat off Aden. It was also conceivable that if there was a dialogue with the YAR regime, those republicans who opposed the Egyptian occupation could be exploited. With support from the Foreign Office, recognition was looking increasingly likely. [41]

Meanwhile, Imam al-Badr arrived in Hajjah only to find that the garrison had declared for the republic. More worryingly, he then failed to raise the powerful Bakil federation of tribes in the north so had to move on farther and cross the border into Saudi Arabia. Together with 2,000 troops, al-Badr headed for the border town of Najran to meet up with his uncle, the popular Prince Hassan, who was rallying tribesmen to the royalist cause.[42] Hassan's most zealous supporter was the young King Hussein of Jordan, and while he was no admirer of al-Badr, Hussein realised that if the Imamate collapsed Nasser would then attempt to destabilise Jordan, Saudi Arabia and the Gulf sheikhdoms. It was an argument that had persuaded King Saud of Saudi Arabia to become a committed supporter of the Imam. Saudi and Jordanian officers were soon training royalists in Saudi camps and supplying them with recoilless guns, together with mortars and heavy machine-guns for use against aircraft. Although the military assistance of Saudi Arabia and Jordan fell short of air support, as both monarchs suffered unreliable air forces, the equipment al-Badr received was sufficient to enable him to return to north-west Yemen and set up a Command HQ in caves in the Jebel Qara.[43]

The Saudis also put pressure on the United States to support the royalist cause. Even before the coup Crown Prince Feisal, the Saudi Foreign Minister, had travelled to America to chide President Kennedy for his aid to Nasser, which was the largest US aid package to any Arab country. Despite this, Nasser remained highly sceptical of American motives, chiding Miles Copeland, the Central Intelligence Agency (CIA) Officer with the barb, 'the genius of you Americans is that you never make clear-cut stupid moves, only complicated stupid moves that make us wonder that there may be something we are missing'.[44] In an attempt to prise America away from Nasser, Feisal had a further meeting with Kennedy on 6 October 1962 and using the carrot of oil, strongly urged him not to recognise the YAR. But Kennedy was not persuaded, and his State Department continued to be critical of agencies of countries, including Britain, that sought to destabilise governments using covert means. Many felt this was a double standard especially as America's CIA had recently given clandestine support to rebels trying to topple President Sukarno of Indonesia.[45] It was fortuitous that the CIA often took a different line to that of the State Department and on the issue of Yemen the agency was against recognition. Jim Critchfield, Director of CIA Mideast, was convinced that the West could ill afford to give Nasser free rein in Yemen, stating that the Egyptian involvement was 'a strategic move, a two pronged effort by Moscow to make the Red Sea into a Russian lake'. And to back up his assessment Critchfield put in a

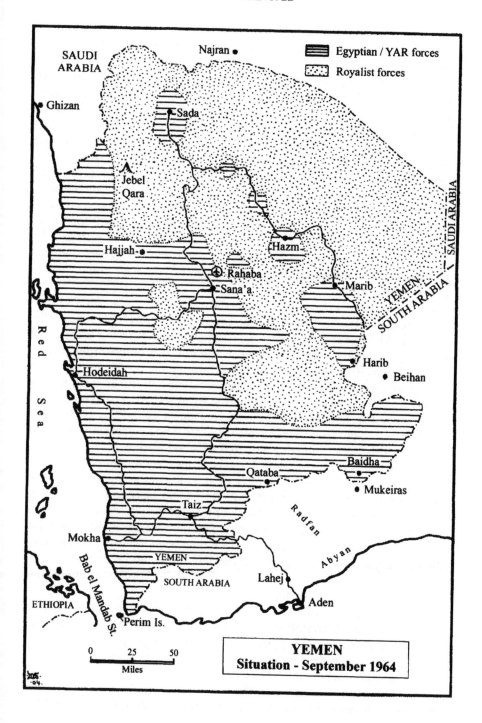

SAUDI ARABIA

Najran

Egyptian / YAR forces

Royalist forces

Ghizan

Sada

Jebel Qara

Hajjah

Hazm

Rahaba

Sana'a

Marib

SAUDI ARABIA

YEMEN

SOUTH ARABIA

Red Sea

Hodeidah

Harib

Beihan

Baidha

Qataba

Mukeiras

Taiz

Radfan

Abyan

Mokha

YEMEN

SOUTH ARABIA

Lahej

Aden

ETHIOPIA

Bab el Mandab St.

Perim Is.

| 0 | 25 | 50 |

Miles

YEMEN
Situation - September 1964

competent Arabist, James Fees, to act as the CIA officer in Taiz – a move that resulted in intelligence on YAR troop deployments coming into American hands.[46]

The dire shortage of British intelligence from royalist-held areas of Yemen was suddenly rectified by the appearance of a remarkable paladin and adventurer, Billy McLean. Lieutenant-Colonel Neil 'Billy' McLean, DSO, MP was originally commissioned into the Royal Scots Greys in 1938 but found regular soldiering too tame. During the Second World War he volunteered for guerrilla operations in Abyssinia where he served with Orde Wingate's 'Gideon Force'. Later in the war he became involved with the Special Operations Executive (SOE) in Albania followed by employment in MI9, another secret organisation dealing with escapees and prisoners-of-war.[47] When the war ended McLean became MP for Inverness, specialising in fact-finding missions. Through these missions he made invaluable contacts with heads of state: these, together with his wartime friendships, were to make him a central character in the story of the Yemen Civil War.

One of McLean's close contacts was King Hussein, who, on a visit to London, urged the Scotsman to visit Yemen and report first hand on the situation. McLean soon left Britain, staying briefly with King Saud on 23 October, where Hussein's message was reinforced before travelling to Aden. He was then spirited into Yemen, through the border Federal state of Beihan, whose ruler the Sharif was providing a useful channel for the covert supply of arms and support to the royalists.[48] McLean soon found that the royalists had organised themselves and were fighting back under the direction of the 56-year-old Prince Hassan, who had recently returned from his duties as Yemeni delegate to the United Nations.

The royalist forces were split into six armies, each commanded by a royal prince. They held most of the eastern region of the country and were fighting for control of the west, inflicting 1,700 Egyptian casualties in December alone.[49] However, the lack of royalist air power was a serious drawback and McLean was in no doubt that the royalists would need this air support as well as ground weapons if they were to wrest control from the Egyptians. After three days McLean left Yemen and travelled back to Riyadh where he saw King Saud: he confirmed the Saudi assessment, and reported back to Lord Home.

The Americans continued to pressure Britain to recognise Sallal's regime, but Macmillan stalled recognition. He was unimpressed both with the State Department's arguments and Kennedy's grasp of the situation, recalling that Kennedy disclaimed any knowledge of Yemen, admitting 'I don't even know where it is'.[50]

The United States recognised the Sallal Government on 19 December 1962 but, as Macmillan recorded, it was not long before they realised the implications:

It is getting pretty clear that the Egyptians mean to use the Yemen as a jumping-off ground for Saudi Arabia – a great prize. They are dropping arms inside Saudi Arabia, and obviously are in touch with subversive elements there. What is ironical is that the Americans, who accepted the threat to Aden and the Federation (especially an old colony!) are now tremendously alarmed about Nasser going for Saudi Arabia and all the vast American oil interests involved.[51]

Another powerful reason for Britain withholding recognition was the desire to resume diplomatic relations with Saudi Arabia, broken off since 1956. King Saud had made it quite clear that memories of Suez and the Buraimi dispute could be put to one side in order to deal with Yemen, the common enemy. But resumption of these relations would undoubtedly result in Yemen closing the British Legation. Despite the pleadings of the Chargé d'Affaires, Christopher Gandy and sections of the Foreign Office, the British Government felt that any intelligence links lost as a result of the closure could be made good by men like Billy McLean, now on the ground in Yemen. Lord Home was able to report that relations were resumed with Saudi Arabia on 16 January 1963, the same day that Aden Colony formally acceded to the Federation of South Arabia. It was a relief that the Federation merger passed off without much incident but, as predicted, Sallal was furious about the *rapprochement* between the British and Saudis and closed down the British Legation.[52]

On 11 January 1963 Nicholas Elliott, who had relinquished the Beirut SIS station in favour of Peter Lunn, returned to the Lebanese capital on a special mission. He came to confront Kim Philby over his traitorous activities, and after a series of meetings with Elliott, Philby proffered a luke-warm confession in return for the promise of immunity from prosecution. SIS 'street-eyes' must have been monitoring Philby's movements, but on 23 January he failed to appear at a dinner party hosted by Glencairn Balfour-Paul, a First Secretary at the British Embassy. Philby had slipped away to Moscow on a Soviet freighter. Whether Philby escaped through Elliott's irresolute tactics or by the design of SIS is uncertain, but when it became public knowledge, it brought unwelcome criticism of the intelligence agencies.[53] Beirut continued to be a crossroads for intrigue, and shortly after Philby's flight, Anthony Blunt, who would become the 'Fourth Man' in the celebrated spy scandal, arrived in the city ostensibly to stay with his old friend Sir Moore Crosthwaite. Ironically, like Philby, Blunt was also related to a famous Arabist and adventurer, in his case, the outrageous Wilfred Scawen Blunt.[54]

The Yemeni royalists began to attract some unlikely supporters. In March 1963 a delegate from the Imam visited Israel to ask for help and was officially rejected, but privately the matter was pursued. Jews in Yemen had once been a significant community, especially in the silver trade and enjoyed special privileges such as exemption from military service and the veiling of their wives. But in 1948 over 48,000 were airlifted to the new state of Israel in an operation known as 'Magic Carpet' and their numbers in Yemen had since dwindled. It was not the protection of the few remaining Jews that concerned the Israeli Intelligence Service (Mossad), but the next move in its constant battle with the Egyptians. In a meeting held with Lord Home to discuss the Yemen War, the Israeli Foreign Minister, Golda Meir, made it clear that her major concern was the development of Egyptian rocket systems capable of a range of 400 miles. This was within striking distance of both Israel and British targets in the Arabian Peninsula.[55] Consequently, in an attempt to bolster the Imam, a series of supply drops were made into royalist positions, from unmarked planes out of Djibouti, while Israeli instructors reportedly began operating with royalist tribesmen. Although the idea of Jewish support for an Islamic cause was uncomfortable to many, the Israelis were keen to keep a civil war fermenting in Yemen, thus drawing Egyptian troops away from the Israeli border.[56]

Billy McLean's mission to Yemen though, was firmly imbedded in the conservative Arab cause and he had the support of a substantial pro-royalist lobby connected to the Macmillan Government. This network included many who were involved in special operations during the Second World War, and although these irregular units were substantially reduced after the war, their former members remained in close contact and 'on call'.[57] Central to this caucus was Macmillan's son-in-law, Julian Amery, son of the legendary imperialist, Leo Amery, a past Secretary of State for India. Julian Amery had enjoyed a colourful past including a spell as a war correspondent in the Spanish Civil War; his active service in the Second World War was spent in irregular warfare in Albania. It was there that he again met up with McLean, his old schoolboy friend from Eton, and together with Captain David Smiley of the Royal Horse Guards (The Blues) they embarked on a number of SOE operations. Post war and running concurrently with a political career, Amery immersed himself in military 'think tanks' and pressure groups, such as the Army League to ensure that Britain maintained her military strength in the face of the Soviet threat.[58] His apogee came when he was appointed Minister of Aviation in July 1962 and from that official position he became known as the unofficial 'Minister for Yemen'.

Macmillan's son, Maurice, was another member of the network. Married to the Hon. Katherine Ormsby-Gore, sister of David, the British Ambassador in Washington, Maurice was an MP and director of the Cairo (Middle East) branch of the Arab News Agency (ANA). This proved to be an extremely influential news agency throughout the Arab world. Originally created by SIS out of an old war-time propaganda agency, it numbering among its executives Alan Hare and Lord Gibson, as well as Tom Little, the noted Middle East authority.[59]

While this group continued to exert political influence on the Prime Minister and his Foreign Secretary, little had been done to offer actual military assistance to the royalists in Yemen. In London, al-Badr was not held in high esteem and overt government assistance was out of the question, but McLean's optimistic reports gave hope of some covert military operations to keep the Egyptians at bay.[60] To this end, a meeting was held in April 1963 at White's Club in London, attended by Amery, McLean, Lord Home and two prominent figures in the Special Air Service, the founder and President, Colonel David Stirling and the Colonel-Commandant of 22 SAS, Colonel Brian Franks.[61] At this meeting McLean, who had just returned from his third visit to the royalist lines in Yemen, was able to inform his colleagues that there were six royalist armies engaged in the counter-revolution. They controlled the whole of east Yemen, but to make any headway in the west, they needed military training together with bazookas and mortars, as well as air support. His treks through the Yemen highlands, surrounded by 'kilted and turbaned tribesmen, festooned with bandoliers, pistols and hand-grenades, and with enormous curved daggers in their belts', were not without danger. McLean was machine-gunned by Egyptian helicopters and witnessed Russian Ilyushin bomber raids, but was clearly anxious to get back to the action.[62]

The meeting agreed that intervention in Yemen was to be an 'unofficial' operation for Special Forces who would offer military training and mount intelligence gathering operations. Senior figures in SIS, such as Nicholas Elliott, realised it would have to involve 'retired members' of the SAS rather than SIS. He calculated that it would take months to establish the necessary SIS agents in Yemen and there was uncertainty whether the organisation even had the resources to mount an operation in time to stop the Egyptians' consolidation of power. The head of SIS, Sir Dick White, was initially opposed to Amery's agenda, insisting that his organisation 'should not go on the offensive, but just stick to the job of intelligence gathering'.[63] Nevertheless, the Prime Minister appeared keen to involve SIS officers in a more central role and created a task-force of old Arab hands headed by John Da Silva (ex head of station, Bahrain) and supported in London by Desmond Harney and Dennis Womersley (ex head of station, Baghdad).[64]

By the spring of 1963 units of the regular 22 SAS had already started operations in the Borneo Campaign, but the sensitive nature of the Yemen War demanded that only SAS Territorials 'on leave' or retired, should be committed.[65] Stirling subsequently called on the services of Lieutenant-Colonel John Woodhouse, CO 22 SAS, as well as Lieutenant-Colonel Jim Johnson, recently retired CO 21 (Territorial) SAS.[66] In a series of secret meetings, well documented in recent books by General Sir Peter de la Billière and Alan Hoe, Stirling co-ordinated the military adventure from offices in London using a cover company, Television International Enterprises (TIE), together with Saudi finance and British logistics. Safe passage of operatives and weapons from Aden to the Yemen was arranged by Stirling, using his friendship with the High Commissioner, Sir Charles Johnston, to gain access to facilities at Government House.[67] With the support of the Deputy High Commissioner, Kennedy Trevaskis, Stirling was provided with the services of Johnson's ADC and Private Secretary, 28-year-old Flight-Lieutenant Tony Boyle, while Captain de la Billière directed the transfer of men and equipment through Aden.[68]

In his account of an SAS soldier, codenamed 'Taffy', which included service in Aden and Yemen, Peter Stiff disclosed the simple system of recruitment of ex-SAS servicemen available for unofficial operations:

> When you leave the SAS of your own choice, it is traditional for you to have a last interview with the Colonel. He calls you by your first name, while you address him as 'sir'. I had my final interview with the Colonel . . . he offered me tea and we had a chat and a few laughs about the good times in Singapore. I stood up and we shook hands while he wished me luck for the future.
>
> 'Would you,' he asked casually, 'like to be on the list?'
>
> 'Thank you sir,' I replied just as casually, 'I would.'
>
> 'All right then, Taffy,' said the Colonel, 'I'll see to it then,' and I left.
>
> . . . Not everyone, particularly men who were often in trouble, was asked. It was considered a great disappointment if the question was not put. It represented a sort of final failure. Once on the list, you might be called to immediately go on an operation for MI6. On the other hand, you might wait for three years, or you might never be called. You had no say in the matter anyway and could not ask.[69]

Lieutenant-Colonel Johnson set about recruiting ex-SAS men including 'one of the originals', Major Johnny Cooper, who was one of the handful of men who formed David Stirling's original 'L' Detachment in the Second World War. This legendary unit that was to form the nucleus of the SAS had carried out a number of successful raids on enemy airfields in North Africa. Cooper, who is sometimes incorrectly described as Stirling's driver, was in fact his desert navigator and gunner and earned the respect of all who served with him. Following the war, he obtained a commission with 22 SAS in Malaya in 1951, and after commanding two of its squadrons there, he went on to join 'D' Squadron in its magnificent action at Jebel Akhdar, Oman in 1959. It was while he was serving with the Muscat Regiment of the Sultan of Oman's Armed Forces that he received a telegram from Stirling in May 1963, which just read, 'Please join me in Aden soonest possible'.[70]

It was a summer of scandals for the Conservative Government. There were rumours of a well-known politician in the Duchess of Argyll's divorce case and the Profumo affair threatened to escalate. Consequently, Duncan Sandys moved to distance the government from the Yemen operation.[71] This may have been a public relations ploy but Stirling was determined to proceed with the Yemen mission and Cooper was instructed to set about organising the small force assembled for him by Lieutenant-Colonel Jim Johnson. The group comprised three SAS volunteers who had been granted one month's leave for the operation, together with four French intelligence officers, and they were soon on their way out of Aden through Beihan to Yemen. After training royalist troops throughout June, mainly in the use of the Bren Gun, Cooper's first large action took place when he set up an ambush in a wadi to the east of Sana'a. He later recalled:

At about 0900 hours the Egyptians moved into the wadi in con- siderable strength with a parachute battalion leading, followed by T-34 tanks and light artillery. They were unaware of our presence further up the valley, and about halfway up, the tanks and artillery halted. The infantry, burdened with a lot of bulky kit and dragging Soviet heavy machine-guns on wheels, advanced shoulder to shoulder in a tightly packed extended order. The royalist gun sections' orders were to hold their fire until the Egyptians were well onto the killing ground below our positions. As the enemy reached our markers, our men opened up with devastating effect, knocking down the closely packed infantry like ninepins. Panic broke out in the ranks behind and then the tanks started firing, not into our positions but among their own men. Then the light artillery opened up, causing further carnage ... as night fell they retreated back towards Sana'a with a very bloody nose indeed. We counted eighty-five bodies, which were left where they fell, remaining there for some two years before an agreement was reached to permit the Red Cross to collect the skeletons.[72]

So successful were Cooper's operations that it was not long before Sana'a Radio was announcing a reward of £5,000 for his capture or his head. Meanwhile, the group of foreign mercenaries had expanded and control of operations was now vested in another old Arabian hand and contact of Billy McLean, Colonel David Smiley. The ex-CO of The Blues had retired from commanding the Sultan of Oman's army after successfully suppressing the rebellion in 1959, and in the meantime had taken up the unlikely role of an inspector for *The Good Food Guide*. When McLean suddenly asked Smiley to accompany him to Yemen and make a report on the military situation for the Saudis, Smiley needed little encourage- ment.[73] Under the cover of a correspondent for *The Daily Telegraph*, he entered Yemen and was introduced by McLean to the royalist commanders. King Feisal of Saudi Arabia soon asked Smiley to take command of not only the ex-SAS men recruited by Johnson, but also the increasing band of international mercenaries. Smiley recalled:

> At the height of the mercenary effort, when I was commanding them, they never numbered more than 48, of whom 30 were French or Belgian and 18 British. They were broken down into small missions – usually one officer, one NCO wireless operator, and one NCO medical orderly – and deployed according to the wishes and needs of the royalist commanders. [74]

These 'advisors' were spread over the entire royalist army, which was estimated to number 30,000 tribesmen and was still commanded by Royal Princes, some of whom had just returned from university. Although a fearless soldier and committed to the cause, Smiley had his own methods of stress-relief. When he needed rest he would block out the sound of distant machine-gun and mortar fire by tuning his transistor radio to the BBC and listening to the familiar Hampshire burr of John Arlott commentating on the latest Test Match.[75] The contest at Lord's seemed a long way away from the bitter struggle in the Yemen highlands.

Once it was clear to Sallal that Britain would defer recognition of the YAR, he launched a series of verbal attacks describing Britain as, 'a hideous old woman whose power was finished'.[76] There was now the clear prospect that the republicans would ratchet up their support for the dissident tribes in South Arabia and the British received intelligence that 'Stalin's organ' type rockets were installed in the Yemen and pointing at the Federation. If these rockets heralded an all-out attack on the Federation, the British defence forces looked decidedly thin.[77] The High Commissioner, Sir Charles Johnston, felt beleaguered, sending an urgent appeal to the Prime Minister, 'the fact is that the Egyptians intend attacking the Federation by one means or another and you and we must take the necessary steps beforehand'. Sallal's deputy, Baidani, piled further pressure on Britain declaring over Radio Sana'a that plans were afoot to establish a republic for the whole of the region.[78]

Johnston had good reason to feel insecure, as the only troops available in the Federation were four battalions of the local FRA supported by British units consisting of one Commando Company, a battery of Field Artillery, a half battery of Light Anti-Aircraft guns, and a squadron of Armoured Cars. With troops from the Aden Garrison needed for internal security in Aden, protection for the States of the Federation would rely on the dubious method of RAF 'proscription bombing'.[79] And if retaliation had to be carried out by the RAF against Yemen, the pilots would now have to contend with anti-aircraft guns, recently installed by the Egyptians.

Sometimes actions by British forces played into the hands of the YAR. The June 1963 'picnic disaster' proved an unnecessary fillip to cross-border tensions when a party of forty-five service men and women strayed into Yemeni territory. The group, mostly RAF office staff, had been allowed leave to camp and picnic in a designated area just outside Aden, but a long way from the Yemen border. Inexplicably, the convoy of six vehicles, commanded by Major Ormerod of the Aden Garrison, lost direction in the vicinity of Shu'aybi, and as darkness fell on 22 June the party careered on towards the Yemen border. As the vehicles crossed into Yemen they were ambushed by tribesmen who opened fire on the forward vehicles, wounding some of the female clerks. There was chaos in the darkness. Some of the British troops managed to crawl back into friendly territory, but four of the men went forward to assess the situation and were shot dead. The eighteen survivors were soon captured by the Yemenis and marched to Taiz, where they remained in captivity pending negotiations to secure their release.[80]

While Baidani attempted to control the local political situation in Yemen, his brother-in-law, Anwar Sadat, directed the overall course of the Egyptian campaign from Cairo. Among the members of Egypt's Revolutionary Command, Sadat was the keenest proponent of the war in the Yemen. He not only saw the campaign as a good training ground for Egyptian troops for a future war with Israel, but also saw it as a means to pressurise King Saud, whom he held responsible for the previous year's collapse of Egypt's union with Syria.[81] Accordingly, he provided large resources, estimated to be costing nearly $1 million per day to enable his military commander, Field-Marshal Hakim Amer, to increase ground troops in the Yemen. These troops were even supplemented by a battalion of Palestinians, styled a 'Frontier Defence' and raised in the Gaza Strip.[82] The idea of an international force, along the lines of the one employed in the Spanish Civil War, was discussed but Nasser came down in favour of increasing regional proxy forces. Consequently, Colonel Mahmud Atyia of the Egyptian Military Intelligence organised the issue of rifles, mortars and machine-guns to dissidents in the Federation. He also initiated the training of Yemeni and dissident commandos who could slip over the border into the Federation to harass and attack FRA forts and British patrols.

In January 1963 there were over 15,000 Egyptian troops in Yemen and Field-Marshal Amer visited the country to personally organise a series of operations, known as the Ramadan Offensive. Using armoured columns, Egyptians swept the royalists from the town of Marib, which fell on 26 February, closely followed by Harib, which surrendered on 4 March. Although the royalists were pressed back into their mountain strongholds, the Egyptian military success was only achieved by large reinforcements, which increased troop numbers from 20,000 men in

February to 30,000 in March. This army was supported by large armoured contingents and over 200 aircraft, which operated from local airfields.[83]

Nevertheless, despite their increasing numerical superiority, the Egyptians made little progress in the mountains and by June 1963 their offensive petered out. The Egyptian ranks were poorly led and morale started to suffer among units despatched to the highlands, which was not helped by their enemy's practice of slicing off the ears and noses of those they captured. Young Egyptian conscripts were terrified to be confronted with the bodies of fallen comrades, decapitated and horribly abused.[84] This low morale was admitted by Field-Marshal Amer but was hardly helped by his ensuing purge among the Egyptian officer corps, which resulted in the arrest of over fifty officers on charges of 'plotting'. Amer pressed on, increasingly at odds with both the Egyptian Revolutionary Command and Nasser, and determined to develop Yemen as his personal power base.

The Egyptians faced considerable problems. While they had captured the towns of Marib, Harib and Sada, they were hardly welcomed by the local urban population, who were happy enough to support the new republican regime but were often sullen in their reception for the outsiders. The very geographical position of Yemen proved an even bigger obstacle. The vast stretches of the 'Empty Quarter' to the north, the Hadhramaut to the east and the Red Sea to the west had always favoured the isolation policy of the Imams. The terrain was inhospitable to an occupying force and although there was a coastal plain that reached forty miles inland and which was soon occupied by Egyptian and YAR forces, the interior comprised high mountain ranges running from north to south, reaching heights of over 10,000 ft. Furthermore, to the east, these mountains verged into a desert, one of the hottest places on earth.[85]

Consequently, living and fighting in these conditions was appallingly hard and communications were impossible for troops unfamiliar with the country. Wounded men on both sides could expect little medical help, and with bad hygiene and endemic tuberculosis, survival rates were poor. Prisoners were usually butchered and a code existed, especially among the royalist tribes, that damned all prisoners as cowards and only worthy of death. Even the International Committee of the Red Cross (ICRC), well used to humanitarian disasters, was alarmed at the findings of their medical missions to the Yemen. Two Red Cross doctors recorded the appalling condition of casualties found in the mountains:

> En route we found two badly wounded men in a cave, suffering from shrapnel wounds. For five days they had been lying waiting for care on sheepskins stained with blood and pus, one half unconscious. There was practically no water and no soap in this stinking hole. We

administered Chloromycetin and arranged for their evacuation. We also found a little girl of 10 with acute pneumonia and a boy of 12 who was dying ... Then another consultation: 20 patients whom we treated for malaria, pneumonia and a combatant wounded in the thorax by a sword.[86]

Sallal's own YAR troops were badly equipped. None of the planes or tanks inherited from the Russians had been maintained and their small arms consisted of Czech pistols, 1914 Mauser rifles and curve-bladed *jambiyas*. It was hard to make good soldiers out of urban Yemenis and their numbers rarely exceeded 5,000. Furthermore, this YAR army was so short of educated men that the Egyptians had to occupy all the staff jobs, as well as supplying the officers.[87] With poor pay the loyalty of the YAR troops to their president was questionable, although their uniforms did appear to instil some pride. One witness reported a turnout of troops, which showed off a variety of uniforms including those from the British Air Training Corps, a Petty Officer in the Royal Navy, and one of a guard of the old London and North-Eastern Railway Company.[88] Uniforms worn by the opposing royalist forces often showed the same theatrical leanings. Colonel David Smiley observed one tribesman sporting an Air Vice-Marshal's tunic, while another was seen in the uniform of the General Manager of the Southend-on-Sea Transport Corporation.[89]

Government Communications Headquarters (GCHQ) at Cheltenham, which monitored regional wireless networks, picked up indications that Egyptian commanders in the Yemen highlands were experiencing serious difficulties. Their mechanised units were succumbing to extremely simple but effective royalist tactics. As convoys of Egyptian tanks were blocked in mountain passes, ambushers stuffed rags into the tank exhaust pipes: the resulting fumes forced the tank crews to clamber out and once exposed, they were machine-gunned from the royalist positions.

During the early months of 1963 the Egyptians had used their long-range Ilyushin and Tupolev bombers, operating from Aswan in Egypt and employing mixed Egyptian and Russian crews to attack strategic royalist targets. However, by September 1963 with the help of 500 Soviet technicians, an airfield was built at Rahaba, near Sana'a, which could accommodate the heavy bombers. Five squadrons of fighter planes, including Yakovlev 11 piston-engine aircraft and MiG 16 and 17 fighters, used airfields within Yemen.[90] The republicans were winning the air war and the royalists were desperate for outside help from Saudi Arabia. But the Saudi Air Force, stung by the defection to Cairo of its commander and several pilots, was still weak and had to rely on South African pilots to bolster its force.[91] The possibility that the Saudi involvement in the Yemen War could escalate deeply alarmed President Kennedy, who cabled Macmillan:

Nasser and Sallal may well try to ferment trouble in Saudi Arabia or elsewhere. We've already seen them try to cow the Saudis by bombing Najran, and only the strongest words from here appear to have temporarily turned them off. If Nasser escalates and the Saudis hit back with mercenary pilots, we may have the Near East aflame. I'm sure this will suit the Soviets, but you and I would surely be the losers.[92]

As the Egyptians continued to bomb the Saudi towns of Najran and Ghizan, the US attempted to mediate between Egypt and Saudi Arabia and arrange a cease-fire. During the spring and summer of 1963, teams from the United Nations arrived to monitor the withdrawals but, while Saudi Arabia and Jordan ceased activity, Egypt merely withdrew a brigade only to replace it the following month.[93] The British Government publicly acquiesced with this intended truce but this outraged those still fighting in the field for the royalists. A telegram (subsequently heavily 'weeded') to 'Fisher', from a senior royalist supporter (possibly McLean), complained that 'there is an indication of a radical change of policy. I understood we were all agreed that prolonged stalemate would best suit British interests'.[94] However, the UN mission foundered, and the Egyptian air force continued to use their Russian-built TU-20s to bomb royalist villages.

In July 1963 it was even reported that the Egyptians were dropping poisonous gas onto royalist positions and those close to the action, such as Johnny Cooper, recalled seeing areas of ground 'covered with a black gooey substance that was giving off vapour'. But tests on specimens returned to the British Government's Porton Down Research Station proved inconclusive. Despite worldwide press coverage, the bombs probably only contained a phosphorous agent.[95]

In August 1963, due to his wife's ill health, Sir Charles Johnston retired. His tenure, initially as Governor and then as the first High Commissioner, was contentious. Socially, he was well connected and wielded great charm. He had a profound grasp of foreign affairs and was an expert planner but failed to impress Denis Healey who judged him 'a languid cynic', while others felt that as an experienced career diplomat, Johnston should have been better at overriding government attempts to delay decision-making.[96] That criticism could not be levelled at his successor and former deputy, Sir Kennedy Trevaskis.[97] He was an experienced Arabian official, having for many years occupied the role of Agent in the WAP, and he was determined to bring the hinterland into all discussions about the future of South Arabia. As a first hand observer of Nasserism for many years, he was under no illusions that should the YAR Government consolidate its hold on the Yemen, then Nasser would immediately order an all out assault on 'the seat of Imperialism' in Aden, as well as British interests in the wider Gulf region. By comparison, the old Imamic designs on British interests would seem amateurish. He implored Duncan Sandys, Secretary of State for the Colonies, to provide greater investment and for an immediate bolstering of the British military presence in South Arabia before it was too late.[98]

As long as the Egyptian regime had to wait for Britain's decision over formal recognition of the YAR, they became wary of overtly supporting dissidents in the Federation. By the autumn of 1963 it was clear there would be no recognition. The royalist camp was also buoyed by the assassination of President Kennedy in November 1963, an event that caused much rifle firing among the royalist tribes who clearly hoped for a change in US policy. Furthermore, the war in Yemen had reached a stalemate, which the royalists were attempting to break with a new offensive. The Egyptians knew this could only be mounted with the assistance of supplies reaching the royalists through the Federation states of Beihan and Dhala. It was now time for the Egyptians to move the war to the British. The wild and remote Radfan region was a good place to start.

NOTES

1 Despite his horrific injuries, Ronald Bailey went on to become British Ambassador to Bolivia and Morocco. Fortunes changed rapidly in Yemen, and when the revolutionary republic gained power later that year, the assailant became the regime's Chief Executioner. However, he was later murdered by the family of one of his victims. Ronald Bailey to Author, 2 July 2002.

2 Even today, the Military Museum in Sana'a displays horrific photographs of the beheadings of revolutionaries after the 1955 failed coup. Public beheading was discontinued by decree in 1964 and replaced by the firing squad: see *The Salt Lake Tribune*, 26 January 2003. Also Edgar O'Balance, *The War in the Yemen*, Faber & Faber, 1971, p. 27.

3 The resources of the British Legation were extremely limited. Staff consisted of the Chargé, his wife and a 'no 2' who would act in his absence. On the insistence of the Imam, the First Minister could only be titled Chargé d'Affaires, and the coat of arms could not be displayed. Ronald Bailey to Author, 2 July 2002.

4 Balfour-Paul, op. cit., p. 73, and Sultan Nagi, 'The Genesis of the Call for Yemeni Unity' in Pridham, op. cit., pp. 240–59.

5 Imam Ahmed continued to insist that non-Arab states could only enjoy legation status and had to be based in Taiz, while the embassies of Arab states remained in the northern city of Sana'a. US economic assistance to Yemen in 1960 amounted to $3m; see p. 25, MF81, Documents of US National Security Council 1947–85, LHCMA.

6 Ronald Bailey to Author, 2 July 2002.

7 It was true that some 80% of Yemen's exports did pass through the British-controlled port of Aden, but total exports were pitifully small in the first place.

8   Memorandum, JIC (57) 102, October 1957, CAB 158/30, NA.
9   Pridham, op. cit., p. 144. Also Yezid Sayigh & Avi Shlaim (eds), *The Cold War and the Middle East*, Clarendon Press, 1997, p. 280.
10   Most commentators indict Egypt for its role in the coup, with the exception of Professor Fred Halliday. The connection between Sallal and the Egyptians at Hodeidah is stressed by Harold Ingrams, *The Yemen*, John Murray, 1963. For Sallal see Dana Adams Schmidt, *Yemen: The Unknown War*, Bodley Head, 1968, pp. 20–8. Also Fred Halliday, *Arabia Without Sultans*, Saqi Books, 2002, pp. 101–2 and Holden, op. cit., pp. 93–5. See also David Ledger, *Shifting Sands: The British in South Arabia*, Peninsular Publishing, 1983, p. 42.
11   One local irritant was the imposition of Eastern Bloc employment practices. See W E Griffith, 'Soviet Influence in the Middle East', *Survival*, Vol. XVIII, 1976. Also Page, op. cit., p. 49.
12   Halliday, op. cit., p. 98.
13   Robert McGregor to Author, 29 January 2003. David Holden, in *Farewell to Arabia*, p. 84, scotched other rumours about the Imam's syphilis. Holden was *The Sunday Times* Foreign Affairs correspondent before he was murdered in Cairo in 1977. For details of his mysterious death, see Downton, op. cit., pp. 341–2.
14   Ronald Bailey to Author, 2 July 2002.
15   Captain P Boxhall, 'The Yemen – Background to Recent Events', in *Army Quarterly*, July 1964, pp. 201–9. Also Pridham, op. cit., p. 78. For the Red Sea, see Lieutenant-Commander Youssef Aboul-Enein, 'The Egyptian–Yemen War (1962–67): Egyptian Perspectives on Guerrilla Warfare' in *The US Army Professional Writing Collection*, www.army.mil/prof.
16   O'Balance, op. cit., pp. 70–2. By this time, there was ample opportunity to mix with Egyptians through the Egyptian military mission in Sana'a.
17   Salahaldin al-Bitar, 'The Rise and Decline of the Ba'ath', in *Middle East International*, June 1971. See also Tom Little, *Modern Egypt*, op. cit., 195–6, and Tariq Ismael, op. cit., p. 27 and Tabitha Petran, *Syria*, Ernest Benn, 1972, p. 161.
18   Halliday, *Arabia*, op. cit., pp. 98–9. Also Page, op. cit., p. 64.
19   The rebels had surprisingly little armour and ammunition. The coup was staged using thirteen tanks, six armoured cars, two mobile artillery guns and two anti-aircraft guns. Each tank only had five rounds of ammunition; see Youssef Aboul-Enein, op. cit.
20   Because the average height of most Yemenis was about 5ft, doorways and staircases were tiny. Al-Badr, certainly no colossus, kept cracking his head in palace doorways.
21   There were several plots in preparation at the time, including the one hatched by Sallal. The 26 September coup was carried out by Lieutenant Ali Moghny with the assistance of Egyptian Intelligence. It was not long before Sallal joined forces and took over the new regime. Many saw it as no coincidence that the revolution had occurred on the very day that Aden agreed to merge with the other states of the Federation of South Arabia. For a detailed account of the coup, see Dana Adams Schmidt, op. cit., pp. 20–35.
22   Dresch, op. cit., p. 237.
23   Schmidt, op. cit., p. 74.
24   Under the 1946 Attlee Doctrine, the UK mainland and Empire territories were to be defended against subversion by the Security Service (MI5). The collection of intelligence in the rest of the world was covered by SIS. This split broke down where Commonwealth countries became involved with foreign

powers. See Tom Bower, *Sir Dick White and the Secret War 1935–90*, Heineman, 1995, p. 243. Also Stephen Dorril, *MI6: Fifty Years of Special Operations*, Fourth Estate, 2000, pp. 31, 679.

25   Major O'Bryan-Tear served in 'The Jedburghs' under the *nom de guerre*, 'A J Forrest', and was wounded in an ambush in France in 1944. See Arthur Brown, 'The Jedburghs: A Short History, www.ww2-TheJedburghs. Also Dorril op. cit., p. 242.

26   Gandy to Foreign Office, 10 January 1963, PREM 11/4356, NA. West Germany also retained an agricultural mission in Taiz, staffed by six of their nationals who were all Arabists. They made frequent trips into the hinterland, which may have generated intelligence useful to the West.

27   Johnson to Secretary of State, 4 December 1962, PREM 11/4356, NA. Chauvel was the son of the French Ambassador to London.

28   It was later revealed that some senior executives at *The Economist* together with Lord Astor, proprietor of *The Observer*, all knew that while Philby was working on their assignments, he was also reporting to SIS: see Eric Downton, *Wars Without End*, Stoddart, 1987, p. 339.

29   St John Philby had died in Beirut two years earlier, by which time his legendary influence with governments had vanished due to an opinionated nature. During the Lebanese Civil War, his grave in Beirut was despoiled and given over to a PLO casualty: see MI5 file ref. 'St John Bridger Philby', KV 2/1118/9, NA, and Anthony Cave Brown, *Treason in the Blood*, Robert Hale, 1995, p. 496.

30   *The Observer*, 22 October 1962.

31   Downton, op. cit., pp. 331–5.

32   Ibid, op. cit., pp. 252–3.

33   Ann Cuthbert correspondence, 6 November 1962, Cuthbert Papers. BP employees were accompanied by their wives. Servicemen, with certain exceptions, were unaccompanied.

34   Soviet and Czech advisors could always monitor any war; see Anwar el-Sadat, op. cit., pp. 143–4. Also J E Peterson, 'The Yemen Arab Republic and the Politics of Balance', in *Asian Affairs*, Vol. 68, October 1981. See also O'Ballance op. cit., p. 73 and Page, op. cit., p. 75.

35   Hennessy, op. cit., p. 40.

36   Harold Macmillan, op. cit., pp. 267–8.

37   For details of the network that bound the Egyptian regime, see Imad Harb, 'The Egyptian Military in Politics', *Middle East Journal*, Vol. 57, # 2, Spring 2003. For al-Baidani, see Rahmy, op. cit., p. 90.

38   The initial Egyptian force numbered 3,000 and by the end of October it was estimated at 10,000; see Aboul-Enein, op. cit., O'Balance, op. cit., p. 72, 85, and Bidwell, op. cit., pp. 198–9.

39   David Ormsby-Gore to Lord Home, 27 February 1963, PREM 11/4357, NA.

40   Gandy's policy in Yemen was at odds with Trevaskis, the architect of the Federation. They had entirely different attitudes and, although they were contemporaries at both Marlborough and King's College Cambridge, Trevaskis had been a sporting and gregarious 'hearty' whereas Gandy was an aesthete. John Malcolm to Author, 8 May 2004.

41   Successive Heads of the Arabian Department, Robert Walmsley (1961–3) and Frank Brenchley (1963–7) together with the Prime Minister's Private Secretary, Sir Philip Zulueta (1955–64) were all for recognition: see Zulueta to PM, 27 December 1962, PREM 11/4356, NA. For Gandy, see Gandy to Foreign Office, 10 January 1963, PREM 11/4356, NA. For Sallal's

overtures, see Rahmy, op. cit., p. 124. Also John Malcolm to Author, 8 May 2004.

42 Prince al-Hassan also served as Imam al-Badr's Prime Minister. He retired from the fray in 1968 due to ill health. He spent the next thirty years in the US and Saudi Arabia, where he died in 2003. For an appreciation by A B Eagle, see *British-Yemeni Society Journal*, Vol. 11, 2003.

43 Gandy to Foreign Office, 10 January 1963, PREM 11/4356, NA; also Johnston to Defence Secretary, 4 December 1962, PREM 11/4356, NA. See also Schmidt, op. cit., pp. 48–51. Rising oil revenues bolstered the House of Saud but the loyalty of its US trained armed forces was suspect and had to be bolstered by a 'white army' of *Bedu* tribesmen. Saudi pilots on missions in support of royalists had recently defected to the UAR.

44 Copeland, op. cit., p. 204. Copeland knew that such moves were often made for very good tactical reasons.

45 David Holden and Richard Johns, *The House of Saud*, Sidgwick & Jackson, 1981, pp. 226–7. For Indonesia, see A & G Kahin, *Subversion as Foreign Policy: The Secret Eisenhower & Dulles Debacle in Indonesia*, New Press, 1995, p.92.

46 Quoted in Bower, op. cit., pp. 250–1.

47 McLean died in 1986. Four years later, Xan Fielding, a close friend and kindred spirit, wrote a comprehensive biography, *One Man in His Time: The Life of Lieutenant-Colonel N L D 'Billy McLean, DSO*, Macmillan, 1990.

48 For McLean see Xan Fielding, op. cit., pp. 130–4. Also Holden & Johns, op. cit., p. 229. For the Sharif, see Gandy to Foreign Office, 10 January 1963, PREM 11/4356, NA, and Jedda Embassy to Foreign Office, 27 October 1963, FO 371/168809, NA.

49 Casualties quoted in Dana Adams Schmidt, op. cit., p. 234.

50 Report by Burke Trend, 10 January 1963, CAB 129/112, NA; also Harold Macmillan, op. cit., p. 271.

51 Macmillan Diaries, 7 March 1963, MS Macmillan, Bodleian Library, Oxford.

52 Sir Charles Johnston to Foreign Office, 23 January 1963, PREM 11/4357, NA. Also Foreign Office Memo to Prime Minister, 22 January 1963, PREM 11/4357, NA.

53 In another remarkable coincidence, Peter Lunn, the SIS Head of Station in Beirut, was away skiing at the time of Philby's escape. Philby gave an interesting interview, post escape, about his activities in SIS, in *Kodumaa*, No. 41, p. 3, 13 October 1971, published by the Soviet Committee for Cultural Relations with Compatriots Abroad, Estonia (translated by FBI). See also Tom Bower, *The Perfect English Spy*, Heinemann, 1995, pp. 296–305 and Anthony Cave Brown, op. cit., 504–9.

54 Rather than meeting the British Ambassador, Blunt's mission was more likely to see his old Soviet controller Yuri Modin. By this time, the Security Service (MI5) had already interviewed Blunt more than a dozen times,

55 Minutes of meeting between Golda Meir and Lord Home, New York, 2 October 1963, PREM 11/4928, NA. See also Major E O'Balance, 'Middle East Arms Race, in *Army Quarterly*, July 1964.

56 It was a tactic the Israelis reportedly used some years later when they supplied weapons and medicine to the Anya-nya rebels fighting a Nasserite regime in Sudan; see Bloch & Fitzgerald, op. cit., p.128; also Halliday, op. cit., p. 140 and Holden & Johns, op. cit., p. 229. In 1948 the Jews in Aden Colony had also declined, from over 7,000 to under 1,000.

57 Colonel David Smiley to Author, 16 September 2003. Also Richard Aldrich, 'Unquiet in Death: The post-war survival of the SOE, 1945–51', in Gorst & Lucas (eds), *Politics and the Limits of Policy*, Pinter, 1991, pp. 193–8.

58　For Amery's military correspondence with Captain Basil Liddell Hart, see File GB99 Amery, LHCMA. Julian Amery's brother John founded the pro-Nazi British Free Corps and was hanged for treason in 1945.

59　Little was Managing Director of ANA in the 1960s and wrote a series of authoritative books on the Middle East, including *South Arabia, Arena of Conflict*. For ANA, see Bloch & Fitzgerald, op. cit., p. 95.

60　For London's low opinion of al-Badr, see Ormsby-Gore to Foreign Office, 22 November 1963, PREM 11/4928, NA.

61　Lieutenant-Colonel Franks was also the first Commanding Officer of 21 SAS Regiment, the Territorial unit formed in 1947. For accounts of the meeting at White's, see Alan Hoe, *David Stirling: The Authorised Biography of the Founder of the SAS*, Little Brown, 1992, pp. 356–9 and Dorril, op. cit., pp. 684–5.

62　Feilding, op. cit., pp. 133–42.

63　Verrier, op. cit., p. 255 and Bower, op. cit., pp. 244–9.

64　Kim Philby, article in *Kodumaa*, 13 October 1971, translated by FBI, 25 April 1972. Also Dorril, op. cit., p. 687. Denis Womersley was posted to Aden in 1966. His distinguished career ended with postings to Beirut, and Bonn in 1974.

65　For a detailed account of 22 SAS in Borneo, see Peter Dickens, *SAS: The Jungle Frontier*, Arms and Armour, 1983.

66　It was Woodhouse who, together with Major Dare Newell, established the SAS as a modern fighting force in the early 1950s. 22 SAS was the regular unit, while 21 and 23 SAS were Territorials, set up after World War II. 21 was the successor to David Stirling's wartime desert group, whereas 23 was the successor to the wartime MI9, which had helped British soldiers and airmen escape from occupied Europe. For an analysis of SAS post-war operations, see John Newsinger, *Dangerous Men: The SAS and Popular Culture*, Pluto, 1997.

67　As from 18 January 1963, the date of the merger of Aden with the Federation, the Governor was titled High Commissioner. For TIE, see Hoe, op. cit., p.359. Also Halliday, op. cit., p. 149.

68　Boyle was the son of Marshal of the Royal Air Force, Sir Dermot Boyle. Boyle (junior) retired as ADC in October 1963 but continued his association with the operation: see de la Billière, op. cit., pp. 202–7 and Dorril, op. cit., p. 685. Also David Smiley, *Arabian Assignment*, Leo Cooper, 1975, p. 154.

69　Peter Stiff, *See You in November: The Story of an SAS Assassin*, Galago, 2002, p. 50. Stiff goes on to refer to Stirling's company, Watchguard International, as the main conduit for post-war recruitment, but this company was not formed until 1967. However, there were other organisations available in the early 1960s. For an analysis of the myriad of companies used by Stirling, see Bloch and Fitzgerald, op. cit., pp. 46–50. Colonel Slim (later Viscount Slim) commanded 22 SAS Regiment 1967–70. He was GSO1 (Special Forces) HQ UK Land Forces, 1970–2.

70　Obituary, *The Times*, 13 July 2002. Also Johnny Cooper, *One of the Originals*, Pan Books, 1991, pp. 157-9.

71　The Profumo affair had serial repercussions; see *The Sunday Times*, 28 April 2002.

72　Cooper, op. cit., pp. 163–4.

73　For his time as Commander of the Sultan of Oman's Armed Forces, see Colonel Smiley corres. 1958–9, Ref. 43251 Middle East Centre, St Antony's College, Oxford University. David Smiley returned to Yemen in 2003, meeting some old adversaries and assisting with the Yemeni Official History of the conflict. See *British-Yemeni Society Journal*, Vol. 11, 2003. For his fascinating career, see David Smiley, *Irregular Regular*, Michael Russell, 1994.

74   Smiley, *Arabian Assignment*, op. cit., p. 154.
75   Ibid, p. 137.
76   Cabinet Memo, 10 January 1963, CAB 129/112, PRO.
77   An undated (probably April 1963), secret intelligence assessment later discounted the idea that these rockets were long-range missiles. They were identified as Czech rocket launchers, type RL130, with an effective range of five miles, PREM 11/4928, NA. Also Johnston to Prime Minister, 16 February 1963, PREM 11/4357, NA.
78   Johnston to Macmillan, 16 February 1963, PREM 11/4357, NA. For Baidani, see Schmidt, op. cit., p. 76. Baidami's outbursts even alarmed Cairo and he was soon removed and posted to the Legation in Beirut.
79   Memo by Chief of Defence Staff, 7 January 1963, PREM 11/4356, NA. See also Johnston to Prime Minister, 16 February 1963, PREM 11/4357, NA.
80   This account has been based on a description in Michael Crouch's memoir, *An Element of Luck*, Radcliffe, 1993, pp. 135–9. See also James Lunt, *The Barren Rocks of Aden*, Herbert Jenkins, 1996, pp. 185–6 and O'Balance, op. cit., p. 113. Among those killed were Lance-Corporal R Jeffery (Royal Marines), Driver R Morley (Royal Army Service Corps) and Signalman R Leech (Royal Corps of Signals).
81   Anwar el-Sadat, *In Search of Identity*, Collins, 1978, p. 162. Although Sadat accepted that the Egyptian military campaign was a failure, he cited the eventual replacement of King Saud by Feisal as a useful outcome.
82   For Palestinians, see note in memo from Arabian Department, Foreign Office, by B R Pridham, 26 September 1963, FO 371/168809, NA. For funding, see Arabian Department Memo, 3 October 1963, FO 371/168809, NA.
83   *The Egyptian Invasion of Yemen*, Legation of Moutawakilite Kingdom of Yemen, London, 1964, Yem. 3a.Mou., AWDU.
84   This practice was not allowed in operational areas controlled by foreign mercenaries. The Imam also attempted to curtail the practice, to little effect. See Schmidt, op. cit., p. 171. See also Bidwell, op. cit., p. 208 and O'Balance, op. cit., p. 118.
85   Lieutenant-Colonel N McLean, 'The War in the Yemen,' lecture given to RUSI, 20 October 1965, Yem (N). 3/MCL, AWDU.
86   *The ICRC and the Yemen Conflict*, International Red Cross, Geneva 1964, Yem.2c.ICRC, AWDU.
87   O'Balance, op. cit., p. 88.
88   'In the Yemen – A Crisis for Nasser', *Topic* Magazine, 1 December 1962; also Captain Boxhall, 'The Yemen – Background to Recent Events', *Army Quarterly*, July 1964.
89   Colonel David Smiley to *The Household Brigade Magazine*, Spring 1966. .
90   Schmidt, op. cit., pp. 167–9.
91   Gandy to Foreign Office, 10 January 1963, PREM 11/4356, NA. Due to the Yemen threat, Western arms companies, including Northrop, Lockheed and the British Aircraft Corporation, all vied for sales of air defence systems to Saudi Arabia. See Anthony Sampson, *The Arms Bazaar*, Hodder & Stoughton, 1977, pp. 158–64.
92   Kennedy to Macmillan, 26 January 1963, and Macmillan to Kennedy, 14 February 1963, PREM 11/4357, NA. See also Memo, Macmillan to Foreign Secretary, 18 September 1963, FO 371/168809, NA.
93   Ahmed al-Shamy, *The Egyptian Invasion of Yemen*, Legation of the Moutawakilite Kingdom of Yemen, A/Yem.3a.MOU, AWDU.
94   Telegram 501, 5 March 1963, PREM 11/4928, NA. Sender and recipient have

been deleted under Section 3 (4) Public Records Act. Indications are that it was sent to Nigel (later Sir Nigel) Fisher, Under Secretary of State for the Colonies. See also unsourced (possibly Brenchley) memo to Prime Minister, 21 November 1963, PREM 11/4928, NA.

95   The first report appeared in *The Daily Telegraph*, 8 July 1963. Also Colonel David Smiley to Author, 16 September 2003. See also Holden and Johns, op. cit., p. 234 and Cooper, op. cit., p. 170.

96   Correspondence, John Malcolm, December 1998. See also Denis Healey, *The Time of My Life*, Michael Joseph, 1989, p. 283. Johnston's wife was a member of the old Georgian royal family, later supplanted by the Tsars of Russia. He finished his distinguished diplomatic career as the UK High Commissioner in Australia (1965–71).

97   Trevaskis received a KCMG upon his appointment as High Commissioner.

98   Letter 14 October 1963, to Duncan Sandys. Sender's name removed under PRA, but letter issued from High Commissioner's Office. See PREM 11/4928, NA. See also Trevaskis to Sandys, 22 October 1963, FO 371/168809, NA and Sir Kennedy Trevaskis, *Shades of Amber*, Hutchinson, 1968, pp. 194–6.

CHAPTER IV
Operation 'Nutcracker'
(4 January–28 February 1964)

By late 1963 intrigue was rife in Sana'a, not helped by the fact that President Sallal was ill, spending much time in Cairo undergoing treatment for ulcers and a heart condition.[1] The US and the Soviet Union made sure they were well represented in Yemen and, although many of those collecting intelligence operated under diplomatic or press cover, opponents usually knew the identity of each other. It was not the Brooks Brothers' suits and button-down collars that gave the Americans away but the fact they were in such close proximity to the Soviet agents, sometimes sharing the same accommodation. David Holden, Foreign Affairs correspondent for *The Sunday Times*, witnessed the chief Russian security officer for Yemen tormenting Robert Stookey, the American representative, in the sordid confines of a government guesthouse. Both had just taken it in turns to burn their confidential documents in the overflowing lavatory, when the Russian appeared and proceeded to pick up Stookey's briefcase exclaiming, 'Ah, Meester American, what carry you here? Gold so-overrreigns?' Stookey must have had an anxious moment, for the case carried far more valuable items than sovereigns. Holden maintained that the case contained the top-secret American cipher books.[2]

Egyptian Intelligence was also extremely busy in the Yemen during 1963. Their attention was turning to a small chubby agricultural engineer, who was proving adept at organising nationalist dissent. Qahtan al-Sha'abi did not look like a revolutionary firebrand. Personable and nearing middle age, he was almost a generation older than his companions, but his benign image, rather like that of his nationalist opponent, al-Asnag, was misleading. For when he was inciting a crowd or mob, al-Sha'abi slipped easily into the mould of enraged agitator. Like many nationalist revolutionaries, he was literate and erudite. Born in Lahej in 1920, he was educated at Aden College and later graduated from Khartoum University as an agricultural engineer. He returned to Lahej where he became a state agricultural officer and soon became close to the nationalist al-Jifri clan. Through a literary club in Sheikh Othman, he gathered together a group of young radicals and immersed himself in the nationalist politics of the South Arabian League. But in 1958 British pressure forced out the turbulent Sultan of Lahej and the al-Jifris, and al-Sha'abi, fearing arrest, bolted to Yemen together with state funds. He soon moved on to Cairo, where he revitalised the South Arabian League and became its Public Relations Officer. But allegations over the misappropriation of party funds forced him out of the group and he fled back into Yemen, where he joined a motley crowd of disaffected Yemenis and Adenis in Taiz. His younger charismatic cousin, Feisal Latif al-Sha'abi, soon joined him and together they attracted a small dedicated band of radicals.[3]

However, it was the 1962 revolution and the arrival of the Egyptians that had really changed Qahtan al-Sha'abi's fortunes. With the dissidents soon mobilised and formed by the Egyptians into a 'National Liberation Army', al-Sha'abi assumed the role of their commander. This became the military arm of a new and more radical movement called the National Liberation Front (NLF), which was set up under Nasser's guidance. The NLF, known in Arabic as al-Jabha al-Qaumia, was a different and more formidable movement than either the South Arabian League or ATUC and its political offshoot the People's Socialist Party (PSP). The NLF's formation took place in Taiz in June 1963, and was formally announced by Radio Sana'a on 28 July 1963. The membership had largely evolved from a group of exiles from Aden and the Federation who had already been active in the south, particularly as members of the Arab Nationalist Movement (ANM), the forerunner of so many Arab nationalist and terrorist groups.[4] Importantly, the NLF enjoyed wide support ranging from tribes in the hinterland of South Arabia, especially in the Radfan, to port and refinery workers and intellectuals in Aden State. Conversely, the other main nationalist group, the ATUC, was predominantly an urban organisation based in Aden State. Said Nasr, a southerner who later became a communist official, recalled his recruitment to the NLF in Yemen:

> With the revolution in the North in 1962, we knew the time had come for decisive action. The ANM was small but was strong among the youths and intellectuals. We had political study groups and had much debate about what to do, since the old methods of strikes and demonstrations had reached the limits of their usefulness. We looked to Algeria and to Cuba. After Radfan broke out, those of us in this area who were part of the ANM went to Taiz. After political and military training, I returned to my hometown while others went to take part in operations in the Radfan. We had been trained in an isolated camp near Taiz. There were two kinds of training: tribesmen were trained to be a liberation army fighting in the mountains and border areas: youths from towns like us were trained to work as

fedayeen with explosives, and we learned how to do commando actions.[5]

In another innovation, the NLF was set up with secret cell structures, similar to those in Nasser's revolutionary organisation. The members of each operational unit were unknown to the next one and only the cell leader had knowledge of objectives and contact with the next level of command. Cells spawned until all levels of local administration and the army were penetrated, but throughout 1963 and 1964, British intelligence was still unaware of the extent of NLF influence and intentions.[6]

After the official launch of this formidable movement, its first object was stir up rebellion within the Federation. One of the assets of a nationalist inspired rebellion is often the terrain and climate, as the terrorist FLN movement had recently proved in Algeria, and the mountainous Radfan region was ideal country in which to launch a revolt. Its poor communications would deny Federal troops access, and allow NLF cells to work with impunity among tribal areas. The climate assisted the dissidents, most of whom were used to living and fighting in intense heat, while their knowledge of the terrain was invaluable to them in launching night attacks. But it was the provision, leading from the 1962 revolution, of a major safe base in Taiz in the south of Yemen, that proved to be of paramount importance to the success of the NLF.[7] The mediaeval city of Taiz had been the seat of the Imam and vied with Sana'a as the capital, although it only numbered 15,000 inhabitants compared to 50,000 in Sana'a.[8] With a maze of square, dun-coloured houses and white mosques, it allowed a guerrilla movement like the NLF to operate freely and to recruit young operatives for future campaigns. Fadhl Ali Abdullah, another future communist official, remembered:

> I had friends in the ANM, but I was against them for reasons that were unclear to me at the time. I think now that I doubted their ability to go beyond Arab nationalism. I also came to feel that the defeat of the British could only come through armed struggle. After the NLF was announced, I went to Taiz around December 1963. I spoke to Qahtan al-Sha'abi and others there. I said that we wanted to struggle with them because we agreed with their principles. After four days we reached an agreement and I came back to Aden.
>
> After one month some NLF people contacted us here in Aden. We formally joined in February 1964. At first I was involved in commando activities, but after I graduated in 1965, my comrades insisted that I become General Secretary for the Aden Port Trust Union. I was working as a clerk in the port. I was against becoming General Secretary so early but my comrades insisted that it was necessary.[9]

At this stage, the NLF was not an overtly leftist organisation. It was true that there were Marxists within its membership and much of its rhetoric was studded with talk of 'comrades' and 'imperial lackeys'. But its main political slant followed that of al-Sha'abi – Arab nationalism of the Nasserite brand, vaguely to the left and anti-imperialist.[10]

Recruits to the military arm of the NLF were either sent up to Cairo for military training or attended a training camp set up near Taiz. It was not long before they were dispatched to the Radfan and by the autumn of 1963, clad in combat fatigues, the cadres of the NLF set about instructing and co-ordinating tribal rebellion. The anti-British campaign had started in the summer of 1963 in Upper Yafa, an area within the Federation boundaries but independent of it. In October, it spread to part of the neighbouring state of Dhala, particularly the central area of Radfan, which bordered the only road passing through Dhala linking Aden to Yemen.

The Radfan took its name from the Jebel Radfan at the centre of the tribal territory, nominally controlled by the Amir of Dhala. It was an extremely rugged and isolated tract of country about 400 square miles in total and lying sixty miles north of Aden and twenty miles south of the turbulent Yemen border town of Qataba. In a land of deep narrow wadis and jagged peaks, the local people lived a meagre and wretched existence. Brigadier James Lunt, Commander of the local Arab FRA, was well acquainted with the population:

> The vale contained some of the most vicious blood feuds in all Arabia. Its inhabitants dwell close-cooped in their stinking hovels, the accumulated manure of generations rotting beneath their noses and their animals stabled immediately below their living quarters. Riddled with disease, suspicious of every foreigner, their withered and stunted physique bears witness to their under-nourishment. Instead of growing food in their fields, they choose instead to cultivate *qat*, which they chew from noon until sundown, by which time their minds are sufficiently stupefied to commit any crime.[11]

Nonetheless, the tribesmen's superb marksmanship seemed to be little affected by the mild narcotic and neither was their energy dulled when it came to protecting their livelihood. The area was dominated by the Qateibi tribe, a fierce and independent clan who had never signed any treaty with Britain and had no sense of allegiance to anyone. They held many grievances against the new Federation, primarily over the issue of tariffs. These were collected together with booty often extorted under duress from the caravans and convoys that passed through their territory. Historically, half the tolls were retained by the tribes while the other half were handed over to their notional ruler, the Amir of Dhala. But, as Lieutenant-General Sir Charles Harington later admitted to the Chief of

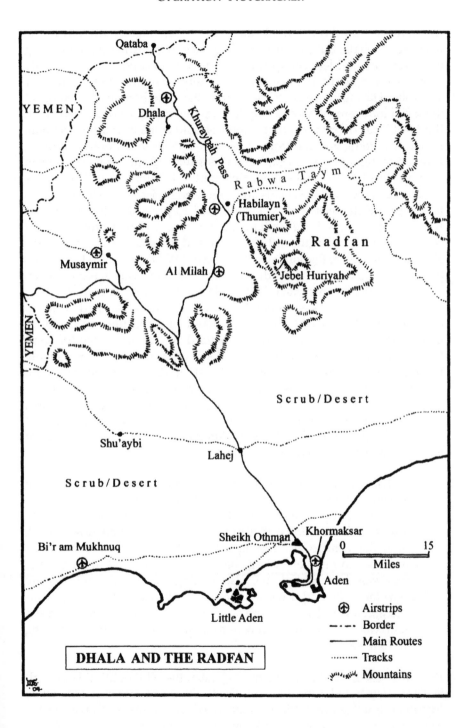

Qataba

YEMEN

Dhala

Khurayjah Pass

R a b w a   T a y m

Habilayn
(Thumier)

R a d f a n

Musaymir

Al Milah

Jebel Huriyah

YEMEN

Scrub/Desert

Shu'aybi

Lahej

Scrub/Desert

Bi'r am Mukhnuq

Sheikh Othman   Khormaksar

0   15
Miles

Aden

Little Aden

DHALA AND THE RADFAN

⊕ Airstrips
–·–· Border
—— Main Routes
········· Tracks
⸌⸍⸌⸍ Mountains

the Defence Staff, Lord Mountbatten, 'the tribes might form part of the Amirate of Dhala, but they pay no allegiance to the Amir, a man lacking in personality and leadership and quite unable to cope with this unruly area'.[12] Consequently the Qateibi tribe rarely accounted to the Amir for any tolls. Harington recommended that the time-honoured method of 'financial inducement' would help to keep the rebellious tribesmen quiet. But HMG was determined that income should come in from the Radfan, rather than going out, and from the date of Dhala's incorporation into the Federation, random violent extortion was outlawed and legal tolls were to be paid direct to the Federation. Despite the intention that these funds were to be reinvested in schools and irrigation projects, the tribes refused to accept the changes. The NLF continued to press the charge that the British had neglected the Radfan for too long and that any proposed changes would upset the tribal values and structures.[13] Furthermore, although the area of Radfan lay within the old WAP, the seven local tribes prided themselves on their independence and there was agitation when they were officially integrated into Dhala State and the Federation.

These tribes were a considerable force within Dhala, and from an estimated total of 30,000 Radfanis, a band of 7,000 fighters could be mobilised.[14] And they were well practised in the art of feuding and fighting. British officials in the area had sometimes been victims, notably Peter Davey, a political officer murdered in 1947, and the near fatal stabbing in 1950 of the British Agent for the WAP.[15] Even those who knew the area well and had a rapport with the Arabs, like Lieutenant-Colonel Sandy Thomas, were at risk. In June 1962 he was stabbed in the back by a zealot and escaped death only by the intervention of a political officer. It was an experience he vividly remembered:

> Suddenly, without the slightest warning, I felt a tremendous blow in the centre of my back, near my spine. It was as though a very heavy man had thumped me there with all his might. It felled me to the ground with such force that my knees were skinned raw. Dazed, somewhat winded and feeling a rather familiar wartime nausea, I clambered to my feet. A large bearded Arab dressed in long white robes was just behind me, also getting off the ground. To my amazement, he had a wicked looking *jambiya* [curved knife] in his hand and it was dripping with my blood . . . As the dagger was raised again, Godfrey Meynell threw himself on the fellow's back, bringing him to the ground.[16]

From his base in the border town of Qataba, the NLF political leader, al-Sha'abi, distributed arms and supplies to the dissident tribesmen, while Egyptian Intelligence Officers supervised recruitment. It was fertile ground as the town was a well-known reception area for tribesmen who had fallen out with their sheikhs, and when penniless and alone, they became easy targets to mobilise. Sedition was also encouraged by the large number of cheap transistor radios, afforded by even the poorest tribesmen, which poured out continuous exhortations from Radio Cairo and Radio Sana'a, to 'throw off the shackles of the colonial oppressors and their federation lackeys'. Saif Hassan Ali, the premier Radfan sheikh, suddenly claimed he was being 'oppressed' by the Amir of Dhala and demanded that the area dominated by his tribe, the Qateibi, should be recognised as a separate state.[17] Soon afterwards, a confederation of tribes led by the Qateibi, the self-styled 'Red Wolves of Radfan', went into action from their heartland in the Wadi Misrah. They were formidable opponents. As tough, fit warriors, they could travel great distances and tolerate severe hardship and now that they were receiving new rifles from the Egyptians, their marksmanship was even more deadly.

Between October and December 1963 the NLF military commander, Ali Antar (alias Mohammed Nasser al-Bishi), organised the blocking of the Dhala road through a series of ambushes and mine-laying operations.[18] Ironically, many of these mines were old Mark 7 British anti-tank mines left behind by the British in the Suez Canal Zone. There were also attacks on FRA positions, notably an assault by 200 dissidents on a fort at Thumier. With this outright challenge to the Federation and with the severing of a vital route into Yemen for royalist support, British military retaliation was inevitable. Time was limited and local security in the Radfan was too poor to allow a 'hearts and minds' civil operation. Proscription bombing was ruled out for such a wide area and a decision was made to launch a land offensive into the Radfan, with air and naval support. The aim of the operation, which was heavily endorsed by the High Commissioner, Sir Kennedy Trevaskis, was to expel certain well-known dissidents and demonstrate that the Federal Government had the will and the means to enter Radfan whenever it liked. To this end, the track that ran along the Wadi Rabwa at the base of the mountains was to be improved to take armoured cars and jeeps. This would enable any future Federal or British forces to move into the more distant and fertile Wadi Taym in the centre of the Radfan. It was also hoped that such a demonstration of force would receive wide publicity and thereby aid local recruitment to the FRA, as well as sending a clear message to the Egyptians in Yemen that the British were committed to the Radfan.[19]

But there were many critics of this plan who felt that any short-term military successes would be negated by a lack of political strategy in the region. Without a follow-up of capital investment in roads and social welfare they argued, the British would fail to consolidate any military gains. And due to the lack of intelligence on the NLF, the true motives of the rebellion were masked from military planners who assumed that they were dealing purely with a repetition of old tribal agitation.[20]

While the British were preparing military plans for the Radfan, power began to shift within the nationalist camp. By late 1963 Nasser was beginning to tire of al-Asnag and the Cairo sponsored PSP, calling them 'too moderate'. While the Egyptian President continued to publicly support the PSP and its leader al-Asnag, he was also keen to promote his latest client, the NLF leader, al-Sha'abi.[21] In October a confidant al-Sha'abi was able to announce that the NLF was the only group who could offer armed resistance to the British. Consequently, in an effort to keep pace with his dissident competitors, al-Asnag decided on a terrorist spectacular.

During the evening of 9 December al-Asnag, together with a group of plotters from the PSP cell in Aden Airways, assembled on the beach at Khormaksar to finalise plans for the assassination of the High Commissioner and his leading Federalist Minister, the Sharif of Beihan. They knew that the forthcoming London Conference, called to harmonise Aden and the other federated states, would focus world attention on South Arabia and would be a good time to commit an outrage. They struck on 10 December, just as Trevaskis was about to leave for the Conference. As he was talking with a group of officials and civil servants on the tarmac at Khormaksar Airport, the plotters dropped a grenade into the gathering. Just before the explosion, which killed one person and wounded forty-eight others, George Henderson, the gallant and effervescent aid to Trevaskis, pushed his chief aside but caught a grenade splinter in his lung and later died.[22]

Henderson's death was a severe blow to the British administration and particularly to its forthcoming campaign in the Radfan. Robin Bidwell, himself a former political officer in the WAP, lamented the loss, noting that several experienced hands were now dead and most of the other political officers were consumed with their new role as advisers to Federal Government ministers.[23] The Federal Government reacted just as the dissidents hoped they would, by declaring a State of Emergency, deporting a number of Yemenis and arresting over fifty members of the PSP, including al-Asnag. There followed a carefully orchestrated round of condemnation from the UN and Soviet satellite countries, and calls for the release of the plotters. A large number of political tracts were issued by the ATUC. Most were published in Cairo, with such indigestible titles as 'A Curtain Raiser to Repression by British Colonialism Against Workers of Aden and Their Families'.[24] While these were probably only read by the students and literate Yemenis in South Arabia, the rhetoric coming out of Cairo Radio and Sana'a Radio reached a much wider audience. The broadcasts branded Arab pro-Federalists, such as Zein Baharoon, the Chief Minister of Aden State, as 'servers of colonialism'. The cause was even taken up by a group of British Labour MPs who visited Aden and lobbied the case of those detained over the airport attack. Understandably, this alarmed the Federal Rulers whose morale slumped at the prospect of a future Labour Government.[25]

For the moment however, both the Federal Rulers and the royalist leaders in Yemen had the ear of the British Prime Minister. On 17 December Colonel David Smiley, fresh from combat in the Yemen, visited Downing Street to update the new Prime Minister, Sir Alec Douglas Home, on the royalists' supply requirements.[26] Smiley was able to report that the Egyptians had suffered over 10,000 casualties since their involvement in Yemen and he then pressed the royalist case, reminding the PM that the Saudis were considering buying Canberra bombers.[27] And a month later, the Imam al-Badr was making further overtures to the PM, pleading in a letter from his camp at Mansur, that 'we have learnt lessons we will not forget from our experiments in international relations'.[28]

There was also support from an enthusiastic SIS station in Aden. The new chief was John Da Silva, a 45-year-old ex-Army Intelligence Officer who had already distinguished himself in Rome, Hamburg and Bahrain, and was now a vigorous campaigner for action against the Egyptians. He saw them as a legitimate enemy of British interests and a part of Soviet strategy in the region, an argument that now found wholehearted support from his chief, Sir Dick White. In a series of successful operations in cooperation with GCHQ signals intelligence, SIS started to play a prominent and well-directed role in cross-border activities.[29]

Any strike into rebel-held territory in the Radfan would need RAF support and by the winter of 1963/4, the RAF had a formidable establishment based at Khormaksar airfield. Considering there was only one runway it was still the station for nine squadrons and two flights, totalling eighty-four aircraft and was even able to accommodate 'V' bombers visiting on 'Lone Ranger' flights from the UK. The offensive potential of the Khormaksar base was considerable, consisting of thirty-six Hunter FGA9 fighter/ground attack aircraft, with 8 and 208 Squadrons, supplemented in March 1963 by the arrival of 43(F) Squadron ('The Fighting Cocks'). There were now also four Shackleton MR2 bombers, which could dispense large quantities of 4½ inch flares and 20lb fragmentation bombs for night operations.[30] Furthermore, the newly arrived 26 Squadron was equipped with the new Belvedere helicopters, twin rotor machines which could lift guns and small vehicles into inaccessible territory.[31] The profile of the RAF Command was further enhanced by the appointment in October 1963 of the legendary fighter ace, Air Vice-Marshal Johnnie Johnson to AOC, Air Forces Middle East (AFME). Johnson would bring his panache and drive to a role that would see British forces engaged in mountain warfare for the first time since Korea.

The Radfan offensive operation, christened 'Nutcracker', was scheduled to commence on 4 January 1964. It was essentially an FRA operation and as such would be handled by the British Commander, FRA, Brigadier James Lunt. Although the FRA was still gaining strength, it was important that it was seen to be capable of handling rebellions largely on its own. Estimates of its strength made in 1964 showed that there were 189 Officers, 4,075 Other Ranks (OR), 133 boys and 250 enlisted followers, with an annual budget of £4¾ million. However, little outside assistance was available, for HQ 24 Brigade was still in Kenya and even its units such as Four Five Commando, which normally operated in South Arabia, were on standby to defend the recently independent African colonies against army mutinies. The other brigade-sized unit, Aden Garrison, commanded by Brigadier Michael Harbottle, was fully occupied on security duties in Aden town and the rest of Aden state.[32]

Above brigade level, staffs were still bedding in after the restructuring, and there were also new Commanders. In May 1963 Major-General John Cubbon was appointed as General Officer Commanding (GOC), Middle East Land Forces (MELF) and this coincided with the appointment of his superior, Commander-in-Chief, Middle East Command (MEC), Lieutenant-General Charles (later Sir Charles) Harington. The engagement of General Harington, who had taken over the unified command from Air Chief Marshal Sir Charles Elworthy, saw the continuation of the custom of rotating the post through each of the three Services.[33] MEC covered a vast area and had to oversee not only South Arabia but also the rest of the Persian Gulf and British commitments in Africa, even extending to Mauritius.

Brigadier Lunt was not convinced that a purely military operation like 'Nutcracker' was the answer to rebellion in the Radfan, sensing that it would play into the hands of the dissidents, as well as committing the FRA to a permanent role in the region. He was a forceful character and, although a great proponent of the role of Arab soldiers, he made plain to Trevaskis that this operation held too many risks.[34] As a portent of trouble to come, there were political problems concerning the deployment of the local FRA. The Federal Government could not decide whether to keep all the Radfani members of the FRA out of the operation. In the end, just the Radfani officers took part, leaving the Radfani OR to return home on leave, where they were subjected to NLF taunts that their officers were part of 'the imperial conspiracy'.

Despite these difficulties, the operation commenced with the assembly of 2, 3, and 4 Battalions FRA at Thumier, a village on the Dhala Road near the start of the Radfan mountains, where they were joined by the FRA squadron of armoured cars. The British support comprised a troop of Centurion tanks from 16th/5th Lancers, the regiment which Brigadier Lunt had previously commanded and whose troop was now commanded by his son, 2nd Lieutenant R Lunt. Artillery support was provided by 'J' battery, 3rd Battalion Royal Horse Artillery (3 RHA), while the road building exercise was to be carried out by 2 Troop, 12th Field Squadron, Royal Engineers. A Brigade Air Support Officer (BASO) was also based at Thumier with HQ 24 Brigade, to co-ordinate air cover by Hunter fighters and Shackleton bombers.[35]

In an innovation, two of the new Belvedere helicopters from 26 Squadron, as well as four Wessex helicopters from 815 Squadron RN, airlifted men from 2 FRA up onto picquet positions, high on the ridges above the Rabwa Pass. Here the heat reflected off rock faces and could exceed 130°F, harsh for both humans and machines. Unfortunately, British helicopter operations were still in their infancy and lagging behind the Americans and Russians. But the successful operation involving the landing of Four Five Commando at Port Said during the Suez Crisis had given a fillip to the concept and there had been further helicopter operations in Malaya and Cyprus.[36] Nevertheless, there was much deliberation over the deployment of the Belvedere helicopter, or the 'Father of Two Fans' as it was known to the Arabs. Brigadier James Lunt reflected:

> There was, of course, some risk attached to the employment of these machines, since no one was certain how they would perform at that height [over 4,000 ft] and in the blazing temperatures of midsummer. There was also the risk that the tribesmen might regard their appearance as a heaven-sent opportunity to try out their marksmanship and even the blunderbuss can do a deal of damage to a helicopter when it is coming in to the 'hover'.[37]

Such caution was well founded, for during 'Nutcracker' a second Belvedere was landing picquet troops when the pilot heard a loud crack. Holes appeared in the cabin behind his co-pilot and snipers' bullets punctured the engine bay and front fuel tank. The pilot managed to take off again, but as soon as the BASO at Thumier heard about the incident, he ordered all the helicopters back to base. This timidity clearly angered Brigadier Lunt who saw his plan in danger of collapse, leaving both picquets and the main force exposed. After a furious row, Lunt demanded, and secured the return of the helicopters. In some extraordinarily skilful manoeuvres, the pilots of 26 Squadron proceeded to land further picquets on the ridge tops together with the 105mm guns of 3 RHA. They managed to lower the guns, even facing them in the right direction to save the crews struggling to turn them in the confined space.

The horse gunners of 'J' Battery were the regular artillery support for the FRA throughout the Federation. They had come out to South Arabia in July 1963 with their 105mm pack howitzers to replace 'D' Battery who had used the 25-pounder gun. One advantage of the 105mm was that it could be broken down into thirteen pieces for camel transport, but in 'Nutcracker' they were airlifted in one piece. A gun battery comprised three sections of two guns each. Each section had a compliment of two officers and thirty-five men, and two sections were committed to Operation 'Nutcracker', while the third section found itself constantly employed with the FRA in border clashes in the state of Beihan.[38]

As soon as 2 FRA picquets landed they came under fire from much larger numbers of dissidents, attempting to re-take command of the heights. Despite determined resistance the picquets started to take casualties and had to fall back along the ridges above Wadi Rabwa, but not before they had allowed the main FRA force to advance up and clear the wadi. These dried riverbeds, which carved through the sheer mountain passes, were not comfortable terrain in which to operate. Being infested with flies and mosquitoes, malaria was a constant threat and in the rainy season, water would pour down the steep rock faces and into the wadis, creating a sudden flash flood, powerful enough to sweep vehicles away. Even the wadi water was undrinkable as it was infested with bilharzia, so troops had to rely on their daily personal allowance of twelve pints of water. This had to be supplied from their own refilled water bottles, which were often near boiling point in the midday heat.[39] Despite the conditions, 12 Field Squadron Royal Engineers were now able to start building the road through this hostile territory. Local labour had to be recruited for this task and the same tribesmen who worked for the Engineers during the day would then snipe at the FRA force during the night.

After two weeks the Wadi Rabwa was secured and then 4 FRA moved forward and advanced up the Bakri Ridge. With the help of the Belvedere and Wessex helicopters, picquets, guns and supplies were moved quickly along the ridge despite the hazards of enemy sniper fire. But the troops also had to contend with poor maps with no height markings and, with water in such short supply, taking the wrong route could have dire consequences.[40] Meanwhile, the rebellious 'Wolves' kept their distance. They were well concealed in rocks and crevices and eschewing close-quarter combat, they would usually open fire from half a mile away. Despite intensive Hunter rocket fire, the rebels would doggedly hang onto their positions and still fire back. And even though many appeared elderly, they could still run down steep mountains at an extraordinary speed. While some were kitted out in NLF green combat fatigues, most dissidents still sported a shaggy jacket, baggy Moslem trousers and as many bandoliers of ammunition as they could carry. The kit was then topped off with a skull-cap covered with khaki cotton, wound round in the form of a turban, and plastic 'flip-flops' which seemed incongruous for their role of negotiating sharp mountain ridges. Although the look was the opposite of the smartly turned out FRA, it was 'the Wolves' who proved to be the more determined and ferocious fighters, and who earned the respect of their British opponents.

By the beginning of February, the road into Wadi Taym was finished, allowing the second part of the operation to commence. Much of the road, often incorrectly described as a tarmac road, was in fact constructed from sand and gravel but was still a great feat of engineering.[41] Under the codename 'Operation Rustum', the force now swept deeper into the Radfan and through the fertile area of the Danaba Basin and Wadi Taym. They met only light opposition, and in mid-February the main FRA force withdrew from the interior back to the base at Thumier. They left behind one battalion of FRA together with the artillery to garrison the forward area. But with helicopter support now withdrawn, it was impossible for this battalion to patrol the high ground and the dissidents started to move back along the ridges. It was a dangerous time for those left patrolling the valleys, especially as the FRA were dominated by tribal ties rather than Federation loyalties. Major Tony Stagg, Commander of J (Sidi Rezegh) Battery 3 RHA, realised that most Radfan villages were potential death traps:

> A platoon patrol going into the village of Danaba was badly ambushed and shot up. Living in the village was an officer of the Federal Guard on leave, who apparently gave no warning of the ambush. Subsequently he was arrested and a court of inquiry was convened in Danaba itself. A company group was detailed to accompany and protect the court, taking with them a section of 3-inch mortars and Vickers machine-guns, carried by camels. About a thousand yards from the village, the group came under heavy and accurate rifle fire. They were almost completely in the open and a number were hit in the fusillade, including the Forward Observation Officer [Captain M F Bremridge]. Off also went the camels with most of the support weapons. The dissidents, about eighty to a hundred strong, were on the high ground above and around the basin. For over three hours the group were pinned down and throughout this time, the FOO remained in the open and kept the rear support gun battery firing from target to target and controlled Hunter aircraft brought up from Aden in a series of strikes. The patrol finally managed to withdraw under cover of fire. For this action, the FOO was awarded the Military Cross.[42]

The FRA had insufficient manpower and resources to effectively patrol the area and the last battalion was withdrawn to Thumier at the end of February. However, with FRA losses of only five killed and twelve wounded, 'Nutcracker' was hailed a success. It had certainly been a valuable experience for helicopter pilots, infantry and gunners to operate

together at such high altitudes. 'J' Battery 3 RHA had acquitted themselves well and many of the 3,000 rounds fired had found their mark. For
the first time, helicopter pilots had encountered the problems of high
wind turbulence at midday on the mountain peaks, which cut out flying
between 0900 hours and 1600 hours. Even at low levels and in wadis, the
pilots found that rocks and dust obscured everything, especially when
attempting to land Belvederes. Indeed, one alarming feature of such
mountain warfare was the extent to which all weapons and hardware
rapidly deteriorated when exposed to the dust.[43] The FRA Arab troops
had proved their worth in the operation, especially those working in Air
Control Posts (ACP), who accurately guided in Hunters from 208
Squadron to cannon and rocket the dissidents, often lodged in remote and
inaccessible crevices. And 'Nutcracker' had demonstrated, albeit briefly,
British resolve to back the Federation by force. [44]

Despite the valuable lessons learned from the operation, there was
continuing disquiet among some military commanders, notably Brigadier
James Lunt, that the operation was a waste of money. And the fact
remained that the FRA would be stretched to patrol and maintain a
Federal presence in such inaccessible terrain. Progress through the Radfan
mountains could be unbelievably slow and supplying picquet posts
required plenty of resources. A new road was all very well, but it would
be unusable unless the heights all around were under Federal control.
And now that the NLF were directing many of the dissident tribes,
rebellions could be co-ordinated throughout the Federation, so as to
stretch the FRA to its limits. To the frustration of political officers and
agents in the field, few resources were allocated to back up any military
success in the Radfan. Because there was little attempt to win over the
local population in any 'hearts and minds' campaign, the Federal
influence would soon evaporate once the troops had left. Consequently,
the Qateibi tribe moved back into Wadi Taym in March, closed off the new
road and started to break it up. There was also political capital to be made
out of the use of 'excessive force' by the British, and Radio Cairo and
Radio Sana'a soon claimed a victory for the dissidents, announcing that
the 'Red Wolves had driven out the imperialists and their Federation
lackeys'. Shortly after, the dissidents resumed their attacks on convoys
using the Dhala Road, and reasserted their control of the Radfan, hardly
having to rely on their old established methods of fear and extortion.[45]

This was an orchestrated plan by the NLF to put pressure on the Federal
forces and was not, as the British thought at the time, a sign of old tribal
turbulence. Indeed, it was the ability of the NLF, through its cell structure,
to conceal the extent of their influence in Radfan that enabled them to
carry on their subversion work.[46] While British eyes seemed to be firmly
fixed on al-Asnag and agitation from the ATUC, the NLF quietly extended
their web. The militant Awad al-Hamad recalled:

I started out as a police officer in Aden because we were so poor in the mountains. Yes, I was what the British would call a tribesman, from the Aulaqi tribe. Because we were fierce and large, the British used many of our tribe to control the people. But I was not a stooge and deserted. After the 1962 Revolution, we Yemenis in the ANM separated ourselves from the ANM and formed the National Liberation Front, committed to armed struggle. We organised in the South at that time too, in all the provinces. We infiltrated the tribal leadership and politicised the people from within. I worked here in this province [Lahej] from the very beginning, although I am not from here. But this is my home. I have fought on this land since Radfan, and from the beginning we have been totally dependent on the people here.[47]

However, even though the Egyptians and the NLF claimed that events were moving their way in the Radfan, over the border in Yemen their military progress was grinding to a halt. This was in part due to weaknesses within the Egyptian military machine. Their Commander-in-Chief, Field-Marshal Amer, undoubtedly had plenty of warning to prepare an expeditionary force for the Yemen, yet Egyptian staff work was poor and their peasant army was hopelessly ill equipped for mountain warfare. No altitude training had been given and with poor maps and badly maintained transport, groups of Egyptians were often left beside their crippled convoys in highland passes. The arrival of garishly clad tribesmen, as dusk fell, must have terrified the shivering conscripts. Colonel David Smiley often came across the outcome from these confrontations:

> There was a wrecked T34 Russian tank and the burnt-out shells of several armoured personnel carriers, and I counted – with my handkerchief to my nose – more than 50 decomposing bodies, half buried by sand and half eaten by jackals. I saw, also, six decapitated corpses – executed republicans.[48]

As most tribesmen were poor, the prospect of booty was a further inducement to attack the Egyptians, and after an ambush a tribesman could capture several rifles and perhaps even some heavier arms, which could be sold to provide a windfall. Sometimes there were even bigger prizes. When Prince Hassan launched an offensive near Marib, to the east of Sana'a, the Egyptians dropped four groups of paratroops to try and stem the royalist advance. But they fell wide of the mark into royalist positions and were duly slaughtered, while the royalists captured three of their helicopters, together with their Russian crews.[49]

With a succession of small victories during 1963, the royalists seemed to be closing in on the capital, Sana'a, defended by an Egyptian garrison of 7,000 troops. Despite Egyptian air superiority, Egyptian offensive operations were usually blocked and even when the Commander of Egyptian forces in Yemen, Lieutenant-General Anwar al-Qadi, personally commanded an expedition in December 1963, it was ambushed and al-Qadi was wounded by mortar fire. David Holden, an experienced observer of the region, felt that the problems confronting the Egyptians in Yemen were of their own making, for they believed that training and logistical difficulties would soon disappear if they were ignored:

> There is a general Arab tendency to take the word for the deed, the wish for the accomplishment, and to believe that obstacles can be overcome most easily by being overlooked. It follows from this that to call attention to obstacles is to be more of a traitor than a critic, because it automatically diminishes, in Arab eyes, the chances of wish fulfilment. As an example, it is part of the Nasserite and Arab nationalist faith that tribalism or any other traditional source of Arab disunity is in some way an invention of imperialist reaction that will be swept away as soon as the truth of revolutionary Arab unity is revealed ... To admit that the undesirable does exist, is a very un-Arab trait.[50]

The royalists were still receiving most of their supplies via the Federal State of Beihan and the Egyptians were anxious to cut off this route using the weapon of American pressure. On 22 November 1963, the very day that President Kennedy was assassinated, Sir David Ormsby-Gore, the British Ambassador in Washington, telegrammed Whitehall reporting that Kennedy felt his own 'prestige' was at stake over Yemen and that the Sharif of Beihan should be restrained. It remained to be seen whether the new President, Lyndon Johnson, would take such a personal interest in the war in Yemen.[51]

The other dilemma for the British Government was how to restrain King Feisal from starting a direct confrontation with Nasser. Angered that the Egyptians had made no attempt to reduce their involvement in Yemen, King Feisal was ready to strike back.[52] The risk of escalation leading to direct Russian intervention alarmed the British Government and was highlighted when the Yemeni President, Sallal, visited Moscow in March 1964. A Treaty of Friendship was signed in the Kremlin between Sallal and President Brezhnev for 'economic, technical and cultural cooperation' between their two countries.[53]

Events taking place on the Federation/Yemen border were rapidly making that escalation more likely. The exact border between the federal state of Beihan and Yemen had always been disputed. In 1934 there was an attempt to establish a *status quo* frontier based on tribal boundaries, but since then the line was frequently ignored and the scene of constant incursions.[54] During the early 1960s the Russian-built 'Moose' trainer aircraft was a common sight in the border area, and in 1963 and early 1964 Egyptian Yak interceptor aircraft made a number of bombing raids into this sector in support of raids made by Yemeni tribesmen. Even after repeated warnings from the British Government not to stray into Beihan, two aircraft from Yemen strafed a *Bedu* encampment on 13 March 1964. As the British considered their retaliation, there was another incursion on 27 March when an Egyptian helicopter attacked the Federal fort at Jebel Bulaiq, followed by machine-gun and grenade attacks on Federal positions along the Beihan border.[55]

During this period the British High Commission was active in dealing with the border threat from Yemen. Michael Crouch, who was acting political officer for Dhala (in Godfrey Meynell's absence), recalled a meeting with Robin Young, the Senior Adviser WAP, in the spring of 1964. Young confided that he was involved in laying anti-tank mines on the Yemen side of the border but was disturbed at what might be their indiscriminate results.[56] His chief, Sir Kennedy Trevaskis, was more resolute. In a telegram to Duncan Sandys, Trevaskis confirmed intelligence reports that the Yemeni Commander at Harib had asked for Egyptian air strikes into the federal territory of Beihan. But, he added, he thought that the object of the Egyptian strike was to teach a lesson to renegade republican tribes who had sought sanctuary in Beihan. As such, there was no strict military imperative to retaliate, but the High Commissioner felt compelled to act; a gesture was needed to satisfy the federal rulers that British force would always back them up. In turn, the rulers needed to show their tribes, especially those in north Beihan that they still had the power to bring about military action.[57]

The Acting Commander-in-Chief agreed with Trevaskis that an RAF strike should be carried out, preferably against a target just over the Yemen border such as Harib Fort, with its republican garrison and military supplies. But while Middle East Command agreed with the High Commission over retaliation, there were still concerns about whether Egypt really had intended to over-fly the border on some of the occasions.[58] John Bushell, the Political Advisor to MEC, was worried about the way Trevaskis interpreted intelligence reports. Writing to Frank Brenchley at the Arabian Department of the Foreign Office, he confided:

> I am afraid it will always be difficult as long as Trevaskis is High Commissioner, if only because he is such a forceful personality. His staff do not care to argue much with him and since, as you know, he is convinced that the Egyptians have a great plot against the Federation, he naturally tends to interpret any incident of this sort according to his theory.[59]

Whatever the private misgivings, on 28 March the RAF were ordered to attack Harib Fort. Four Hunters from 43(F) Squadron and four from 8 Squadron scrambled, and within twenty minutes were diving on the fort. In the words of one pilot, 'we went in low and plastered it – got 92% direct hits with 3 inch rockets'.[60] The operation was a success but despite the usual preparatory leaflet drop, the Yemenis claimed eleven killed and seven wounded. The response from the Arab world was immediate and vitriolic. Radio Sana'a erroneously claimed that the town of Harib was attacked and that women and children were killed. Newspapers in many Arab states carried headlines about 'British Imperial Aggression' and the Arab League, a council of Arab countries, called for all Arab governments to 'reconsider their relations with Britain in the light of her aggressive attitude in Yemen'. More alarmingly, they called for 'the liquidation of British bases in Arab areas'.[61] The pressure on Britain mounted with the Yemen Government calling for a meeting of the Security Council of the United Nations, where Sir Patrick Dean, Britain's Representative, had to make a spirited defence of his country's actions.[62]

That same month Nasser visited Sana'a for the first time and declared that 'we swear by Allah to expel the British from all parts of the Arabian Peninsula'.[63] It was confirmation, if confirmation was needed, that the Harib Incident had played into Nasser's hands and was a public relations disaster. Meanwhile, another display of British force was being planned. But this time it would pack a much bigger punch.

NOTES

1   Report on Intelligence, British Embassy Bonn, to B R Pridham, Foreign Office, 15 October 1963, FO 371/168809, NA. See also Political Office, Middle East Command to Foreign Office, 19 December 1963, PREM 11/4928, NA.

2   Holden, *Farewell to Arabia*, op. cit., p. 107. The cipher books were extremely sensitive as they contained the means to translate coded messages emitting from the American Legation.

3   When the British finally left in 1967, al-Sha'abi became President and Latif was appointed Premier. Within eighteen months, internal strife in the NLF saw al-Sha'abi placed under arrest and Latif, murdered. Al-Sha'abi died in 1979 after ten years of house arrest. See J Bowyer Bell, 'South Arabia: Violence and Revolt' in *Conflict Studies*, No. 40, November 1973. For al-Sha'abi, see Little, op. cit., p. 182.

4   The NLF comprised nine other groups, including the Yemeni Free Officers and the Hadramaut Socialist Party, see Pridham op. cit., pp. 48–52. Dr George Habash founded the ANM in 1954 at the American University of Beirut. As a result of the 1967 Arab–Israeli War, the ANM split into rival factions. Habash then endorsed more extreme terrorist action, forming The Popular Front for the Liberation of Palestine. For details of the gestation and birth of the NLF, see Lackner, op. cit., pp. 36–42.

5   Quoted in 'Socialist Revolution in Arabia', Merip Reports No. 15, March 1973, Yem. 3, AWDU. For the inspiration derived from the Algerian Revolution, see also Tareq Ismael, *The Arab Left*, Syracuse University Press, 1976, p. 94.

6   Glen Balfour-Paul to Author, 31 January 2003 and Sadat, op. cit., p. 100; also Colin Beer, *On Revolutionary War*, Galago, 1990, p. 11.

7   Abdul Ismail (one of the founders of the NLF), 'How we liberated Aden', in *Armed Struggle in Arabia*, The Gulf Committee, London, 1976, Yem. 3, AWDU. For the importance of terrain and bases, see Bard O'Neill, *Insurgency & Terrorism*, Brassey's, 1990, pp. 56 & 114–23. The 1962 Yemen revolution also inspired the 1965 Oman rebellion, Halliday, op. cit., p. 145

8   Peter Somerville-Large produced an interesting social record of the Yemen during the Republic, in *Tribes and Tribulations*, Robert Hale, 1967.

9   Quoted in 'Socialist Revolution in Arabia', Merip Reports No. 15, March 1973, Yem. 3, AWDU.

10 Stookey, op. cit., p. 60. The drift to the political left, which accelerated rapidly in 1967, is covered in detail in Tareq Ismael, *The Arab Left*, op. cit. and Walid Kazziha, *Revolutionary Transformation in the Arab World*, Charles Knight, 1975, pp. 65–81.

11 Lunt, op. cit., p. 53.

12 Harington to Mountbatten, 11 June 1964, DEFE 13/570. Harington was appointed C-in-C, Middle East Command in 1963. He was awarded a KCB in 1964.

13 It seems that economic changes implemented by the British in Oman were more successful in retaining existing tribal structures. See O'Neill op. cit., p. 134.

14 'The Radfan' in *People's Socialist Party Background Paper, No. 4*, London 1964, Yem. 3a. Soc., AWDU. While PSP publications contain many embellishments, they also provide useful details of tribal structures.

15 Peter Davey's life and work in South Arabia is described in Aidan Hartley, *The Zanzibar Chest: A Memoir of Love and War*, HarperCollins, London, 2003.

16 Thomas Chronicle, op. cit., p. 75. See also Incident Report A10/04, July 1962, DEFE 25/17, NA, and Lunt, op. cit., pp. 61–2.

17 'Lecture Notes II', File 2/5, Brigadier Dunbar Papers, Liddell Hart Centre, KCL. Also Trevaskis, op. cit., p. 207, and Day, op. cit., introduction to *Sultans of Aden*.

18 Ali Antar became Minister of Defence in the post independence NLF Government. He was killed in January 1986, during bloody infighting that cost over 4,000 lives. For events in South Arabia after 1967, see Fred Halliday, *Revolution and Foreign Policy: The Case of South Yemen 1967–1987*, CUP, 1990.

19 Middle East Command to Foreign Office, 19 December 1963, PREM 11/4928, NA.

20 Lee, op. cit., pp. 203–5 and Bloch & Fitzgerald, op. cit., p.131.

21 There was also Chinese support for the radicals, comprising an intensive aid programme that rivalled the Russians, see Page, op. cit., p. 78 and 86.

22 He was awarded a posthumous bar to his George Medal. For an account of his bravery in an earlier ambush, for which he won the George Medal, see Trevaskis, op. cit., p. 104.

23 Bidwell, *Two Yemens*, op. cit., p. 151.

24 Published by ATUC and printed by Dar el-Hana Press, Cairo, 1963, Yem. 3a. SOL, AWDU.

25 'Report on Radio Sana'a', A10/04, 8 January 1964, DEFE 25/17, NA.

26 Douglas-Home had disclaimed the peerage he held while he was Foreign Secretary, in favour of a descent to the Commons as Sir Alec, which allowed him to be appointed Prime Minister.

27 Unsigned Memo, Prime Minister's Office, 18 December 1963, PREM 11/4928, NA.

28   Al-Badr to PM, 25 January 1964, PREM 11/4928.
29   For Da Silva, 1966 Diplomatic List, and Stoic Register. For SIS clandestine operations, see Bower, op. cit., pp. 253–4.
30   For information on fighter and weapons technology, the author is indebted to Chris Golds, who was a Flight-Lieutenant and later Squadron Leader with 43(F) Squadron, and is now an aviation artist and replica designer. From its inception in 1916, 43(F) Squadron had an illustrious record in two world wars and into the jet age.
31   Statistics from Air Chief Marshal Lee, op. cit., pp. 200–4.
32   'Report of the Ministry and Force HQ, Federation of South Arabia', June 1964, DEFE 13/570, NA. Battalions of the FRA were spread between semi-permanent camps at Dhala, Mukheiras, Beihan and Ataq. See also Brigadier G S Heathcote, 'Operations in the Radfan Mountains', Lecture to RUSI, November 1965, Hargroves Papers.
33   The Royal Navy was the last of the Services within the unified command to move their HQ to Aden. Flag Officer Middle East moved to Steamer Point, Aden after the 1961 Kuwait crisis.
34   See Obituary, The Daily Telegraph, 22 October 2001. Lunt made clear, in conversation with T Mockaitis, that 'Nutcracker' happened 'only because Trevaskis wanted it'. See T Mockaitis, British Counterinsurgency in the Post Imperial Era, MUP, 1995, p. 51. After he retired, Lunt wrote the biographies of two men he knew well, Glubb Pasha (1984) and Hussein of Jordan (1989).
35   There was no representation from 45 Commando. Although based in Little Aden, their resources in January were employed in helping to quell a mutiny in Tanganyika. See also T Stevens, 'Operations in the Radfan 1964', in RUSI Journal, 1965. See also Lee, op. cit., pp. 206–7.
36   Major A Stagg, (later Lieutenant-Colonel, CO 3 RHA), 'Gunners in the Radfan' in The Journal of the Royal Artillery, March 1965. For helicopters, see also Captain T M P (Paddy) Stevens, 'Troop-Carrying Helicopters' in Army Quarterly, January 1958, and James Ladd, By Sea, By Land, The Royal Marines 1919–1997, HarperCollins 1998, p. 293.
37   Lunt, op. cit., p. 164. For Brigadier James Lunt & correspondence with Captain Basil Liddell Hart, 1967–70, see Liddell Hart Papers, LH1/464, KCL.
38   Prior to 'Nutcracker', the three battery sections were normally split between Dhala, Mukeiras and Ataq. For a full account of the RHA in the theatre, see Brigadier David Baines, 'Gunners in South Arabia 1957–67', Baines Papers and also Imperial War Museum, London (IWM).
39   Major Stagg, op. cit. Bilharzia is a potentially fatal tropical disease caused by worm larvae in the water, which can pass through human skin and multiply in the body.
40   Brigadier Baines, op. cit., p. 20. Also Lee op. cit., p. 207.
41   Comments by Major-General Charles Dunbar, on Lieutenant-Colonel Julian Paget's draft of Last Post, 25 September 1968, 2/6 Dunbar Papers, LHCMA.
42   Major Stagg, op. cit. This would appear to be the same incident recounted by Peter Hinchcliffe, the political officer who escorted the party, in his talk 'Dhala' Diary', given to members of the British–Yemeni Society, 12 April 2000. Hinchcliffe recalls that the court of enquiry comprised Jim Ellis, Colonel Chaplin and Richard Holmes. Jim Ellis displayed great gallantry by recovering a wounded FRA soldier and later completed the work of the wounded FAC officer.
43   Being originally volcanic ash, the dust was extremely abrasive and caused much damage to gun parts, especially the muzzle brake and gearing.

44 See Lee, op. cit., pp. 205–7, Paget, op. cit., pp. 46–50, Stagg, op. cit.

45 For Lunt, see Balfour-Paul, op. cit., p. 183. For propaganda, see 'Out of Aden Colonialists', published by International Committee for Solidarity with the Workers and People of Aden, Yem. 3a. Sol, AWDU.

46 The British authorities did not outlaw the NLF as a subversive group until 1965. For an analysis of early NLF infiltration tactics, see Lackner, op. cit., p. 39.

47 Quoted in *Merip Reports*, No. 15, March 1973, Yem. 3, AWDU.

48 Smiley, op. cit., pp. 163–4.

49 O'Balance, op. cit., p. 93.

50 Holden, *Farewell to Arabia*, op. cit., p. 103.

51 Ormsby-Gore to Arabian Department, Foreign Office, 22 November 1963, PREM 11/4928, NA. Also 14 December, PREM 11/4928, NA.

52 In a UN Mission Plan, agreed by Egypt and Saudi Arabia, disengagement was to be carried out by both sides. Feisal felt that Nasser had totally ignored the agreement; see Ormsby-Gore to Foreign Office, 13 December 1963, PREM 11/4928, NA.

53 *Tass*, 22 March 1964.

54 Foreign Office memo, 21 October 1963, FO 371/168809, NA.

55 Colonial Office to UK Mission, New York, 28 March 1964, FO 371/174627, NA. Also Chris Golds to Author, 10 June 2003.

56 Crouch, op. cit., pp. 124–5. Robin Young, like Ralph Daly, another senior advisor, was a product of the old Sudan Political Service. With impeccable manners, in the opinion of his chief, Trevaskis, 'he affected the lifestyle of an Edwardian country gentlemen'.

57 Trevaskis to Secretary of State for the Colonies, 16 March 1964, FO 371/174627, NA. Also Foreign Office to Washington, 26 March 1964, FO 371/174627, NA. There were sections of the Foreign Office who were unhappy at the influence of the Sharif of Beihan, see Bidwell, op. cit., p. 153.

58 R Posnett (Foreign Office) to R Shegog (Colonial Office), 24 March 1964, FO 371/174627, NA.

59 Bushell to Brenchley, 19 March 1964, FO 371/174627, NA.

60 For the Harib raid and reaction, see J Beedle, *43(F) Squadron*, Beaumont Aviation, 1985, p. 310.

61 Quoted in Sandys to Prime Minister, 31 March 1964, See also Trevaskis to Sandys, 31 March 1964, both FO 371/174627, NA.

62 UN Office of Sir Patrick Dean to Foreign Office, 2 April 1964, FO 371/174627, NA.

63 Quoted in Bidwell op. cit., p. 153.

CHAPTER V

The Radfan Campaign

Part I: (30 April–11 May 1964: Operation 'Cap Badge')

The Radfan remained an area of strategic importance to the British because of its proximity both to the border and to the Dhala Road, the only navigable route running up from Aden to the Yemen. Since Operation 'Nutcracker' the area had become lawless again, with constant ambushes of military and commercial convoys on the road and, more importantly, interruptions to the flow of British and Saudi weapons to the Yemeni royalists. It was time for a more resolute military operation.

The overall political objectives were to reassert Federal Authority and make the Dhala Road safe for traffic.[1] The military aim was to 'end the operations' of the dissidents within 'the defined area' of the Radfan, and it was intended to clear out the enemy from their territory and destroy their means of support – the millet crops and livestock on which they depended. The drawback was that such destruction could hand the NLF a propaganda coup, resulting in defections by locally recruited FRA men.[2] As it was, the NLF had enough material to agitate rebellion, with road building high on the list of concerns for the Radfan tribesmen, as one dissident explained:

> Roads enable infidels and wheeled traffic – a most unnatural work of the devil – to penetrate our tribal mountains. What will happen to those tribes who have lived for centuries by transporting goods across the mountain passes? What will happen to the camel drivers, breeders and muzzle makers? They will all be redundant and then all that is left for them to do is to become rebels.[3]

While the Aden–Dhala road was the source of much anger, it was also the scene of a worrying new development. Tribal tactics were changing and due to NLF influence the dissidents were now fighting a more co-ordinated campaign. There were signs that battle plans were emerging and that they were using wireless communications. Mines were regularly laid on the roads, which caused a steady stream of British casualties. On 4 April 1964 Corporal Davis MC, serving in an FRA signals squadron, was killed and three Arab soldiers were wounded, when their vehicle was blown up near Thumier. Several days later, Sir Kennedy Trevaskis admitted, 'after 14 guerrilla attacks, the Aden–Dhala Road is unusable as the area is now under guerrilla control'.

Such guerrilla tactics bore all the hallmarks of classic revolutionary warfare espoused by Che Guevara and Mao Tse Tung. The dissidents in the Radfan were closely following Mao's creed of, 'enemy advances, we retreat – enemy halts, we harass – enemy tires, we attack – enemy retreats, we pursue'.[4] In order for the operation to be a success, the British force needed to decisively crush the dissidents within their own territory. Merely forcing them out might satisfy military objectives but it would also fit in with NLF tactical plans. For having retreated to their safe Yemen sanctuaries, they could later trek back over the ridges to repeatedly harass British patrols.

In order to preserve the veneer of a Federal military operation, the Federal rulers asked for British military assistance under the terms of their Defence Treaty.[5] Major-General John Cubbon, GOC MELF was appointed to oversee the new Radfan operation. This short, stout ex-paratrooper was a competent and trusted commander, and although his most recent appointment was home-based, as GOC South-Western District, he had much experience of the Middle East. Known affectionately as 'The Red Ant', he was originally commissioned into the Cheshire Regiment and during the Second World War became renowned for 'driving like Jehu' to get his men back to Dunkirk. After the war, he commanded successively, the 1st Battalion The Parachute Regiment in Palestine, the 1st Battalion The Cheshire Regiment in Egypt, and finally assumed command of 18 Infantry Brigade during the Malayan Emergency.[6]

On 14 April 1964 Major-General Cubbon appointed 47-year-old Brigadier Louis (later Sir Louis) Hargroves to control the operation and to come up with a suitable battle plan.[7] Brigadier Hargroves, a dapper, suave Commander who had the reputation of being accessible to his subordinates, had only recently arrived in South Arabia to take command of the Aden Garrison. He had considerable experience of mountain operations, having served on the North-West Frontier, and grasped the vital importance of picqueting the high ground. Despite his appreciation of the terrain, he was still faced with welding together a new team to direct the operation and was surprised to learn that he had just three days to put a plan together.[8] The operation needed to start by the end of April as temperatures were rising rapidly and fighting a campaign in the hot season would seriously disadvantage British troops. Going into late May or June would see personal water consumption rise dramatically and there would be severe acclimatisation problems for new troops.

In an extraordinary feat of organisation, 'Radforce' was swiftly put together with a small HQ based at Thumier, where the force was to

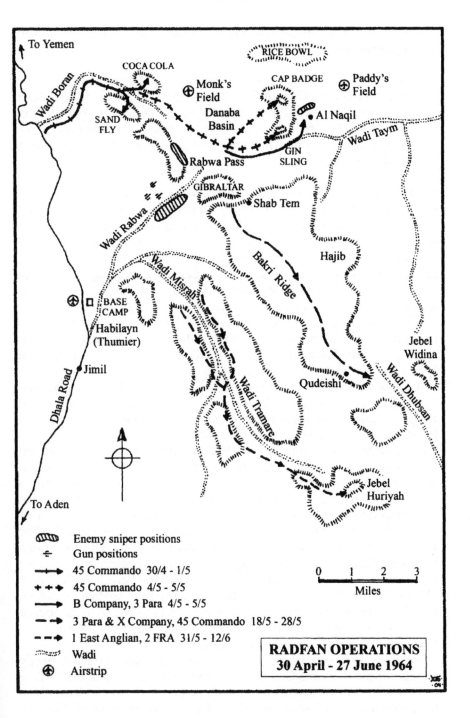

RADFAN OPERATIONS
30 April - 27 June 1964

assemble. Brigadier Hargroves was in bullish mood and announced to waiting pressmen at Thumier:

> There is a tremendous traffic in wireless communication, probably across the border. Our aim is to strike at the hard core, who have been interfering with and threatening the road. We hope to put them in such a position that they will ask the political authorities [in the Federation] for terms. Then we could get down to the business of a stable government.[9]

But there seemed to be confusion at HQ, MEC, as to the real scope of the operation. General Cubbon had only limited forces at his disposal and 'Radforce' was only ever intended to be a temporary unit, to last for the three weeks duration of the campaign. A press conference placed the emphasis very much on 'reconnaissance' rather than offensive operations and the GOC stated 'there is no concept of any large-scale operation'. But another spokesman talked of operations 'at a guess, lasting a year'. The problem facing military planners, when determining the size of their force and length of operation, was the chronic shortage of intelligence on the strength of the dissidents and NLF cadres. A political officer was appointed to the Force HQ to advise on local tribal affairs, and although he was a great asset, lack of resources limited his role.[10]

Another difficulty was the shortage of helicopters. With 'Nutcracker' this had created enough problems, but the impending 'Operation Cap Badge' required the movement of even larger numbers of troops to inaccessible points. The Army did have the new Scout helicopter from 13 Flight and the Search and Rescue (SAR) Flight had the more powerful Whirlwinds, but they were designed for a re-supply role. Consequently, the plan and the composition of Radforce went through several changes until Brigadier Hargroves presented a final draft on 17 April. Units from 24 Brigade, still based in Africa, were required to remain there to ward off any local army mutinies but Four Five Commando were available. The Force, which was now able to draw on support from the FRA and Aden Garrison, finally amounted to brigade strength. It comprised Four Five Commando, a company from the 3rd Battalion, The Parachute Regiment (3 PARA), a company from the 1st Battalion, The East Anglian Regiment, together with two battalions of FRA. Support was provided by armoured cars from D Squadron, Royal Tank Regiment, 'J' Battery 3 RHA and a troop from 12 Field Squadron, Royal Engineers.[11]

Suddenly, before the plan could be put into operation, the rebels nearly wiped out the Radforce Commanders. On 25 April some of the leading officers were on a reconnaissance mission when the front Landrover hit a landmine and was blown up. Major Linfoot (Quartermaster General, FRA) was killed instantly and Major John Monk (Brigade Major, FRA) later died of his wounds, while Lieutenant-Colonel Roy Watson, who had contributed much to the planning of the operation, was severely wounded. Brigadier Hargroves, the Commander of Radforce, narrowly escaped death as he was travelling in the following Landrover.[12]

The plan was for a night-time assault on 30 April/1 May to occupy the fertile area of the Danaba Basin, which was about four miles in diameter, together with the adjacent 'Rice Bowl' ridge near Wadi Taym. It was essential to capture the high ground before dawn and therefore the hill known as 'Cap Badge', which towered over 3,700ft and divided the two areas, was a prime objective. As there were insufficient helicopters available to land the Royal Marines, it was decided that their three Companies would night march to their objectives. Night operations had significant advantages, for temperatures were considerably lower than the daytime, which could average 120°. It was known too that the enemy disliked defensive night operations and such a plan would also negate their normal advantage of good observation.[13]

There were two obvious routes into the area, one being the Wadi Rabwa from the south-west and the other, through the narrower Wadi Boran to the north-west. After consultations between Lieutenant-Colonel T M P 'Paddy' Stevens, Commander of Four Five Commando, and Brigadier Hargroves, it was decided that the Marines would advance along Wadi Boran. It was a tougher route but Lieutenant-Colonel Stevens, a veteran of the Normandy *bocage* fighting in World War II, considered it would be more lightly defended. 'Z' Company, RM would seize 'Sand Fly', a hill flanking the Wadi Boran, while 'X' and 'Y' Companies, RM would advance through the Danaba Basin to occupy the ridge of 'Rice Bowl' to the north. Meanwhile, B Company, 3 PARA were to parachute onto the main objective, 'Cap Badge', using Beverley aircraft. To facilitate the drop, 3 Troop 22 SAS were to operate ahead of the force to collect intelligence and mark a drop zone (DZ) for 3 PARA.[14]

The Station Commander at Khormaksar airfield, Group Captain (later Marshal of the RAF Sir Michael) Beetham, supervised air cover. The main aircraft at his disposal were the Hawker Hunter, Fighter/Ground Attack (FGA) 9, used by 208 Squadron and 43(F) Squadron. The FGA 9 was a rebuild of the earlier Hunter F Mk 6 and had been in service in South Arabia since January 1960. This new mark included tail break parachutes for short runways and an increased weapons load. This allowed delivery of 1,000 lb bombs together with 2 inch or 3 inch rockets and 100-gallon napalm bombs. In addition, the FGA 9 had, as its standard fixed weapons, four 30mm Aden cannons, which made it a formidable machine. It was a 'classic' aircraft that both mechanics and pilots relished.[15] For bombing missions, 37 Squadron would provide four Shackleton MR3s, which were the only aircraft available for offensive night operations, but as they were unable to operate below 3,000ft, their gun armament was not utilised. 78

Squadron and its Twin Pioneer aircraft would carry out re-supply.[16]

As the road up from Aden was so tortuous, the bulk of the force had to be airlifted. The trusty Vickers Valetta C Mk 1,[17] known as 'The Pig', had recently been withdrawn when 233 Squadron was disbanded; so 84 Squadron flew the Blackburn Beverley in its place. At this time the Beverley was the largest plane in the RAF, being designed to carry outsize cargo, and with a vast freight hold of 170 m^3, it could accommodate a load of twenty tons, which also unfortunately made it a large target for ground-fire.[18]

While the main force advanced from the north-west, artillery support would be provided by 3 RHA, sited in the Wadi Rabwa and within range of 'Cap Badge'. The horse gunners were in good heart and their morale was boosted by the arrival of six new 105mm guns, which had recently been moved up to Thumier by tractor.[19]

Just before the operation started, Forward Observation Officers (FOO) were despatched to the various assault and picquet companies and then a section of guns was moved forward along the Wadi Rabwa. Accompanied by two armoured car troops and a rifle platoon of East Anglians, the gun section soon came up against a road block, which was only cleared by calling in Hunter strikes. Incoming mortar shells and sniping continued, though the artillery section that remained in Thumier pounded the enemy with HE shells and smoke to help the gunners get into the forward positions. A second gun section was then brought forward and by 13.00 hrs on 30 April, 'J' Battery were in their final gun positions at the head of Wadi Rabwa. As well as providing fire support for the main assault, the activity in the Wadi Rabwa would create a diversion.[20]

The revised plan had also called for 120 men from B Company 3 PARA to parachute from two Beverleys at midnight on 30 April/1 May. The drop was to be made near 'Cap Badge', and instead of using the Paras' normal pathfinder company, an SAS patrol was to mark a suitable DZ and guide the Beverleys in.[21]

The SAS involvement had resulted from lobbying by the commander of 'A' Squadron 22 SAS, 30-year-old Major (later General Sir Peter) de la Billière. Known as 'DLB', he had always been something of a rebel with a non-conformist streak, which stood him in good stead when he was selected to the SAS in 1956. With combat experience in the closing stages of the Malayan Campaign in 1958 and the taking of Jebel Akhdar during the Oman rebellion in 1959, he had topped up his experience of South Arabia with a recent two-year spell as an Intelligence Officer with the FRA. He now saw the opportunity for the SAS, as 'deep-penetration' troops, to be introduced into the Radfan Operations. South Arabia was familiar territory to units of 22 SAS who, together with 'C' (Rhodesian) Squadron, had trained in the mountains the previous year. After obtaining the agreement of General Sir Charles Harington and the CO 22

SAS, Lieutenant-Colonel John Woodhouse, de la Billière arranged for 'A' Squadron to leave their base in Hereford and fly out to Aden on 22 April.[22]

While the families of the SAS squadron were under the assumption that their men were exercising on Salisbury Plain, their arrival in Aden was no secret. It was common knowledge among civilians as well as military personnel. Writing home to her parents about the stories surrounding the Radfan build-up, Ann Cuthbert related the local news:

> We hear we're to be driven out of Aden – Ismail seems to think that it's all ballyhoo and there's no likelihood of a holy war. We also hear that there are no Egyptians in the centre of Yemen – they're all massed along the Federation border – no wonder the SAS have arrived.[23]

The nominal strength of 'A' Squadron 22 SAS at this time was about seventy-five officers and men and the Commander was assisted by both a Squadron Sergeant-Major and a Quartermaster-Sergeant, in addition to a support team including drivers, signallers and medics. The Squadron comprised four troops of sixteen men each, which were led by a Troop Captain assisted by a Troop Sergeant, and each troop was further split down into four-man patrols, which always included a medic, signaller, and sometimes an Arabist.[24]

Shortly after their arrival at Thumier Camp, the squadron went on a training mission and engaged a uniformed enemy party of some forty men, inflicting casualties.[25] For the 'Cap Badge' operation, Major de la Billière decided that a pared down troop of nine men would suffice for the immediate operation. He selected No. 3 Troop, commanded by 27-year-old Captain Robin Edwards of the Somerset and Cornwall Light Infantry, 'a big broad-shouldered Cornishman who softened his otherwise rugged appearance with a winning smile', and who had earned the respect of all in the Regiment by conquering polio to join them.[26] Edwards, who in line with SAS practice bore no badge of rank either at base or in the field, had a dependable team with him. Every man was trained to Regimental Signaller standard, had his own speciality and was also cross-trained in one other troop skill. Most were tough veterans of Malaya and Borneo and were attached to the SAS from units including The Royal Signals, Parachute Regiment, Royal Engineers and various infantry regiments.[27]

On 29 April, at last light, three sorties of Scout helicopters, each carrying three SAS men, took off from Thumier and swooped into rebel territory, while a short artillery barrage kept the enemy occupied.[28] The plan was to drop the patrol off well short of their target, after which they would night march into position before dawn on 30 April, lie up during the day and appear that night to mark a suitable DZ.

Once the helicopters had left them, the patrol moved off in diamond formation, with a lead scout out on point followed by Captain Edwards, while his 2IC, Troop Sergeant Reg Lingham, brought up the rear and covered the back of the patrol.[29]

As they started on their six-mile march towards Wadi Taym, the patrol's movements were monitored from an enemy watchtower; an Arab house perched high on a ridge above Habilayn Village, which curiously had been left untouched by the RAF. Some hours later, dissidents were observed slipping out of the fortified base and making their way in the direction of Shab Tem, a village near the proposed DZ.[30]

As the SAS patrol skirted the mountain ridges, the Signaller, Trooper Nick Warburton, started to slow up with stomach cramps. Despite keeping him in the middle of the formation and relieving him of his wireless, the food poisoning took its toll and by 0200 hours Captain Edwards contacted base to say the patrol would have to stop. He found a good defensive position on the slopes of the Bakri Ridge, on high ground and in a hollow, to lie up for the night and following day. By nightfall on 30 April he hoped Warburton would recover enough for the patrol to make it down to the Wadi Rabwa and three miles across to the DZ. But as dawn broke they found they were about half a mile above the hamlet of Shab Tem, near the point where the Wadi Rabwa led into Wadi Taym. Over the wireless Trooper Nick Warburton could hear radio chatter from a nearby village house, obviously used as a rebel HQ, and in the vicinity they counted twenty-two Arabs in green combat fatigues.[31]

The SAS men lay undetected in two old sangars on the hillside. Then, at 1100 hours, goats started wandering up towards the SAS position followed by their goatherd. The goatherd was talking to a woman who appeared to be rounding up strays when he glanced up and caught sight of the SAS men crouching in the sangars. Startled, the goatherd turned and alerted the woman. In a split second, the nearest SAS Trooper determined the risk of exposure, and with a single round, shot him. The rifle shot echoed around the hills and the woman disappeared, tearing down the hillside to tell the rebels in Shab Tem. Edwards and his men knew what was coming next and contacted base HQ.[32]

Within ten minutes, armed rebels started clambering up towards the sangars and as soon as they were in range, Edwards gave the order to engage the enemy. Every trooper marked his target and in the opening salvo, six of the nearest tribesmen fell. The rest scattered, some returning fire from behind boulders while others tried to work their way around and along the ridge above the SAS position. Meanwhile, back at 'A' Squadron base at Thumier, Major de la Billière realised that with enemy numbers increasing, the patrol needed swift air support. Major Mike Wingate Gray, 2IC of 22 SAS, then co-ordinated air attacks with the beleaguered patrol using the BASO in the Radforce HQ. It was not the quickest of relay systems, for the message came from the Edwards patrol to Major Wingate Gray before passing to the BASO who then talked the pilots in.

Pairs of Hunter FGA9s from 43 (F) and 208 Squadrons were scrambled at Khormaksar airfield, and after flying low level through the approaching wadis, the aircraft climbed to 3,000 ft above the Bakri Ridge.[33] The SAS patrol had identified a map bearing for the target, and a colour code for the smoke marker to be laid down for the air strike. But the maps were notoriously inaccurate and as the first Hunter went steaming down into a dive, the pilot had just ten seconds to pick out the smoke marker and hit his target. At 500mph, one ravine or mountain looked just like another, and tribesmen behind boulders were almost invisible. Lining up the target on the bottom diamond of his Reflector Sight, the pilot slid the catch on his control column to live and, within seconds, released all six of his 60lb rockets and pulled sharply back up to 3,000ft. His No. 2 was following on, and even before the first salvo of rockets had hit, the second aircraft had released another six 'drain pipes'. As the second Hunter pulled away from the dive, some of the rebel positions below disintegrated in a cloud of bursting rock and dust. Some rockets had struck home but several slewed off target, as each trajectory was affected by the air turbulence from the salvo. Further pairs of Hunters were now coming in, queuing up like a taxi rank, taking radio instructions and diving to attack, while those who had discharged their weapons returned to base. On the tarmac at Khormaksar, three technicians rushed to refit each Hunter with fuel and ammunition and within ten minutes the planes had taken off on the next sortie.[34]

The repeated Hunter attacks were keeping the rebels at bay, but despite the punishment they were receiving, it was remarkable how the tribesmen kept up their rate of fire, let alone their orientation, as the slopes were shrouded in clouds of dust and debris from the rocket strikes. It was difficult for the RAF pilots to achieve high casualties among the scurrying rebels in these conditions, and probably no more than ten per cent of the attackers were killed by these air strikes.[35]

Meanwhile on the ground, in the fierce heat of the afternoon, the SAS men were conserving their ammunition, trying to eke out their resources until darkness might allow an escape. The patrol only had a command set wireless, which meant that their calls for artillery support had to be passed through their squadron HQ at Thumier, then to 'J' Battery Commander and then to the guns in the Wadi Rabwa. 3 RHA continued to pound the enemy between RAF sorties, but eventually they had to cease firing when the tribesmen advanced too close to the SAS position. An attempt was also made to reach the men by helicopter, but the aircraft was soon shot up by enemy fire and had to return to base.[36]

By late afternoon, several enemy .303 rounds found their mark. In the sangar holding Captain Edwards, Trooper Paddy Baker was hit in the back of his knee, with the round passing through him and killing Trooper Warburton behind. Incoming rounds also smashed the wireless, rendering it useless. Then as several rebels finally rushed the sangars,

Trooper Bill Hamilton was hit, the round creasing his shoulder blade. The enemy charge was only stopped when Sergeant 'Geordie' Tasker opened up with bursts from his Bren, killing several of the attackers. Baker was now bleeding profusely, but the patrol medic, 'Darkie B', darted across to him and despite the fire, was able to staunch the wound. More tribesmen had joined the attack and the enemy now numbered about seventy, some closing from twenty yards away.[37]

The light started to fade and it was soon obvious that air support could not continue for much longer. Without communication with their base, the patrol decided to make a break for it in two groups and under cover of darkness. One group, under Sergeant Reg Lingham, would give covering fire as Edwards' group zigzagged down the hill. There was nothing they could do for Trooper Warburton, and they had to leave his body in the sangar. Everything that could not be carried was destroyed and the Morse set and remains of the wireless were disabled. As Captain Edwards jumped up to leave his cover, he was shot in the stomach and fell backwards, his pack wedging him between the rocks. Sergeant Lingham rushed to his side but it was too late. Edwards was severely wounded and murmured to Lingham, 'get out of it and leave me alone'.[38]

The three survivors from Edwards' sangar, Sergeant 'Geordie' Tasker, Trooper Baker and 'Darkie B' made it clear of the position to some cover twenty yards away. They then gave covering fire as the remaining group of four, including Sergeant Lingham, Lance Corporal 'Taffy B' and the wounded Trooper Hamilton, made their escape. The whole group then made off into the night as the rebels stormed what was left of the sangars. Keeping to the high ground with the Wadi Rabwa down below them, the men kept ahead of any enemy trackers. But as the exhausted party marched on, groups of rebels closed in on them. However, the wounded Troopers, Paddy Baker and Bill Hamilton acting as back markers, twice set up ambushes and despatched the pursuers.[39] All through the night the men kept up their pace, never ceasing their vigilance, and having shared the last of their water with the wounded, they descended into the Wadi Rabwa, now only several miles from base. It was still dark and they were extremely cautious in case FRA picquets mistook their identity and shot them as rebels. But as dawn came, an armoured car in the wadi met the ragged patrol and the wounded were hauled aboard while the other five survivors marched the mile back into camp. While the SAS debrief started at Thumier, the rebel tribesmen were taking grisly revenge on the bodies of Captain Edwards and Trooper Warburton.[40]

Full confirmation of the SAS disaster reached the advance parties of Four Five at about 2400 hours. Z Company had already peeled off to take 'Sand Fly' but X and Y Companies were already in enemy territory on the edge of the Danaba Basin. Lieutenant-Colonel Stevens arranged a revised plan, which recalled X and Y Companies and sent them off to scale the adjacent hill, christened 'Coca Cola'. Even those men loaded with Vickers machine-guns and mortars still managed the task of the 1,500ft ascent in quick time and by dawn on 1 May the commandos from Four Five were overlooking the Danaba Basin.

Meanwhile, back at the artillery positions in the Wadi Rabwa the crews were under constant sniper fire, crawling or running at the double around the position. They were firing over open sights at rebel snipers across the valley, pinning them down and inflicting casualties. While a new plan was prepared following the aborted Edwards Patrol, the pack howitzers were still employed in supporting new SAS four-man patrols working the Rabwa Pass. This time, the SAS were equipped with A41 wireless sets, enabling them to contact the guns direct, and when combined with accurate spotting, enabled many rebel positions to be destroyed.[41] However, enemy numbers continued to build and to allay the threat of the guns being surrounded, they were withdrawn, with two sections returning to Thumier to support the continuing SAS operations to the east. The remaining 3 RHA section then laboriously trundled their guns up and around the northern route to cover the Danaba Basin and 'Cap Badge'.

After the survivors of the Edwards Patrol had made it back to base, it was clear that the enemy were holding the proposed DZ area, south of 'Cap Badge'. Although 3 PARA were prepared to drop into an unmarked zone, Brigadier Hargroves decided it was too risky. There was now nothing for it but to night march 'B' Company 3 PARA, together with Four Five, to take the main objective of 'Cap Badge'.[42]

At sunset on 4 May the 1 East Anglians on 'Sand Fly' and 'Coca Cola' relieved Four Five. Then the commando units, X Company (Major Mike Banks) and Y Company (Captain Gavin Hamilton-Meikle), started the arduous five-mile journey down into the Basin to guide 3 PARA towards the heights beyond. Major Banks, an experienced mountaineering officer who had recently returned from the Yukon, was another World War II veteran and like Captain Hamilton-Meikle, was typical of the high calibre officers that 45 Commando attracted. Physical hardship or injury mattered little to Banks, and when on one occasion he had returned to duty following a bad climbing accident, with his back red-raw and badly scarred, he just pressed on as if nothing had happened.[43]

After three miles, Y Company split off together with the Commando tactical HQ and scaled the 1,000ft 'Gin Sling', just below 'Cap Badge'. As X Company and 3 PARA continued on their mission, they remained unchallenged, passing empty sangars, which the dissidents had left for the night in order to return to their villages to sleep. However, the Radforce movements were still observed. Dogs yapped in the nearby villages and flickering lights were seen.[44]

While X Company Four Five started the steep ascent of 'Cap Badge' from the south-west, the Paras skirted the lower levels and descended the

Wadi Taym beyond, in order to attack 'Cap Badge' from the south-east. However, this was real mountaineering and the only available maps were simple and gave no indication of the extremely arduous going over gullies and crags. As dawn broke on 5 May the exhausted Paras found themselves in the open and in front of the hostile village of Al Naqil. They couldn't hope to conceal themselves and soon rifle and machine-gun fire erupted from the mud houses and forts.

Using Marine FOOs, high up on the neighbouring hill of 'Gin Sling', the Paras called in artillery support from the 105mm guns near Danaba. But it was an extremely difficult target and because the enemy village was sandwiched between units of Four Five and the Paras, only a few rounds could be fired without hitting friendly forces. Hunter strikes were then called in to rocket the rebel forts, and this was shortly followed by a 3 PARA assault on the village led by 'B' Company Commander, Major Peter Walters. The enemy then tried to flank this attack and cut it off, but Captain Edward Jewkes followed up with the remaining platoons and blocked the rebels, killing most of them in a fierce firefight. The Paras now partly occupied the village but were pinned down by enemy sniper fire from the hills above and were starting to take casualties. Twenty-one-year-old Private Michael Davis was shot and killed and Sergeant Baxter was severely wounded. As Baxter lay in the open, Captain Jewkes ran over to him to administer morphine but as he bent over the wounded Sergeant, Jewkes was shot and killed.[45]

Meanwhile, the Paras' supplies of water and ammunition were running low, even though the Army Air Corps' Beavers had braved the fire to drop fresh supplies. Some of the wounded also needed urgent attention but there was no way to evacuate them. Then in an ambitious move, 'Z' Company Four Five, who had been holding 'Sand Fly', were flown across by helicopter and landed on 'Cap Badge'. They then climbed 1,500 feet down the mountain to mark a drop zone near El Naqil for a 'casevac' by Belvedere helicopter. This was a very difficult task, for although the Belvedere had many advantages, such as its large capacity, it was also an easy target for snipers when manoeuvring to land. And until a suitable integrated radio network could be established, incoming helicopters would have to contend with not only enemy fire but also friendly artillery and mortar bombardments. The Belvedere also needed a large landing zone, which was a rare facility on steep mountainsides. However, one site was eventually identified and a helicopter soon arrived, carrying 3 PARA medics and the battalion Padre, who set about comforting the eight wounded men and burying the two dead. Once the remaining rebels had been cleared, the weary Paras, who had endured a ten-hour night march followed by fierce fighting for the best part of a day, then climbed to the summit of 'Cap Badge' before nightfall.[46]

In the following days, dissident resistance died down enabling a battalion of FRA to replace 1 East Anglians on 'Coca Cola' and 'Sand Fly', who in turn went forward to replace Four Five on 'Cap Badge'. The East Anglians had some extraordinary encounters in some of the hamlets in the surrounding area. Because the area was so inaccessible, some villagers had never seen a white face before and the arrival of the soldiers prompted several women to commit suicide by throwing themselves down a well.[47]

The lull in the fighting now gave Middle East Command (MEC) time to assess the progress of the Radfan Campaign. Although the military operations to date were successful, it was clear that only a long drawn out commitment would contain the Radfan rebels. The interior had proved as tough an opponent as the tribesmen and ignorance of the true conditions had severely hampered troops and aircraft. MEC planners admitted:

> The country is deceptive, even those parts which appear flat. Almost invariably the time taken to get from one point to another was underestimated, even after air reconnaissance and the study of air photographs. Initially, the maps available were of poor quality, inaccurate and with few details. Eventually Commanders were considerably more cautious in their estimation of time and space problems.[48]

This problem was further exacerbated by the shortage of suitable helicopters to land guns, picquets and supplies onto hilltops. There were periods when Wessex helicopters from HMS *Centaur* were available but Belvedere helicopters were in short supply. Even this machine had its limitations, with one commander divulging, 'the Belvedere is a useful cargo lifter but it is really too big and too high off the ground for quick loading and unloading'.[49]

As British patrols traversed the rock-strewn wadis and sheer mountain passes, they became frustrated with the continuing distance of their enemy. Consequently, no prisoners were captured and intelligence suffered. If the SAS had been introduced into the Radfan earlier, before operations commenced, their intelligence-gathering role would have been properly utilised and enemy strengths more accurately assessed.[50] Another difficulty encountered was that tribesmen, well used to the terrain, would often fire at the extent of their rifle range and in familiar territory they often marked these ranges before an engagement.[51] Because the Forward Air Controllers (FACs) and FOOs on the ground could not always advance close enough to accurately spot the enemy positions, expenditure of British ammunition was high. This in turn affected re-supply, and this problem was aggravated when artillery and air support was sometimes called upon too frequently. The physical difficulty of re-supply was crucial as the depth and timing of any operation was usually governed by how quickly ammunition, water and food could be brought forward. The water requirement alone was twelve pints per man per day, and a Company needed three helicopter sorties for an extended operation.[52] For inaccessible valleys or wadis, no organised pack transport seemed to be available and although the FRA were able to control camels, the British re-supply teams would have benefited from the use of some sturdy mules. Where camels were used to transport the pack howitzers, the camel train could be unworkable as fourteen beasts would be needed per gun and each animal could only carry four shells.[53] In addition, British troops often had to operate beyond their artillery cover and therefore had to carry additional support weapons. Trooper Jim Buchanan, serving with Four Five, recalled:

> During 'Operation Cap Badge' I was with the support company as a Vickers machine-gunner. With its water-cooled barrel, it was a very heavy gun to carry around but it was robust and accurate, which was important when you think that most of the enemy fired at you from over 1,000 yards away. The gun had served us well in two world wars, and I was sorry when it was replaced the following year with the GPMG (General Purpose Machine-Gun). The GPMG had more rapid fire, but it was not as good as the Vickers in the desert conditions of Radfan. There were more stoppages because there were too many moving parts and the sand and dust got into everything.[54]

These operational difficulties were to become more acute as the campaign pushed farther into the wild interior.

Part II: (11 May–27 June 1964)

By 11 May reconnaissance had confirmed that the enemy was far from beaten but it was clear that the scope of future operations was beyond the capabilities of the small HQ of 'Radforce', which had only ever been a temporary command. Considering that it comprised only about a third of a normal Brigade staff, 'Radforce' HQ had been a remarkable achievement, due in no small part to the work of the Brigade Major, Major Clive Brennan.[55] While Brigadier Hargroves had to return to the pressing needs of Aden Garrison, it proved difficult to find a Regular brigade to replace 'Radforce' as the British Army was already heavily committed with emergencies in Cyprus, East Africa and North Borneo.[56] Neither was there any slack in the BAOR, so the only available formation was 39 Brigade, serving in Northern Ireland and commanded by Brigadier (later General Sir Cecil) 'Monkey' Blacker.[57] The former cavalryman was whisked out to South Arabia and briefed that the Radfan Campaign was to be extended deeper into enemy territory. He immediately set about a plan to secure the Bakri Ridge, a mountain feature to the south, which dominated the nearby rebel stronghold of Wadi Dhubsan.

To mount further operations, improvements had to be made to landing facilities and the airstrip at Habilayn was enlarged to take Medium Range Transport (MRT), while new airstrips were constructed near Wadi Taym, named 'Monk's Field' and 'Paddy's Field'.[58] The old military adage that 'there are never enough sappers' was particularly relevant in the Radfan and the engineer troop was subsequently enlarged to two field squadrons and a field park. Reconnaissance was also stepped up, with 'A' Squadron SAS mounting a number of successful operations in the Wadi Taym. They were assisted by 15 Intelligence Platoon from the Intelligence Corps, who were now on hand to study the SAS reports as well as air observation reports, and to analyse captured weapons. However, the enemy again proved to be elusive, and although some were killed in engagements with the SAS, no rebels were captured alive.[59]

With regard to the fighting force, 'B' Company 3 PARA were rested after their tough action and replaced with the remaining 3 PARA companies under the command of Lieutenant-Colonel Tony Farrar-Hockley. Infantry strength was further bolstered by the arrival of the 1st Battalion Royal Scots, while armoured car support was also increased and Lieutenant-Colonel Bryan Watkins, CO 4 RTR, was brought in to control future armoured operations. He knew that driving and maintaining the Saladin armoured cars and Ferret scout cars in the Radfan was a rough and ready business:

> The main problem was seized suspensions, clogged with salt-laden sand, which needed a quantity of grease and some vigorous bouncing over a rocky strip of desert to free them. This done and the cars liberally painted with red lead to counter the effects of the salt on their metal, they were ready to learn the tricks of desert driving and navigation. The heat was such that the troops could literally fry an egg on the armour at midday and motoring became impossible, because the petrol vaporised in the carburettors, often forcing the crews to wait until the cool of the evening before they could get moving.[60]

These preparations for future operations started even before official Government sanction was given. Earl Mountbatten, in his position as Chief of the Defence Staff, wrote to the Secretary of State confirming that although Government authority for an extension of the Radfan Campaign had yet to be given, 'the Chiefs of Staff have examined requests for reinforcements in order to ensure that there should be no delay if the operations are approved'. It was anticipated that actual operations could only start after 22 May, when HMS *Centaur* arrived in Aden with its compliment of Wessex helicopters.[61] She was also to deliver two much needed 5.5 inch guns for the RHA, ordnance whose range was over ten miles, almost double the distance of the existing 105mm guns and which could destroy enemy caves.[62] However, in the meantime, events in the Radfan were developing fast. Probing patrols on the Bakri Ridge had brought back information that the area was, for the moment, lightly defended. Brigadier Blacker decided on a quick assault by 3 PARA, even if it meant dispensing with helicopters. 3 PARA were ready for any eventuality, and using one company as porters, the paratroopers swiftly scaled the Bakri Ridge. Despite carrying personal weapons and packs of over 80lbs, they nevertheless reached the Hajib escarpment within two days. They met isolated pockets of resistance but the fiercest fight lay ahead.

As 'C' Company, under Major Tony Ward-Booth, moved towards the highest point of Qudeishi, they encountered heavy enemy fire. Leading sections were met by a barrage of fire coming from several forts and an extraordinary network of caves in and around the escarpment. Ward-Booth called in Hunter air strikes and also artillery support from J Battery, who had meanwhile hauled their guns into the nearby Wadi Misrah. As Hunter rockets crashed into the enemy forts and artillery rounds slammed into the labyrinth of cave entrances, 'C' Company attacked and captured the settlement. The defenders had fought a determined action, bravely defending their positions, even after repeated rocket attacks had demolished their sangars. They lost some thirty warriors, with the survivors melting away down into the Wadi Dhubsan to try and regain the initiative.

The following day, Lieutenant-Colonel Farrar-Hockley ordered 'C' and 'A' Companies, 3 PARA to continue their advance into the Wadi with the intention of capturing Jebel Huriyah, a 5,500ft unconquered peak, which lay beyond. He also had under his command the Royal Marines of 'X' Company, who were to accompany the Paras down the steep descent of 3,000ft into the wadi bed. Major Ward-Booth and his Company HQ, together with other Para units, abseiled down the sheer side of the wadi while the Marines swept down and around the riverbed, keeping in front of the assaulting party. Concealed rebel snipers and machine-guns then opened up, scattering the Marines who took to the higher ground before returning fire. In such circumstances, the junior leadership showed excellent initiative and the Non-Commissioned Officers were incisive in their control over fire and movement.

As the Marines and Paras engaged the enemy, a Scout helicopter on a reconnaissance mission flew low overhead and was repeatedly hit by rebel bullets. The aircraft, piloted by Major 'Jigs' Jackson, contained Lieutenant-Colonel Farrar-Hockley and his Intelligence Officer who were on an urgent reconnaissance mission. As the bullets ripped through the fuselage, the Intelligence Officer was wounded but by skilful control, Jackson managed to bring his shuddering machine down to land near the Marines who formed a cordon while the occupants escaped.[63]

As enemy fire continued, the Marines called in a Hunter strike. As always, this required laying out orange direction markers for the incoming aircraft, but as Captain Roger Brind, Second-in-Command of 'X' Company, completed this job, he was shot through the leg and stomach. Other casualties were suffered as the Marines advanced. No. 1 Troop lost their Signaller, Marine Wilson, who was shot through the chest and collapsed dying into the arms of his troop leader, while Marine Dunkin lost a leg in the enemy fusillade. All the while, Marine Wade clambered around boulders, going from troop to troop, braving the sniper fire to administer first aid to the wounded. The tribesmen kept up their accurate fire, continually moving position and height, but as the afternoon wore on, 3 PARA managed to edge around the top of Wadi Dhubsan. Hammered by Hunter rocket strikes and contained by Marine and Para ground fire, the rebels started to fall back. Dusk fell and once the wounded were 'casevac'd' out of the area, Lieutenant-Colonel Farrar-Hockley's force could be airlifted out. After giving a fine account of themselves and securing their military objectives, 3 PARA and Four Five Commando were now withdrawn from the Radfan. However, although the British force was in the heart of Radfan, the key features of Jebel Radfan and Jebel Huriyah, lying to the south, remained to be captured.[64]

Before Jebel Huriyah, which stood at over 6,000ft, lay Wadi Misrah and Wadi Tramare, both of which had to be cleared, allowing the *jebel* to be scaled. In early June the 1 East Anglians picqueted the Wadi Misrah, allowing 4 RTR to clear the Wadi through to its junction with Tramare. At that point, they were joined by 2 FRA and covered by the 105mm and 5.5 inch guns of 3 RHA. But as 2 FRA advanced to the lower slopes of Huriyah on 7 June they were met with heavy fire from the village of Shaab Sharah. The leading FRA company, together with a FOO, had to advance up the steep sides of the *jebel*, sheer in many places, as enemy fire came down on them from the flanks and from above. The gunners had managed to set up three positions to the rear, enabling the FOO to call down artillery fire onto three enemy positions at once. With this excellent cover and the help of further Hunter air strikes, the FRA overcame the rebel stand and finally occupied Jebel Huriyah on 12 June. It was the last pitched battle of the campaign, and with the occupation of Jebel Widina on 27 June, the dominant features of Radfan were under the control of the Federation. The 'Red Wolves' had melted away, having suffered several hundred casualties but it remained to be seen whether they had been defeated.

While the military operations in Radfan were hailed a success, the achievement of one of the objectives, 'to provoke the dissidents to fight and so to suffer casualties, resulting in a lowering of morale', was open to doubt. The dissidents had, with the exception of the actions at Al Naqil, Wadi Dhubsan and Huriyah, made a conscious effort not to engage the British Army in a set piece battle. The temptations must have been strong, especially as they were fighting in their heartland. But the NLF had learned the lessons of previous guerrilla wars, where rebels had stood their ground and been destroyed by superior firepower.[65] In fact the NLF leadership had felt comfortable enough, even during the military engagements of May, to send a delegation under al-Sha'abi to a nationalist conference in Beirut.[66]

The Radfan Campaign had also been expensive in terms of ammunition expended compared to enemy casualties. Air strikes had resulted in over 600 sorties, leasing off 2,500 rockets and expending nearly 200,000 cannon rounds, while the artillery had fired 20,000 shells. There were criticisms from MEC that too often the infantry called up air strikes and artillery bombardments. But the availability of this support was understandably tempting to any patrol ambushed in a ravine or mountain pass, by almost invisible tribesmen who could inflict wounds for which no rapid aid was available.

One inherent weakness in the plan to pacify the Radfan was that the NLF was still able to maintain its Yemen sanctuaries at Qataba and Baidha, reinforced from Taiz whenever necessary.[67] The maintenance of such 'active sanctuaries' across a frontier has been common to many successful post-war insurgencies. The FLN in the Algerian War sought sanctuary in neighbouring Tunisia, while Cambodia and Laos provided boltholes as well as supply routes for the Vietcong in their insurgency in South Vietnam. Similarly, despite the extensive British operations in the Radfan, large Yemeni arms caravans were still entering the Federation during the summer of 1964, even escorted by Egyptian intelligence officers as they made their way to handover points in Yafa State. Intercepting these caravans was sometimes beyond the resources of the FRA, and even the Federal National Guard, responsible for internal security, did not have the means to pursue them. MEC privately admitted, 'the vehicles on loan to the FNG are all well worn and their arms are obsolete'.[68]

Another important facet of the counter-insurgency war was mobility. Helicopters were considered to be too valuable to risk in an assault role, and the few available were committed to re-supply and transport work. Nevertheless, the operations in the Radfan could not have been contemplated without them. The enemy always maintained the advantage of the harsh terrain, allowing them to keep their distance and they also benefited from the requirement, under the proscription code, for British troops to warn hamlets and villages of impending attack, by leaflet drop. However, this effort to appear 'fair' to Arab and world opinion was sometimes negated by the British Army's clearance methods in the fertile areas of the Danaba Basin and Wadi Taym. For it won few 'hearts and minds' when local crops and village grain stores were destroyed and livestock slaughtered in an attempt to deprive the enemy of sustenance. Such methods were also designed to be punitive exercises, and although MEC recorded reservations among some British servicemen, most were not sorry to see the destruction of the enemy's support system.[69]

The Radfan operations had highlighted the importance of good communications between infantry platoons or companies and their artillery and air support, resulting in continual harassment of the enemy. But despite the 'talking up' of the individual successes in Radfan, by the end of June, after two months campaigning, Middle East Command privately conceded that 'there are as yet no signs of submission by the tribes and the latest intelligence reports indicate that supplies continue to be sent from Yemen into Radfan.[70]

NOTES

1 The artist David Shepherd immortalised the Dhala Road in a painting that now hangs in the School of Infantry, Warminster.
2 In a report in *The Times*, 5 May 1964, a Corporal of the Dhala garrison defected to Yemen with a Saladin armoured car.
3 Anonymous dissident to Clare Hollingworth, May 1964. Translated in her autobiography, *Front Line*, Jonathan Cape, 1990, p. 207.
4 'Field Tactics of Guerrilla Warfare' in Colin Beer, *On Revolutionary War*, Galago, 1990, pp. 32–41.
5 Report of Press Conference, HQ MIDEAST, 3 May 1964, DEFE 13/569, NA.
6 *The Oak Tree* (Journal of 22nd (Cheshire) Regiment), Vol. 81, 1996.
7 In Brigadier Hargroves' absence, Lieutenant-Colonel S Palmer was appointed temporary Commander Aden Garrison. Major-General Cubbon to Brigadier Hargroves, 14 April 1964, Hargroves Papers.
8 Paget, op. cit., pp. 53–4. Similar heat restrictions faced those planning the start of the Second Gulf War in 2003.
9 *The Times*, 4 May 1964. Also Major-General Cubbon to Author, 6 June 1995.
10 Press Conference, HQ MIDEAST, 3 May 1964, DEFE 13/569, NA. The weakness of intelligence was admitted by the GOC. See also 'Report on Radfan Operations', HQMEC, 29 September 1964, DEFE 25/190, NA.
11 The 1 East Anglian was only formed in 1959 from an amalgamation of The Royal Norfolk and The Suffolk Regiment. It arrived in Aden in February 1964 for a twenty-month tour, initially to act as an Aden Garrison battalion and was commanded by Lieutenant-Colonel (later Major-General) Jack Dye MC. On 1 September 1964 the 1 East Anglian was itself redesignated the 1st Battalion, The Royal Anglian Regiment. Michael Barthorp, in his history of The Royal Anglian Regiment, *From Crater to the Creggan*, defers to Sir Julian Paget's, *Last Post*, for an account of the EA in the Radfan. Also Brigadier G S Heathcote, 'Operations in the Radfan', Lecture to RUSI, November 1965, Hargroves Papers.
12 MEC to MOD London, 4 April 1964. Trevaskis to MOD, 7 April 1964. MEC to MOD, 25 April 1964, all DEFE 25/17, NA. Lieutenant-Colonel Watson had

identified the strategic importance of the mountain christened 'Cap Badge'. Brigadier Sir Louis Hargroves to Author, 3 October 2003.

13   'Army Lessons from Radfan', 9 October 1964, DEDE 25/190, NA.

14   'Army Lessons from Radfan', op. cit. Also *Globe & Laurel*, June 1964, and David Young, *Four Five*, Leo Cooper, 1972, pp. 326–9. Ironically, the SAS had often fought during World War II alongside popular resistance groups, but in the post-war years, they had developed into a tough, professional counter-revolutionary force, fighting home grown nationalist movements.

15   Mike Rudd, former Chief Technician on Hunter Hawkers (Hunter Flying Club) to Author, 28 May 2003. The last FGA 9s remained in service with the RAF until the early 1980s. The last Hunter mark was the FR10, used for reconnaissance.

16   The Shackletons were also used to drop leaflets before proscription bombing raids.

17   The Valetta, which was a version of the civil 'Viking', originally took over from the Dakota in 1948 and did sterling service in the Malayan Campaign and also took part in some of the paradrops during Suez in 1956. It had been used in South Arabia since 1949 to transport men and supplies.

18   The sole intact example of a Beverley (No. XB259) remains on display at The Museum of Army Transport, North Humberside.

19   Moving the guns as 'portee' on tractors reduced the excessive wear generated by towing. Brigadier Baines to Author, 28 June 2002.

20   Brigadier Baines, op. cit. Also Brigadier Sir Louis Hargroves, op. cit.

21   Lee, op. cit., p. 210. In Peter Stiff's first person account of the Edwards patrol, published in South Africa, he states that the real mission was cross border intelligence and that the patrol was split into two, comprising four- and five-man teams, inside 'North Yemen'. He then switches the action to 'Jabal Ashquale'. This appears to be a reference to Jebel Ashqab, the large peak near the proposed DZ in Radfan. He further states that the two teams built new protective sangars to lie up in during the day. This would be unusual as it was highly likely that the dissidents, with their acute knowledge of every crag and crevice, would spot any new sangars at daybreak; see *See You in November*, Galago Publishing, revised 2002 edition.

22   General Sir Peter de la Billière, *Looking for Trouble*, HarperCollins, 1994. John Newsinger, in his study, *Dangerous Men: The SAS and Popular Culture*, Pluto Press, 1997, examines the literature and memoirs of 'The Regiment', much of which contain details of the Edwards Patrol and the SAS in South Arabia.

23   Ann Cuthbert correspondence, 28 April 1964.

24   Peter Dickens, *SAS: The Jungle Frontier*, Arms and Armour Press, 1983, p. 38. At this time, 'A' and 'D' were the two operational squadrons in 22 SAS. Between them, they alternated four-month tours in Borneo.

25   'Operations by A Sqn 22 SAS', Hargroves Papers. Also confidential source.

26   De la Billière, op. cit., p. 214. Despite his polio, Edwards looked 'every bit the SAS soldier' and when he came home on leave, always seemed to be suntanned and fit, even in winter. Confidential source.

27   Officers and men are only ever 'attached' to 'The Regiment' and can be returned to their original units (RTU) at any time.

28   In Tony Geraghty, *Who Dares Wins: The Story of the Special Air Service 1950–80*, Arms & Armour Press, 1980, and Anthony Kemp, *The SAS: Savage Wars of Peace*, John Murray, 1994, the SAS patrol are recorded as arriving in enemy territory by armoured cars. However, it was the new Scout helicopter that was favoured for SAS operations as it was stable when hovering, allowing troops to abseil to the ground if necessary.

29 Each Trooper carried a 60lb backpack together with another 40lb of weapons and ammunition. There was an assortment of firepower, with most of the patrol carrying either an SLR or the M16A1 assault rifle together with four magazines containing a personal allocation of 120 rounds. In addition to this, bandoliers of rounds for the Bren light machine-gun were shared around. Another man carried a L42A1 bolt-action sniper rifle.

30 Stephen Harper, *Last Sunset: What Happened in Aden*, Collins 1978, p. 48.

31 Harper, op. cit., pp. 47–8. As a foreign correspondent, Harper later interviewed two wounded members of the patrol, including Sergeant Reg Lingham. However other published reports refer to the wounded as Trooper Paddy Baker and Trooper Bill Hamilton, see *The Times*, 4 May 1964.

32 There are a number of published accounts of the Edwards Patrol, including both fact and 'factoid'. Among the former are, Peter de la Billière, *Looking for Trouble*: Peter Stiff, *See You in November*: John Strawson, *A History of the SAS Regiment*: Ken Connor, *Ghosts: An illustrated Story of the SAS*: Anthony Kemp, *The SAS: Savage Wars of Peace*: Tony Geraghty, *Who Dares Wins*. Among the latter are Pete Scholey, *The Joker*, and Shaun Clarke, *Soldier 'J' SAS*.

33 Because of the intense heat, pilots could only sit in their cockpits, in readiness, for a maximum of ten minutes. Brigadier Sir Louis Hargroves to Author, 3 October 2003.

34 The decision on whether to use rocket or cannon fire would normally be taken at command level, and confirmed at the operation briefing, but because of the speed of the operation it may well have been decided on by the leader of the formation. If there was a risk of ground fire, rockets were usually all fired at once, in one pass. David Malin to Author, 14 June 2003.

35 It was difficult to accurately determine enemy casualty rates, due to their practice of removing their dead. However, after one air strike, it was calculated that out of thirty-five dissidents attacking, three were killed. This was considered the norm, Brigadier Charles Dunbar to Lieutenant-Colonel Julian Paget, 25 September 1968, File 2/6, Dunbar Papers, LHCMA.

36 Major Stagg, op. cit., and de la Billière, op. cit., p. 220.

37 Conference Report, op. cit. DEFE 13/569, NA.

38 Report from SAS survivors at GOC, MELF conference, 3 May 1964, DEFE 13/569, NA. See also Peter Stiff, op. cit., p. 36.

39 Lance-Corporal Baker was awarded the Military Medal for his part in the operation.

40 There is a comprehensive account in 'Aden/Yemen Situation', DEFE 13/569, NA, but much of the report together with enclosures has been 'weeded' by the MOD under Section 5 (1) as recently as July 1995. For accounts of the patrol, see also Geraghty op. cit., pp. 77–8 and Stiff, op. cit., p. 36.

41 Major Stagg, op. cit. Introduced in 1960, the A41 became the standard British Army tactical radio. It was carried in a backpack and weighed about 17lbs including one battery. Also 'Report on Operations of Radfan Force 13 April–11 May 1964', Hargroves Papers.

42 3 PARA were no longer volunteers from other regiments. Since 1953 direct enlistment into the Parachute Regiment was the norm, and since 1958 officers could be directly commissioned.

43 Major Chris Smith (Adjutant, 45 Commando) to Author, 28 May 2003.

44 David Young, op. cit., pp. 328–35 and James Ladd, op. cit., pp. 322–5. Also Brigadier GS Hargroves, 'Operations in the Radfan', November 1965 Lecture to RUSI, Hargroves Papers.

45 Lieutenant Jewkes, aged 25, from Blackpool, served with The Lancashire Fusiliers and was attached to 3 PARA. See *The Times*, 7 May 1964.

46   *Globe & Laurel*, June 1964. *The Times*, 6 May 1964. Also Major Stagg, 'Gunners in the Radfan, in *Journal of the Royal Artillery*, March 1965 and Julian Paget, op. cit., pp. 70–1. For helicopter problems, see 'Army Lessons', op. cit.

47   Brigadier Sir Louis Hargroves, op. cit.

48   'Army Lessons from Radfan Operations', 9 October 1964, DEFE 25/190, NA.

49   'Short Report on Operations of Radfan Force 13 April–11 May 1964, Hargroves Papers. Surprisingly, the Radfan terrain offered better conditions for helicopters than Oman and the Gulf, where operational areas were virtually all desert, rather than rock. Even the Wessex, which had performed so well in Radfan, suffered chronic sand ingestion problems in Sharjah in 1968.

50   'Employment of SAS' in 'Army Lessons from Radfan Operations', 9 October 1964, DEFE 25/190, NA.

51   Confirmation that no prisoners had been taken up to 3 May was given at a press conference of GOC, MELF, 3 May 1964. See DEFE 13/569. Also Brigadier Sir Louis Hargroves, op. cit.

52   The SAS daily requirement was no more than eight pints per man per day. Brigadier G S Heathcote, 'Operations in Radfan', 24 November 1965 Lecture to RUSI, Hargroves Papers.

53   For transport problems, see Major Stagg, 'Gunners in the Radfan', op. cit.

54   Jim Buchanan to Author, 3 May 2003.

55   Brigadier Sir Louis Hargroves was fulsome in his praise for the work of Major Brennan.

56   By mid-1964, ten British battalions were committed to Borneo. For the JIC view of these deployments, see Percy Cradock, *Know Your Enemy: How the Joint Intelligence Committee Saw the World*, John Murray, 2002, pp. 210–23.

57   A former ADC to HM The Queen, Blacker later became GOC Northern Ireland and Vice-Chief of General Staff 1970–3; see William Jackson, op. cit., p. 221.

58   The two airstrips were named after Major John Monk and Colonel Paddy Stevens. Even with the arrival of new Scout helicopters, it was still months before sealed helicopter pads were constructed. These hessian and PSP pads prevented helicopter engines from ingesting the enormous amounts of dust and debris found on Arabian airstrips. See 'RAF Lessons from Radfan Operations', 29 September 1964, DEFE 25/190, NA.

59   John Strawson, *A History of the SAS Regiment*, Secker & Warburg, 1984, p. 198.

60   George Forty, *The Royal Tank Regiment*, Spellmount, 1989, p. 225. 4 RTR maintained three squadrons in South Arabia, while the fourth covered the Persian Gulf.

61   Mountbatten to Secretary of State, 13 May 1964, DEFE 13/569, NA.

62   Brigadier Baines op. cit., p. 25. Also Brigadier Sir Louis Hargroves, op. cit.

63   Obituary, Major-General Ward-Booth, *The Times*, 31 August 2002. *Life* magazine featured an illustration of Ward-Booth in action on the Bakri Ridge. He shared the issue with Sophia Loren, which caused much amusement.

64   During the Radfan Campaign, a total of 116 casualties were casevac'd, see 'RAF Lessons', DEFE 25/190, NA. For the fight in Wadi Dhubsan, see *The Dhow* (Services Newspaper), 24 June 1964, and *Globe & Laurel*, August 1964. See also Lee, op. cit., pp. 212–14, Paget, op. cit., pp. 91–4, Young, op. cit., pp. 337–42.

65   In the Greek Civil War, guerrillas had staunchly defended their base at Grammos and were virtually destroyed as a fighting movement. See E R Wainhouse, 'Guerrilla Warfare in Greece, 1946–9' in F M Osanka (ed.), *Modern Guerrilla Warfare*, Glencoe Press, 1962.

66   The ANM conference was held in Beirut in May 1964 to determine the ideological direction of Arab nationalist groups.
67   Captain D M Miller, 'The Theory and Practice of Contemporary Insurgencies', *Army Quarterly*, January 1966.
68   Acting High Commissioner to Colonial Secretary, 24 June 1964, DEFE 13/570, NA. Also C-in-C, MEC to MOD, 11 August 1964, DEFE 13/570, NA.
69   Report on Radfan Operations, HQMEC, 29 September 1964, DEFE 25/190, NA.
70   C-in-C Mideast to MOD, 22 June 1964, DEFE 13/570, NA.

CHAPTER VI
*'Semper Occultus'**

In the days following the SAS action, rumours circulated in Aden about the fate of the bodies of Captain Robin Edwards and Sapper Nick Warburton that had to be left behind on the slopes of Bakri Ridge. Middle East Command received details, via impeccable American intelligence sources, that two European heads had been displayed on stakes in the central square of Qataba, the NLF stronghold, just over the border in Yemen. A cross-border camel train had confirmed this sighting, and a border post manned by the Federal National Guard claimed to have seen rebel tribesmen crossing into Yemen with two European heads.[1] News was spreading fast among the British, especially as there were sixty-eight journalists with access to the military base at Thumier. In Yemen, Radio Taiz reported the incident and to pre-empt further press speculation and to ensure that MEC, rather than Radio Cairo, gave the account of events, the GOC MELF called a press conference in Aden. On the evening of Sunday 3 May 1964 Major-General John Cubbon addressed a packed meeting of journalists. The room fell silent as he started;

> We had an officer and a trooper of the Special Air Service Regiment killed last Thursday and since then we have had reliable information of decapitation and of the exhibition of their heads on sticks in Taiz. If this is true, I would open this conference at once by expressing, on behalf of all three services in Arabia, our deepest and heartfelt sympathy to all their relatives at home, and to the regiments who have lost them.[2]

The GOC's report should have referred to Qataba rather than Taiz. However, regarding the intelligence reports, Major-General Cubbon was careful to stress the words 'if this is true', but unfortunately he was unaware that the families of the SAS men had not been notified.[3] Quite why the families had not been told that the men were out of the country even mystified the CO, 22 SAS Squadron, who later confided, 'it is no use

* 'Always Secret' – the motto of the Secret Intelligence Service.

117

telling wives that a squadron is on training if it is on operations. We never did this previously'.[4]

The press conference continued with the GOC giving an account of the recent Radfan operations. Yemeni Army uniforms, which were found during the initial fighting in the Radfan, were also displayed, together with captured Russian weapons. But it was the story surrounding the decapitations which unfortunately attracted most press interest. Details of the SAS action were duly given out by Lieutenant-Colonel Cooper, who mentioned the names of some of the patrol members as well as details about the wounded but stopped short of disclosing sensitive operational information. The story was gaining momentum, fuelled by denials from the American Embassy in Taiz that any heads were displayed there. This was strictly true, as the incident had taken place in Qataba, but American attempts to distance themselves from the drama hardly helped Middle East Command. Major-General Cubbon was forced to defend himself, retorting 'I can only add the initial report received by me came from the usually reliable sources'.[5]

To further muddy the waters, Ahmed Almarwani, the Yemen Minister of Information, denied that any decapitations had taken place. 'Britain', he said, 'was still living in the era of the Imam, when heads were chopped off and exhibited in public.'[6] In the British Parliament, the Labour Party took its cue from such sentiments and Denis Healey, the Labour Defence spokesman, together with George Wigg lambasted Major-General Cubbon and MEC for disclosing information based on 'scanty evidence'.[7] Much to the concern of MEC, physical confirmation of the atrocity was hard to come by. Several days later, on 5 May, 3 PARA and 45 Commando took control of Shab Tem and the area where the SAS engagement took place but no trace was found of the bodies of either Captain Edwards or Sapper Warburton.

Then, on Wednesday 13 May two headless bodies were found by an FRA patrol. The bodies were in British denims and from the personal belongings found on them, they were identified as the SAS men and their families were informed.[8] However, the final piece of evidence was understandably not made public. For in early June tribesmen retrieved the heads from a confidential source inside Yemen and although identification was not possible, it was established beyond doubt that they belonged to the SAS men.[9] Denis Healey 'expressed regret' for attacking the GOC for 'disclosure without evidence' and Major-General Cubbon was vindicated. But the whole affair had caused a rift between the media, the Labour party and the military, and had brought into sharp focus the difficulty of using intelligence without compromising sources.[10] The immediacy of the problem was accepted by Middle East Command and the C-in-C privately admitted that 'our public relations has at times given cause for alarm and concern'.[11] The Ministry of Defence were also voicing concern:

> There was an embarrassingly obvious lack of liaison and under-
> standing between the military and the High Commission during the
> early stages of the Radfan operation. Practical difficulties can account
> for a good deal of this but it really looked from London as if the High
> Commissioner [Sir Kennedy Trevaskis] and the Commander-in-Chief
> [MEC, Lieutenant-General Sir Charles Harington] were not in
> touch.[12]

It was becoming clear that the public relations battle was proving every bit
as difficult as the military campaign. The UN, Communist Bloc and Third
World opinion were all lining up behind the nationalists and Britain was
being cast as a colonial oppressor. Furthermore, both the Federation and
MEC had been caught off guard in 1964 by the huge influx of journalists
and reporters arriving in Aden and Radfan, and appeared to have neither
the manpower nor the expert guidance to handle their press enquiries.[13]
Yet there was an established department, operating within the British
High Commission, which was designed to deal with this very problem.
However, as Sir Henry Hardman of the Ministry of Defence (MOD)
conceded, public relations in South Arabia were still in their infancy:

> Apparently Trevaskis believes little is to be gained by cultivating
> journalists. I am told that Ashworth, his PRO, does good work. But
> this cannot be a substitute for a properly conceived press policy,
> implemented with active and public support at the highest level . . .
> During Radfan the press felt they were given inadequate assistance
> by the High Commission, so they got details elsewhere in Aden. They
> also badger the C-in-C and MEC who cannot comment on the
> political situation. Can we strengthen the PR staff?[14]

It was a request that was not pursued due to Treasury strictures. For
despite the concern over PR problems, they were only 'high priority' and
there was a need to 'sacrifice things of high priority in favour of things of
emergency – absolute priority'.[15] There was, after all, an existing
department, which was considered adequate for the purposes.

An Information Department in Aden had been producing 'white
propaganda' since the 1920s. In 1939 the celebrated traveller, Freya Stark,
took part in preparing open-air broadcasts to the crowds thronging
Crater, and during the Second World War the department's output was
increased to counter the Italian threat. However, after the war the section
almost ceased to exist and was only saved by the creation of a new secret
government information department in London. The Information
Research Department (IRD) was formed in 1948, as a secret anti-
Communist propaganda section of the Foreign Office (FO), though the
Russians knew of its existence through the defection of Guy Burgess.

Many of its staff, especially those who worked for its 'action desk', were ex-SOE, ex-SIS officers or journalists with intelligence links. These ties with SIS became closer during the 1950s with the appointment of John Rennie, a Foreign Office man who went on to become head of SIS.[16] The department faced some serious challenges, notably from the Malayan Emergency and the Suez Crisis, but reached the early 1960s with a formidable staff of over 400 operatives worldwide.[17] In 1962 IRD operated from offices in Millbank, London, and was headed by Christopher 'Kit' Barclay, an Eton and Oxford educated diplomat with extensive knowledge of the Middle East.[18]

As IRD expanded, it breathed new life into the information services in many of the colonies and in 1954 the Aden Information Office was resurrected together with its broadcasting facility, the Aden Broadcasting Station (ABS).[19] It was unfortunate timing for just as its competitor, Radio Cairo, came of age in the early 1950s, cheap transistor radios became available to both the poor tribesmen and urban dwellers of South Arabia. Radio Cairo (now renamed 'Voice of the Arabs') exhorted Arabs everywhere, to throw off 'the colonial yolk', and encouraged Arab FRA soldiers to desert.[20] It was an easy message for them to digest, for Nasser's message touched Arab emotions and expressed exactly what they felt but were often too inarticulate to express. However, those promoting the new Federal case realised that they had a new, difficult and nebulous idea to put across to listeners who were reared in a tribal and clan society that had existed for centuries.[21] The other difficulty facing the broadcast producers was the fine line between pushing HMG's case and denigrating an Arab or Arab government, which usually resulted in Arab listeners closing ranks, even if they opposed the Arabs concerned.[22] As threats to security mounted during 1964 and 1965, it became more difficult to get Arabs to work for the Aden Radio and Television Services. It was not until 1966 that a number of Yemenis, who were disillusioned with the Egyptian domination of the north, eventually offered their services as broadcasters.[23] But from the start, ABS was hindered by a lack of financial support. As late as 1963, old transmitters were still in use with short broadcasting ranges, which failed to reach Yemen or the remoter parts of the Federation. Consequently, Radio Cairo and Radio Sana'a remained technically superior to ABS until the mid-1960s.[24]

Another layer was soon added to the information armoury with the creation of an Aden Public Relations Department. This was staffed entirely by Arabs, and after federation in 1959, the section came under the jurisdiction of an Arab Minister. While this encouraged local Arab input, it also meant that the department became cautious about pushing HMG's interests and wary of offending nationalist opinion. In the light of the 1962 merger between Aden and the Federation, this was a weakness that had to be rectified and a British Information Advisor was sought, who together with a senior British Technical Officer, would have access to highly confidential material and could ensure a steady flow of well-sourced circulars and radio broadcasts.[25] However, the usual wrangling over which Government Department should pay for the new Information Advisor seriously delayed his appointment. There were also concerns that the information sector might suffer, as intelligence had, over the duplication of efforts by too many agencies. The Treasury became alarmed that the new Advisor would overlap with the Aden Public Relations Department and they were also worried about 'the odd arrangement of the Governor's Office putting out British propaganda'.[26] Nevertheless, in late 1962 Major Ben Leckie was appointed as the first Advisor.[27] The post was subsequently covered by Lawrence Hobson and in late 1963 by another ex-servicemen, 'the able and energetic' Colonel Tony Ashworth.[28]

The importance of news film was also recognised by IRD and the new Information Advisor was to oversee the output of news and documentaries about military activities, for broadcasts to the troops in South Arabia and worldwide. This meant having access to the highest possible contacts at HQ, MEC, while still remaining part of the establishment controlled by the High Commissioner. At HQ, MEC, this liaison was handled by the new appointment of a GSO 1 (Civil Affairs) who took on much of the role of the previous GSO (Psy Ops).[29] There was also the need to stem the import of subversive films. In a policy similar to that used by the British Film Censor in London, a small censorship panel was set up in Aden to cut out 'all subversive propaganda items from film reels' that might be shown in Aden's cinemas. The panel, which liaised with cinema proprietors and Abdul Girgirah, the Federal Minister of National Guidance and Information, were kept busy sifting newsreels from Egypt that sometimes contained details of how to prime bombs and throw grenades.[30] But surprisingly little concern was shown over films that might upset local religious sensibilities, such as the feature film *El Cid*, depicting a conflict between Christians and Muslims, which was repeatedly shown at the Regal Cinema in Aden.

However, written propaganda was also a useful weapon employed by both sides in South Arabia. In addition to radio broadcasts, the NLF and ATUC used a number of journals and circulars to influence literate Arab opinion, together with constant lobbying within the United Nations and among Third World organisations. For their part, IRD would circulate friendly journalists with material derived from intelligence sources. The journalists would then write their copy for their newspapers without attributing their source and IRD could then quote the journalists' articles for onward transmission. An early example was the Arab News Agency (ANA), an SIS front organisation that became a useful conduit for anti-Nasser activities, before, during and after the Suez Crisis. It was funded by the British Government, and was one of the most reputable Middle

East news agencies, putting out and disseminating stories relevant to the British position in the region. For a time it was run by Tom Little, a highly respected journalist and London correspondent of *al-Ahram*, whose contacts extended as far as direct access to Nasser.[31]

As the propaganda war heated up, IRD 'beefed up' the Office of the Information Advisor in Aden by recruiting several assistants who were fluent in Arabic. One was Derek Rose, who arrived in South Arabia in April 1965. His background was sound and eminently suitable for a Foreign Office career. After five years at Downside School, he spent a year at the Middle East Centre for Arabic Studies (MECAS), in Beirut, as a prelude to joining his family commodities business in the Middle East. But contact with scholars like David Jackson made Rose interested in pursuing a career in the Foreign Office. After studying alongside business graduates and SIS officers such as George Blake[32], Rose went up to Pembroke College, Cambridge. He achieved a First in Arabic before the FO sent him on the Advanced Course at MECAS, followed by a posting to Aden.[33] He was a personable and likeable man with a ready wit and he achieved an instant rapport with the 'local nationals', be they Arab, Somali or Indian, which earned him much respect. He was an obvious candidate for public relations and shortly after arriving in Aden, was seconded from the FO to IRD, ostensibly to work under Tony Ashworth at the High Commission.[34] Individuals were moved or lent to other departments as the FO privately conceded:

> Mr Ashworth is of course lent through the Colonial Office to the High Commissioner by the FO; the main purpose of this arrangement was that Mr Ashworth should work mainly on IRD-type work while at the same time, for cover purposes, playing a more normal role as Information Advisor.[35]

IRD also had an important role to play in winning 'hearts and minds'. In his capacity as Assistant Information Advisor to the High Commissioner, Derek Rose wrote articles promoting the success of British sponsored agricultural schemes. In an attempt to make the Federation more self-supporting, such schemes were created to increase the pitifully small areas under cultivation. Rose calculated that over £2,500,000 was spent on subsidies and the provision of education, health and irrigation projects to the federal states. While this was dwarfed by the £8,200,000 spent on military aid, by 1964/5 there were signs that projects like the Abyan Cotton Scheme could provide decent returns for local farmers.[36]

But although IRD's manpower allowed for local successes in the propaganda war, it could hardly handle the massive influx of pressmen and journalists who arrived during the Radfan campaign. Trevaskis blamed his 'military colleagues' for encouraging this scale of press interest, but if this was the case, the FO singularly failed to provide IRD with sufficient resources to deal with public relations disasters like the 'decapitation incident'.[37]

During the 1960s worldwide press comment was moving in favour of nationalist movements and against colonial powers. Elements in British society were starting to question the established order, and sections of government that had always enjoyed secrecy were coming under the spotlight. The work carried out by SIS and MI5 had received unwanted exposure as a result of recent espionage scandals and these agencies, like all British institutions, had become targets of the new satire boom. *That Was The Week That Was* was broadcast regularly on Aden TV and the record, *Fool Britannia,* which had been banned in Britain, received regular plays on the new 'radiograms' in air-conditioned rooms throughout Aden.[38] The record, which was a daring departure from traditional comedy, featured Peter Sellers and Anthony Newley lampooning the recent Macmillan and Douglas-Home governments, as well as 'The Secret Service'. The Profumo Affair revealed to the public for the first time that SIS were responsible to the Foreign Office, and MI5 to the Home Secretary.[39] In the world of entertainment, the release of the James Bond films fed the public's appetite for the stories about espionage. Stephen Day, who as a young political officer, had some contact with the intelligence agencies in Aden, recalled an evening at the Bureika Cinema in April 1964:

> The cinema was showing the James Bond film, *Dr No.* As the spy film finished, the lights went up and heads started turning around. I saw what must have been about 15 familiar faces from the various intelligence agencies. Goodness knows what they thought of it all. It was quite surreal.[40]

The heart of the intelligence community in South Arabia was the Aden Intelligence Centre (AIC). Originally housed in Crater, it moved in 1965 to a more secure base at Steamer Point, near to HQ Middle East Command and Government House. It was also close to the Interrogation Centre inside Fort Morbut. The AIC had about thirty intelligence officers and clerks, who worked for the myriad of agencies that operated in Aden and the Federation. There were representatives from Police Special Branch, Military Intelligence, Information Research Department, Local Government Intelligence, High Commission, Secret Intelligence Service (MI6), and the Security Service (MI5). The compliment included a Somali 'listener' and an Arab-speaking Israeli, but apart from the IRD officers and an additional translator, few of the Britons could speak fluent Arabic.[41]

As it had always been a Crown Colony, Aden continued to support a representative from the Security Service (MI5). He had a small secretarial staff but there were also a number of other officers within the Civil Administration who reported to MI5, and as the terrorist actions increased through 1965, more recruits to MI5 were taken on. The recruitment process in London featured a bizarre interview, as one officer discovered:

I had been involved in some security work and a colleague suggested I might like to apply for a job he had recently vacated. I was invited to attend an interview in offices in Curzon Street, London. Having arrived, I was ushered up to a second-floor room and found myself before a panel of three smartly dressed interviewers. As I sat down, I noticed that there was also a man behind my left shoulder and one behind my right. The chairman of the panel asked me softly, 'do you know where you are?' I told him I did, and he then asked me, 'have you ever had communist sympathies?' I replied 'no', and then there were further questions that came from behind me. I had to crick my neck to answer them, but perhaps they wanted to see how I reacted. They also asked me, 'are you a homosexual?' and after a negative reply, they tried, 'or are you promiscuous?' I replied that I wasn't, but even if I had been, would I have told them? The questions seemed so unsubtle, but I must have satisfied them, for in due course I was recruited and sent out to Aden.[42]

The MI5 representative in Aden, otherwise known as the 'Security Liaison Officer', was Sandy Stuart, a personable and experienced intelligence officer who had previously served in Ankara, Turkey. As with many other intelligence officers, Stuart was accompanied in Aden by his wife, Judy. But he was not the archetypal MI5 officer who had glided into the service through the 'I knew your father' system of vetting. He was an officer who had risen through the ranks.[43] Part of his brief was the security of the High Commissioner and his staff, and together with the SIS representative, he maintained an office in Government House, sending his daily reports back to London in diplomatic bags.[44] But he worked for a Service that had recently suffered morale problems and self-doubts over the espionage scandals and resulting mole-hunts. This unsettled period was far from over, for just as the Radfan operation was getting under way, in London, Sir Anthony Blunt confessed to spying for the Russians. Even the Director-General, Sir Roger Hollis, was subjected to scrutiny and during the 1960s, the agency spent much time and energy in assessing the extent of damage caused by Soviet infiltration.[45]

For much of the time, intelligence work involves tedious surveillance operations, painstaking analysis, and a determination to continue operations even in the face of disappointments. Aden was no different. Officers were divided into two categories, with 'mobiles' following targets around the back streets of Crater and 'statics' who sat in apartments, offices or cars and watched suspects who might be meeting conspirators or moving weapons. Occasionally, even a simple job could have terrifying moments, as one officer revealed:

> There were certain parts of Ma'alla that later became 'no-go' areas, but they still had to be watched. One night, I drove with a colleague in one of the sequestrated terrorist cars from the pound, to keep an eye on activities. We drove into a school yard, parked to one side and waited. It was a fairly nerve-racking business and when activity started, it could become quite tense. It was a full moon that night and in Arabia, full moons are much larger and lighter than in Britain, and shadows are more dramatic. Suddenly, I was conscious of a large shadow coming across my side window. It moved back and then forward as if stooping. I knew that I was 'a sitting duck' and however quick I turned to fire, he could shoot first. I was done for.
>
> Then, to my huge relief, the shadow showed two large ears – it was a donkey that had quietly come up to the car to scratch himself.[46]

With the incorporation of Aden State into the Federation, the area could also be claimed as operational territory for SIS and there was inevitably some overlap between the two agencies. But SIS was well established in the area, having expanded its operations in support of the British mercenaries in the civil war in Yemen as well as gathering intelligence within the Federation.[47] SIS was normally split between the 'Requirements' section, which assessed the demand for particular types of information, and the operational arm or 'Production' (P) section, which acquired the information. In Aden, P17 was controlled by a Head of Station who operated under the Controller, Middle East. Normally for cover, the Head would be accredited to the High Commission, as a First or Second Secretary, and his office would just consist of several assistants and secretaries.[48] Heads were rotated every two or three years and since O'Bryan Tear's departure in 1963, the Aden Station had been run by John Da Silva, a Trinity man and ex-Major in the Intelligence Corps, previously in charge of successful operations in Oman.[49] Below the Head, there were a number of 'Case Officers' or 'handlers', but confusingly within SIS, the rank of the officer did not correspond to the importance of the operation he was running, and neither did it relate to the rank of the cover he was given. However, the title 'Advisor' in most colonial situations usually implied a degree of intelligence involvement.[50]

The success of intelligence gathering could hinge on the ability of the SIS 'Case Officer' to assess the reliability of information passed on by his agents. These agents were invariably Adeni locals or Yemeni immigrants, with whom the SIS officer would attempt to build a personal bond, which could take considerable time. Once a relationship was successfully established between the officer and his agent, a money inducement usually produced information. This was always of more value if backed up with written evidence, and with this straightforward cash payment, the officer or 'handler' could at least determine his agent's motive, and thereby the reliability of the information. But if fear was ever introduced into the relationship, it could destroy any 'trust' established between agent and handler, and ironically in this devious world, it was trust that bound the agent to his handler.

The selling of information had always been a recognised trade in South Arabia and the large number of intelligence agencies certainly boosted the trade. This worked to the detriment of the security forces when an informant might sell the same piece of information to several agencies at the same time. This gave the information multiple confirmation and a credence it may not have warranted.[51]

The scarcity of Arabists within SIS in the Middle East was a serious problem. The spread of this speciality was indeed thin, with John Christie, Head of Station in Jeddah, being one of the few who could speak the language fluently. In Aden, translators could be called in for interrogation or interpretation of captured documents, but communication with Arab middlemen or tribesmen from the hinterland was difficult. This affected 'deception operations', which were delicate manoeuvres designed to plant false information with known contacts of the NLF or the Egyptian Intelligence Services.[52]

It was not only local Arabs who could act as agents. British businessmen operating through the large financial network surrounding Aden Port would often approach SIS. This use of 'cut-outs' or middlemen was not unusual, for Dick White, then Chief of SIS, remarked on the large number of businessmen who approached his organisation, wanting to 'do a little espionage on the side'. His French colleague remarked that this highlighted the difference between the British and French, for when 'a French businessman goes abroad, it's not a bit of spying he wants on the side'.[53]

GCHQ also played a valuable role in intelligence assessments, especially as communications intercepts were generally considered more reliable than agents' reports.[54] The work was carried out in Aden by operators from the 'Overseas Staff' (C), a secret division within the 'Directorate of Organisation and Establishment'. They were assigned to clandestine listening posts within the High Commission and Aden Intelligence Centre, and were given cover titles, such as the 'Diplomatic Wireless Service'. Much of their work consisted of jamming radio broadcasts from Cairo and Sana'a but this had its limitations, for once the output was jammed, it could no longer be monitored. Other operations consisted of copying and analysing Egyptian cipher traffic between Taiz, Sana'a and Cairo and interpreting the special tap of Arab operators, known as 'Baghdad Morse'. Sometimes American intelligence benefited from the strategic position of the British listening post in Aden. After the Ethiopian Emperor, Haile Selassie, formally annexed Eritrea in 1962, the American National Security Agency (NSA) became concerned about the future intentions of their ally. As they were prohibited under agency rules from eavesdropping on a friendly host country, they requested help from GCHQ. Under a reciprocal agreement forged in 1947, GCHQ monitored Ethiopian military 'traffic' and analysed the ciphers for onward transmission to the CIA. It is highly probable that under this agreement, details of Yemeni wireless traffic, routinely monitored by NSA, were passed on to GCHQ.[55]

However, one of the main British intelligence sources for the war in Yemen remained the small band of military advisors organised by Colonel David Smiley. Both he and Major Johnny Cooper paid a number of visits to Yemen during 1964, monitoring the progress of a civil war that had inflicted large casualties on the Egyptian Army. Estimates of Egyptian and YAR losses vary considerably according to sources, but after eighteen months of war the Egyptians admitted to losing 456 officers and 1,028 NCOs, as well as thousands of other ranks. If a median is taken of 10,000 killed, and the wounded estimated at four times the death rate, then a total of 50,000 Egyptian/YAR casualties were probably suffered. No estimates are available for the royalist losses but they were undoubtedly considerably less.[56]

The impact of such losses on the Egyptian Army was significant and part of the credit for the royalist advances in late 1964 and early 1965 was attributed to the mercenary training teams. Consequently, Major Cooper found that on his return to Britain for de-briefings, the press were waiting for him. Investigative journalists had pursued stories of clandestine British involvement in the Yemen War after Egyptian Intelligence placed articles about Cooper in the Arabic newspaper, al-Ahram. Letters to Cooper from other Yemeni royalist supporters were subsequently published in The Times and he was constantly hounded by the press, only finding relief by returning to Yemen.[57] From there, he kept in contact with John Da Silva and SIS, as well as senior political officers, Ralph Daly and Bill Heber Percy.[58] But other officials in the High Commission were strangely uninterested in hearing about developments in Yemen, even when they came from reliable sources. John Malcolm, a Shell Executive, made a number of visits to republican Yemen including one in 1964 when he met the Prime Minister, General Hasan al-Amri:

> Al-Amri arrived by car with sirens and outriders and strode up the
> steps – a little shrimp-like fellow. We sat down at the table, and after
> the usual courtesies, he pressed me hard on what message I had
> brought from the British Government in Aden. Naturally enough, I

127

played a straight bat and resisted the urge to give my private opinions. The truth was of course that I had absolutely no instructions from the Aden Government. When I returned to Aden, I reported this meeting to the authorities, who predictably took not the slightest interest (as they hadn't on a previous report, which I made to them in late 1962) – this, despite the fact that to my knowledge I was the only person holding a British passport who visited most parts of republican-held Yemen, on at least six occasions over a two year period (1963–5).[59]

Sir Alec Douglas-Home, in the final months of his premiership, had felt the Gulf region might well succumb to the 'domino effect' – the fear that one ally after another would fall to revolutionary forces. America was beginning to identify this threat to her allies in south-east Asia, but it was now a real fear for Britain that Yemen would fall, to be followed by Saudi Arabia and then the Federation and military base of Aden. Consequently British covert support for the royalists was as vigorous as ever. In fact, the Government's monetary contribution was thought to be escalating. Anthony Verrier, Defence Correspondent for *The Observer* and *New Statesman*, carried out a detailed audit of payments made under the Colonial Development and Welfare Acts, via the South Arabian Federation Treasury. Deducting sums paid to the South Arabian armed forces, he estimated that £30 million was unaccounted for.[60] A quantity of arms for the royalists in Yemen was certainly sanctioned by the Prime Minister, with 'RAB' Butler confirming that 'the supply of a small quantity of bazookas and ammunition to the Sharif of Beihan for onward transmission to a dissident group in Taiz, was authorised'.[61] However, the Sharif's shopping list asked for much larger quantities of arms, with a request including '11,000 rifles and ammunition, 20 mortars with bombs, 20 heavy machine-guns, 20 bazookas, 500 anti-tank mines, together with artillery ammunition'. This was enough to carry out a royalist offensive against the Egyptian-held town of Harib, but whether this constituted 'a small quantity' is open to conjecture. However, the Sharif was certainly putting pressure on the British Government, reminding them that he might have to make a premature peace with the YAR if he wasn't supported in his attempts to reclaim contested border villages near his State of Beihan.[62]

In fact, the Sharif's proposals went further. Following his prolonged talks with both Prince Feisal of Saudi Arabia as well as royalist commanders, plans were proposed for covert British aid of £2 million to the royalists. This amounted to a serious escalation of 'Operation Rancour', the existing British attempt to 'exploit dissident tribes up to 20 miles into Yemen, in order to neutralize Egyptian subversive action against Aden'.[63] Through British 'advisors', the royalists also requested that the arms be dropped by RAF aircraft into hard-pressed royalist positions, north-east of Sana'a, as it would take too long to transport weapons overland from Saudi Arabia. The problem facing British Ministers was still one of denial:

> The objective is, that without closing the door to a possible deal with Nasser, to make life intolerable for him, with money and (? arms) – to deny as far as possible, but if activity becomes undeniable, it is no more than we are already accused of.[64]

Nonetheless, if this could be overcome, the 'advisors' recommended a combination of an RAF weapons drop into Beihan, within the Federation, and supplies parachuted into Yemen from unmarked aircraft, chartered in Africa.[65] The progress of covert action was detailed in a memorandum for British Government Ministers:

> Action is already being undertaken at Baidha [Yemen], with some success. A preliminary attempt to organise it at Qataba has not been successful but a further attempt is being made. Action of this kind is carried out under the control of British officers within the Federation who can hand out arms and money in instalments according to the local situation. British responsibility for these actions is thus likely to become known but can be explained on grounds of self-defence against Egyptian and Yemeni subversion.[66]

Despite the resources allocated to tying down the Egyptians in Yemen or fighting the dissident tribes in Radfan, success or failure in the intelligence war in South Arabia ultimately depended on the willingness of local Arabs to assist the security forces. While this had not happened in Palestine, where both Jews and Arabs were ready to attack the British, the recent Malayan Campaign had been a success.[67] However, much to the despair of serving intelligence officers, the operational lessons learned in Malaya were never applied in South Arabia and when changes were implemented, it was often too late.[68] This was particularly true concerning the spawning of intelligence agencies in Aden. Sir Robert Thompson, who had been Director of Security Operations in Malaya, warned:

> There should be one single organisation responsible for all security intelligence within the country. If there is more than one, it is almost impossible to define the respective responsibilities of each organisation or to devise any means of co-ordinating their activities. All sorts of things will start to go wrong. For example, agents, especially the less reliable, will get themselves onto the payroll of several organisations and feed them the same unreliable information.

Such information seemingly confirmed from different sources will be accepted as authentic. The different organisations will withhold information from one another in order to exploit it and obtain credit for themselves . . . Mutual suspicion and jealousies will arise, quite likely with the result that the separate organisations merely end up by spying on each other.[69]

While an attempt was made to pull the strands of intelligence together by the appointment of Brigadier Tony Cowper as Director of Intelligence, this did not take place until 1965. By this time, the NLF had made serious headway in South Arabia.

Although there was hope in Middle East Command that the 1964 Radfan campaign had thwarted the rebel threat, the reality was different. The High Commission in Aden was alarmed at the resurgence of terrorist activity in the hinterland and fired off frequent telegrams to Duncan Sandys:

The Egyptian effort put into the training and equipping of the rebels is paying handsome dividends to our enemies and we are faced with better organised and more daring attacks than we have experienced in the past. In the matter of fire-power the Federal Guard finds itself inferior to the rebels who now dispose of heavy machine-guns, in addition to bazookas, automatic rifles, mines and grenades. The determination with which attacks are carried out and the advent of daylight ambushes are indications of a bleak future . . . Of all the areas Dhala gives the greatest cause for concern. The situation there is thoroughly unhealthy. Out of the 98 incidents in the past fortnight, 47 have occurred in Dhala. The Assistant Advisor has had to be temporarily withdrawn after a near-mutiny by the Federal Guard.[70]

It was fortunate timing, as during the night of 25 September about thirty dissidents fired on the Assistant Advisor's compound, using LMGs and a rocket launcher.[71] It was one of many NLF assaults between June and September 1964, as the terrorist movement expanded its armed operations. It also carried out constant sniping and mining attacks against companies of 1st Battalion King's Own Scottish Borderers and 1 Royal Scots operating in Wadi Taym, Danaba Basin and Wadi Rabwa.[72] There were further attacks beyond the Radfan and Amirate of Dhala, which extended into the border Sheikhdom of Sha'ib, resulting in a weekly toll of damaged or destroyed Landrovers, Ferret Armoured Cars or 3-Ton trucks, together with the inevitable army casualties. While it would take another year for the NLF to establish fronts in the federal states of Lower Yafa, Lahej, Dathina and Audhali, Egyptian Intelligence officers were already established and training NLF cadres in the town of Baidha in

Yemen. With the plan for the hinterland under way, in August 1964 the NLF transferred its violent campaign to Aden town.[73] Abdul Ismail, a founder member of the NLF, recalled the move:

> After the struggle began in Radfan, we started to think about extending armed struggle to Aden, especially since the struggle in the countryside did not absorb all our resources, given the favourable geographical conditions existing in the mountain areas of Dhala, Mukeiras, Yafa and the like. We reckoned that if guerrilla activity could be developed in Aden itself, this would alter the balance of forces in favour of the revolution; the British were not too concerned about the struggle in the countryside and were willing to endure it for years. But they did not want it spread to Aden itself.[74]

The opening of the NLF campaign in Aden coincided with the splintering of the PSP, whose leader, the trade unionist al-Asnag, was still in prison. There seemed to be little enthusiasm among the Adenis for cash contributions to the trade union coffers, for rumours of embezzlement were rife and the apparent affluence of many union leaders rankled with the ordinary members. Besides, in the absence of al-Asnag, there were plenty of young radicals from Aden College coming forward to challenge his grip on the ATUC.[75]

Student radicals were just one of the groups whom the NLF nurtured. Abdul Ismail continues:

> We consolidated our support within the ranks of the Yemeni working class. In the same way, we gained support within the student, women and sports organisations. We were able to remove the opportunist leaders and new ones supporting the revolution, took over. These organisations played an important part in the struggle: for example, women used to distribute pamphlets, relay correspondence and internal directives, and in the country, they transported arms and provided guerrillas with food. The students carried out numerous strikes and resisted the educational policies of the colonialists.[76]

While the NLF spread its subversion like a cobweb over the institutions of South Arabia, HMG was making efforts to bolster the Federal Government. Duncan Sandys reconvened the constitutional conference for June 1964, after it was postponed because of the plot to kill Trevaskis. Despite heated opposition from al-Asnag and his PSP[77], the conference went ahead and its deliberations were quite clear:

> The delegates requested that as soon as practicable the British Government should convene a conference for the purposes of fixing

a date for independence not later than 1968, and of concluding a Defence Agreement under which Britain would retain her military base in Aden for the defence of the Federation and the fulfilment of her world-wide responsibilities. The Secretary of State announced the agreement of the British Government to this request.[78]

This deal was the best the Douglas-Home Government was prepared to offer and the Federal rulers had little option but to accede to it. But while it allowed a few years for the Federation to establish its independent credentials, it also confirmed a date for the final British withdrawal, and allowed the NLF to work to a timetable. The future of the Federation looked uncertain and should the terrorists topple it, any local Arabs connected with it, or with the British administration, would have to answer to the terrorists.

Three months after the constitutional conference, the opponents of the Federation received another boost. In October 1964 Harold Wilson and the Labour Party won the British general election. While this new Labour Government were prepared to support the Federation of Malaysia in its fight with Sukarno, they were not so well disposed towards the rulers of the Federation of South Arabia. One of the first acts of the new Labour Government was to remove the man most closely associated with the Federation – the High Commissioner, Sir Kennedy Trevaskis. As the instigator of the Federation, he had believed passionately in maintaining the ties between the hinterland and Aden in order to eventually achieve full sovereignty for South Arabia and his removal meant that this policy lost momentum. His departure also facilitated attempts by the Government to bring old Trade Unionist opponents, like al-Asnag, into the mainstream in the belief that the Adeni nationalists and the Labour Party shared a common objective. To reflect this change in direction, the Labour Government appointed Sir Richard Turnbull as the new High Commissioner. Turnbull, who had won the accolade 'Hammer of the Mau Mau' for his political role in their suppression in Kenya, had just retired as High Commissioner in Tanganyika. In the recently independent African country, he was successful in establishing good relations with the nationalist leader Nyerere and thereby ensured a peaceful transition of power. The government hoped that with suitable sympathies for nationalist aspirations, Turnbull could achieve the same result in South Arabia.[79] Despite the shift of direction, the new Secretary of State for the Colonies, Anthony Greenwood, confirmed the Labour Government's commitment to granting independence to the Federation in 1968, and to maintaining the military base together with the Defence Treaty.[80]

October 1964 also saw a change in the command of land forces in South Arabia, when 39 Brigade HQ returned to the UK and its units were taken over by 24 Brigade HQ, which was gradually transferring from Kenya to

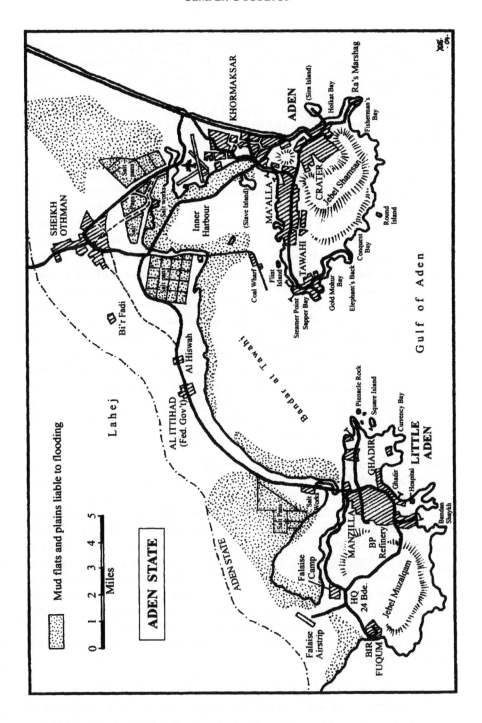

its new base in Little Aden. 24 Brigade now assumed responsibility for 'up-country' security as well as Little Aden and the Federal Government complex at Al Ittihad. Meanwhile, Aden Garrison, which was re-styled as Aden Brigade and was still under the command of Brigadier Louis Hargroves, was about to be confronted with a violent NLF terrorist campaign in Aden town.[81] Corporal Collings, who carried out RAF personnel vetting, at RAF HQ in Steamer Point, recalled the upsurge in violence:

> I lived with my wife Mary and our daughter, in an apartment in Ma'alla Straight and we used to meet up socially with other RAF and Army colleagues on our rooftop balcony. One evening in November, and thinking back this was odd, our *Chowkidar* [apartment house-boy and janitor] was missing and so it turned out were all the other houseboys in the Straight. Anyway, we'd just put our children to bed in the one air-conditioned room in the apartment and there was a terrific explosion and the whole building shook. They'd attacked the 'Oasis Bar', two doors down, with either a bomb or rocket and there was devastation everywhere. It was popular with military personnel – it was before the time that you were banned from certain places – and there were several killed and many wounded. If it was a grenade, it would have been thrown from one of the alleys opposite. Because of the strong light in Aden, passages between the houses were almost black and anyone could hide and then make off. From then on, whenever our *Chowkidar* went missing, we knew the locals had been warned, and sure enough there was an incident.[82]

Much of the ensuing violence involving grenade and bazooka attacks was timed to coincide with a number of visits from British politicians. For it was also the start of the official 'cool season', which always heralded a large number of visitors on 'fact finding missions'. Lord Carrington, First Lord of the Admiralty, arrived, followed by the British Defence Minister, and then in November Anthony Greenwood arrived. He appeared in Aden at a moment of surprising unanimity between the Federal rulers and the members of the Aden State Legislature, who appeared to have agreed on the need for a unified, democratic state, with a central elected government. However, the motives of the two power blocs were entirely at odds. A H 'Barney' Dutton, the energetic ex-Colonial Officer and former Aden Financial Secretary, was sceptical about the motives of the sultans as they embraced federalism:

> In Aden State, all parties and shades of political thought recognise that, having gone into the Federation as merely one of a number of States, and being overshadowed by the Protectorate rulers, their only

way of predominant influence is through a system which will remove the sultans and make way for an elected government which they hope to dominate. It follows that their idea of a unified State is one in which rulers will be retired to the wings, political parties will be free to operate in the protectorates [hinterland], and elections will be for party representatives, not area representatives.

The leaders of the Federation are in favour of a unified State because they think it will enable them to consolidate their position and create a more powerful government. They have, however, very different ideas about what is a democratically elected central government. The sultans do not envisage removing themselves to an ineffective 'House of Lords' but to a House of Lords, which will dominate. (The Sharif of Beihan, not being a 'ruler', would of course not mind rulers giving way to *eminences grises* like himself). They do not contemplate elections being for persons on national party lists but rather for local endorsement of the persons whose candidature they themselves approve.[83]

Meanwhile, as some members of the Aden Assembly espoused a political solution, other Adenis were supporting the more violent agenda. To combat this, as 1964 drew to a close, British troops began foot patrols and roadblocks were set up to thwart the movement of terrorists and their weapons. However, enemy spectaculars did not always go according to plan. Ann Cuthbert described one of the December attacks in a letter to home:

One of the terrorists who blew himself to bits in Crater the other day, was a BP employee – he was about to throw his grenade when it went off, and the friend with him had a leg blown off. The pictures of his torso – all that was left – were screened on local TV, presumably to try and frighten the other bomb throwers.

. . . This evening, Derek had to leave home to help search the Refinery for a terrorist. I don't know whether the papers wrote it up, but 3 terrorists tried to blow up the BP radio mast on a mountain-top beyond the Refinery. Three off-duty soldiers saw them and tried to catch them but they escaped and one climbed the Refinery fence and disappeared inside. There is no proof that the Arabs knew it was BP property – they probably assumed it was an Army radio mast.[84]

On Christmas Eve a grenade was thrown into a children's Christmas party at Khormaksar, killing 16-year-old Gillian Sidey, daughter of Air Commodore (later Air Marshal Sir Ernest) Sidey, Principal Medical Officer, MEC. In this strike against the families of High Command, four other children were wounded, including the son of the Commander-in-

Chief. The last two months of 1964 saw thirty-six terrorist incidents, resulting in thirty-nine casualties, but the most dangerous threat that surfaced was the forthcoming NLF campaign to eliminate the Aden Special Branch.

NOTES

1 *Globe and Mail* (Toronto), 4 May 1964, *The Times*, 5 May, 7 May, 8 May 1964. See also Ledger, op. cit., p. 48.
2 Minutes of Press Conference, HQ MIDEAST, 3 May 1964, DEFE 13/569, NA. See also press report, *The Times*, 4 May 1964.
3 Brigadier James Emson to Author, 17 April 2002. Also Brigadier Sir Louis Hargroves to Author, 30 October 2003.
4 Quoted in de la Billière, op. cit., p. 223. The news came as a terrible shock to the parents of Robin Edwards, who were enjoying lunch in the London Inn, Padstow, when they were informed of their son's death. It was assumed he was still in England. Confidential source.
5 Major-General Cubbon to Author, 4 April 1994. Also *The Times*, 6 May 1964. Certain enclosures within file DEFE 13/570, NA, relating to 'the heads' incident will not be released until 2040, an unusually long retention and seventy-five years after the event. These records are retained under the provisions of a document known as 'The Lord Chancellor's Instrument.'
6 Quoted in *The Times*, 5 May 1964.
7 In his autobiography, Denis Healey declined to mention his part in the furore, stating it was just press agitation. See *The Time of My Life*, Penguin, 1990, p. 232. When Wigg entered Wilson's Government, he also changed his perspective on intelligence and security matters.
8 Confidential Memorandum, A Hockaday to Sir Timothy Bligh (PPS to Prime Minister), 14 May 1964, DEFE 13/569, NA.
9 Top Secret telegram, HQ MIDEAST to Ministry of Defence, 18 June 1964, DEFE 13/569, and MOD to C-in-C, MIDEAST, 18 June 1964, DEFE 13/570, both NA. Understandably, the press were told not to follow up reasons for non-identification.
10 Obituary, Major-General Cubbon, *Daily Telegraph*, 3 February 1997. The large and distinguished presence at his funeral was testament to a much-respected Commander.
11 Lieutenant-General Sir Charles Harington to Lord Mountbatten, 11 June 1964, DEFE 13/570, NA.
12 P Noakes to C Roberts, MOD, CO 1027/701, NA.
13 Brigadier G S Heathcote, 'Operations in the Radfan', 24 November 1965 Lecture to RUSI, Hargroves Papers. Also Paget, op. cit., p. 110.
14 Sir Henry Hardman (MOD) to Permanent Under Secretary of State, 10 July 1964, CO 1027/701, NA.
15 Handwritten memo attached to C Roberts memo, 5 October 1964, CO 1027/701, NA.
16 Paul Lashmar & James Oliver, *Britain's Secret Propaganda War 1948–1977*, Sutton, 1998, pp. 67, 140. Also Bloch & Fitzgerald, op. cit., pp. 90–101. In 1966 Nigel Clive, a former SIS officer who was active during the Suez Crisis, took over as Head of IRD.
17 In 1977 Labour Foreign Secretary, David Owen, closed down IRD because of its right-wing contacts who were attacking the Labour Party.

18 Barclay attended MECAS at the end of the Second World War, when it was based in Jerusalem. This was followed by postings as a Political Officer to Iraq, and as Information Officer, to Beirut. It would appear that he was still Head of IRD in 1966. P Batterbury to D Barker, 14 November 1966, File 108, BP Archives, UW.

19 Molly Izzard, *Freya Stark: A Biography*, Hodder & Stoughton, 1993. Also Gavin, op. cit., pp. 333–5. One compensation was the BBC maintaining its Arabic Service.

20 A more recent example of this 'psywar' tactic in the Middle East was the Hizballah Radio campaign during the 1990s, to encourage fellow Muslims to desert from the South Lebanese Army (SLA). See F M Wehrey, 'A Clash of Wills: Hizballah's Psychological Campaign Against Israel in South Lebanon', in *Small Wars & Insurgencies*, Vol. 13, Autumn 2002, No. 3, p. 63.

21 Local Intelligence Committee Report on 'Radio & Press Propaganda', 6 September 1960, CO 1027/392, NA.

22 See Gary Rawnsley, *Radio Diplomacy and Propaganda: The BBC and VOA in International Politics 1956–64*, Macmillan, 1996. Also Tiffany McKinney, 'Radio Jamming: The Disarmament of Radio Propaganda', in *Small Wars & Insurgencies*, Vol. 13, Autumn 2002.

23 Philo Wasburn, *Broadcasting Propaganda: International Radio Broadcasting and the Construction of Political Reality*, Praeger, 1992, pp. 47–9. Also Ledger, op. cit., pp. 155–7.

24 It was unfortunate that the transmitter did not come onto full power until after the Radfan operations, Brigadier Sir Louis Hargroves to author, 30 October 2003. Also 'Broadcasting – The Aden Transmitter', CO 1027/663, NA, and Gillian King, op. cit., p. 59.

25 'The Establishment of British Information Services in Aden', 23 August 1962, CO 1027/521, NA. See also, Charles Johnston to Colonial Office, 18 May 1962, CO 1027/392, NA.

26 By 1963 it was the office of the High Commissioner. See D Smart to Colonial Office, 11 September 1962, CO 1027/392, NA.

27 Major Leckie had served (and was wounded) in the Second World War and subsequently Malaya. He retired from the Army and entered the Foreign Office in 1961. He later became HMG's Ambassador to Sana'a and Djibouti 1977–8, followed by Lebanon and Algeria. For his appointment as Advisor, see Treasury to Colonial Office, 18 October 1962, CO 1027/392, NA.

28 P Noakes to C Roberts, MOD, 16 July 1964, CO 1027/701. See also Ledger, op. cit. p. 155. After Aden, Anthony Ashworth went on to IRD campaigns in Hong Kong and Northern Ireland. Shortly after IRD's closure in 1977, he became Public Relations Advisor to the Sultan of Oman.

29 'Psychological Operations in the Middle East', in Minutes of Chief of Staffs' Meeting, 19 June 1962, CO 1027/392, NA. Also, Johnston to Colonial Office, 18 May 1962, CO 1027/392, NA.

30 Ashworth to Colonial Office, 18 August 1964 and 4 September 1964, CO 1027/696, NA.

31 Tom Little was spared when Nasser launched an assault on ANA and British intelligence operatives in 1956. When the ANA network was dispersed, SIS lost an important weapon in its fight against Nasser. See Richard Aldrich, *The Hidden Hand, Britain, America and Cold War Secret Intelligence*, John Murray 2001, pp. 482–5. Also, see Bloch & Fitzgerald, op. cit., pp. 94–7; Little, op. cit., *South Arabia*, p. 36; Downton, op. cit., p. 341; Nigel West, *The Friends: Britain's Post-War Secret Intelligence Operations*, Weidenfeld & Nicolson, 1988, p. 96; Hugh Walford, 'The Information Research Department: Britain's Secret Cold

War Weapon Revealed', in *Review of International Studies*, Vol. 24, No. 3, 1998.

32 Blake, who was later exposed as a double agent, had important Middle East connections. He lived with his cousin, Henri Curiel, who was a founder member of the Egyptian Communist Party.

33 Bill Rose to Author, 26 February 2002, and David Ledger to Bill Rose, 23 October 1967; Derek Rose Papers.

34 Ibid.

35 P Noakes to C Roberts, MOD, 16 July 1964, CO 1027/701, NA.

36 The annual cotton revenue from this cooperative of landowners and tenant farmers amounted to £1,250,000. See D Rose, 'Agricultural Progress in South Arabia', in *Port of Aden Annual 1965–6*, Aden Port Trust. Also Stephen Day to Author, 25 April 2002.

37 Thomas Mockaitis, *British Counterinsurgency in the Post-Imperial Era*, MUP, 1995, pp. 54–5. Also Trevaskis, op. cit., p. 208.

38 *Fool Britannia* (Ember Records) featured Joan Collins, Leslie Bricusse and Daniel Massey.

39 Phillip Knightley, *The Second Oldest Profession*, Andre Deutsch, 1986, p. 343

40 Stephen Day to Author, 26 March 2002.

41 Confidential source to Author.

42 Confidential source to Author.

43 Memorandum, D J McCarthy, 1 March 1967, FC08/206, NA. Also Foreign Office memorandum, 3 March 1967, FC08/206, NA.

44 For pen-portraits of typical MI5 recruits, see Stella Rimington, *Open Secret*, Hutchinson, 2001, pp. 67, 101.

45 Hollis retired in December 1965 and was succeeded by Sir Martin Furnival Jones.

46 Confidential source to Author, 17 June 2003.

47 For the background to SIS involvement in British colonies, see Philip Murphy, 'Creating a Commonwealth Intelligence Culture', in *Intelligence and National Security*, Vol. 17, Autumn 2002, pp. 143–5.

48 The State of Emergency, declared after the bomb attack at Khormaksar in December 1963, removed the diplomatic cover enjoyed by SIS officers. Confidential source. Also Anthony Cavendish, *Inside Intelligence: The Revelations of an MI6 Officer*, HarperCollins, 1990, pp. 3, 77. An older practice allowed cover for the SIS Head as the Passport Control Officer attached to the British Consulate. If military rank was used as a cover, it invariably meant 'promotion' from any rank the officer previously held.

49 After service in SHAPE, John Da Silva was appointed 1st Secretary in Bahrain, 1960–2 before his secondment to the 'Political Office, Middle East Command', 1963–6. He was appointed Counsellor, Washington, 1966. He died in May 2002.

50 Cavendish, op. cit., p. 78. Also Bower, op. cit., p. 252.

51 'Military Problems of Counter-Insurgency', File 2/5, Dunbar Papers, LHCMA. Also Cavendish, op. cit., p. 4.

52 One of the few English texts dealing with Egyptian Intelligence is Yaacov Caroz, *The Arab Secret Service*, Corgi Books, London, 1978.

53 Quoted in Knightley, op. cit., p. 289. Despite its problems, SIS was still considered by the Russians to be their 'toughest and worthiest opponents'. See Hennessy, op. cit., p. 42.

54 Philip Davies, 'Intelligence Scholarship as All-Source Analysis: The Case of Tom Bower's *The Perfect English Spy*', in *Intelligence and National Security*, Vol. 12, July 1997.

55 James Bamford, *The Puzzle Palace: America's National Security Agency and its*

Special Relationship with Britain's GCHQ, Sidgwick & Jackson, 1983, pp. xvi–xvii. For Yemen, see Nigel West, *GCHQ: The Secret Wireless War 1900–86*, Weidenfeld & Nicolson, 1986, p. 240, and Aldrich, op. cit., p. 542.

56   The high casualty figures are supported by Dana Adams Schmidt, op. cit., p. 234 and also quoted by Dr Ibrahim El-Shourek, in *The Bloody Strife*, AWDU. David Holden, op. cit., p. 110, quotes lower rates for Egyptian casualties of 3,000 killed and 20,000 wounded.

57   For details of Egyptian coverage of the mercenaries, see *al-Ahram*, 1 May 1964. For French coverage, see *Le Monde* 30 January 1967. See also *The Times*, 5 July 1964, and Cooper, op. cit., pp. 178–80.

58   Cooper, op. cit., p. 178. Ralph Daly was ex-Sudan Political Service, then Senior Advisor East and later Permanent Secretary to the Federal Minister of the Interior. Bill Heber Percy was political officer, Beihan, and later a founder President of the British–Yemeni Society.

59   On this one occasion John Malcolm was accompanied by a senior colleague from Shell. As an Arabist, Malcolm conducted the discussion with al-Amri, who was later removed by the Egyptians in 1965, due to the poor performance of the YAR army. John Malcolm to Christopher Gandy, 28 December 1998, John Malcolm Papers.

60   Anthony Verrier, 'British Military Policy on Arabia', in *RUSI Journal*, November 1967.

61   Trevaskis to Colonial Secretary, 19 July 1964, DEFE 13/570, NA.

62   For arms request, see undated, unsourced 'Top Secret' memos, DEFE 13/570, NA. For the Sharif, see Trevaskis to Colonial Secretary, 19 July 1964, DEFE 13/570, NA.

63   Hand-written note on unsourced report, 'Aid to the royalists', 19 July 1964, DEFE 13/570, NA.

64   Unsigned Memorandum to Colonial Secretary, 20 July 1964, DEFE 13/570, NA. The enclosures surrounding this memo were removed from the file in 1995, under Sec. 3 (4).

65   Unsourced Top Secret Report, 'Aid to the royalists', 19 July 1964, hand delivered to various offices including CDS; see DEFE 13/570, NA.

66   'Memorandum for Consideration by Ministers', 22 July 1964, DEFE 13/570, NA.

67   According to some sources, because the issue of independence was conceded at an early point. See West, *The Friends*, op. cit., pp. 41–9.

68   Confidential source, and West, *The Friends*, op. cit., p. 50.

69   Robert Thompson, *Studies in International Security: 10. Defeating Communist Insurgency: Experiences from Malaya to Vietnam*, Chatto & Windus, 1966. From 1961–5, Sir Robert Thompson headed the British Advisory Mission to Vietnam.

70   Acting High Commissioner to Secretary of State for the Colonies, 8 September 1964, DEFE 25/190, NA.

71   'Sitrep' for week ending 28 September 1964, DEFE 25/190, NA.

72   C-in-C Mideast to MOD, 22 June 1964, DEFE 13/570, NA.

73   'Sitrep' for week ending 6 October 1964, DEFE 25/190, NA. Also C-in-C Mideast to MOD, 22 June 1964, DEFE 13/570, NA, and Pridham, op. cit., pp. 66–7.

74   Abdul Ismail was a founder member of the NLF. A radical, he later assumed power as President after 1967. He was ousted in 1980. See Ismail, 'How we liberated Aden', in *Armed Struggle in Arabia*, The Gulf Committee, London, 1976, Yem 3a., AWDU.

75   Ledger, op. cit., p. 53.

76   Ismail, *Armed Struggle*, op. cit.

77   Al-Asnag arrived in London during the conference and proceeded to voice his opposition at a number of meetings. See 'This Conference is a Farce', published by the PSP, June 1964, Yem. 3a. Asn, IAIS. Also *The Guardian*, 17 June 1964.

78   *Federation of South Arabia – Conference Report,* July 1964, HMSO, London. During the course of the conference, the states of Muflahi, Upper Aulaqi and Alawi applied to be admitted to the Federation. Invitations to join were also issued to the remaining states of Upper Yafa, Qa'iti, Kathira and Mahra.

79   Sir Richard Turnbull, 'Obituary', *The Daily Telegraph*, 24 December 1998. For details and anecdotes of Turnbull's career, hear R F Eberlie (Private Secretary), Tape # 926, Oral History Department, Empire & Commonwealth Museum, Bristol.

80   *Aden and South Arabia*, Central Office of Information, Yem. 26/BRI, AWDU. Also Balfour-Paul, op. cit., pp. 5, 82; *Army Quarterly*, July 1968, p. 257; Trevaskis, op. cit., pp. 224–5. The British military base in Aden had a significant impact on the local economy; over 6,500 civilians were employed at a total annual cost in wages of £2.82 million.

81   Brigadier Hargroves handed over command in February 1966 to Brigadier Richard Jefferies. For NLF involvement, see *The Daily Telegraph* and *The Daily Express*, 30 November 1964. Also Brigadier Sir Louis Hargroves to Author, 13 October 2003.

82   Mervyn and Mary Collings to Author, 11 May 2003. Two servicemen were killed and one severely injured in the attack on the 'Oasis' Bar.

83   A H Dutton to Maurice Banks (later Deputy Chairman, BP), 14 December 1964, 60293, BP Archives, UW. Dutton was an administrative officer in Nigeria (1936–9), before serving in Bomber Command (1940–5) and rising to acting Wing Commander. His post-war career in the Colonial Office was followed by thirteen years with BP. He was an acute observer of events in South Arabia and died prematurely in 1974.

84   Ann Cuthbert correspondence, 5 & 16 December 1964.

1. 'British influence in the Middle East'. Staff and students at MECAS. Derek Rose (standing extreme left), George Blake (standing fourth left). *Bill Rose*

2. 45 Commando on patrol in the foothills, Little Aden (near the future site of Silent Valley cemetery, created in 1965). *Imperial War Museum, R.32542*

3. Colonel David Smiley with royalists, notably Prince Hassan (second right), at his mountain HQ near Sada, Yemen, 1963. *Colonel David Smiley*

4. 'Vulnerable to ground fire'. A Wessex from HMS *Albion* unloading supplies. *Imperial War Museum IN81062*

5. 'Picqueting the high ground'.
Observers from 1st Battalion
The Royal Scots spotting enemy
movements in the Radfan.
Imperial War Museum RS64/01/7

6. Hunter rockets strike a target
during Operation 'Cap Badge'.
Robin Cubbon

7. 'An exhilarating experience'. A Sioux helicopter perches on a ridge in the Radfan. *Brigadier David Baines*

8. A Royal Anglian dog handler about to seek out a wounded enemy. *Imperial War Museum TR24800*

9. A soldier from 1st Battalion The Royal Sussex Regiment returns fire during a night attack, 1965. *Imperial War Museum ADN 65/355/103*

10. 'Irregular warfare'. An Army Special Branch Unit operating in Aden State. *Terry Cheek*

11. Captain John Fleming, OC Air Troop, 1st Regiment Royal Horse Artillery, killed 6 December 1966. *Brigadier David Baines*

12. Lieutenant-Colonel David Baines, CO 1st Regiment Royal Horse Artillery, with British and FRA soldiers on Jebel Jihaf, above Dhala. *Brigadier David Baines*

13. 'Bait for the terrorists'. A foot patrol of 1st Battalion The King's Own Yorkshire Light Infantry moves through Tawahi. *Imperial War Museum ADN 65/524/22*

14. Second Lieutenant John Davis, 1st Battalion The Royal Northumberland Fusiliers, killed in Crater, 20 June 1967. *Pamela Davis*

15. In mountain convoys or street riots, the Ferret Scout Car and Saladin Armoured Car proved their worth. *Geoff Richards*

16. Derek Rose (right) on the waterfront in Aden. He was assassinated near this spot on 20 October 1967. *Bill Rose*

17. A Buccaneer of 800 Naval Air Squadron flying over Ma'alla. In the background Main Pass emerges from Crater. *Imperial War Museum A/35119*

CHAPTER VII
Hearts and Minds

On Sunday 27 December 1964 Inspector Fadhli Khalil attended the Aden *Qat* market in Crater. It was a good place for the policeman to meet contacts and pick up local gossip. But on that Sunday, NLF terrorists had received a tip-off about the time that Khalil would be arriving. As he stood chatting in the market, a car using false number-plates drew up alongside. By the time Khalil saw the masked occupants it was too late. He was hit by several bursts from a machine-gun and died instantly. Abdul Ismail, an ex-teacher and NLF leader in Aden who ordered the killing, revealed what happened next:

> After Khalil was machine-gunned to death, the popular response was one of great curiosity so we had to throw a smoke bomb to cover the getaway, and people ran away or fell to the ground believing it was a hand grenade. After that, we assassinated a number of Special Branch officers, and thereby removed the obstacles to our developing guerrilla activity.[1]

Khalil's death marked the start of a brutal assassination campaign by the NLF in an attempt to wipe out the British intelligence network in Aden. The murders were rarely done quietly, for it was an important psychological tactic for 'collaborators of the British' to be shot in public. During the next eighteen months the NLF murdered sixteen Arab Special Branch (SB) officers and incapacitated many more, a tactic that both intimidated the local population and dashed British efforts to collect local intelligence. A typical murder would involve the kidnapping of a local Arab SB officer, torturing him for information and then dumping his bound and gagged body in Sheikh Othman or Crater. The bullet-ridden body would have a note pinned to it announcing, 'executed by the NLF'.[2]

Historically, Special Branch was staffed mainly by local Adeni Officers, with a mix of ex-Colonial policemen – veterans of the Palestine, Malaya and Kenya emergencies. Having eliminated most of the Arab officers, the NLF then targeted Senior British SB officers. On 4 September 1965 Harry Barrie, an ex-Palestine policeman and Deputy Head of Aden Special

Branch, drove to his office at SB Headquarters at 0715 hours. The HQ was then based in the Aden Intelligence Centre in the heart of Crater and there were only two routes in and out, both watched by NLF gunmen. Continuing on his way, Barrie paused at a traffic junction near the office and was shot dead.[3] The next target was Bob Waggitt, the Head of Special Branch. An experienced policeman, he had no doubts about the chain of terrorist command and often commented, 'we are fighting a snake – the head is in Cairo, the body wriggles down through Yemen and the tail is right here in Aden'. He was high on the terrorist 'hit-list' but miraculously survived. On one occasion, an NLF assassin managed to creep inside Waggitt's house at the same time as the Inspector was taking a shower, but luckily the would-be assassin was intercepted by Waggit's burly body-guard.[4]

Such was the effect of the NLF campaign that Sir Richard Turnbull had to plead with Greenwood, the Colonial Secretary, for twelve new Deputy Superintendents to fill the gaps, admitting, 'not only is the internal security function of the Aden Police gravely impaired but normal police work is also suffering'.[5] However competent these replacements were, they were not Arab and very few of them spoke Arabic. The knowledge of local meeting places and nationalist families started to dry up and increasingly the best source of intelligence for the British was to be gained from the interrogation of suspects.[6]

The new police reinforcements came from an already stretched Colonial Special Branch. In the early 1960s there were still twenty-one SB Forces spread over Colonial and ex-Colonial countries, with the Malayan Force taking up the greatest share of resources. In addition there were nine smaller territories where SB personnel worked under senior police officers. With a worldwide complement of thirty Assistant Commissioners, 500 Inspectors and officers and 1,300 Other Ranks, there were not large reserves of manpower to call upon. Yet just before violence escalated in South Arabia, there was still optimism that the local SB could stem the tide of terrorism. Writing to the Colonial Secretary, the Security Intelligence Advisor confided, 'in territories where Special Branch is fully developed, it would be very difficult for organised subversion to be planned without the colonial government, and hence HMG, receiving early warning'.[7]

British police officers were introduced to all-important institutions, including the BP Refinery in Little Aden. To the wives of BP employees, like Ann Cuthbert, it was a welcome, if bizarre experience:

A European Police officer has been brought over here to bolster up the frightened Arab who was in charge. He's an enormous chap called Crossley – a real character – who comes from Otley! Derek and he have already met over acts of sabotage (which still continue) in the

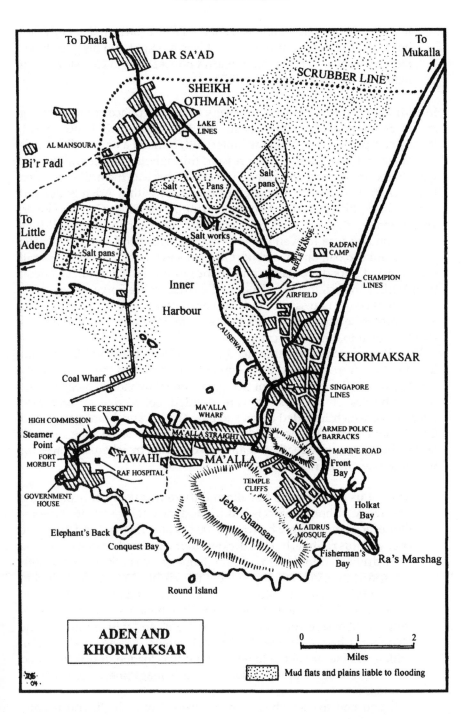

To Dhala
DAR SA'AD
To Mukalla
SHEIKH OTHMAN
'SCRUBBER LINE'
LAKE LINES
AL MANSOURA
Bi'r Fadl
Salt pans
Salt Pans
Salt pans
To Little Aden
Salt works
Salt pans
RIFLE RANGE
RADFAN CAMP
Inner
CHAMPION LINES
Harbour
AIRFIELD
CAUSEWAY
KHORMAKSAR
Coal Wharf
SINGAPORE LINES
THE CRESCENT
MA'ALLA WHARF
HIGH COMMISSION
MA'ALLA STRAIGHT
ARMED POLICE BARRACKS
Steamer Point
MARINE ROAD
FORT MORBUT
TAWAHI
MA'ALLA
Front Bay
RAF HOSPITAL
TEMPLE CLIFFS
GOVERNMENT HOUSE
Jebel Shamsan
Holkat Bay
Elephant's Back
AL AIDRUS MOSQUE
Conquest Bay
Fisherman's Bay
Ra's Marshag
Round Island

ADEN AND KHORMAKSAR

0   1   2
Miles

Mud flats and plains liable to flooding

143

Refinery. He and his family were at the Falaise party and at one point he hissed in Derek's ear that his suit was too tight, did his gun show? Derek was able to reply that it wasn't noticeable and Crossley said it itched all the time! Quite like 007.[8]

In addition to Special Branch, there were two other police units operating in the Federation of South Arabia. The Federal Armed Police (FAP), largely comprising men from the hinterland, fulfilled a para-military role of riot control and guerrilla suppression throughout the Federation, but were based in barracks in Crater.[9] The other unit was the ordinary Aden Police (AP) who dealt with general duties just within Aden State, and were subject, like the other two, to control by the High Commissioner. Traditionally, the Police Force contained an element of small-time corruption and was uneven in performance, with good units in Ma'alla and Tawahi and bad ones in Sheikh Othman and Crater. However, overall the force had a good reputation and, in the words of the Brigadier General Staff MELF, 'the original excellence of the Aden Police Force is something that cannot be overstressed'.[10] But, the constant infiltration of NLF agents and sympathisers into the Aden Police from 1965 onwards ensured its steady slide into the enemy camp.

The SB brief was different to that of the police in mainland Britain, for in Aden they were part of the government machine and their prime duty was to prevent the overthrow of that government by violent means.[11] The responsibilities of the officers were divided between desk and field operations, which included areas such as Airport and Immigration and Court Movements. Public buildings were starting to become terrorist targets but the narrow roads and alleys were often treacherous places for the SB as one officer remembered:

> Most of us lived around Ma'alla and there was really only one route into work, although officers did try and vary it for security reasons. Our official hours were between 0700 hrs and 1300 hrs and again we changed this routine, but the trickiest moments could come when you were driving around town. Although one or two of the boys had soft-top sports cars, others felt you were too visible. You certainly had to be careful when you stopped at a petrol station or when you approached traffic lights as you were then hemmed in, but you kept your pistol beside you, not always on 'safe', and with a round in the chamber. I had a Walther PPK pistol, which was an excellent gun with a reliable signal pin to tell you if it was loaded. It was light and had reasonable stopping power, using a magazine of seven 9mm rounds.
>
> If you had to visit shops when tensions were high, you usually went in a threesome to give you cover, and sometimes, if a visit had

to be made to a sensitive area, a Marine would be allocated to you, to sit in the back of your car with an SLR rifle.[12]

One of the SB routines was to infiltrate agents into the same clubs, associations and Unions that the enemy were infiltrating, which meant using the dwindling band of Arabic-speaking agents. Technical officers were also required to organise the host of robot cameras and audio equipment needed for surveillance operations, but in order to obtain information from local Adenis, SB had to be able to offer protection to their informants, and as the security situation deteriorated, this protection was difficult to enforce. In what became a vicious spiral, local intelligence started to dry up, which in turn reinforced the ability of terrorists to commit outrages. Furthermore, it became difficult to take terrorists to court as witnesses and juries were routinely threatened by the NLF. Combating these problems was hardly helped by the inadequate training of police in counter-insurgency operations – training which suffered from the same limitations that dogged the other security and intelligence forces. For the lessons of previous British campaigns were hard to find in any Aden police training manual. A former Malayan police officer despaired:

> After nearly every campaign an official report is produced, duly classified and entombed in a thousand safes. I cannot remember any of these reports being put to any practical use although once, during the Borneo campaign, I was allowed a quick glance at a highly classified booklet on the Emergency in Cyprus. Whatever lessons were learned there, were not to be divulged to anyone actually engaged in counter-insurgency.[13]

The introduction of new British SB officers into Aden, after the assassinations, had mixed results. Many of them were extremely competent and officers such as Len Sutton, an experienced Head of Special Branch, did much to stem the tide. But changes at the top of the Police Force did not always meet with approval from HQ MELF. In 1965 Peter Owen was appointed Commissioner of Police but his subsequent handling of security matters caused Brigadier (later Major-General) Charles Dunbar, Brigadier General Staff at HQ MELF, much concern. In a forceful letter to the Commander-in-Chief, Dunbar launched a blistering attack on Owen, accusing the Commissioner of 'untruthfulness and evasiveness' coupled with a desire 'to keep his skin whole and to avoid giving anyone offence'. It was a fierce indictment, and Dunbar clearly felt that security and the Police/Army relationship had suffered as a result.[14]

At brigade level, there was machinery in place for communication between the Police and Army, utilising a number of Military Liaison Officers. The Commander of the Aden Brigade, Brigadier Hargroves, even had a joint Army/Police HQ for operations within the main Aden Police Station and he established a good working relationship with his police counterpart, Arthur Wiltshire. But at lower levels of command, the relationship lapsed again. Disquiet at this uneven cooperation was especially apparent when terrorist incidents had to be investigated, with one security official bemoaning, 'there is poor liaison between Police and Army, and even between separate Army units'.[15] Furthermore, the assassination of competent Military Intelligence Officers, like Major Mike Pearman of The Staffordshire Regiment, prevented such links from flourishing.[16]

Superintendent Bill Fairholme, of Aden Special Branch, felt that the root cause of such poor liaison was an inherent rivalry between the services:

> In Malaya, Kenya, Uganda, Cyprus and Aden – the pattern was ever the same. The Army definitely 'looked down' on the Police, who not surprisingly responded with reserved, and often open bloody-mindedness. Sharing information was seldom if ever done willingly, by either side. Nor did the Army and Police tend to mix socially, after 'office hours'. Of course this pattern has a much longer history, for the Colonial Police was never a career chosen by the sons of gentlemen.
>
> Another aspect of this poor Army/Police relationship was that in many comparable ranks (especially the lower ranks), the Police were far better paid. Also, to the fury of the lower paid in the Army, the Police picked up large extra pay by being entitled to overtime.[17]

Rivalries like these were difficult for the local security commanders to overcome, but the appointment of a new 'Director of Intelligence' in 1966 heralded an attempt to unite the intelligence gathering agencies. There had been previous 'Heads' of Intelligence – Hilary Colville-Stewart, prior to 1965 and Brigadier Tony Cowper (the first Director of Intelligence) during 1965–6 – but with the appointment of the ebullient John (later Sir John) Prendergast, progress really was made in pulling together the strands of intelligence gathering. His enlistment was an inspired choice. He had vast experience of intelligence work in colonial situations, having seen service in the Colonial Police Service in Palestine followed by Security Intelligence Middle East (SIME) in the Canal Zone in 1952. He was appointed Director of Intelligence in Kenya in 1955 and played a significant role in subduing the Mau Mau rebellion before repeating the same success in Cyprus during the EOKA campaign in 1958. He then spent six years with Special Branch in Hong Kong, immediately before arriving in South Arabia. The big Irishman had a reputation for 'getting things done' but events in South Arabia would test the reserves of even the most competent operator.[18]

Women working for the High Commission may have been a novelty to local Arabs, but they were still fair game to the terrorists. Susan de Heveningham Baekeland, who had been involved with security at Khormaksar airport at the time of the Trevaskis attack, was careful to protect herself. She had learned to be tough and independent, having lived through the Kenyan Mau Mau Insurgency, and was taught to shoot with both hands in case she was wounded in one, by Dabo Davidson, the former bodyguard to Al Capone. After a spell in the Kenyan Special Branch and study at MECAS, she was pitched into security work in Aden:

> I always used a bulletproof jacket, because two of my colleagues had been shot in their VW in a traffic-jam. I purchased my BP jacket from Wilkinson Sword, who made them for King Farouk – they were made of interlocking titanium plate and weighed about 30 lbs. I was walking to my office with this thing on and I saw an Arab come out from the Steamer Point Tourist Office. He started to pull the pin on a grenade. I never hesitated. I just shot and the grenade exploded and killed him. I didn't cross the road because he could have had an accomplice. I just went straight into my office and phoned General Cubbon, who I knew.
>
> On another occasion, I was walking down a street and a grenade exploded behind me. The shrapnel split and hit the two people either side of me. It was all very dangerous. I had a flat over one of the shops in Steamer Point and I rigged up a bell and cotton, so if anyone came up the steps at night, I'd hear them. I once leapt out of bed, revolver in hand, only to see goats coming up the steps, looking for rubbish to eat.[19]

Another problem that helped increase support among Adenis for the terrorist groups was the narrow franchise of the Aden Legislature, the body that notionally represented Aden State. In an attempt to keep control of the assembly, Britain had restricted the right to vote to those born in the Colony. There were no accurate figures for the Aden State population in the 1960s but the 1955 Census had shown 36,910 Adeni Arabs, 18,881 Protectorate Arabs, 48,088 Yemenis, 15,817 Indians and 10,611 Somalis.[20] Since 1955 the population had swollen, mainly from Yemeni immigrants and there were large numbers of semi-skilled youths in Aden without a vote. In the 1959 elections, it was estimated that there were only 21,500 qualified registered voters out of 200,000 inhabitants, and of those entitled, only 6,000 voted.[21]

Even with this limited control, the Legislature soon started to spin out of Britain's orbit. In its early days, the assembly was fortunate to have as its leader Hassan Bayoumi, who was one of the few Adenis who understood the rivalries of the hinterland. However, he died of a heart attack in 1963 and was replaced by Zein Baharoon, another pro-Federalist, but one who did not have Bayoumi's breadth of vision. He resigned in February 1965 after a row with the British Government over the Eastern states, and was in turn replaced by Abdul Mackawee, an affable but indecisive nationalist who supported the increasingly radical PSP.[22] By now, the Aden Legislature had a nationalist rump, sympathetic to terrorist aims and including men such as Khalifa Abdullah Khalifa, the Aden Airways employee who was accused of the 1963 bomb attack against Trevaskis.[23] With such radical nationalists at the heart of government, the Federal officials and supporters felt even more isolated, especially as HMG appeared to sympathise with the radicals. Donal McCarthy, the High Commission's External Affairs Advisor despaired:

> When Mr Greenwood became Colonial Secretary in 1964, it was widely known both among 'our friends' and the radical nationalists in South Arabia that he was sympathetic to the latter. It was widely spread in Aden, with what truth I do not know, that the PSP representative in London had ready access to him. It was widely assumed by the Federalis, even before they had met him, that he was hostile to them . . . They [the Federalis] were dealing with a government, which either did not understand, or was not prepared to work within, what they regarded as the power realities in South Arabia.[24]

Meanwhile, in Taiz in May 1965, a restructuring of forces was taking place within the nationalist camp. At the conference, which excluded the NLF, al-Asnag and his supporters from the PSP, together with the South Arabian League agreed to form a new movement called the Organisation for the Liberation of the Occupied South (OLOS). To counter this new contender on the nationalist scene, the NLF held its first Congress in June 1965 and produced a Charter dedicated to the expulsion of the British base in Aden coupled with the destruction of the Federation and merger with the YAR. Moreover, the Charter was the first tangible evidence of the rising influence of the left wing within the NLF, a section at odds with al-Sha'abi's more pragmatic leadership.[25]

In the summer of 1965 al-Asnag was thwarted by NLF supporters in his bid for re-election as Secretary-General of the ATUC. Realising he was outmanoeuvred by his rivals, he withdrew OLOS from its overt political activities in Aden, and re-grouped in Yemen. His statements became more bellicose and he stirred up industrial action by calling strikes at the Khormaksar air base and Aden Port. At the same time, the NLF kept up its violent campaign with the assassination of the ruler of Shaib State outside his house in Crater.

Protection was consequently offered to all members of the Aden Legislature and they were issued with firearms, but with a minimum of training there were some fatal and near-fatal accidents. Pistols on the hips, where the hammer caught an obstruction, or carried in the trousers, were the usual culprits. When one Legislative member hurriedly put on his trousers one morning, he forgot he had a loaded pistol in the pocket, and shot off his penis.[26] Even familiarity with firearms did not always prevent accidents. A Cook Sergeant in 45 Commando was removing his .38 revolver, attached to a lanyard, when he dropped it and it fell onto a table beside him. There was just enough movement in the firing pin to strike a round, and the weapon fired, shooting him through the head.[27]

Danger was never far away for the many British families who lived in Little Aden, and for children, it proved an exciting diversion, as Ann Cuthbert wrote to her parents:

> Yesterday, a mine or bazooka went off at the far end of the beach. We were playing a game of 'Monopoly' with Charles, when there was a terrific explosion. We flung ourselves out into the garden with binoculars, and could see a lot of activity but couldn't determine what the three military jeeps were doing in the dusk. It's the last bit of road before the pass and the jeeps have roadblocks there every afternoon and night. I watched them yesterday pm through binoculars, searching a dustbin lorry and going over the same piece of sand. So whatever it was must have been laid afterwards. Young Charles was thrilled with all this, of course – especially as they'd had a talk at school by an explosives expert, and a demonstration of the booby-traps in use. Now all the children allegedly know what not to pick up or kick.[28]

Prominent figures in public places ran an increasing risk. Every Wednesday afternoon at 1400 hours, Sir Arthur Charles, the British Speaker of the Aden Legislature, played tennis at the public courts in the Hai-al-Qati district of Crater. During the afternoon of 1 September 1965, no one saw Hasan al-Zaghir loitering near the courts, and as Sir Arthur finished his game and returned to his car, al-Zaghir approached him and called out his name. Sir Arthur, courteous as ever, answered the call and moved towards the Arab. The NLF 'commando' stepped forward and shot him through the neck. Sir Arthur fell to the ground, and as he lay dying, five further rounds were fired into his back.[29] It was another killing in a public place, of a much respected representative of the Federation. A dawn to dusk curfew was imposed in Crater and Anthony Greenwood called on Chief Minister Makawee to condemn the callous murder. Mackawee expressed sorrow, but failed to condemn the attack, saying 'I put the entire onus for this deteriorating situation on Britain'.[30] After Sir Arthur's murder, the atmosphere in Aden became charged. Stella Rimington, who later became Director-General of MI5, recalled stopping at Steamer Point on RMS *Caledoni*, on her way to India:

Aden brought further excitement – the troubles there were in full swing, the Speaker of the Legislative Council had been shot a few days earlier by terrorists demanding independence and an explosion on shore greeted the ship as we sailed in. That didn't stop us going ashore to bargain for watches and a camera at duty free prices but all the time I felt an uneasy sensation in the small of my back, wondering if anyone had a rifle trained on it.[31]

The escalating violence and obstructive actions of Mackawee and the Aden Assembly pushed HMG into suspending the Aden constitution on 26 September 1965. The Aden Assembly was also dissolved and the High Commissioner assumed 'direct rule'. Although the Federation Council continued, its existence was compromised by the fact that the High Commissioner could only persuade two Adenis to accept nomination as Ministers.[32] Mackawee fled to Cairo, complaining of 'British oppression', but 'direct rule' did little to suppress the terrorists and the assault on Civil Servants continued apace. Nigel Pusineli, who as Director of Establishments was at the heart of the High Commission in Aden, learned to handle the morning post with care:

> There were three Assistant High Commissioners. The man who was running the Aden side, opened the post one morning and had his hands blown off. A telephone message quickly went round, alerting everyone to the threat, and the secretary to the man running the Federation side, suddenly exclaimed, 'I've just put a parcel like that, on Ian's desk'. It was quickly retrieved and so was the parcel posted to me, but it was a close call.[33]

Sometimes the terrorists would target an off-duty 'Tom' or 'Jock' as opposed to a more high-profile official and outings in 'civvies' could sometimes be more dangerous for soldiers than when they were in uniform. Brigadier Louis Hargroves, Commander of Aden Brigade, encountered the sordid end to one soldier's off-duty activities:

> One day in 1965, I was driving around Aden, when I was told by my HQ on the radio that a Private of the ****** Regiment had been murdered. As I was quite near the place, I went in to see what had happened. The soldier on guard at the entrance to the hotel told me that it was, in fact, a brothel. Inside, covered by a blanket, there lay the fresh-faced lad, who had been shot through the head. It transpired that he had gone to the resident prostitute and while on the job, had been shot. The awful old hag thought I was another customer and started to remove her clothes.[34]

An increase in the number of terrorist attacks during 1965 did not always suit the NLF. More unreliable bomb-throwers had to be recruited, many with the capacity to blow their fingers off when fiddling with the detonator. And statistically, the greater the number of terrorist operations, the more likely it was that some would fail and luck would be on the side of the security forces. And luck, rather than intelligence, sometimes played a part. On 19 June 1965 Second-Lieutenant W Hawkins, a young officer from the 1st Battalion The Royal Anglian Regiment, happened to be driving near the Seamen's Mission at Steamer Point, just after terrorists had thrown two grenades inside the building. It was luck that Hawkins was on the spot, but then he promptly ordered his driver, Private M Richardson, to chase the getaway car. Richardson drove fast and with great skill and the Royal Anglians soon cornered the terrorist car. Hawkins tackled one of the men, brought him down and held him captive with his revolver, while Richardson went for help. A hostile crowd soon formed but Hawkins held onto his man. When help finally arrived, the terrorist together with the contents of the car enabled a complete enemy cell to be destroyed. Luck had played a part initially, but it was the bravery of the two Royal Anglians that achieved the success.[35]

A group whom the military, intelligence and federal communities all heavily relied upon were the political officers. Considering the historic strategic importance of South Arabia, it was surprising that this breed of Empire servant was a relative newcomer to the region, first arriving in 1933.[36] Traditionally, political officers in British colonies and protectorates were administrators and had some form of executive power. But in South Arabia there were few formal guidelines and the growing numbers of political officers found themselves acting as advisors, negotiating with local chiefs and encouraging them to build basic forms of administrative machinery. By the time of the Federation in 1959, the political officer's role was somewhat complicated as the new Federal authority assumed responsibility for most legal and administrative issues. As the old advisory treaties were still in force with many of the Federated States, the officers continued to act in their former capacity as Assistant Advisors, responsible to HMG rather than the Federation.[37]

To the new generation of political officers who arrived in South Arabia in the early 1960s, it was the legendary figures from the period before the Second World War – R A B Hamilton, and the EAP 'advisor' W H 'Harold' Ingrams – who were the role models. According to Sir Kennedy Trevaskis, these pioneers set a standard, which their successors found difficult to emulate:

> It was not easy to recruit political officers or retain them. Our establishment was never filled and the rate of wastage was such that in a span of two years, seventeen out of twenty-six officers had come

and gone. Two resigned within a few weeks of arrival, one refusing to 'kow-tow' to any 'five-rupee sheikh' and the other complaining of our excessive colonialist zeal. Some – particularly those from Africa – complained of a lack of authority; others that they could not lead normal lives.[38]

However, despite Trevaskis's reservations, there were political officers from the old Sudan Political Service, like Robin Young and Ralph Daly, who proved remarkably stoical and provided wise council during the worst days of the Aden Insurgency. Daly, a great raconteur, also had a military background with the Welsh Guards, and others who had done military service, including Jim Ellis, Peter Hinchcliffe and James Nash, appreciated the difficulties involved in army and RAF operations in the hinterland.[39] There were other political officers who became steeped in the lore of South Arabia, men such as Robin Bidwell, who was equally at home at Lord's or Twickenham as in the arid mountains of the Western Aden Protectorate, and who went on to write the authoritative *Two Yemens*.[40] Others like Stephen Day, who became an authority on the tribes and social customs of the hinterland and set up the Abyan Museum of Yemeni Artefacts, immersed themselves in the culture and soul of the region. Another political officer, and one who became something of a legend in the hinterland, was Godfrey Meynell.[41] The Derbyshire landowner was based with his wife, Honor, in a fort at Dhala with the intention that he should pursue development projects in the Radfan and repair some of the public relations damage from the Radfan Campaign. Meynell enthusiastically tackled these local problems and was not afraid to go into hostile environments where he managed to generate goodwill even in his adversaries. However, he was often thwarted, like his colleagues, by a constant lack of financial as well as moral support:

> Generally speaking, the non-Arabist, frequently changing and largely administrative Colonial Service in Aden did not match the limited but active intelligence and drive of most of the Protectorate Service up-country. There was practically no interchange between the Colonial Service in the field and the Colonial Office at home, and little or no first-hand knowledge of the Protectorate among politicians and public here [London].[42]

Two of the main requirements for a political officer were an ability to live with the indigenous population and to be fluent in Arabic. Consequently, as Arabists, they were extremely good at communicating with local rulers before and after meals, whereas most army officers, diplomats and other visitors struggled to be understood. Derek Rose, as Assistant Information Advisor, spent much of his time showing visiting journalists what had been achieved in the Federation, especially showcases like the Abyan Cotton Scheme.[43] But writing home to his parents, Rose lamented the communications gulf:

> Yesterday, I took Mr Neville Brown of the *New Statesman* to Abyan. We drove there along the beach in the Land Rover. He is a very solid Birmingham University Lecturer in International Affairs, and carried on a very serious conversation with me in measured tones about Britain's role in the Middle East. Later, we went to see the local ruler, the English political officer [Stephen Day], and the director of the cotton scheme. The trouble was that Mr Brown's questions were so long and intellectual that the ruler had the greatest difficulty in understanding them, let alone answering them.[44]

Glencairn Balfour-Paul, a diplomat with considerable experience of the Middle East, concluded that for HMG's representatives in South Arabia, 'it was possible to combine a dedicated concern for one's job with a light-hearted awareness of the irrationality of the whole business'.[45] This was one way of preserving sanity in a job, which sometimes required living in isolated hill-forts or remote villages. In border areas there was usually military protection, and within individual states the Federal National Guard 1 provided military back-up; but invariably the political officer was left with only an Arab assistant, trained in Morse Code, with a line to 'Head Office' at Champion Lines, Khormaksar. Under the old individual tribal treaties, the sultans were bound to accept the advice of the political officer, but the knowledge that the sultan was something of a permanent fixture while the officer might 'disappear on leave or another posting', sometimes reduced the effect of his advice.[46]

As the violence increased, so did the threats against the political officers and there were casualties. Godfrey Meynell was stabbed and Major Tim Goschen was killed when his Dakota aircraft was blown up in 1966. More extensive casualties were probably averted by the protection of local tribes, who, if they trusted the local officer, would leave him alone, rather than follow the advice of Radio Cairo and murder him. But it was the local Arab Assistant political officers who suffered the heaviest casualties, especially in Aden State where their deaths mirrored those of the Arab Special Branch officers. There were a number of murders that were the probable result of clan feuds, rather than the premeditated assassinations later claimed by the NLF. Nonetheless, there were enough NLF threats in circulation to persuade some Arab political officers to desist from their work. When they bravely ignored the threats, the method of clinical despatch was usually the same – a bullet in the back of the head, fired by a masked gunman, followed by a statement by the NLF on Radio Sana'a.[47]

The political officers were an important link in the information and intelligence chain, as they often had the best local knowledge. General Sir Peter de la Billière, then working as a Junior Intelligence Officer (G3) in Aden, recalled:

> My job consisted largely of correlating intelligence reports from the battalions up country and writing daily 'Intsums', or intelligence summaries. Every morning I would motor to the Federal Government complex at Al Ittihad to attend the daily intelligence meeting, briefing people on FRA [Federal Regular Army] developments. The meeting would be chaired by the Senior political officer. In the corridors there was time for discussion with other political officers such as Ralph Daly and Robin Young, and often those from the out-stations – Bill Heber-Percy, James Nash and Michael Crouch.[48]

However, although there was a consensus on intelligence matters, there was no formal structure that enabled officers to meet together and trade experiences and ideas. They were often too geographically isolated. They did, however, manage to integrate with local tribes, largely because of their fluency in Arabic, which had usually been honed at the Middle East Centre for Arabic Studies (MECAS) in Lebanon. This controversial British establishment had been established in 1948 at Shemlan, a small Maronite Christian village in the mountains twenty miles from Beirut. Stories about MECAS's espionage connections started to circulate because the school was the brainchild of Robin Maugham and its first director was Bertram Thomas, both well-known figures in the intelligence world. The Foreign Office funded the school and during the 1960s under its proficient Director of Studies, John (later Sir John) Wilton MC, it produced about thirty Arabists every year.[49] The syllabus was wide and aimed 'to teach the Arabic of the newspaper and radio as well as the colloquial, spoken by the educated eastern part of the Arab world'.[50] Islamic and Arab history was also covered, and just as importantly, students were taught Arab social customs, including how to deal with a 'mutton crab' – essential learning for future Middle East ambassadors and their embassy staff.[51]

While intelligence officers undoubtedly studied there, and maintained their contacts with diplomatic and business sources, there were a number of other Foreign Office students, as well as those students sponsored by banks and officers from the three Armed Services. Large trading concerns and oil companies, such as BP and Shell, sent young executives to study, and the school also became a useful conduit for promising Arabists, like Derek Rose, to find their way into the more secret departments of the Foreign Office. Consequently, there is no doubt that MECAS was considered extremely important as a means of preserving British influence in South Arabia and throughout the Middle East.[52]

Although the school had survived through the Suez Crisis, the UAR started a campaign of vilification in 1961. The Cairo periodical *Akher Saa* attacked MECAS with the headline 'Secrets of the Spy School in Lebanon' and listed a number of teachers with alleged ties to SIS.[53] The story was soon taken up by other Arab nationalist newspapers and it was unfortunate timing that the Blake spy scandal was breaking. Headlines appeared such as, 'Kifah penetrates the nest of spies', with the 'exclusive' that MECAS was part of a Zionist conspiracy because the spy, George Blake, studied there during 1960–1 and had recently claimed to be Jewish. There were also attempts to link Philby to MECAS after his defection in 1963, but this soon petered out through lack of evidence.[54] Although the school enjoyed a measure of protection from the Lebanese President, Druze leaders soon clamoured for it to be shut down and there were even reports of a UAR MiG fighter, sighted three times on reconnaissance flights over the school.[55]

Another medium for promoting British authority was television. It had only recently arrived in Aden, and although few Arab homes owned a set, one was to be found in most bars and coffee shops. The South Arabian Television Service, funded by the Federation, maintained a regular output and used a number of IRD produced local programmes, including a weekly current affairs programme fronted by the Arabist, Derek Rose. With about half the programmes in Arabic and the rest in English with subtitles, this was a serious attempt to reach the urban Arabs.[56]

In a further effort to win young 'hearts and minds', the Information Advisor, Tony Ashworth, made attempts to provide an Education Television Service for the Federation schools. This, no doubt, would advertise the role of the few British aid and agricultural schemes as well as stressing the advantages of maintaining a military presence. But again, the British Government failed to provide the necessary financial support and Ashworth had to pursue BP for funds to employ a Television Officer, provided by the British Council.[57]

Radio funding fared better, with the Aden Broadcasting Service putting out six hours of local programmes in Arabic each day, together with relays from the BBC Arabic Service. The morale of the British troops was boosted by regular radio output from the Aden Forces Broadcasting Association, operating from RAF Khormaksar. Corporal Mervyn Collings and his wife, Mary, lived in a balcony apartment in the Air India building, in the bustling Ma'alla Straight. As Mary remembered, they were surrounded by Adeni families, all possessing the latest technology:

> We lived opposite the old Aden railway station, which had been converted into a house by a rich Arab with four wives. All the wives seemed to live there together with their twelve children. We used to watch their nightly ritual, when they were all put to bed on the top floor, which was open to the sky. The boys were all kissed and put into

bed first. Then as soon as the parents had disappeared, twelve little figures bobbed up over the parapet and were all soon sitting in a line, swinging their legs and all laughing at the goings on in the street below. The Straight was a busy place at night, with its bars and shops that were much smaller than the stores like Bhicajee Cowasjee in Steamer Point. And you could haggle with the traders, as prices weren't fixed. But whenever the sheikhs from up country came down into town, things changed. Their motorcades, Cadillacs and Mercedes, would sweep down the Straight and in all the shops, it was suddenly, 'prices have risen, Mhem Sahib'. Although I was warned not to, I often travelled on Class C buses. I always felt safe because Ginette, my daughter, travelled with me and she was blonde, which fascinated the Arabs. These buses would travel up behind the Straight where many of the locals lived, in houses made of old wooden packing crates. Hard to imagine, but they lived in these flimsy boxes, yet they always had the very latest 'Frigidaires' radios and TV's.

Up country, although the hectic activity of the Radfan Campaign had given way to smaller operations, artillery still played an important role. During September 1964 'J' Battery, 3 RHA, was relieved by three batteries of 19 Field Regiment and these were split between the FRA and 24 Infantry Brigade. The guns were spread between Radfan, Mukeiras and Beihan as well as providing support around Aden State. However, the increase in rebel activity in Beihan prompted the arrival of additional attachments from 7 Parachute Regiment RHA.

A typical engagement occurred during the night of 18/19 March 1965, when Major Jimmy Ferguson's 28 Battery was in support of 2 FRA near Beihan. Just after midnight, the gun position was fired on by rebel bazookas and machine-guns, and Lieutenant Martin Proudlock swiftly ordered his men to manhandle one of the guns out of its gun pit, swing it into action and fire at the rebel positions over open sights. Having silenced this attack, Proudlock and his men then engaged more of the enemy who were attacking the FRA unit, and successfully saw off the threat. For his brave action that night, Lieutenant Proudlock was awarded the MC.[58] The following night, another British unit came under deadly accurate rebel fire. A 3 inch mortar pit, occupied by men of No 3 Company, 2nd Battalion Coldstream Guards, received a direct hit from an enemy mortar. The round killed three Guardsmen instantly and the resulting fire in the pit threatened to ignite all the HE and phosphorous bombs. Disaster was averted by the brave action of Captain S Barnett and CQMS F Pell, who dashed into the pit, removed the casualties and put out the fire. They then ran across open ground to reach a MOBAT recoilless gun and engaged the enemy positions.[59]

During 1965 the Chiefs of Staff in London realised that MEC had to be reinforced with further ground troops and the 1st Battalion, The Royal Sussex Regiment were despatched from Malta in April 1965. However, there was no show of concern about the deteriorating security situation and press releases stressed that these men were only 'replacements' and not reinforcements. Elsewhere, battalions and regiments continued to be rotated.[60] In September 1965 19 Field Regiment returned to Britain and was replaced by 1st Regiment Royal Horse Artillery (1 RHA) who had spent the last thirteen years as part of the British Army of the Rhine (BAOR) in West Germany. Although terrorist activity was escalating, it was surprisingly, an 'accompanied' tour, and some 200 RHA families arrived at Falaise Camp, Little Aden. With this responsibility in mind, the CO of 1 RHA, Lieutenant-Colonel David Baines, organised each battery to tour three months up country followed by six weeks down in Little Aden. The horse gunners were soon in action, even engaging in approved cross-border artillery duels. In night fighting, the 'Green Archer' radar tracking system proved extremely useful, and unexpectedly helped air traffic control in guiding pilots in bad weather.[61]

There were also changes in Four Five Commando. On 21 November 1964 Lieutenant-Colonel Paddy Stevens handed over command to Lieutenant-Colonel Robin McGarel-Groves, his former Second-in-Command. The following month, McGarel-Groves moved up from his base in Little Aden, to organise Commando operations around Thumier, Dhala and Wadi Rabwa. He was determined to keep his men occupied as much as possible: to move them away from stationary OPs towards patrolling and reconnaissance work, but still mindful that up-country, all his operations had to be approved by the Commander FRA, and carried out in conjunction with the local political officer.[62]

Four Five were also involved in 'hearts and minds' operations, which were inevitably drawn out. Bringing local tribes 'on side' was usually the result of individual trust, for if a tribal chief liked and trusted a political officer, he would cooperate with a British military operation or civil project. He did so because of the personal relationship and not out of any loyalty to HMG. However, there were times when a political officer had the ground cut from under him and a military solution was deemed expedient:

> The most serious long-term consequence of the ready availability of air control was that it developed into a substitute for administration ... the speed and simplicity of air attack was preferred to the more time-consuming and painstaking investigation of grievances and disputes.[63]

'Hearts and minds' was only part of a possible solution. Major-General John (later Sir John) Willoughby, who had taken over as GOC, MELF, from Major-General John Cubbon, commented on the stark choice facing the population of South Arabia:

> Fundamentally, the purpose of terrorism is to force the head of every family to commit himself to ask this question, 'Can this Government save me from being killed? Is it going to win?' Because, quite simply, if the answers are 'no', he must join the terrorists or die.[64]

Major-General Willoughby brought drive and experience to one of the most difficult commands in the British Army. He had started his military career with the Middlesex Regiment and had shown early promise by driving his Austin car up to the first floor of the officers' mess. He commanded battalions of both the Middlesex and Dorset Regiments during World War II and went on to serve in Korea and Cyprus, with a subsequent appointment in 1961 as Chief of Staff, Land Forces Hong Kong.[65]

As the new GOC MELF wrestled with the deteriorating situation in South Arabia, ironically across the border in Yemen, peace talks were in the offing. This state of affairs had arisen largely because military operations on both sides were stagnating. Egyptian forces had risen to a high-water mark of 60,000 during 1965, but even with their thirteen infantry divisions, one artillery division, one tank division and assorted paratrooper and Special Forces units, they failed to make inroads into royalist strongholds. Field units were only supplied with aerial navigation maps so Egyptian Commanders could not properly organise land operations; when they suffered casualties, the wounded could not be evacuated quickly without correct map coordinates. Added to this, Egyptian lines of communication were frequently cut, thwarting their efforts to hold onto important strategic towns like Harib, which was re-captured by the royalists in March 1965.[66]

Furthermore, British support for the royalists, through their covert supply of arms and unofficial advisors, had kept the Egyptians at bay and Nasser even conceded to the Arab Socialist Union that his troops 'continued to face military problems through the activities of British mercenaries'.[67] This support, though still energetically pursued by Conservative mavericks such as Billy McLean, Julian Amery and Peter Thorneycroft, was no longer endorsed by the British Labour Government. Thorneycroft, the ex-Defence Secretary and now in opposition, was something of a favourite on Radio Sana'a and was regularly singled out in their broadcasts:

> O Peter, announce and declare whatever you wish because you will quit our land and the people of South Arabia have resolved to get rid of you. O Peter we have raised our arms and shall not put them down

until we achieve our freedom, dignity and honour, or die. We are not afraid of your mercenaries or your tanks. We shall not follow your mean Amirs who sold themselves and their honour for the devil, in lieu of a handful of Derhams thrown to them as bones thrown to dogs.[68]

Meanwhile, the Prime Minister, Harold Wilson, saw Billy McLean purely as 'a leading mercenary' but was concerned that Amery might 'get mixed up with mercenary activity' during his continuing visits to South Arabia.[69] Amery was clearly considered a 'loose cannon' and obstacles were now placed in his way by the Foreign Office, who suggested to the High Commission:

That a responsible official should accompany Amery and McLean . . . aircraft might not be available to them, because of 'operational' or 'maintenance' reasons. It is of course essential that person named [Amery] should be given no, repeat no, reason to suppose that we have misgivings about him or that there is surveillance over his movements.[70]

Amery's opponents within the Foreign Office and Ministry of Defence also stamped on any intelligence reports from Yemen that exaggerated the Russian threat.[71] Amery nevertheless continued to promote the royalist cause, but despite his efforts and those of the military 'advisors' in the field, Imam al-Badr did little to inspire his own followers. The fact that he was an alcoholic hardly helped, and Colonel David Smiley despaired at seeing the royalist HQ, which shifted from cave to cave, always littered with empty gin bottles. Furthermore, the royalist leader rarely showed decisive leadership, and unlike previous Imams, he never led his troops in battle. This did little to enhance his prestige, which was further dented by his failure to stop certain tribal chiefs selling royalist arms to their republican opponents.[72]

Meanwhile, three years of attrition in Yemen had drained the Egyptian Treasury at the rate of $1 million per day and sapped the Egyptian Army's morale. Nasser was also keen to mend fences with fellow Arab states, however conservative they might be, to ward off the growing military threat from Israel.[73] He also faced unrest at home over the Yemen War, and when this was combined with international pressure, it brought him to discuss a peace agreement with the Saudis in August 1965. As the main royalist broker, King Feisal demanded that Egyptian troops be withdrawn from Yemen at the rate of 10,000 per month. A ceasefire of sorts even came into operation, but by December 1965, peace talks stalled, the fighting erupted again and no Egyptian withdrawals took place.

Both the republicans and royalists in Yemen now had a network of international support. As well as succour from Egypt, the YAR could count on other Arab 'progressive' states such as Iraq and Algeria, while the communist giants, Russia and China continued their programme of economic aid. The conservative Middle Eastern states of Saudi Arabia, Jordan, Morocco and Iran lined up behind the royalists, who enjoyed continued support from Britain, the only major western state to oppose the YAR.

However, one major international power was still playing a double game. In an attempt to court Arab and developing countries, the United States had been one of the first countries to recognise Sallal's regime in 1962. But by 1965 the US relationship with Egypt had seriously deteriorated, in no small part due to Egypt's acceptance of large Soviet weapons deals. President Johnson, mindful of both his large American Jewish lobby and also of the need to influence and control Israel's nuclear development programme, had moved towards a pro-Zionist policy. The US continued to recognise the YAR, but American arms were finding their way, via Saudi Arabia, to the Yemeni royalists. At the same time, US sponsored military programmes were also training royalists in Jordan and the Najran Oasis.[74]

It was becoming clear that both Britain and the US were now hoping for a stalemate in Yemen: to sap Egyptian resources would suit America's new ally, Israel, as well as keeping pressure off the new Federation. At the end of 1965, Britain still appeared intent on keeping her military base in Aden, and ominously, a new British Military Cemetery was being constructed in Silent Valley, a stark and dramatic glen, near Falaise Camp in Little Aden.[75]

NOTES

1   Abdul Ismail, 'How We Liberated Aden', in *Armed Struggle in Arabia*, The Gulf Committee, April 1976, Omm. 3a, AWDU. According to Ledger, op. cit., Hashim Umar, the recently elected member for Sheikh Othman North, played a part in the killing.
2   Pieragostini, op. cit., p. 130.
3   Bill Fairholme to Author, 13 August 2002.
4   Ledger, op. cit., p. 65. Waggitt quoted in Pieragostini, op. cit., p.101.
5   Turnbull to Greenwood, 17 September 1965, CO 1037/226, NA.
6   By 1966 interrogation was considered just about the only source of information. See Dunbar Lecture Notes II, p. 4, 2/5 Dunbar Papers, LHCMA.
7   MacDonald to Colonial Secretary, 8 November 1957, 'JIC Intelligence', CAB 158/30, NA.
8   Ann Cuthbert correspondence, 8 February 1965.
9   The Armed Police were established in 1929. In the 1960s they had a complement of seventeen Officers and 350 OR. After 27 March 1967 there were no British officers, and on 1 June 1967 all police units were amalgamated into the South Arabian Police.

10 Dunbar to Paget, 25 September 1968, File 2/6, and 'Report on Commissioner of Police', File 2/4 – both Dunbar Papers, LHCMA. David Ledger details some of the problems with the Aden Police in *Shifting Sands*, op. cit., p. 147.
11 S Hutchinson, 'The Police Role in Counterinsurgency Operations', in *RUSI Journal*, December 1969.
12 Confidential source to Author.
13 Hutchinson, 'The Police Role', op. cit.
14 Dunbar to Commander-in-Chief, 8 March 1967, 2/4 Dunbar Papers, LHCMA. Dunbar was the Principal Staff Officer in Army HQ but was not referred to as Chief of Staff, to avoid confusion with the C-in-C's own Chief of Staff.
15 Ann Cuthbert correspondence, 17 March 1965.
16 Major Pearman was assassinated on 18 September 1965.
17 Bill Fairholme to Author, 25 October 2002.
18 Major-General Charles Dunbar to Lieutenant-Colonel Julian Paget, 25 September 1968, 2/6 Dunbar Papers, LHCMA. Also Lady Prendergast to Author, 23 September 2002. Sir John Prendergast was awarded the George Medal for his service in Kenya. See also West, op. cit., p. 75, and Crouch op. cit., pp. 204–5.
19 Baekeland, op. cit.,
20 *Census Report 1955*, Government Press, Aden.
21 Franchise qualifications also stipulated voters to be male, resident for two years preceding registration, to own immoveable property and to have an average monthly income of at least 150 shillings. See 1963/64 Research and Information Commission, ISC, Netherlands, Yem. 3a, AWDU. Also Karl Pieragostini, *Britain, Aden and South Arabia: Abandoning Empire*, Macmillan, 1991, pp. 41–2.
22 Mackawee was also appointed a local director of Besse, a large trading company in Aden, to provide a token Arab presence on the board.
23 Khalifa was in custody at the time of his election to the seat of Crater (North), and ten members of the Legislature demanded his immediate release. He was subsequently appointed Finance Minister.
24 Donal McCarthy to Sir Richard Beaumont, 20 November 1967, FCO 8/41, NA.
25 The left wing of the NLF was supported by the radical ANM in Yemen, with some members espousing Marxism. Al-Sha'abi and the leadership belonged to the Nasserite wing that controlled the organisation. See Lackner, op. cit., pp. 40–2. Also Pridham, op. cit., p. 52, and Tareq Ismael, op. cit., pp. 25–7.
26 Ledger, op. cit., p. 59.
27 Colonel Leslie Hudson to Author, 3 September 2001.
28 Ann Cuthbert correspondence, 13 May 1965.
29 Nigel Pusineli, Tape # 652, Oral History Archive, Empire & Commonwealth Museum, Bristol. Also Major-General Sir John Willoughby, 'Counterinsurgency', op. cit., and Sir Gawain Bell, *An Imperial Twilight*, Lester Crook, 1989, p. 152.
30 *The Observer*, 5 September 1965.
31 Rimington, op. cit., p. 55.
32 A H Dutton, 'Aden and the UN', 7 July 1966, File 47740, BP Archives, UW.
33 Nigel Pusineli, op. cit. This probably relates to the incident involving Robin Thorne, Ministerial Secretary to Aden's Chief Minister 1963–5 and Assistant High Commissioner 1966–7. He reportedly lost several fingers when a parcel bomb exploded. Ann Cuthbert correspondence, 17 January 1966.

34 Brigadier Sir Louis Hargroves to Author, 30 October 2003.
35 Michael Barthorp, *Crater to the Creggan*, Leo Cooper, 1976, p. 39. Also Willoughby, 'Counterinsurgency', op. cit. Second-Lieutenant Hawkins was awarded the MBE and Private Richardson, the Queen's Commendation for Brave Conduct.
36 Colonel M Lake, the first political officer outside Aden, was only appointed in 1933 to cover the vast area of hinterland, known formally as the Western Aden Protectorate, and was succeeded the following year by Lieutenant-Colonel R A B Hamilton; see R A B Hamilton, as The Master of Belhaven, *The Kingdom of Melchior*, John Murray, 1949, p. 59.
37 Peter Hinchcliffe, 'Dhala Diary', Talk to British–Yemeni Society, 12 April 2000. See also Bidwell, *Two Yemens*, op. cit., p. 93 and Lunt, op. cit., pp. 166–8.
38 Trevaskis, op. cit., p. 109.
39 There are interesting pen-portraits of political officers by Michael Crouch, Assistant Advisor EAP; see *An Element of Luck*, Radcliffe Press, 1993, pp. 126–9.
40 Bidwell was also Secretary of the Middle East Centre, Faculty of Oriental Studies, Cambridge University. For an appreciation, see G Rex Smith, 'Robin Bidwell – Obituary', in *British–Yemeni Society Journal*, 1994.
41 Godfrey Meynell attracted more recent publicity when he offered himself as a 'human shield' to Iraq, prior to the War in Iraq, 2003. See also '1 RHA Return to Aden', *Gunner*, February 1998.
42 Donal McCarthy to Sir Richard Beaumont, 20 November 1967, FCO 8/41, NA.
43 A huge watershed near Taiz came down onto the Abyan plain, depositing silt and resulting in over 100,000 acres of rich, fertile soil. The cotton cooperative was run by the landowners and tenant farmers and administered by the British. It was one of the success stories of South Arabia. See Paul Dresch, op. cit., p. 63.
44 Derek Rose to Bill Rose, 1 August 1966, Rose Papers. Proposals for Abyan agricultural development were suggested as early as 1926, but only paltry funds were provided.
45 Quoted by Sir Anthony Parsons in his foreword to Glen Balfour-Paul, *The End of Empire in the Middle East*, op. cit.
46 Stephen Day to Author, 25 April 2002. Also Bidwell, *Two Yemens*, op. cit., p. 93.
47 For details of clan murders, see Dresch, op. cit., pp. 97–8. Also Crouch, op. cit., p. 183.
48 General Sir Peter de la Billière, *Looking for Trouble – SAS to Gulf Command*, HarperCollins 1994, p. 193.
49 *The Sunday Telegraph*, 22 March 1961. The school was expanded in 1959. For details of the MECAS administration, see John Wilton to Foreign Office, 22 February 1961 and 3 March 1961, FO 371/157595, NA. See also Verrier, op. cit., p. 174. John Wilton was subsequently appointed Deputy High Commissioner.
50 'MECAS 1965', FO 366/3539, NA. See also EH Cookridge, *Shadow of a Spy*, Leslie Frewin, 1967, pp. 183–6.
51 Consists of two large mutton carcases that are eaten with the right hand. Bill Rose to Author, 26 February 2002.
52 'MECAS 1965', FO 366/3539, and D McCarthy to Secretary of State, 21 October 1967, FCO 8/206, both NA. Also Susan de Heveningham Baekeland, op. cit., and Derek Rose Papers, op. cit. The 'long course' of 1963/4,

comprised 50% Foreign Office, 22% Banks and 28% Oil and Trading Company students. See also Richard Beeston, *Looking for Trouble*, Brassey's, 1997, pp. 33–7.

53 The list is shown in telegram from British Diplomatic Mission, Cairo, to Foreign Office, 16 March 1961, FO 371/157595, NA.

54 For Blake, see *Kifah*, 17 May 1961. Also British Embassy to Foreign Office, 27 May 1961, FO 371/157595, NA. The Foreign Office sent Blake to MECAS in September 1960 to study Arabic. He showed promise and was recommended for the Advanced Course. It is probable that he was under surveillance at MECAS and was suddenly summoned back to Whitehall on 3 April 1961. He was charged with treason. For Philby, see A J Wilton to Foreign Secretary, 13 June 1965, FO 366/3539, NA.

55 The school was subsequently moved to Cyprus.

56 Derek Rose correspondence, 1 August 1966, Rose Papers.

57 Ashworth to G Keeting (BP), 9 December 1965, 47740, BP Archives, UW.

58 Brigadier Baines, 'Gunners in South Arabia', Baines Papers.

59 Those killed in the engagement were Guardsmen A Edge, M Reynolds and D Wilkins. For their courage, Captain Barnett was awarded the MBE and CQMS Pell, the BEM; see Julian Paget (ed.), *Second to None: The Coldstream Guards 1650–2000*, Leo Cooper, 2000, p. 210.

60 CRO to Malta HQ, 17 March 1965, PREM 13/1017, NA. There were some gaps in the rotations of battalions, such as The Royal Anglians, whose 1st Battalion left Aden in September 1965 and were not replaced by a Company from their 2nd Battalion until May 1966.

61 Ibid. Counter-battery retaliation against targets in Yemen was considered acceptable, but any other Yemeni targets had to be approved by the appropriate Federal Minister. See Foreign Secretary to Prime Minister, 14 September 1964, DEFE 13/570, NA.

62 Colonel McGarel-Groves to Author, 14 September 2001.

63 Captain David Parsons, 'British Air Control', *Aerospace Power Journal*, summer 1994.

64 Major-General Sir John Willoughby, 'Problems of Counter-Insurgency in the Middle East', in *RUSI Journal*, May 1968.

65 Just before his appearance in Aden, Willoughby had successfully completed a military logistics study in southern Africa, in the wake of the Smith Government's declaration of UDI in Rhodesia; see 'Obituary', *The Times*, 8 March 1991.

66 Youssef Aboul-Enein, op. cit.

67 Quoted in Rahmy, op. cit., p. 197.

68 Transcript of broadcast by The Ministry of National Guidance and Information, Sana'a Radio, No 111/64, DEFE 13/570, NA.

69 Memorandum of meeting between PM and Colonial Secretary, 6 January 1965, PREM 13/488, NA.

70 Marnham (FO) to High Commission, Aden, 8 January 1965, PREM 13/488, NA. For restrictions see MOD Air to HQ, Mideast, 19 January 1965, PREM 13/488, NA.

71 Colonel Michael Webb's claim that 'the heaviest and latest Russian tanks, guns and aeroplanes were in use by the Egyptians' was discounted by the MOD. See MOD to Private Secretary, Defence Secretary, 16 September 1964, DEFE 13/570, NA.

72 Manfred Wenner, *The Yemen Arab Republic*, Westview Press, 1991, p. 135. Also Colonel David Smiley to Author, 16 September 2003.

73   For the external and domestic pressures on Nasser, see Rahmy, op. cit., pp. 195–204.
74   On 31 May 1965 Nasser announced at the second PLO conference that because Egypt still had 50,000 troops in Yemen, the time was not right for a conflict with Israel. See Moshe Gat, *Britain and the Conflict in the Middle East, 1964–1967*, Praeger, 2003, pp. 68–9, 116. Also Wenner, op. cit., p. 133.
75   Although the cross that stood on top of the rocky pinnacle has been demolished, Silent Valley Cemetery is still maintained today by Mr Nadir Ali. See '1 RHA return to Aden', *Gunner*, February 1998.

CHAPTER VIII
Hill Forts and Hunters

On 14 February 1966 a BOAC flight took off for Aden. On board was a party of three men, travelling under the name of Mr A Butler, and their mission was to have a profound effect on the fortunes of the Federation of South Arabia. The party consisted of the recently ennobled Frank Beswick, together with John Marnham and Alan Butler of the Foreign Office. The Federal Ministers were given little warning of Beswick's visit, with FO advisors cautioning 'we shouldn't even tell them that Lord Beswick is coming until at the earliest a day or two before he arrives'.[1] On arriving in Aden, the party had a meeting with the High Commissioner and at 0930 on 16 February Lord Beswick addressed the Federal leaders:

> When South Arabia comes to full independence, that is not later than 1968, the British forces should be withdrawn from the Aden Base. Consequent on this, I am afraid, is that after independence, we shall not be able to accept any further military commitment in South Arabia. The Treaties of 1959 and 1963 with the Federation and the advisory treaties with individual states will terminate on independence.[2]

This devastating announcement came a week before the British Government's new Defence White Paper was formally published. It was the outcome of a defence review that the Labour Government had undertaken when it first came to power in 1964, and it drastically altered British defence commitments East of Suez. While the overriding cause of the cut backs was economic strictures, it was still a terrible blow to the host of tribal leaders and government officials who had placed their trust in British promises of continued military assistance. Denis Healey, the Labour Defence Secretary, had declared only the year before that 'it would be politically irresponsible and economically wasteful to abandon Aden', and even the month before Beswick's fateful visit, Healey confirmed that 'Britain had no intention of reneging on her commitments in the Middle East.'[3] There had even been recent attempts at constitutional reform in South Arabia, with the commissioning of Sir Ralph Hone and Sir Gawain

Bell to look at ways of bonding Aden to the Federation and encouraging the Eastern Protectorate to join them. However, this was a forlorn gesture, which soon fell apart after Beswick's visit.[4] The Labour Peer's mission had no crumbs of comfort for the Federal Ministers, as even post-independence aid to the Federal Government was to be withheld. Prior to the meeting with the rulers, John Marnham's FO superiors had briefed him that 'in the text given to Federal leaders, even the assistance after independence should not be specific'. Such was the determination to be out of Aden, that even the derisory 'assistance' only amounted to 'the possibility of a British training mission and also of leaving some guns'. It was this reneging on the commitment to a post-independence defence treaty, more than the closure of the military base, that appalled the Federalists.[5] Those British Army officers, who worked closely with the Federal Ministers, were equally staggered by the pronouncement. Brigadier Paul Crook, Security Operations Advisor to the High Commissioner, recalled:

> These people had been our friends who supported and trusted us. Branded by terrorists as 'lackeys of Britain', they were now being virtually abandoned. Yet they continued to work with us towards some form of stability throughout the rest of the year. Men like the Minister for Security, the stout-hearted Sultan Saleh, and the Foreign Minister, Sheikh Mohammed Farid.[6]

It seemed that the Federation, which was ushered in by the British in the first place, was now being discarded without even a tilt at the outside forces cultivating the situation. Barney Dutton of BP noted the response among those Arabs working for the Federation:

> Many Arabs still find it impossible to believe that HMG means what it has said and a repeated criticism was that the British did not even make any public *démarche* to the Egyptians, let alone initiate counter-measures, for example, against the Egyptian intelligence officers in the Yemen, who are organising the incidents in Aden.[7]

Healey's pruning of British military commitments was widespread and ongoing. There would be short-term increases in troops for the Gulf region, but numbers were cut in Malta, Gibraltar and Cyprus. Pressure from the American President, Lyndon Johnson, for a British presence alongside Australian and New Zealand troops in Vietnam was resisted; while at home, the unwieldy Territorial Army was trimmed to a more efficient TA. But controversy raged over intended cuts in the Royal Navy and internationally, the defence economies were viewed as weakness rather than realism. Nasser, whose fortunes were faring badly in Yemen, greeted the news with a declaration that he would rescind his August 1965 agreement with King Feisal over the withdrawal of Egyptian troops from Yemen. His troops would now remain in Yemen, at least until all British troops were driven out of South Arabia. The Egyptian Commander, Field-Marshal Amer, went even further, declaring that his troops would stay in Yemen to underwrite a pro-Nasser government in South Arabia, once the British had left.[8]

Inside Yemen, the cease-fire collapsed and the conflict was regenerated. Royalist commanders went back to their HQs that were spread across the networks of caves that riddled the Yemen highlands. Colonel David Smiley, who had swiftly returned to monitor the situation, had his own 'star' system for the quality of these command centres. Few qualified for a five star accolade. Most caves were in an appalling condition and were infested with flies and lice, and Smiley had to chain smoke cigars in order to mask the overwhelming stench of human waste and decomposing flesh.[9] Another difficulty he encountered was the language. Smiley was not an Arabist, and while some of the younger royal princes spoke good English, older senior commanders struggled:

> Al-Badr's English was extremely bad but the older Prince Hassan, at least spoke a sort of pidgin English. However even this had its limits. His headquarters were based on a high plateau, where he ran about in a Landrover, which had somehow been carted, in pieces, up the sheer mountainsides. After arriving on the plateau and then climbing up the 120 steps to his lair, I was delighted to be asked if I would like to sit down and enjoy some apple pie. I was therefore rather dis-appointed when a grinning man suddenly appeared with a tin containing pineapple rings.[10]

Following the agreement between King Feisal and Nasser the previous summer, Egyptian troop numbers in Yemen had fallen dramatically from a high of 60,000 to under 20,000. But now that HMG had made its declaration about withdrawal from the Aden military base, Nasser poured troops back into Yemen. However, his new battalions were as unprepared as his former expeditionary force, lacking maps and knowledge of their enemy.[11] The royalists should have capitalised on these weaknesses but Colonel Smiley was not impressed with the condition of the royalist forces marshalled for the next round of hostilities. He located Brigadier-General Kassim Monasir, probably the Imam's most competent Commander, who confided, ' I have no supplies. I have only one 75mm recoilless gun and no ammunition for it; I have very few machine-guns and hardly any bombs for my mortars'. It appeared that since Monasir was a non-royal commander, the other princes were jealous of his military successes and withheld arms from him. Smiley promptly organised a parachute drop of supplies but it was too late. Shortly after

Smiley had left him, Monasir deserted to the republicans.[12] The royalist foot soldiers were loyal enough to Smiley but they thrived on war, violence and booty and as the conflict only spluttered along, they began to lose interest. Political solutions were of little concern to them and they would sooner have a fight to the death. Moreover, King Feisal, who by 1966 was bolstered by British and American arms, felt in a more secure position and was no longer prepared to allow the Imam and his royalist troops such a long leash. Negotiation, rather than outright confrontation with Nasser, seemed more attractive. Even David Smiley knew his contract as a mercenary commander was nearing its end, as increasingly his time was spent on administration in Jedda rather than the field operations he relished.[13]

Contact between Yemen and South Arabia was also being restricted. During 1966 the Federal Government, without consulting HMG, closed off the Yemen border to all trade and passage. This increased the number of guard and patrol duties for the FRA, but ominously, large amounts of traffic still passed through the border, especially in Lahej. It became apparent that this was not a security measure but more a means of securing extra revenue. According to one highly-placed British Official, it was clear that officials and guards under the control of the Sultan of Lahej were taking bribes and exacting tolls, an activity excused by Sultan Saleh as *maftuh*.[14]

While the border region was officially the preserve of the Federal forces, British troops in the hinterland were still largely located in the Radfan area. Thumier, the old base for the 1964 Radfan campaign, was made a permanent camp and renamed Habilayn in 1965.[15] Lessons had been learned from the Radfan Campaign and although most of the camp was out of sniping range from the surrounding hills, camp beds were dug into the ground inside the tents. Long queues for the cookhouse, which might provide the enemy with a target, were dispensed with as the men arranged their own catering. This had its drawbacks, according to Trooper Jim Buchanan RM:

> I was still one of the younger boys in our troop and when we were in camp in Habilayn, I was often sent out from our tent to get supper from an Arab food shop in the 'High Street'. A popular choice was omelette and one evening I was carrying back these take-away omelettes through the camp, when there was a terrific bang behind me, throwing me forward and covering me in egg. The explosion, which was from an enemy rocket fired towards the camp, took the shirt off my back and shook me up. I staggered back into our tent, looking a complete wreck. There was no concern from the others about my condition. They were all too upset about the state of their omelettes.[16]

Habilayn Camp normally supported an infantry battalion or commando from 24 Brigade as well as being the FRA HQ for Area West. From Habilayn, British companies were distributed to strongholds at nearby Dhala, while at Mukeiras in the centre of the border territories, FRA troops formed the main contingent, assisted by a battery of artillery and sometimes supplemented by an infantry Company from Aden Brigade.[17] Lieutenant S D Lambe recalled the pattern of gun support in the Radfan:

> A normal three-month tour up-country will probably include up to a dozen operations with one gun out of camp in support. They do not normally last longer than four or five days and the gun may be airlifted by a Wessex helicopter. If the guns are in a Federal Regular Army camp, the FOO party is likely to become very fit. The FRA plan on short patrols; i.e. fifteen miles round trip, to go at six mph if unaccompanied by British soldiers. A special concession for British troops, that is, the FOO party, is a slower speed of only five mph. Even in Europe this would be formidable.
>
> The climate plays its part. Up-country temperatures rise on occasions to 135° with a correspondingly low evening temperature of 95°. During the 'summer' thunderstorms are frequent and terrifying. Seen from a distance they are a solid wall of sand and rain reaching to nearly two thousand feet, and when they arrive, the deluge fills trenches in minutes and the wind blows down sandbagged walls.[18]

The base and outlying forts had to be constantly re-supplied. The shortage of helicopters meant that vehicle convoys, often called 'The Dhala Convoys', were the usual means of supply up-country. However, they were frequently targets of rebel ambushes, initiated by land mines. Advance picquets on the heights above the tracks through the mountains could do little to combat mines and inevitably the army Landrover, that staple of any mobile column, had to be modified to cope with the threat. The standard short-wheel model was modified locally by welding ¼" mild steel plate on the underside of the front seats, with sandbags laid on the floor. Roll bars were fitted and everything inside was stripped out together with the windscreen. Thus adapted, the Landrover could only carry two men, who would be reasonably well protected, but would still suffer with shock and lacerations if the vehicle hit a mine. In this event, the vehicle itself would be written off. Commanders' Landrovers were also fitted with a wire cage, so that any grenades thrown at them would bounce off. For defence purposes, sometimes a GPMG or a .300 Browning would be rigged-up on a tripod mount with the machine-gun facing forward, which would allow the gunner a fire elevation arc of 35°.[19] Other vehicles such as the Bedford Rear Loader were also protected by steel plate, stripped inside and sandbagged, while the Half Cab vehicle, already converted by RE workshops in the UK, had a separate armour-plated cab and chassis that would separate in the event of a blast.

Tours up-country made a welcome break from security duties in the stifling confines of Aden State, but soldiering in the mountains brought its own special dangers. On 26 May 1966 a Company of the 1st Battalion Welsh Guards came under attack from well-aimed mortar rounds and Energa grenades. The rebels followed this up with a second attack on 12 June but this time the company had advance warning and beat off the tribesmen, killing six and wounding a further six. Meanwhile, Number 3 Company came under attack at Al Milah and a Private was seriously wounded and the Company Commander had a lucky escape when a Blindicide rocket exploded on his bed at 10.15pm. He put his luck down to a glass of 'Johnnie Walker', taken in another bivouac.[20]

Another popular target for rebel tribesmen were the numerous hill forts that dotted the mountains. Often perched on inaccessible ridges or on the edges of vast ravines, they were usually garrisoned by the Federal National Guard 2, who until 1965, were recruited and controlled by local state rulers and maintained an independence from the British Army. It was an isolated life recalled Lieutenant Simon Mort:

> Such forts were sited in spectacular settings. There was a magnificent pass leading up to Dhala called the Khuraybah Pass. It was always said 'this is where The Life Guards (two regiments before us) lost a Saladin' and presumably also the crew.
> The FNG sat all day and all night in forts in exposed and dangerous places. Because they seemed to spend the entire time inside the fort chewing qat, smoking 'hubble-bubbles' and talking, these strong-points stank of stale urine. They were however, very hospitable – probably because visitors relieved the tedium of the day but also because of the natural Arab inclination to be hospitable. We enjoyed the hospitality and soon learned to immune ourselves from the odour. I forget their exact hierarchy and structure, but the FNG were not regulars and we always perceived them as something on the lines of the Yeomanry officered by local upper-class men of laid-back mien.[21]

Up-country patrolling by British infantry units developed as an art rather than an exact science but they faced an enemy who were excellent exponents of the craft. Years of mountain fighting was now honed by more sophisticated tactics employed by the NLF. Egyptian Intelligence units assisted in training rebel tribesmen, teaching them to patrol in groups of between fifteen and thirty men, split into two sections and sometimes accompanied by an HQ unit. Depending on the terrain, the enemy patrol would employ two lead scouts and the sections would keep about 100 yards apart. Each man would carry either a 7.62 Tokarev or Simonov semi-automatic rifle or an older bolt action .303 Lee Enfield together with quantities of No. 94 Energa rifle grenades and the familiar No. 36 Mills grenade.[22] In addition, their support weapons included the LMG (Bren), 61mm mortars and Blindicide rocket launchers.

During 1965 and early 1966 movements of these enemy patrols were increasingly monitored by units from 22 SAS. The SAS squadrons were alternating between jungle warfare in Borneo and desert operations in South Arabia, and the recently reformed 'B' Squadron, under the command of Major (later Lieutenant-General Sir John) Watts, achieved some notable successes in the Radfan mountains.[23] However, there remained the inherent problem that regular infantry battalions often had no knowledge of where the SAS units were operating. The Special Forces were under the direct control of MELF, and consequently units from 24 Brigade would have to contact HQ MELF to be sure that patrols would not conflict and cause casualties by 'friendly fire'.[24]

If rebel patrols were tracked and then surprised by a British ambush, which opened up at some distance, they would normally break and run. However, if they were engaged at close quarters they would retaliate with rocket launchers, which were always loaded and ready to fire. One ambush party from 1st Battalion Prince of Wales's Own Regiment of Yorkshire (1 PWO) discovered this to their cost when 'B' Company, under command of Lieutenant Peter Orwin, set up an ambush site on the approaches to Habilayn airfield. During the night of 27 July 1966, an enemy patrol of some twenty men walked into the fire-zone and Orwin's men opened fire from a range of fifteen yards. Against a conventional enemy the trap could have been a slaughter but the Radfan rebels retaliated instantly, turning four rocket-launchers on the Yorkshiremen, killing Lance-Corporal Bryan Foley and wounding another soldier. The fight turned into a bitter exchange but Lieutenant Orwin gradually got the upper hand, moving among his men and directing a combination of GPMG and mortar fire to drive the enemy back, killing two and wounding six. 'B' Company suffered a total of five casualties and such attacks were ample evidence that even when surprise was on the British side, the enemy could exact a high price for the engagement.[25]

The rebels were also adept at firing the rifle grenade, and although the explosive content was less than a hand thrown grenade, in the open sparse terrain, it mattered little that the grenade could only travel in a straight trajectory. And while the forward section of the enemy patrol was engaged, the rear section would invariably work their way round to outflank the ambush position.[26]

Patrols from 45 Commando were similar in size to enemy parties, but the staple rifle was the L1A1 SLR (Self-Loading Rifle), a popular assault weapon with a 20-round magazine and effective range of 600 yards.

Support weapons would usually include four GPMGs and four Armalite rifles in order to inflict overwhelming and demoralising firepower as soon as possible. Lead scouts were a problem, and although 'Race' Troops could provide experienced men for the purpose, other units struggled. However, reconnaissance was a vital platoon or troop role, as any advance on a hamlet or village would result in barking dogs from a distance as much as 500 yards. Furthermore, maps could not be relied upon and navigation had to be carried out using previous tracking, air photos and information from static picquets.[27] When the enemy was tracked down by a Commando patrol, they always put up a fierce fight and would rarely surrender:

> Three of the enemy were sighted 200 metres to the front, running up a low hill. One of them stopped and fired a number of rounds at our troop. The troop took up a kneeling position and engaged the enemy at about 175 yards with rifles and GPMG. Two of the enemy fell dead and the third disappeared over the top of the hill and could not be located by our troop. However, he was spotted by one of the picquets and he immediately opened fire on the picquet. The picquet returned fire and killed him.[28]

The only integral, indirect weapon available to Commando patrols was the 81mm mortar used by designated Mortar Troops. Twenty-nine year old Lieutenant (later Major-General) Andrew Keeling was a Mortar Officer commanding a troop of thirty men:

> In my Mortar Troop we had three sections of mortars and each section comprised two mortars with a three-man crew. There was also a Command Post Team with a Sergeant using a plotter board to co-ordinate tasks. The mortars themselves were simple but effective. They only had a bipod, base and striker plate, but weighed about 25 lbs and together with two bombs, which weighed the same again, you had a heavy load. Camels were often used in difficult terrain but they were difficult beasts to handle.
>
> The mortars were very effective in the hinterland. We used standard High Explosive (HE) and smoke shells, and because the ground was so hard you got a good clean detonation when the round landed, so the enemy also had to contend with flying rock splinters. In fact anyone caught in the open, within 40 yards of the burst was likely to be a casualty.
>
> When we were on a six-week tour up-country, we spent our time either in Habilayn Camp or out on the mountains. We often passed through hamlets or villages – they were not picturesque – and I will always remember the appalling smell of human and animal waste as we passed through. Many of the villagers appeared to have branding

marks on them. Apparently the local 'doctors' burnt out any illness with a branding iron.[29]

Another heavier weapon available to Four Five was the L6 Wombat. Devised as an anti-tank weapon, it was a popular successor to the older MOBAT (itself derived from the Battalion Anti-Tank guns, or BAT series). The Wombat was a recoilless weapon, maintaining the same 120mm calibre, and in the mountains of South Arabia it proved extremely versatile as it could be manhandled over rough terrain and either sited in a gun-pit or mounted on a Landrover, 'portee' fashion. However, as the Australians were finding in Vietnam, the Wombat had a fierce back-blast, visible enough to give a position away to the enemy.[30] But Trooper Jim Buchanan was impressed with the weapon:

> The Wombat was a good piece of equipment. It was designed, of course, to knock out tanks but was effective against any enemy defensive position, particularly sangars. You didn't have to be that accurate and as long as you hit the ground near the target, you could be sure that you would take out anyone inside the sangar – the blast from the 90lb shell saw to that. But you could never be sure of how many enemy casualties you'd inflicted. Afterwards, you'd find nothing at the target site apart from a shoe with a foot still in it, or perhaps a turban with part of a skull still in it. The enemy always took their dead and wounded away.[31]

Because of trickle drafting, much of the experience gained in the Radfan by Four Five could be retained within the commando. However, other regular units who arrived in South Arabia, fresh from Germany or the UK, had to start from scratch. Even their more senior commanders could not rely on recent experiences in Malaya to provide military lessons, for Malaya had enjoyed some circumstances simply not present in South Arabia. The Malayan Communist Party leadership was inexperienced, Malaya itself was geographically isolated and independence was granted in 1957 while the Emergency was still in force.[32] While one of the architects of that success, Sir Robert Thompson, had certainly influenced President Kennedy in his approach to the Vietnam War, he could only offer limited advice about South Arabia.

Another experience that was markedly different to other counter-insurgency campaigns was the air war. To pilots like Flight-Lieutenant David Malin DFC, Operations Flight Commander with 43(F) Squadron, flying in South Arabia was an extraordinary experience:

> It was terrific flying and probably the best you would have in your career. You had a buzz from the pure tactical freedom – air traffic

controls were negligible once you were 20 miles out from the control area of Aden. The country was dramatic in the extreme. Flying low level through long winding wadis and then climbing above the massive mountain ranges was tremendous. And the weather, almost always clear, fine and predictable, was a great boon.

You still had to be careful. It was no good dawdling at low levels through rebel-controlled wadis or you'd be shot at. While most rebels just tried to shoot directly at the plane, some of them got the hang of it and gave some lead before they shot at you. We lost one aircraft this way from small arms fire, but luckily the pilot managed to eject, and there were nine other occasions when our Hunters were hit by SAA.[33]

The air war could not have been successfully fought without the teamwork between the fighter pilots, their ground technicians and the Forward Air Controllers (FAC). During the phase 1965–1967, Aden was the first tour for many of the pilots after finishing their conversion training at RAF Chivenor. These 'first tourists' performed remarkably well over such testing terrain, although the fact that virtually all pilots came through the operations unscathed was as much due to the qualities of leadership shown by the Flight Commanders, as individual pilot skills. However, while sorties could not have been carried out so successfully without the ground technicians, pilots also relied heavily on their FACs.

The FACs, who were army officers trained by the RAF, were highly rated by the pilots for their professionalism and bravery. It was a difficult and often dangerous job, for the FAC would be on his own and usually in hostile territory. To identify the position of the enemy, he would first radio the pilot and tell him the colour of his smoke. Then he would fire smoke bombs from his mortar towards the enemy, and direct the pilot to fire his rockets or cannon '20 yards to the right of the smoke', all the while taking account of the difference in angles on the ground and air. If the FAC moved to avoid enemy fire at this critical moment, he risked death from friendly fire.[34]

It was hard to envisage the FRA taking on this technical role after independence, let alone providing suitable candidates for pilot training. One possibility might have been for the US military mission in Saudi Arabia, which was then training Saudi pilots to fly Hawker Hunters, to also train any suitable South Arabians. It was also conceivable that the Federation could hire foreign pilots, in the way that Saudi Arabia had relied on South African pilots when building its air force, but there would be insufficient aircraft to ward off any future full-scale Egyptian invasion. So any newly independent Federation would remain highly vulnerable.[35]

The other component of successful fighter operations was the aircraft itself. Pilots like Flight Lieutenant Chris Golds AFC, 'B' Flight Commander with 43(F) Squadron, were in no doubt about the quality of the Hunter:

174

The Hunter FGA9, which was based on the Hunter F6 Interceptor, was a very tough aircraft and because of the increasing power of radar it was required to fly at low levels. This was hard on the airframes but the Hunter could take it, and because it was so strong it was also an excellent weapons platform. One of the innovations of the mark was the brake chute. Khormaksar had a 2,700 yard runway and was longer than most, so if there wasn't any headwind the brake parachute was very handy. But you didn't use it unless you had to, because it was a bugger to pack away afterwards and if you were on an operation, it could slow up the turnaround time. Beihan airstrip was tricky for this routine as it was so oily, and if your drag chute didn't work, you were off the end.

But maintaining Hunters in the heat and dust meant that the technicians had to work miracles to keep the Hunters in operational order. There were times when they broke down and when you were flying in pairs, say six pairs in sequence, if one or two failed to take off, there would be a hole in the air cover at the sharp end. Even if this gap were 15 minutes, it would be enough for the enemy to re-establish themselves.[36]

The fighter pilots flew very much on their instincts and their observation had to be acute, for one problem facing the pilots was a lack of navigational aids. Flight-Lieutenant David Malin lamented the quality of the maps that pilots were provided with:

The whole area had been surveyed by Canberra aircraft and converted into maps, but the detail was very inconsistent. Often the key elements of the map would be missing, to be overlaid with 'No topographical details available', which was very helpful if it was the target area you were supposed to hit. One map, I remember, was priceless – it consisted of just a mass of chocolate coloured desert, without one single feature on it, but it was nevertheless dignified with a grid pattern.

To help the formation identify the target – say if it was an undistinguished fort among other buildings – the leader would often fire a burst of cannon fire into it, and the flight pilots would all watch like hawks to mark the spot, and then release their rockets towards it. Sometimes, we didn't need rockets as a three second burst from our Aden cannons could demolish the top of a fort.[37]

Once back at their base at Khormaksar airfield, the pilots attended a mission debriefing and dispersed to their quarters, while the ground crews went through the methodical checks on the Hunters. There was always tight security around the base. Arab guards were mounted at the gates to watch over the 'village' with its clubs, messes, shops, churches and recreational facilities, as well as the more sensitive sites. In turn, the Arab guards were supervised by the RAF Police, or 'snoops' as they were known. Surprisingly, they were not usually armed, but the RAF Police-dog handlers certainly were. They patrolled at night around the airfield perimeters and among the aircraft to combat not only sabotage but also theft of fuel and parts. There were also times when the end of an RAF evening patrol could be 'extended' to include a night spell on the beach. To Acting Corporal Gareth Jones, this provided some memorable images:

> We'd put the Landrover into a safe parking spot on the long beach. Caps off, we would smoke, talk quietly and enjoy the magnificence of the sunset over the water. We watched with similar pleasure, the long slow camel trains walking through into the night – oil lanterns swinging and the beasts growling as they wended their way out into the desert. Or later, the dawn call to prayers, amplified via a 'Sony' speaker, which would waft across the waters of the harbour. It never failed to stir me.[38]

Before 1966 terrorist actions had been brutal and certainly effective when directed against identified targets, but they lacked co-ordination. The Egyptian regime and particularly Egyptian Intelligence began to see the benefit of uniting the disparate nationalist groups in South Arabia, and attempted to combine OLOS and the NLF. On 13 January 1966 an announcement was made that the rivals had indeed buried their differ-ences and would merge into a new organisation called the Front for the Liberation of Occupied South Yemen (FLOSY). But almost immediately, splits occurred within the Egyptian sponsored FLOSY, with local NLF activists and cells denouncing the merger. These radical cells murdered Ali Qadhi, President of the ATUC and al-Asnag's trusted lieutenant, which resulted in bloody retaliation by FLOSY. Heavyweights from ANM, such as George Habash, were brought in to try to hold the merger together, but two months of negotiations failed. Qahtan al-Sha'abi and his cousin Feisal al-Sha'abi, who formed the core and right-wing of the NLF leadership, were detained by Egyptian Intelligence in Cairo for the next fifteen months in order to allow FLOSY to prosper.[39]

Meanwhile terrorist weapons continued to flood into Aden. Military checkpoints barely restricted their passage, so an attempt was made in 1966 to throw a physical cordon across the desert, just north of Sheikh Othman. The responsibility for the construction of the eleven-mile fence lay with the 1st Battalion Coldstream Guards who had arrived the previous October. The Second-in-Command of the battalion, Major P Stewart-Richardson (known as 'Scrubber'), organised his Guardsmen, and particularly the Corps of Drums, to erect the fence from coast to coast, leaving three entry points through which all traffic had to pass. Searching people and vehicles was a time-consuming and frustrating business, made worse by the prohibition of searching Arab women. However, the resourceful Coldstreamers managed to fit mine detectors to the underside of chairs, and when the Arab women were invited to sit down while their men were searched, they detected whether the women were as ample as they looked. Ultimately the Scrubber Line was a very visible show of force, and although it was patrolled by helicopters and armoured cars, as well as foot patrols, it only had limited success in the numbers of weapons captured.[40]

In an attempt to open up separate 'fronts', in the early months of 1966, the terrorists turned their attention to disrupting Aden's commercial life and particularly its duty-free trade. They struck just as port traffic was returning to normal after a union go-slow had forced commercial shipping towards the rival port of Djibouti. Tourists from the passenger liners were also returning to shop in Aden, but a series of well-timed murders in and around Tawahi soon stopped their visits ashore.[41] Economic concerns were now being hit in conjunction with military targets.

NOTES

1 Lord Beswick, a former Labour MP and stalwart of the Co-operative movement was ennobled in 1964. He had no experience of the subtleties of Middle Eastern politics, but later found favour as the Lords' Chief Whip – much to the displeasure of Dick Crossman. See *The Diaries of a Cabinet Minister, Volume II*, Hamish Hamilton, 1976. For secrecy provisions, see Memorandum, J Marnham to A Galsworthy, 27 January 1966, CO 1055/307, NA.
2 Transcript of Meeting with Federal Supreme Council, CO 1055/307, NA. See also Notes to Meeting of 17 February 1966, also CO 1055/307, NA. The High Commissioner, Sir Richard Turnbull, had been made aware of the Government's intentions from the beginning of February 1966. See Turnbull to Marnham, FO, 5 February 1966, CO 1055/307, NA.
3 Quoted in Balfour-Paul op. cit., pp. 84–5.
4 For details of the Hone/Bell mission, see Sir Gawain Bell, op. cit., pp. 151–70.
5 R Belcher to J Marnham, Colonial Office, 11 February 1966, CO 1055/307, NA. For 'assistance', see Lord Beswick to Colonial Secretary, 16 February 1966, CO 1055/307, NA. Also 'Confidential Political Situation Report', Hargroves Papers.
6 Brigadier Paul Crook, *Came the Dawn: 50 Years an Army Officer*, Spellmount, 1989, pp. 120–1.
7 Memo, A H Dutton, 15 April 1966, File 28693, BP Archives, UW.
8 For details of Healey's defence cuts, see Sir William Jackson, *Withdrawal from Empire*, Batsford, 1986, pp. 229–33. For Nasser and Amer, see *al-Ahram*, 19 May 1967. Also 'Presentation on South Arabia to JSSC by Brigadier C G T Viner and Brigadier R L Hargroves', 21 March 1966, Hargroves Papers.
9 Colonel David Smiley to Author, 16 September 2003.

10 Ibid.
11 The Egyptians only had one Commander, General Talaat Hassan Ali, who knew the terrain well; see Youssef Aboul-Enein, op. cit.
12 Monasir was executed soon after by his own tribe, who were disgusted at his disloyalty. See Smiley, op. cit., p. 210.
13 Smiley, op. cit., p. 213.
14 Donal McCarthy to Arabian Department, FO, 13 October 1967, FCO 8/41, NA.
15 Thumier was also the name of a local village.
16 Jim Buchanan to Author, 3 May 2003.
17 In the summer of 1966, four Troops from 1RHA trained FRA gunners on 25-pounders. In early 1967, the FRA gunners were then moved up-country to provide artillery support to their own battalions. Colonel M J Richards to Author, 5 May 2004.
18 Lieutenant S D Lambe, 'Night Action', Brigadier Baines Papers.
19 'Vehicles used in South Arabia', 2/1 Dunbar Papers, Liddell Hart Centre, KCL.
20 *The Household Brigade Magazine*, autumn 1966.
21 Simon Mort to Author, 15 March 2004. In 1965 FNG 2 were merged into the South Arabian Police, though because of their connections with state rulers they often maintained their independence.
22 The No. 36 was a more recent variant of the classic pineapple No. 5 Mills grenade. Although the segments on the case did aid fragmentation, their original intention was to aid handgrip in the slippery conditions of the Western Front.
23 'Obituary: Lieutenant-General Sir John Watts', *The Daily Telegraph*, 15 December 2003. Watts was appointed Commander of 22 SAS Regiment in December 1969.
24 Colonel McGarel-Groves to Author, 14 September 2001.
25 Lieutenant Orwin was awarded the Military Cross for this action. '1 PWO Sitrep', July 1966, Dunbar Papers, Liddell Hart Centre, KCL. Also, Major-General Michael Tillotson, *With the Prince of Wales's Own*, Michael Russell, 1995, p. 37.
26 45 Commando HQ, 'Ambush Patrols', 11 May 1967, ADM 202/578, NA.
27 Ibid.
28 '45 Commando, Operation Vanguard V', File 2/1, Dunbar Papers, LHCMA.
29 Major-General Andrew Keeling to Author, 14 September 2001.
30 John Norris, *Brassey's Anti-Tank Weapons*, Brassey's, 1996, p. 108. The BAT series of guns had replaced the heavy wartime 17-pounder.
31 Jim Buchanan to Author, 3 May 2003.
32 See Professor Ian F W Beckett, 'Robert Thompson and the British Advisory Mission to South Vietnam, 1961–1965', in *Small Wars & Insurgencies*, Vol. 8, 1997.
33 David Malin DFC to Author, 14 June 2003.
34 Chris Golds to Author, 10 June 2003. See also 'Forward Air Controlling is not a Mystic Art', *Globe & Laurel*, December 1965.
35 Humphrey Trevelyan to Sir Maurice Bridgeman, 10 June 1966, File 47740, and A H Dutton to M Banks, 16 June 1966, File 47740, BP Archives, UW.
36 Chris Golds to Author, 10 June 2003. In early 1964 Golds was reluctantly transferred to RAF Chivenor, to train new pilots. He returned to Aden in July 1966, as Squadron Leader and Junior ('shiny shoes') Staff Officer.
37 David Malin to Author, 14 June 2003.

38 Gareth Jones to Author, 21 May 2003.
39 Lackner, op. cit., p. 43.
40 *The Household Brigade Magazine*, spring 1966.
41 Memo, A H Dutton, 15 April 1966, BP Archives, UW.

CHAPTER IX
Street Fighting

One of the most important jobs in internal security in Aden was the locating of terrorist arms caches. This could be a long and frustrating business in the 'rabbit warren' of Crater and, as one Superintendent discovered, sometimes involved some elaborate schemes:

> *Qat*, the mild narcotic that all the locals seemed to chew, could not be legally imported from Yemen. So, a lot of dealers used to import it 'through the back door' using couriers. As a result, they knew the local scene well and their illegal activities naturally spilled over into connections with the terrorists. If we paid them enough, they would inform us where the terrorists were living. One day, we pulled in a well-known dealer, got the Crater map out in front of him and told him to point to these places. As an Arabist, I was able to translate for him, but it was immediately apparent, he hadn't a clue how to read a map. The only way was for him to point these places out to us by making a tour of Crater. Naturally, it was far too dangerous for him to be seen with us, so several of us dressed up in veils and pretended to be his wives. One night, he drove us around the back streets of Aden in an old VW Beetle, discreetly indicating terrorist safe houses. Our disguise seemed to work, but every officer kept his hand on his pistol underneath his *chador*.
>
> If you had a tip off about an arms cache, it would only be a general location. Finding the actual cache often took a long time. Weapons and ammunition were usually hidden in hessian sacks, but buried very deep in the ground and they could easily be missed in a cursory sweep. Before you could arrest and detain anyone for a month, you had to obtain a Governor's Order, and once this was done, the detainee's property was confiscated. This often resulted in more arms finds and usually their car was also impounded, and more often than not, it was a VW Beetle. These cars were popular with the terrorists because they were supposed to have the largest car body voids, in which the terrorists could hide their mortars and Blindicides.[1]

181

Sometimes it was a mistake by the terrorist which exposed an arms cache. On 13 June 1966 there was a tremendous explosion in Crater, at a house owned by a member of the Mackawee family. Security forces arrived at the smouldering ruins to find a headless and armless corpse, together with course notebooks from a sabotage tutorial conducted in Cairo. The terrorist had blown himself up while priming a bomb, having inadvertently set the timer to the current time. Luckily, the explosion had unearthed a huge arms dump in his house including Schmeissor Machine pistols, Stenguns, Russian grenades and blocks of TNT.[2]

This lucky discovery must have prevented many incidents from taking place, but Crater and Sheikh Othman were awash with weapons. When a terrorist attack occurred, the culprit was usually lost in the maze of back alleys and narrow streets – escape routes that required sealing off. 518 Company, Royal Pioneer Corps did some sterling work in constructing concrete block walls which closed off many exits but as fast as the walls could be thrown up, the terrorists would knock holes through to make good their escape.[3]

If they were foiled in one getaway plan after an attack, the terrorists could always find sanctuary in a Mosque. Pleas by the security forces to the local Imam usually failed and when the time came for the Mosque to empty, the assassin had usually changed clothes. Women were sometimes handed small arms after an attack and swiftly hid them under their voluminous clothes, knowing that male security forces could never search them. While possession of radios gave the British troops some advantage, Intelligence officers knew that modern equipment had its limits:

> We thought that because we had the technology, we could easily handle the local dissidents and with our radios, could control any situation. But they knew their terrain – every dark back alley and covered cellar. Often their simple 'bush telegraph' system was far quicker than our sophisticated communications.[4]

Another restraint imposed on troops, in line with the policy of minimum force, was the 'Blue Card', which gave 'Instructions to Individuals for Opening Fire in Aden'. Warnings had to be shouted out in Arabic and English, but if a soldier was confronted by a grenadier, reaction had to be instant or the life of the soldier and innocent bystanders could be jeopardised. If the terrorist grenadier pulled the pin on a British-made grenade he had four seconds before ignition, but if it was a Chinese or Soviet weapon it would explode in half that time. Sometimes it was the grenadier's own instincts that sealed his fate:

> In Aden, the terrorists had money from their various protection rackets and they paid local Arabs, what must have been a pittance, to

throw grenades at British Army patrols. There was one instance when one of these bomb throwers appeared out of an alley and, taking a grenade from under his *futah*, pulled the pin. He raised his arm to throw the weapon, when he was suddenly spotted by the patrol. Instinctively, he quickly stuffed the grenade back under his *futah* pretending nothing was happening. Of course, the thing exploded, blowing him to smithereens. It was callous the way the terrorists would exploit these simple Arabs.[5]

For stop and search operations, the Army had not yet developed the sophisticated checks later seen in Northern Ireland. These involved stopping everyone at checkpoints, stripping all suspects and looking for shoulder bruises from weapon recoil, powder burns on arms and silver linings around the cuffs from firearm propellants. There were also language problems, for few units had enough Arab speakers to spread around. And while a heavy Scots or Geordie accent might be totally unintelligible to the Arab at a checkpoint, the Arab's far from 'Modern Standard' Arabic was unlikely to register with the soldier.[6] Despite these limitations, service in Aden did help many soldiers hone their observation skills, invaluable in street patrolling or urban skirmishing. While there were many distractions in the backstreets and markets of Crater or Sheikh Othman, troops did learn how to look 'into' crowds and scan the bobbing heads and scurrying figures for any sign of the unusual. And when the unusual was spotted, they could respond with 'quick accurate shooting at the fleeing target, from the standing position'.[7] Sometimes the task was made more difficult when witting or unwitting locals, and even children, provided cover for terrorist 'grenadiers'. A report into a grenade attack in the Tawahi district revealed:

> At 2020 hours, on 2 March 1966, Lieutenant ******* was with a party of Royal Marines at the south end of Kuwar Street, dismantling a cordon, when a crowd of children came towards the party, jeering and catcalling. He saw a grenade (Mills 36 Type) bowled at the Marines from behind the children. It came to rest about 6 ft away. The Lieutenant gave a warning and took cover as the grenade exploded, wounding three Marines. Just after, he ran towards the crowd from which the grenade was thrown, and saw a man aged about 20, run from behind the crowd. He fired one shot at the man with his 9mm Browning pistol.[8]

A man was later found dead near the scene with a bullet wound to the head. The Marine's training had paid off and the dead man was later identified as a known terrorist.

After the Aden Special Branch was seriously weakened by the NLF assassination campaign, the job of identifying and detecting individual terrorists fell increasingly on the Aden Intelligence Centre. Enemy networks still had to be penetrated and agents placed within the NLF and FLOSY organisations. It was also vital to discover the enemy techniques and operational plans, so a buttress had to be given to the ailing police Special Branch. This support was to be found among the 'recce' platoons of army Companies, who were swiftly converted into army 'Special Branch' units. Lance Corporal Terry Cheek, serving with the 1st Battalion Somerset and Cornwall Light Infantry, recalled his service with such a formation:

> We came out to Aden in April 1966, straight from exercises in Norway, so it took some time to acclimatise. Our 'recce' platoon had already received some basic training before we came out – unarmed combat and pistol shooting – but the best training for Special Branch work was being out there in Aden, in the back streets. We used to paint our Army Landrovers in gaudy colours and hang all sorts of baubles and streamers from them to make them just like the local Arab vehicles. We were in plain scruffy clothes for most operations, and only wore uniform for proper search and cordon operations. We had the choice of a 9mm Browning or a Sterling Machine-Gun, which was popular as the butt could fold-up, making it like a long-nosed pistol, and it had a larger magazine but it wasn't very accurate.[9] Nor did the SMG have much stopping power. One of our men shot a grenadier running away and, at a range of 50 yards, dropped him with a burst from his SMG. But of the four rounds that hit the terrorist, three merely flattened against his body. Only the fourth did the business.
>
> When we had a tip-off from an informer about an arms cache, it was usually to be found in Sheikh Othman under the floor of a 'kutchi' hut, which were hovels made from old packing crates. The informer would arrive wearing a long black robe with a huge hood to disguise him from the locals and was usually accompanied by a police SB officer. In about 50% of the cases, we found what we were looking for – grenades, small arms and ammunition.[10]

As a result of these combined army and police Special Branch swoops on cinemas, offices, cafes or clubs, arrests could sometimes be made. Corporal Charles Russell, of 1st Battalion The Queens Dragoon Guards describes a typical operation:

> The 'op' was arranged between the Military Intelligence Officer at 24 Brigade and SB officers. We were ordered to report to the guardroom at Falaise Camp where we were collected in a civilian van, taken to

the site to be searched to meet up with a uniformed member of the Arab Police Force. I was involved in two separate night searches at the BP social club in Little Aden. We were briefed in the van at 9.30pm, before entering the Refinery. We were all armed with Sterling Machine-Guns (SMGs) and wearing plain clothes, so that the SB officer wouldn't stand out. There were about six or seven of us, plus the SB man and the Arab constable. Two men guarded the rear exit while we went in through the main doors, collected all the Arab occupants and body-searched them for weapons. They stayed put while we searched cupboards, under furniture and the wood panelling and floorboards to see if it was disturbed to hide explosives. The civilian policeman was there if any arrests had to be made.

Other daylight searches were in a back street area of Tawahi, a shantytown area backing into Crater, just off the Ma'alla Straight leading down to Steamer Point. We had 'mug shot' type photographs of wanted terrorists and basically just walked through the area looking out for notables and hoping to stir up a reaction. When I look back on these ventures they seem amateurish, but I suppose SB knew what was wanted, though dressing in civvies did cause problems. One of our men, Lance-Corporal Ahmed Thomas had Arab parents and looked like a local. A military checkpoint soldier at the end of the street leading into Tawahi saw Lance-Corporal Thomas, thought he was an Arab terrorist with a weapon in a known hard area, and cocked his rifle, ready to shoot. This soldier obviously hadn't been warned that we were in the area. We shouted and luckily the soldier stopped just in time.[11]

Once the NLF had crippled the police Special Branch they moved against the remaining methods of intelligence gathering – the Interrogation Centre at Fort Morbut and the Detention Centre at al-Mansoura. As both centres were heavily defended, physical attacks were ruled out in favour of propaganda and subversion tactics. This was allied with a policy of intimidation against the local police, who by 1966 realised that after independence they would have to account for their actions to their new masters.[12] Such was the climate in which allegations of torture against British soldiers began to proliferate.

Combined parties of troops and Special Branch officers carried out the arrest of suspects. A house would be encircled in the early morning hours, when the suspects were sleeping. Troops would then break down the main door or a window, charge in and the SB officers would swiftly arrest the suspect, while others searched the house for weapons or incriminating documents. The suspect was then taken straight to Fort Morbut, described by David Ledger as:

A narrow two-storey building situated within an army cantonment perched high upon the cliffs overlooking the harbour entrance. It commanded one of the most beautiful views in Aden. Originally it had been the headquarters of the Military Special Investigation Branch but was now surrounded by barbed wire. The upper floor was used for interrogation and offices, the lower contained six cells.[13]

Under the Aden Emergency Regulations of 5 June 1965, the High Commissioner could authorise the detention of suspected terrorists. A man could be held in the Interrogation Centre at Fort Morbut for seven days without warrant and for a further twenty-one days, under a 'holding order', if a senior officer considered it necessary in order to obtain the necessary evidence. This soon became the norm and even after this, the suspect could be held for a further period under a 'detention order' and incarcerated at the al-Mansoura Detention Centre. While this further detention might be requested because evidence was not forthcoming from frightened or hostile witnesses, there was another more advantageous reason why suspects were held for long periods. For the institution of proceedings would cut short valuable time, during which interrogators could glean information from suspects about the NLF's revolutionary cell structure. This organisation was notoriously difficult to break into, and attempts to put in undercover agents often failed due to their cover being exposed by nationalist sympathisers within the local police, including those in command. On 23 June 1966 29-year-old Hussein Jawee was arrested and detained as a suspected terrorist sympathiser. He was the Chief of Police in Crater.[14]

Allegations of mistreatment were made against the security forces, with nationalists and trade unionists taking their claims to the United Nations and Amnesty International. The British Government, alarmed at the bad press it was receiving, despatched Roderic Bowen QC to Aden. Bowen, who had recently lost his Liberal seat in the 1966 General Election, arrived in October 1966 to investigate procedures (but not allegations against individuals) at Fort Morbut, where thirteen men were in custody and at al-Mansoura where there were 110 detainees. At both centres virtually all the staff were from the Armed Forces and therefore came under military law, a practice he recommended should be changed to the employment of civilian interrogators. This would create problems, as Fort Morbut had come to increasingly rely on the interrogators from the Counter Intelligence Company of the Army Intelligence Corps. However, although Bowen found some irregularities in the medical records between Fort Morbut and al-Mansoura, he ultimately found little foundation for the accusations of cruelty.[15]

Bowen's findings did little to placate the growing anger of organisations like Amnesty International. Their Swedish delegate, Dr Rastgeldi, held meetings in Cairo before proceeding to Aden, where he pursued the case of Abdul Khalifa, a member of Mackawee's Aden government.[16]. Rastgeldi then stopped off at Cairo on the way back, which compromised his position of impartiality. However, it was not long before the British Press picked up the Khalifa campaign, with the *Daily Mail* accusing Brigadier Tony Cowper, the first Director of Intelligence of 'refusing to aid the torture enquiries'.[17] Although the two centres had come under his control, Cowper had left the post in late 1966, and had subsequently taken up the position of Defence Advisor in Malaysia. In such a sensitive post, it is questionable whether Cowper could be expected to enter a public debate on allegations made by individual detainees.

Peter Bennenson, a British barrister and President of Amnesty International, further stoked the controversy by claiming that his offices were broken into, and Aden files were stolen. He followed this up with an investigative trip to Aden where he made a number of allegations about individual breaches of detention procedures – breaches which Sir Richard Turnbull categorically denied.[18] He further lobbied the Premier, Harold Wilson and aired his grievances on BBC television, using the '24 Hours' programme on 18 November 1966 to attack British detention and interrogation techniques. A transcript of the programme reported that Bennenson named three interrogators, whom detainees accused of using torture to extract confessions.[19]

Further accusations of torture, which inflamed British troops attempting to keep order against orchestrated civil rioting, came from surprising sources. Corporal G Lennox, a clerk in the Royal Army Ordnance Corps claimed in a letter to *The Sunday Times* that while on guard duty at Fort Morbut, he heard and witnessed 'screams of pain and the howling of the detainees' during the night when interrogations took place. He further alleged that following the brutal killing of an RAF serviceman behind Ma'alla Straight, Special Branch officers brought suspects into Fort Morbut and he witnessed one suspect being severely beaten.[20]

This incident probably relates to the aftermath of the murder of Sergeant Hatton, RAF, who, while shopping off-duty, had been approached from behind by his assassin who pressed a 9mm pistol to his neck before calmly pulling the trigger. As was the norm, all witnesses suddenly vanished but Special Branch knew it was the hallmark of a local terrorist who had recently assassinated a West German businessman and two policemen.[21] The suspect was duly apprehended but his captors knew full well that because of intimidation, no witnesses would ever come forward and there could be no trial. Ill-treatment of suspects was unacceptable but no doubt frustration at the lack of official retribution did affect the judgement of some guards.

Torture is an extremely emotive issue, and there were attempts by the nationalist press to compare the Aden allegations with the systematic torture that was carried out by French forces during the Battle of Algiers.[22] Even al-Asnag was initially muted in his support for the torture allegations, but after receiving some reported telephone death threats from the nationalist camp, he soon strengthened his language. Through his membership of the 'Prisoners' Review Tribunal', al-Asnag then joined in the condemnation of the predominantly British Army interrogators. However, doctors from the Royal Army Medical Corps who regularly attended both Fort Morbut and the al-Mansoura Detention Centre strenuously denied the allegations. Furthermore, the Aden branch of Red Cross International, who constantly monitored detainees, found some inconsistencies but no material evidence of systematic brutality.[23]

It was usually the more subtle interrogation methods which produced results but even these had their limitations, as Brigadier Charles Dunbar realised:

> It is of course a pretty poor substitute for intelligence agents because it [interrogation] is most expensive in troops and is short term. When an Arab is picked up with a grenade or a pistol, the majority will sell their mothers down the river at once. You may be lucky and from the interrogation pick up three or four others. It may run on from these but the scent soon goes stale. Warnings have gone round and the affair dries up.[24]

Relations between the Adeni locals and the Army were often strained and made worse by occasions of off-duty violence. On 17 September 1966 Guardsman Gabriel murdered a local taxi driver after a drunken spree and found himself facing the death penalty. However, as he was off-duty, he was therefore subject to civil law, and the Aden Penal Ordinance was based on the Indian Penal Code, with marked differences to British rules. After much legal wrangling and a desire to remove the case from the spotlight, Gabriel was spirited to Britain but according to Arab news-papers, not before he had tarnished the image of British servicemen.[25]

Out on the streets in Crater, army patrols faced a problem that became familiar during later operations in Northern Ireland – soldiers were expected to react immediately and correctly to incidents on the street, which were not all they seemed. While it was proper that they or their officers should be responsible for their actions, sometimes the troops' view or position gave them a different interpretation of the events. Newsreels or photographs might show evidence of riots or street contact but they could not convey the tension, fear and sheer electricity in the air that riots produce. A further ingredient of this heady mixture was the instability of the police, whom the troops knew to be disloyal, if not actively working with the enemy. In this atmosphere, the police were rarely given credit for their actions. One example involved a patrol passing through a street cordon in July 1966. Suddenly there was a loud explosion. Royal Marines on the other side of the cordon saw a car accelerate furiously away from the area of the explosion and they shouted at the driver in English and Arabic to stop. The vehicle continued on its way and one Marine fired a round from his SLR rifle while another fired a short burst from his Sterling machine-gun. The car swerved across the road and hit a wall outside the police station. Immediately, a policeman rushed out and shouted into the car. The driver got out and climbed into the back seat, while the policeman got into the car and drove it off at high speed. What had seemed like an escape vehicle for the grenadier, provided by the police, was in fact a car on a family outing, including a pregnant woman. The driver, who was near the explosion, had panicked and driven off to get out of the way, and when the policeman intervened, it was not to help a terrorist escape but to relieve the wounded driver and take the car's wounded occupants to hospital.[26]

One of the most common targets for terrorist grenadiers were military Landrovers, though the vehicle occupants were often spared by inaccurate bomb-throwing, with one witness observing, 'we just managed to miss another grenade in the Ma'alla Straight – as usual it missed the patrol jeep and flew into a group of Somalis and Arabs, killing one and wounding two others'.[27] Another familiar army vehicle on the streets of Sheikh Othman and Crater was the 3-Ton armoured 'Pig'. This was a creation utilising a normal Bedford chassis with a long armoured compartment forming the troop carrier. The armoured section, which could carry up to twenty soldiers, had side slits, side doors and two main doors to the rear but because of the composite weight it failed to boast floor protection. However, a bulletproof glass visor shielded the driver and he could swiftly deposit a section of troops straight into a trouble spot or could equally well evacuate casualties.

A succession of armoured regiments had seen service in South Arabia during the early years of the insurgency. The 10th Royal Hussars, 16th/5th Queen's Royal Lancers, 5th Royal Inniskilling Dragoon Guards, and 4th Royal Tank Regiment had all played their part in internal security operations. During 1965/66 the armoured reconnaissance role was taken over by the 4th/7th Royal Dragoon Guards, while the 1st Royal Tank Regiment provided a strategic reserve.[28] In September 1966 the 4th/7th were replaced by the 1st The Queen's Dragoon Guards (1 QDG), with its squadrons rotating every three months between Aden State and up-country. The regiment, known as the 'First and Foremost', deployed mainly with the Alvis Saladin Armoured Car, which had a crew of three and was equipped with a 76mm medium gun as well as a Browning machine-gun. There was also a QDG Air Squadron, which was based at Falaise Airfield in Little Aden.[29]

Another important reconnaissance vehicle was the Ferret Mark II Scout

189

Car. Crewed by a driver and a Commander, who also manned the 042 radio and the .300 Browning machine-gun, it proved to be a tough and manoeuvrable vehicle for both patrolling 'up-country' and urban street-fighting. In fact, they were so hardy that when they were hit by an out of control terrorist's car, the car would ride halfway up the front of the hull and barely scratch the armour. The terrorist's vehicle would be a complete write-off.[30] When an infantry section needed to be brought in quickly to quell a street riot, the Saracen Armoured Personnel Carrier (APC) was employed. This vehicle, which had a crew of two, could carry ten infantrymen who could dismount from two doors at the rear, and was protected by a Browning .30 machine-gun. It enabled troops to be protected as long as possible from small arms fire, grenades and mortar splinters, while at the same time carrying their supplies and providing reliable communications. But there were disadvantages with the APC, including the vulnerability of whole sections of infantry inside to enemy anti-tank weapons. And in riots in Crater and Sheikh Othman, there were occasions when the infantry section dismounted from the closed environment of the APC and tumbled, disoriented, right into the middle of a storm of rocks and sniper fire. Despite the drawbacks, the crews of these armoured vehicles handled them with much skill, even though, in South Arabia the operating temperature inside was often in excess of 100°.[31]

1 QDG often operated in their Ferret Scout cars with the external bins removed, so any explosion under the vehicle would be deflected upwards and outwards, away from the crew. Sandbags padded out the area below the crew compartment and offered additional protection, which was often called for, as one of their main roles was supporting foot patrols around Sheikh Othman. These patrols usually comprised men from the 1st Battalion, The Cameronians (Scottish Rifles) and 3 Royal Anglian Regiment.[32] But, as Corporal Charles Russell of 1 QDG discovered, it was sometimes difficult to identify who the enemy was:

> The practice of patrolling in Sheikh Othman was done on a round the clock basis at no particular pattern or route. During one patrol, one of the foot soldiers spotted an Arab squatting in a doorway, who hadn't been there on a previous look around this area. The soldier went up to this Arab, who had his headgear covering most of his face. The soldier was about to question this Arab, as was the usual practice, when the Arab said in a very obvious Midlands' accent, 'Fuck off'. A member of Hereford's finest had been found – the SAS on an undercover operation. Which was rather silly because no one had informed us that the SAS were operating in that area that night.[33]

The SAS were in the process of perfecting their street-fighting skills in an attempt to lure terrorists out of the shadows. Their operations in Sheikh

Othman and Crater were similar to the old 'Q' Squads in Palestine and were carried out by no more than twenty men. The swarthy and hook-nosed members of 'The Regiment' were recruited, along with Fijian volunteers, for their similarity to Arab locals. Dressing in Arab clothes they would dissolve into the streets and alleys of Aden. In ones or twos, they would stake-out known terrorist haunts and attempt to eliminate enemy grenadiers or known assassins, sometimes using the bait of army patrols or other SAS men in civilian clothes. By 1966 they were based in Ballycastle House, a block of flats in the Khormaksar complex where they received additional training in close-quarter combat. However, the success of these 'Keeni-Meeni'[34] operations was compromised by their wide territorial scope and the fact that they were rarely dovetailed with the special operations of regular army units. There were a number of stories that circulated concerning 'friendly-fire', and on 25 October 1966 the Arabic daily paper, *al-Ahram*, reported that the previous night two groups of British soldiers in Sheikh Othman had fired on each other, killing one soldier and wounding another. It was apparent that they were on special operations as the casualties were in civilian clothes.[35]

Undercover operations continued in the back streets of Crater and Sheikh Othman but problems continued over communication between army Special Branch units and regular foot patrols. Lance Corporal Terry Cheek, as part of the 1st Battalion Somerset and Cornwall Light Infantry's SB unit feared the approach of other army patrols:

> The trouble was that we usually operated in two-man teams and we had no radio to warn approaching patrols that we were in a house or a side alley. Some of the army units, and the Paras in particular, were tough customers and if they found you with a weapon on you, they didn't check first to find out who you were. So we got used to quickly hiding our weapons if we heard them approaching. We were not completely isolated because there was usually a '3-Tonner' with a support platoon in the area to back us up, but as we were not in radio contact, they usually only responded if they heard rifle shots or an explosion.

The Cameronians had started their recent tour of Aden in April 1966 but they had bitter memories of a previous tour in 1958. Then, one of their companies was ambushed near Dhala with the loss of six soldiers killed and seventeen wounded.[36] This tour involved Internal Security (IS) duties in the western part of Aden town including patrols, manning checkpoints and searching for weapons caches as well as stints up-country in the Radfan. Routine 'cordon and search' operations by the Cameronians, under their CO, Lieutenant-Colonel David Riddell-Webster, yielded a steady flow of enemy weapons and ammunition. In operation 'Purple

Heart' men from 'A' and 'D' Companies set out to trap an enemy grenadier who was operating near the passenger jetty in the Tawahi docks area. After a cordon and search, Rifleman McIntosh uncovered four unprimed No. 36 grenades from a pile of rubbish under the outside stairs of a house. The grenades were removed and the rubbish replaced while the soldiers moved back to a hidden OP post and waited for their man to appear. After a long wait, an Arab appeared in a white shirt and garish pink trousers, walked casually up to the rubbish, looked around and bent down to rummage through it. He was immediately arrested and protested his innocence, but he was found to have placed four grenade-igniter sets in the rubbish, and subsequent checks revealed him to be an NLF member. Such events made it clear that most grenade incidents required more than one terrorist and usually the services of a terrorist quartermaster, courier and any number of available grenadiers.[37]

Good patrolling, whether in Aden or up-country, required efficient signalling and the infantry were well served by the Royal Signals. The Aden Signal Squadron, originally formed in 1959, was integrated with 254 and 255 (Bahrain) Signal Squadrons and 603 Signal Troop to create 15 Signal Regiment in January 1965. The unit had a wide brief, for apart from the provision of operators and linemen to all parts of the Federation it provided communications for Aden Brigade as well as a radio/cipher detachment in Mukalla.[38] In the Radfan it was found that the high frequency wireless sets did not function adequately and the system had to be altered to Very High Frequency (VHF). This problem also bedevilled operations in Aden, where the high ridges around Jebel Shamsan played havoc with reception. However, the close proximity of Observation Posts (OPs) to patrols, at least in urban situations, meant that the A41 wireless set could be widely used and reception problems could be countered by fitting two radio antennae, at different angles to the OP sets. Every soldier in a Company was trained to use the A41 and most Companies had up to twenty sets for use between OPs, vehicles and foot patrols.

Good communications were vital to the role of OPs. When foot patrols, or in times of increasing tension, Landrover 'mobile' patrols were sent into riot situations, the two units worked in tandem. Spotters in the OP, using high-powered binoculars, could often identify a ringleader inciting a mob from 1,000 yards away. They would then radio down to the patrol giving a description such as, 'man in yellow head scarf, red shirt, grey trousers, wrist watch on right hand, now sitting in doorway on your right. Arrest!' The suspect would then be swiftly hauled out of the crowd. Often a terrorist could be spotted firing a shot or throwing a grenade and he could be arrested with the same technique, though the elation of the spotter, having engineered a good arrest, was soon dampened by the hard slog down from the OP to sign a witness statement at the prisoner cage.[39]

While British troops had no respect for their terrorist opponents in the sordid back-street conflict in Aden, in Radfan there was an acceptance that the rebel tribesmen were a brave and resilient enemy. Lieutenant Shaun Lambe, a horse gunner, certainly found the 'Red Wolves' were worthy adversaries:

> All attacks are similar in form. Small arms and Blindicides are the favourite weapons. A Blindicide is very like a rocket launcher though the projectile is nothing like as lethal. Occasionally mortars are used. The enemy is tough and very brave. If his intention is to attack a camp and fire ten Blindicides at it, nothing short of death will deter him. If he is killed during it then Allah has willed it. He has great endurance and will travel many miles to attack a camp and return home carrying his dead and wounded.[40]

The Blindicide RL-83 was a Belgian designed rocket launcher that found favour in the world arms market. They were simple weapons, incorporating a one-piece barrel, with an extended length of 1.7m and a bore of 3¼ inches, with a percussion firing mechanism that loosed off a motorised rocket. A 4 inch model was available but larger rockets meant heavier rocket motors, and as the object was to conceal the weapon until the last minute, the smaller bore was more manageable for terrorists. Although it had to be fired and operated by a crew of two, another advantage of the shoulder-held Blindicide was its quick reload time and its ability to be folded in half for transportation. It became a deadly weapon against either fortifications or vehicles and could penetrate 12 inches of armour or 3 ft of concrete.[41] A typical rocket assault occurred during the night of 28 April 1966, when a section from B Battery 1 RHA, sited at Monks Field Camp, Radfan came under attack. An enemy rocket hit the side of a sangar just as the 105mm gun was firing. The gun slewed and the 105mm round hit the edge of the sangar and exploded, killing Sergeant Dunkley and Gunners Hughes and Bartley, as well as seriously wounding two others. The desperate situation was relieved by the bravery of the gunners, including Sergeant Gall who 'rallied the detachments, put out an ammunition fire and kept one gun firing while the position was swept by enemy fire'.[42] The NLF favoured such night-time operations in the mountains and as Lieutenant Lambe describes, they served to disorientate British soldiers on the receiving end:

> Crash! The ear splitting noise of the explosion blasted sleep away and galvanised the waking men. Scrambling from their beds, they grabbed at clothes and stumbled out into the night. Time to notice the hammering of the .5 Browning thirty yards to the left, spewing out a stream of tracer from the camp. Much more impressive than the pock ... pock ... pock from the distance. But those bullets are coming this way.

Halfway to the guns, and out of the corner of one eye, a flash, crash and a column of dust and sand. Pounding legs, and twenty yards across to the gun position seems like twenty miles. I reach the gun pit and the safety of the sangar wall. Must calm down. The noise is terrific and there's a lot of stuff flying around but everyone reaches their posts. Inside the sandbagged command post the radio and tannoys are switched on. 'Test tannoys'. 'Section Commander relay all orders to 2'. Emergency lighting on, target record book open, we're ready.

The din is awful; I hope they're not using mortars. Too insulated in the command post. A quick look outside. A hissing projectile lands behind the gun position as the Browning and our Bren fire bursts of tracer that splashes together about seven hundred yards out. 'Sir,' calls a voice from the command post, 'Fire Mission'. By the time I reach the tannoy the signaller is checking back. 'Papa Four, at my command, three rounds for effect.' Airburst is at nine hundred yards dead in front of the guns. That'll shake them. With the first rounds away everyone feels better.

Unbelievably, the attack is barely five minutes old. A quick glance – the Surveyor, Bombadier X, naked at the start of the attack, is now wrapped up in the battery flag. Gunner Y, brand new and paler than most, looks like a potential signaller. Our infantry's mortars are inconveniently sited about thirty yards behind the command post and are making a considerable contribution to the clamour. One of our cooks appears and complains that he's run out of ammo for his 3½ inch rocket launcher. He qualifies by about three inches as the most front-line soldier in Radfan.

Another explosion outside No. 1 gun pit. A Sergeant appears in the command post, his pyjama trousers splashed with blood, dark coloured in the dim light. 'They're hurt at No. 1 – a Blindicide,' he shouts, as he goes out again. I follow him out. Near No. 1 sangar, an apparition stumbles into my torchlight. Blood upsets most people and I'm no exception. From head to toe, he's covered in blood and although he's one of my men, he's unrecognisable. They never teach you at first aid lectures how difficult it is to lift and carry a naked man, slippery with blood. Eventually, he's taken into the stores and sheets are ripped up. His moans are heartrending. Where the hell's the medic?

Dust and smoke and the stinking smell of cordite hangs over No. 1 sangar. The section commander cannons into me, shouting 'I can't find Sergeant Z or Gunner Y'. Search the position. Must call a roll. A yell from the command post and another fire mission requested. The Number One in 2 sangar is still in action but Gunner Y is wounded and lying across the gun trails. The men haven't moved him in case they hurt him further, but he's a mess, and at first glance, he appears to be past hurting. Call in a 'casevac'. Gently the men lift him out and carry him away. The firing continues. The layers are marvellous. Cool as ice. 'Ready ... Fire.' The rounds burst on target, a low hill, eight hundred and fifty yards away. Our friends the infantry cut loose with a medium machine-gun and spray the area to discourage further enemy action.

The chopper comes and goes with our covering fire. Big sighs of relief from everyone. It's over. We walk slowly back. The cooks have got a brew on. Everyone is dog-tired but sleep won't come tonight – we're too sad. The body, wrapped in a brown hairy blanket with an ID disc pinned to it, was one of us.[43]

Radio Cairo, in its efforts to boost FLOSY, attributed every terrorist incident up-country or in Aden to its protégé group and ignored the NLF. This further confused the British intelligence agencies, which were trying to establish the strengths of the various armed movements. Consequently, FLOSY continued to be overrated while the NLF was barely recognised and had only been proscribed as a terrorist organisation in 1965, when it was already well established.[44]

The NLF had been busy cultivating the non-Federated states of the Eastern Aden Protectorate. Qu'aiti, Kathiri and Mahra had all refused to join the union, for not only did they consider themselves culturally and geographically separate from the old WAP states, but the prospect of oil in their territories, combined with their tracts of good agricultural land and fish stocks, persuaded them to stay independent. They also failed to be stirred by the Egyptian threat, sensing that events in Yemen would only threaten the nearer states of the Federation. However, the prospect of oil had now receded and the sultans of the EAP were more receptive to British overtures. But unification was still a distant hope and British political officers and military advisors continued their sterling work in these territories. Men like Jim Ellis, Michael Crouch and John Shipman kept open vital communications between the tribes of the EAP and the British High Commission in Aden. Ellis had served on the North-West Frontier with the Baluch Regiment and had been the EAP Military Assistant to the redoubtable Colonel Sir Hugh Boustead. His subsequent, distinguished sixteen-year career in South Arabia included service with the HBL and ended with his appointment as the last Resident Adviser in the EAP.[45]

Although the level of terrorist activity in the EAP never reached that of the Federation, there were sporadic grenade attacks in Mukalla, the capital of Qu'aiti and the home of the Resident Advisor. There were also a number of attacks on British officers. In June 1965 Major David Eales, second-in-command of the HBL, was murdered by one of his own men, and on 28 July 1966 the League's CO, Lieutenant-Colonel Pat Gray, was killed by his own sentry outside his home in Mukalla. Gray's wife, Edith, was seriously wounded in the attack and had to be 'casevac'd' to Britain, while the FLOSY leader, al-Asnag, voiced his approval of the deed on Radio Cairo.[46] But despite some successful operations by the HBL against the NLF, notably on the island of Socotra, the terrorists established a firm base in the EAP. In their stronghold of the Hadhramaut, Ali al-Beedh and his NLF cadres pursued a more radical line than their leadership and during 1966/7 even attempted to promote land reform in tribal areas. Support also surged for the NLF in the region after rumours that the Hadhramaut was about to be annexed to Saudi Arabia with the connivance of Britain.[47]

The EAP was strategically important to Britain, because its eastern state, Mahra, bordered Oman, where, despite the successful defeat of a rebellion in 1959, a new Egyptian-backed terrorist movement had emerged in 1962. The Dhofar Liberation Front (DLF) was becoming increasingly strident and an attempt was made in April 1966 to assassinate the ruler, Sultan Said.[48] The DLF had been allied to the NLF since 1965 and had the use of the two coastal NLF strongholds in Mahra, at Qishn and Hauf. A DLF training camp was in operation in the border village of Hauf and in October 1966 a British assault was planned to break it up and capture the guerrillas.[49] The recently commissioned HMS *Fearless*, an Assault Landing Ship which later played an important part in the Falklands War, was brought in to transport the 1st Battalion Irish Guards together with an SAS party and a unit from Four Five Commando. On 25 October HMS *Fearless* stopped some way off the coast of Mahra, 'opened her stern, took in nine feet of sea water, and the landing craft swept out of the ship'.[50] The SAS went in ahead and took twenty-two prisoners, while the Irish Guards, supported by Wessex helicopters, carried out a successful 'textbook' cordon and search operation.

While these attempts to contain the insurgency were underway in the east, to the north, in Yemen, British agents were still monitoring and 'advising' the royalist forces. Wilfred Thesiger, in the words of Johnny Cooper, 'a most peculiar Major', returned to Yemen in 1966 through contacts of Billy McLean. Although Thesiger had served in the wartime SAS, his mission into a country wracked by civil war was something of a mystery. Clothed in Arab dress, he was nominally attached to the forces of Imam al-Badr's cousin, Prince Hassan. But he ended up roaming the interior, monitoring destruction caused by indiscriminate republican bombing or, on one occasion, observing the 'bloody remains of an entire Egyptian column wiped out by the royalists'. However, Thesiger's commitment to the royalists was lukewarm and Major Johnny Cooper, who was still co-ordinating assistance to the Imam's forces, doubted that Thesiger was officially gathering intelligence. Nevertheless, Thesiger's compassion for the Yemeni people resulted in him despatching medical aid wherever he found the casualties of war.[51]

The struggling Yemen republican government also faced internal challenges. In August 1966 President Sallal returned to Yemen from Cairo to find his Prime Minister, al-Amri, in open revolt against him. The Egyptians promptly arrested Sallal's opponents and some were shot by firing squad, among them Hadi Isa who had gained a reputation for 'killing prisoners for fun when drunk'. Sallal continued the purges for the next few months, with show trials and public executions, some ending with the bodies of those shot, left swinging from the city gates of Sana'a.[52] Sallal's tenuous hold on Yemen was concerning his paymaster, Nasser, who realised that the Yemen civil war could drag on for years while the Israeli threat to Egypt was escalating. The border posts between Israel and her Arab neighbours remained on high alert and, according to Israeli Intelligence, Nasser pulled three army brigades out of Yemen during 1966 for home defence.[53]

However, Nasser's enemy, Saudi Arabia, remained convinced that he was still too strong and a threat to the Arabian Peninsula. King Faisal feared Soviet intentions in the region and pointed to their development of Hodeidah Port as evidence of Communist designs on the Red Sea. Britain's 'about-turn' and intended abandonment of South Arabia merely reinforced his fears of isolation.

NOTES

1   Geoff Richards to Author, 17 June 2003.
2   1 PWO 'Sitrep', June 1966, File 2/1, Dunbar Papers, LHCMA.
3   Ibid.
4   Confidential source.
5   Geoff Richards to Author, 17 June 2003.
6   It came as a shock to some of those who learned Modern Standard Arabic to find how different it was from the spoken forms of the Arabic language.
7   Lieutenant-Colonel Blenkinsop, 'Notes on Aden Mutiny 20 June 1967', Records of The Fusiliers Museum of Northumberland, Alnwick, Northumberland (hereafter FMN).
8   'Grenade Attack on RM –Tawahi', ADM 202/569, NA.
9   The L2A3 Sterling came into service with the British Army in 1956. The gun could be fired from the shoulder with the stock extended, or from the hip, with the stock folded under the barrel.
10   Terry Cheek to Author, 30 October 2003. The Somerset and Cornwall Light Infantry were formed in October 1959 through the amalgamation of The Somerset Light Infantry and The Duke of Cornwall's Light Infantry. In July 1968 the regiment was assimilated into The Light Infantry.
11   Lance-Corporal Thomas later became a helicopter pilot for an oil company and was killed in a flying accident in China. Charles Russell to Author, 6 May 2003.

12   'Notes on the Security Situation in Aden', High Commission, 25 January 1967, DEFE 24/252, NA. Also Mockaitis, op. cit., p. 58.

13   David Ledger, op. cit., p. 87. Also Mockaitis, op. cit., p. 60.

14   For detention issues, see 'Alleged Use of Torture in Aden – The Bowen Report', DEFE 13/529, NA. Also Geoff Richards to Author, 17 June 2003. The powers of the High Commissioner originated in the State of Emergency declared on 10 December 1963. For Jawee, see Amnesty Report, 11 November 1966, PREM 13/1294, NA.

15   The medical records of one suspect at Fort Morbut showed no injuries, but on arrival at al-Mansoura he was reported to have 'traumatic perforation of Tympanic membrane'. See Bowen Report, November 1966, DEFE 13/529, NA. Also Memorandum, Private Secretary to Army Minister, 17 November 1966, DEFE 13/529, NA. For Intelligence Company, see Anthony Clayton, *Forearmed: A History of the Intelligence Corps*, Brassey's, 1993, p. 236.

16   Khalifa had been arrested and interrogated in March 1966 as a suspected leading member of the NLF.

17   For Khalifa, see Graduate Congress to Dr Rastgeldi, 2 August 1966, PREM 13/1294, NA and Turnbull to Arabian Department FO, 17 November 1966, DEFE 13/529, NA. For Cowper, see Defence Planning Staff (Army) memo, 2 March 1967, DEFE 24/252, NA.

18   For alleged burglaries, see FO Memorandums, 17 November 1966, DEFE 13/529, NA. For Aden allegations, see Turnbull to Arabian Department, FO, 16 November 1966, DEFE 13/529, NA.

19   Transcript BBC TV, '24 Hours' programme, transmitted 18 November 1966, DEFE 13/529, NA.

20   For Lennox's allegations, see Intelligence Report, 29 October 1966, DEFE 13/529, NA.

21   'Four Five Commando Sitrep', 1966, File 2/1, Dunbar Papers, LHCMA.

22   There have been recent high-level admissions of the systematic application of torture by French forces in Algeria. See Note 12, Alice Hills, 'Hearts or Minds or Search and Destroy? Controlling Civilians in Urban Operations', in *Small Wars & Insurgencies*, Vol. 13, 2002.

23   For al-Asnag, see Intelligence Report, 22 October 1966, DEFE 13/529, NA. For doctors, see correspondence, 'Torture in Aden', December 1966, DEFE 13/529, NA. For individual cases, see 'Memorandum from the Civil Service Association of South Arabia', DEFE 24/252, NA. Michael Crouch, the Assistant Advisor, EAP, reported witnessing some violent action by staff sergeants. See *An Element of Luck*, op. cit., pp. 194–8.

24   Lecture Notes II, 1966, 2/5 Dunbar Papers, LHCMA.

25   However, they still observed the English rules of evidence. Gabriel's sentence was later commuted to ten years imprisonment in the UK. See WO 32/21278, NA.

26   'Report into Crater Incident, 1 July 1966, ADM 202/569, NA.

27   Ann Cuthbert correspondence, 19 May 1965.

28   1 RTR also found themselves increasingly involved in day-to-day IS operations. See George Forty, *The Royal Tank Regiment*, Spellmount, 1989, p. 226.

29   The Regiment was created from the merger of 1 King's Dragoon Guards and Queen's Bays (2nd Dragoon Guards) in 1959. Its nickname was derived from its seniority. See Michael Mann, *The Regimental History of 1st The Queen's Dragoon Guards*, Michael Russell, 1993, pp. 495–501.

30   'Vehicles used in South Arabia', 2/1 Dunbar Papers, LHCMA.

31 Major D Houston, 'Dismounting from APCs', in *RUSI Journal*, March 1969. Also Charles Russell to Author, 6 May 2003.

32 As the junior regiment in the Lowland Brigade, the Cameronians were disbanded in May 1968 after nearly 300 years of unbroken service.

33 Charles Russell to Author, 11 May 2003.

34 So-called after the Swahili phrase for the slithering movement of a snake in long grass. See Newsinger, op. cit., pp. 22–4.

35 File 108, BP Archives, UW.

36 Thomas Chronicle, op. cit., p. 51.

37 *The Covenanter*, Vol. XLV, 1966 and 'The Cameronian Newsletter from Aden', # 4, September 1966, File 2/1, Brigadier Dunbar Papers, LHCMA.

38 Lord and Birtles, op. cit., p. 62.

39 Lieutenant-Colonel P Downward, DSO, DFC, 'An Infantry Battalion in Aden', in *RUSI Journal*, March 1969. Colonel Downward became acting CO Aden Brigade in 1967.

40 Lieutenant S D Lambe, 'Night Action', Brigadier Baines Papers.

41 Norris, op. cit., pp. 22–3. In the later period of the insurgency, terrorists used the RCL-83, a shorter barrel and longer-range version of the RL-83.

42 Sergeant Gall was awarded the Queen's Commendation for Brave Conduct. Brigadier Baines, 'Gunners in South Arabia', Baines Papers.

43 Lieutenant S Lambe, op. cit. The account is a realistic, dramatic reconstruction of an RHA engagement.

44 Transcript of Cairo Radio, 'Voice of the Arabs', 18 May 1967, FCO 8/252, NA.

45 Lackner, op. cit., pp. 45–7.

46 'Colonel and Mrs Gray case', FO 371/185309, NA. Also Crouch, op. cit., pp. 186–7 and Little, *South Arabia*, op. cit., p. 155.

47 Pridham, op. cit., p. 59. Also Lord and Birtles op. cit., p. 44.

48 In 1970 Sultan Said was toppled by his son Qabous in a British-backed coup. For an account of the Dhofar War, see Major-General Tony Jeapes, *SAS: Secret War*, HarperCollins, 1996.

49 'Confidential Report. Situation in EAP', Aden 30 October 1967, FCO 8/252, NA.

50 HMS *Fearless* was the major ship in the Amphibious Group during the Falklands War. For the Hauf operation, see Crouch, op. cit., pp.190–1.

51 Michael Asher, *Thesiger: A Biography*, Viking, 1994, pp. 474–9.

52 Dresch, op. cit., p. 105. Also Little, *South Arabia*, op. cit., p. 156.

53 Ian Black and Benny Morris, *Israel's Secret Wars*, Warner Books, 1992, p. 217.

CHAPTER X
Front Page

Journalists from many countries were attracted to the danger and intrigue surrounding the civil war in Yemen. The Luxembourg documentary film-maker, Gordian Troeller, arrived at the start of the revolution together with his journalist girlfriend, Marie Claude Deffarge. The pair had already carved out a controversial partnership, writing for *Stern* and attacking French conduct in the recent Algerian War. In Yemen their coverage was no less controversial, and while Troeller took movie film and photo stills, Deffarge interviewed fighters and non-combatants. Their questions to the Yemenis were uncompromising but surprisingly they suspended cynicism when they came across Billy McLean near Marib, describing him politely as a 'journalist'.[1] However, there were others such as Dana Adams Schmidt, the *New York Times* Middle East correspondent, Joe Morris of *Newsweek*, and Richard Beeston of *The Daily Telegraph* who made regular *bona fide* press missions to Yemen, braving not only the cross-fire in battles but also the suspicions of their host country that they might be passing information to the intelligence services. Journalists, after all, act in much the same way as intelligence officers – both enter foreign countries and 'dig around' in the community in order to establish contacts.

Beeston was one of the most experienced South Arabian hands, having first visited Aden in 1957 to cover the unrest near Dhala. He had witnessed the sight of Randolph Churchill, the *Evening Standard* correspondent, in the bar of Aden's Crescent Hotel, 'looking older than his father' and bellowing about the American policy on Yemen. The incident was not enough to deter Beeston and he returned to South Arabia on many occasions, later reporting on the Egyptian use of poison gas.[2] Anthony Verrier came out to write an article for *The Economist* in 1965 as the journal's coverage of South Arabia had diminished since the departure of its old contributor, Kim Philby. The redoubtable Verrier stayed with Michael Crouch, the Assistant Advisor in the EAP, who was reminded by his guest that in his opinion, the former C-in-C, General Harington had spent too much time 'building roads in the Radfan and not enough time fighting rebels'.[3]

The allegations of torture and rough handling of terrorist suspects made good copy for newspapers. If terrorist incidents could be witnessed by a camera or described by a journalist in a national newspaper, they received what later became known as the 'oxygen of publicity' as the broadcast value of the attack far outstripped the military gain. Every report in a newspaper or magazine was investigated by the Foreign Office and if found to be untrue, strenuously rebutted. Usually this involved explaining to the newspaper the full circumstances behind an incident, but restraints on a paper's 'column inches' rarely allowed this rebuttal to be printed. Even if it was, the reader would usually only remember the impact of the original story.[4]

The Observer carried an article in January 1967 concerning an affidavit sworn by Mohamed Shamshir, a detainee at al-Mansoura who alleged rough treatment by prison guards. The allegation appeared to be innocuous and included the detainee 'being pushed' by a prison guard. However, as a later investigation discovered, the detainee was a well-known terrorist quartermaster who was guarded by soldiers from a Company, which the day before had been subject to a grenade attack in Crater. The unit had lost one man killed and nine others wounded in the incident.[5]

During the Aden Insurgency, the MOD conceded that the press had not been handled well during and after the Radfan Campaign. At a meeting held at the MOD on 28 September 1964 it was decided that journalists had been allowed too much access to military areas and that free transport should no longer be available to them.[6] According to an MOD official, this largely unfettered access was allowed despite the objections of the High Commissioner, Sir Kennedy Trevaskis:

> The High Commissioner is not well disposed to the press. Indeed he told me in Aden that he thought Mr Ashworth went too far towards satisfying the Army's desire for publicity for their operations and that it would be better if all correspondents were confined to Aden and were not encouraged to roam around the area of the fighting.[7]

Clare Hollingworth, the Defence Correspondent for *The Guardian*, conceded that access was all too easy for the press and they took full advantage of it. For a journalist could spend a few nights in 'colourful discomfort' up in the Radfan before returning to the comparative luxury of the Crescent Hotel in Aden. Or he could just hop onto an available helicopter and travel on a day-trip to the combat area.[8] There was also the problem that HMG was promoting the independence of the Federation, but when any journalist arrived in Aden, 'he was taken in tow by a British public relations officer' rather than an Arab from the 'independent' Federation. It was clear that the Information Advisor took pains to declare himself as 'a Federal Government spokesman' but the Foreign Office conceded that 'this deceives no one'.[9]

There were memorable images of the war in South Arabia. It was the early era of photo-journalism and magazines such as *Paris Match* and *Life* carried striking war photographs from the world's trouble spots. Photographer Terence Spencer, who had already covered the wars in East Africa, the Belgian Congo and Cyprus, was sent by *Life* to capture images of the 1964 Radfan Campaign. Together with correspondent, Jordan Bonfante, Spencer went right into the heart of the battle for the mountain region and risked his life to photograph the Paras in fierce firefights. After all, raising a camera to shoot a picture looked to the enemy like someone raising a weapon. Cameramen were also more vulnerable because their view was restricted and many admitted that they took more risks because when looking through a viewfinder 'you almost felt you were watching a film rather than being in danger'. Bonfante was nonetheless awed by what he saw, recording how the Paras 'wearing red berets and puttees, rose with fixed bayonets and charged straight into a guerrilla-held village'.[10]

Middle East Command had an ambivalent attitude towards the press with the result that there was no clear policy on access. Journalists found they could get into the middle of cordon and search operations or riot situations inside Crater, which proved unpopular with many in the security forces.[11] Soldiers felt pressmen were often obtrusive during an operation and when situations became overheated, soldiers had to show the utmost restraint in front of the cameras, one complaining 'you felt like you were on the bloody stage'. There was also concern that rioters would play up to the newsmen, yet the photojournalist, Terry Fincher, recalled that he seemed to be allowed access to any flashpoint in Crater and his photographs certainly portray the tension and electricity of riots – images that later proliferated in Northern Ireland. Fincher was also on hand to record the cost of Britain's war in South Arabia, with emotive pictures of military funerals at Silent Valley Cemetery.

The celebrated war photographer, Don McCullin, bought his first twin reflex camera in Aden, when he visited the town during his earlier service with the RAF. In 1967 he returned with the journalist, John de St Jorre, to record the last months of British control. The pair travelled throughout the collapsing Federation interviewing and photographing sheikhs, tribesmen, nationalists and soldiers. They highlighted the 'personal interest' stories, accounts that Cairo and Sana'a had used so skilfully in their propaganda war. Stories like that of Nadia, a local Adeni girl who was faced with the amputation of her leg. Her family knew Abdul al-Asnag, who was then in exile in Cairo and who arranged with Nasser for her to be treated by the best Egyptian doctors. They saved her leg and Nadia was able to dance again. As the article pointed out, it was 'useful propaganda for Nasser's "hearts and minds" campaign'.[12]

Rumour and gossip was often the staple diet of foreign correspondents. *Neues Deutschland*, the German periodical, published an article claiming that there were West German mercenaries fighting for the Federation of South Arabia. The East German propaganda machine picked up the story and boosted it with accusations that these men were also ex-Nazis, a line pursued by broadcasts issued by Radio Cairo. However, it seemed that the source of the story was the appearance of some British sailors in naval dress. They were from HMS *Ashanti*, and were temporarily assisting in security operations in Crater. Local Adenis, who had never seen this uniform before, were alarmed and spread the word that the sailors were German mercenaries and the story spread.[13]

These were news stories that constantly dripped onto a weary public, unlike the subsequent huge Middle East terrorist 'spectaculars' that exploded on the world scene from 1968 onwards. In fact, the Aden Insurgency was one of the last of the old style nationalist campaigns, and many writers have argued that it was only the emergence of mass media and global communications after 1968 that enabled terrorism to be boosted into a higher orbit.[14] Journalists in South Arabia had none of the advantages of digital camera/satellite or phone/laptop equipment demanded by modern foreign correspondents, but they did have wide-spread access to the front-line. This relaxed attitude towards the press was a hallmark of the simultaneous Vietnam War, but it was an outlook that did not last long: the demoralising TV images of urban warfare during the Vietnam Tet Offensive in 1968 were enough to encourage all governments to restrict future press access.

There continued to be disquiet in Britain over the 'torture allegations' made against some British Army interrogators and in response to press interest, a BBC *Panorama* team arrived in Aden in 1966. The 1st Battalion Coldstream Guards were on Internal security duties in Aden at the time, and the film crew shot footage of the Guards on patrol. Such was the novelty of being filmed during military operations that few of the faces betrayed any wariness. Investigative journalism was still a new concept in the front line and few soldiers realised that documentary film-making was no longer uncritical.

There were times when both HMG and the Army gained from press involvement. Journalists often proved to be better intelligence sources than official channels, and in the early months of the Yemen civil war, they were indispensable. Harold Macmillan confided that during the early years of the Yemen civil war he read *The Guardian* articles of Clare Hollingworth and thought they provided better intelligence than SIS.[15] Elements in the Army realised that the media could prove advantageous. Individual regiments understood that with the end of the Empire, there would shortly be a drastic re-structuring of the Services in which many famous regimental names would disappear. By dispensing with their helmets, 'soldiers could display their distinctive cap badges to press photographers' and thereby advertise their regiments.[16] In the UK the

Royal Marines were also busy keeping their name in the spotlight. The Marines' Office, which was responsible for recruitment and PR issues, provided regional newspapers with stories on the activities of local Marines in South Arabia. Young journalists like Angela Rippon, writing for the Plymouth based *Sunday Independent*, flew into Khormaksar airport to write articles on Four Five Commando, visiting Little Aden and flying up-country to Habilayn to cover personal stories.[17]

Industrial unrest in Aden was often recorded in the press as if it was the spontaneous reaction of local workers to oppressive British sponsored employers. Troops and police were usually called in and the strikers, whose ranks were swelled by NLF or FLOSY agitators, turned to violence. Such events required careful planning by activists such as Said Addaqa:

> In 1965 we organised the Federation. We had the youths working secretly also. We had secret meetings and organised demonstrations. We also had political education meetings. The literature was mainly Arab nationalist. I can't say how big the Front [NLF] was then because it was completely secret: each unit had no contact with any other. There were about ten in my unit. We used to meet three times a week. An example of our activities: a ship would come to the harbour. We would demand higher wages from the ship's agent. Not that the work we were doing was necessarily worth more, but so that the agent would either have to accept our demands or refuse. The second step, after his refusal, was to strike. There was violence, especially when the police were called in against the strikers.[18]

Although shipping activities in the Port of Aden were in decline by the 1960s, oil bunkering was still a major activity and it remained a primary target for the terrorists. The Aden Port Trust still presided over the largest oil bunkering port in the world, with a capacity to take twenty-four ships at buoy berths in the harbour, thirteen at pipeline berths and still have room for eleven working ships.[19]

Building work on the BP Refinery at Little Aden had started in 1952 and provided temporary work for over 12,000 men, many of whom were Yemeni immigrant workers. When the plant was finally commissioned in 1954, it provided regular employment for 2,100 people, refining five million tons of Kuwaiti crude oil annually, which was then supplied as fuel oil to the ships calling at the Port.[20] The Refinery also produced motor spirit and kerosene for the markets in the Eastern Mediterranean and Indian Ocean. BP was in the front line of British efforts, which were pursued vigorously by Julian Amery, to prevent oil in the Middle East from being controlled by the American multinationals. Consequently, there was concern that if South Arabia fell to the Egyptians, they would acquire the Refinery, and with it, the ability to disrupt the world oil market.[21]

205

The Refinery was also crucial to the British military base and as the RAF commitment increased during the late 1950s, the oil installation played an important role in supplying gas fuel for the turbines and Heavy Fuel Oil for the Power Station at Khormaksar airfield. The Navy was supplied with Fuel Oil, while HM Submarines were fed directly by pipelines running from the Refinery; and to underline the importance of the Royal Navy, all HM Warships had priority in loading and berthing at the BP berths.[22]

In the light of its future role in an independent Federation, BP was careful to appear 'non-aligned', though in practice its fortunes were inexorably tied to those of the British High Commission in Aden. Even one of the BP non-executive directors, Sir Humphrey Trevelyan, was allowed 'leave' in order to take up his position as the last High Commissioner of Aden, in May 1967.[23]

BP were able to provide much needed accommodation for the Services at Little Aden, where they leased the 'East and West' barracks and a number of 'Riley Newsome' houses. Despite the reduction in maritime trade in the 1960s, staff at the Refinery and bunkering installations still numbered over 2,500 together with over 10,000 dependants. Included in this figure were 177 British staff with an additional 200 dependants, all of whom were accommodated according to seniority, in A, B and C category housing. It remained, socially, a very colonial establishment with the wives and families who accompanied most BP employees becoming immersed in the rounds of the tennis club, dramatic society and beach club (popular, because it boasted its own shark nets).[24] However, under its General Manager, Peter Batterbury, the Little Aden cantonment did manage to preserve some normality until the last year of the British presence.

Despite its value as a local employer, the Refinery came under sporadic attack from both the NLF and FLOSY. During 1965 and 1966 the terrorist groups generated numerous industrial 'walkouts' and there were attempts to blow up the two nineteen-mile pipelines that joined the Refinery to the oil bunkers at the port. In early 1967 KB Wazir, the senior Bunkering Controller, was shot and killed.[25] This terrorist attack alarmed BP executives, who were concerned that despite the vital importance of the Refinery to the region, neither HMG nor Whitehall seemed to consider it in the plans for withdrawal or independence.[26]

BP also provided much-needed medical facilities for the area. Barbara Binns came out to Aden in 1960 with her husband, Charles, who was a Medical Officer with BP and a former MO with the Trucial Scouts. Together with another ex-nurse, Jennie Roberts, and ably assisted by Rachel Littlewood, Barbara ran a Red Cross Clinic in Little Aden that was attended by over 500 local mothers and babies each month, for local infant mortality was high and children were undernourished. Terrorism finally came close to Barbara's home in 1965:

The troubles in Aden between FLOSY and NLF were growling on around us, with Army roadblocks and nightly skirmishes with tracer bullets streaming across the sky, as regular events. The odd tragic event involving people we knew would be dinner-table talk at home in Little Aden, but there was no sense of awareness of the real danger of our situation. Then one day in 1965, we heard the tragic news of our neighbour. After work one day, he had unwisely taken his family shopping in Aden town. We sensed it was unsafe to go into Crater in those days but our neighbour felt secure because he had been there so long and had many friends among the locals. His car broke down and whilst fixing his exhaust he was shot point blank in the face.

Then in 1966 our houseboy, ***** left us to work in Aden. One Sunday morning, not long after his arrival, there was an explosion and it appeared that a bomb had gone off prematurely. A blood trail was followed back to his quarters at the home of a prominent French family and he was found there with a very damaged hand. A search of his flat revealed a veritable arsenal of hidden weapons and although he was arrested, he later escaped from the prison hospital by climbing out of a bathroom window. It was only later that our young son chirped up and said that while working for us, ***** had kept guns under his bed in his quarters, and had proudly shown them off to the children.[27]

There was also a 130-bed BP hospital, where seven British doctors, including Charles Binns and Mark Littlewood, provided medical care for a community of some 12,000 people. This embraced not only BP employees, but also their large network of dependants. Many of these came down from the hinterland where malaria was common and there were cases of leprosy and even one patient who managed to contract both chickenpox and smallpox. But it was combating the endemic disease, bilharzia, caused by parasitic worms in wells and ponds, that consumed so much of the medical resources.[28] There were also maternity facilities at the BP hospital and the company funded a General Practice Surgery in Aden, which looked after a further 3,000 of the local population.[29]

The fact that someone was working in medicine, which might have helped local Adenis, offered no immunity from attack. Davina Daintree, whose husband, John, was a doctor in South Arabia, remembered a potentially explosive round of bridge:

One evening we were playing bridge in our bungalow in Marine Drive, when a grenade was thrown at the house. We heard it hit the roof and John went out into the garden. It hadn't gone off and he nearly trod on it, picked it up and threw it across the road onto the beach. He then phoned the General Manager, who asked him how much he had had to drink that evening. John's reply was unprintable. Four Five Commando bomb disposal unit then came and sandbagged the grenade and blew it up, and as we were British, we resumed our bridge and I remember bidding, and making, seven no-trumps.[30]

During 1965, against a background of rising unrest, BP started a policy of recruiting more local Arabs. Ann Cuthbert wrote home to her parents:

> The go-slow in the Refinery continues. There has been trouble in the Power Station including a potentially lethal act of sabotage, which thoroughly frightened all concerned and has led to the Superintendent there, offering his resignation. We are already desperately short of Europeans of course, owing to the 'Arabisation' programme, so what with the men working on shifts to keep the place going, they really can't do with resignations as well. It wouldn't surprise me if all the Europeans came out on strike soon – they go home to miserable wives and are working like beavers anyway.[31]

Employing more Arabs in the Refinery caused new problems. The remaining 150 Europeans within the Refinery were stretched to fill the technical jobs, but more importantly, as the terrorists' constituency increased in size, so pressure and intimidation from them had more effect within the Refinery.[32] When an employee was suspended because of suspected terrorist activity, the Arabs from his department could be brought out on strike, threatening a close down. On 18 April 1966 Hamid Nabech, a Supervisor of Employment at the BP Refinery, was murdered. But this was not intimidation aimed at a British institution. Nabech was a senior FLOSY member, and the murder was carried out by the NLF as an example of an increasingly bitter feud between the competing terrorist groups.[33]

Between the acts of murder and intimidation, life in Aden State and for the troops in camps around Khormaksar could be civilised. For entertainment, the troops had regular swimming parties and daily feature films were shown in camps. Live shows were put on, though during one show a very drunk Tony Hancock was booed off the stage while Bob Monkhouse fired off jokes considered 'blue' even by an army audience. It was left to Harry Secombe to bring some sobriety to the evening by singing 'Bless This House' to the backing of gunfire coming from al-Mansoura. A chorus line of high-kicking girls then woke everyone up from a sentimental daze.[34]

Another diversion for servicemen was the keeping of bizarre pets. Although it was officially prohibited under service regulations, some airmen couldn't resist bringing back unusual animals from overseas, as Sergeant Bob Douglas, an Air Signaller with 84 Squadron, discovered:

One of our aircrew had enjoyed a drunken night out in Nairobi and returned to Khormaksar bearing a baby crocodile. The animal was christened 'Sergeant Scorpio' and put on a lead. He used to go on flights with his owner, so he must have travelled thousands of miles. He died on active service when one of the locals took offence to him. We had all become very fond of Sergeant Scorpio and he was buried in the Squadron garden with full military honours.[35]

The proliferation of transistor radios in South Arabia coincided with the rise of pop music and in particular, the 'British Hit Parade'. The British Forces Broadcasting Service (BFBS) relayed the latest records and juke boxes in the bars and NAAFI stations in Ma'alla and Tawahi constantly pounded out the favourites. Ferret Scout cars trundled along the streets of Aden to the background beat of The Applejacks' *Have I the Right?* Patrolling soldiers remembered the irony of walking down alleys to the strains of Gerry and the Pacemakers singing *Walk On* or to the more aggressive backing of The Animals' *We Gotta Get out of This Place (if it's the last thing we ever do)*. Up-country, soldiers relaxing in their bivouacs in Habilayn Camp might listen to records from the burgeoning 'flower-power' movement, such as Peter, Paul and Mary's, *Where Have All the Flowers Gone?* Sometimes the melodious Roy Orbison wafted over the camp with the prophetic *It's Over*.

Local television contained regular news bulletins and two BP wives were employed as British newsreaders. There were also several readers from the Services, one of whom was usually inebriated. Ann Cuthbert, herself a newsreader, recalled:

> It was early days in television, and things were not very sophisti-cated. Of course there was no autocue, and news items were read off bits of paper in front of you. One particular naval officer, who read the news, was often drunk. I watched one of his performances, when in the middle of his live broadcast, one of his news sheets slipped off the desk. He tried to catch it and missed. He just stared into space as a hand came up from under the desk, in camera shot, and put the paper back in front of him.[36]

Threats to the safety of British employees in radio and particularly television meant that increasingly Arabs became the mainstay of broadcasting. FLOSY, who were particularly strong in this industry, then made increasing efforts to bring Aden Broadcasting employees out on strike. When they were successful in calling a seven-day strike, some workers were sacked and this brought a fresh round of accusations and threats from FLOSY, especially intimidation of employees' families. Again it was Tony Ashworth of IRD and the late Hassan Bayoumi who were

ADEN INSURGENCY

singled out for abuse together with those employees who had returned to work and were warned in the numerous threats from the FLOSY military command that:

> The Front warns any person from trying to cooperate with ASHWORTH and his gang, or who agrees to work at the TV and broadcasting station in place of those who were dismissed by BAYUMI. They will face the just sentence of the people.[37]

In October 1966 Egyptian hopes of FLOSY becoming the dominant nationalist group were dashed. A militant group within the NLF, including the Aden guerrilla leader, Abdul Ismail and the hinterland commander, Ali Antar, broke away and formed a new militant NLF. In doing so they lost Egyptian financial backing but were soon able to replenish their coffers by bank raids and extortion. But this did not tell the whole story, as an intelligence source admitted:

> The financing of the NLF is still shrouded in a great deal of mystery. They are better financed than an organisation of purely local inspiration would seem likely to be. They have a highly developed and efficient organisation for collecting 'subscriptions' but that alone could hardly have provided all the necessary funds.[38]

If the source of funds for the new, radical NLF remained a mystery, it was clear that Egypt was still financing FLOSY. Nasser was concerned that his investment was about to be eclipsed by a more radical opposition and Egyptian Intelligence set about conceiving a fighting wing for FLOSY (by the creation of the Popular Organisation of Revolutionary Forces – PORF). But it was the new NLF who were quickest to promote an upsurge in violence as they were the group with extensive combat experience as well as an established cell structure.[39] Consequently, from the end of 1966 the split between the Egyptian backed FLOSY and the NLF became irrevocable and soon turned to violence. This further confused an already bewildering array of blood feuds and tribal rivalries that peppered everyday life in South Arabia and it certainly made tracing the source of any outrage almost impossible for the security forces. On 22 November 1966 an Aden Airways Dakota was blown up on a flight from the state of Wahidi to Aden, killing twenty-seven people. Five members of the Uthaiman family from Wahidi were arrested and held at the Interrogation Centre at Fort Morbut. But the ongoing investigations revealed an extraordinary web of intrigue, and the final responsibility for the outrage went much further than any one terrorist group.[40]

Considering the quantity of flights that were made across the hinterland by civilian and military aircraft, it was fortunate that there were not more

210

incidents. 84 Squadron, who operated the large Beverley workhorses, suffered the loss of one aircraft when it hit a mine on an airfield, but otherwise the unit's flight compliment remained unscathed. The squadron airlifted vast quantities of supplies and personnel across the arid hinterland; as Air Signaller Sergeant Bob Douglas points out, the cargo was very diverse:

> Flying up in the highlands was unbearably hot and with swirling sand up to 10,000 ft, the dust and haze clouded the ground below. There was little relief in the terrain as you came in to land. On occasions we used to take the *Bedu* from hill fort to hill fort and we had to take all their goats with them. At the end of the flight there was no landing strip. You just dropped into the desert where you saw a tyre burning to show the wind direction.
>
> Once we went over to Mukeiras to pick up a large red fire engine – one of the big engines, not the little 'Green Goddess' type. We successfully loaded it but we could only get three of the Beverley's engines working, so taking off would be a problem. At that moment, the dissidents started mortaring the airstrip. We had to quickly decide whether to stay and risk getting blown up or to try and take off. We gambled on a take-off and backed up the airstrip to get as much length as possible. We lumbered up the airstrip and just before the end, managed to lift off from the sand dunes. There was a gully beyond and we only just made it out of there.
>
> When we landed at Khormaksar we found that the bloody idiot who put the fire engine on, hadn't taken the water out of it. The weight of those 500 gallons nearly did for us.[41]

Lighter aircraft soon became a more popular means of moving commanders around their units than the time-honoured Landrover, which was so susceptible to landmines. On 3 November the CO of 3 Royal Anglian Regiment, Lieutenant-Colonel (later General Sir Peter) Leng, had a very narrow escape when a landmine blew up his Landrover.[42] Remarkably he survived. But helicopters such as the versatile Sioux offered a safer, quicker, and usually more comfortable trip, with the great advantage that they could move swiftly across inaccessible terrain. They certainly found favour with pilots such as Sergeant Pilot Martin Forde of 1st The Queen's Dragoon Guards, who was attached to Aden Brigade:

> The Bell 47 Sioux was a tremendous machine to fly. It was very slow, which made you vulnerable to SAA and it was basic by today's standards. But it had a turbo supercharger and could be flown hot and high. The flying was amazing over mountains, ravines and open desert, where I sometimes collected tribesmen wounded in clan

feuds. They were like Apache Indians – all gun belts, loincloths and daggers. No guns were mounted in the Sioux and so my only weapon was a .38 Smith & Wesson six-round revolver, which hardly gave you security.[43]

However, there were occasions when this form of transport was also precarious. On 6 December 1966 Captain John Fleming RHA was flying Major John Sharpe, Commander of Chestnut Troop 1 RHA, around his battery positions in a Sioux helicopter. Gunner John Cain sat in the rear, beside a store of grenades and ammunition, cradling his SLR rifle. As they neared Musaymir, along the Yemen border, the helicopter suddenly spiralled out of control and crashed into a gully, the fuel from the ruptured tank showering downwards and exploding the ammunition. The men were all killed instantly and the resulting inferno destroyed most of the aircraft, making any accident investigation extremely difficult. When contact had been lost, a search started, and although Sergeant Pilot Forde spent several hours looking for Fleming's machine, in the end he had to return to base empty handed. He recalled that as he landed, 'a lady rushed out and asked if I had found John Fleming – it was his wife'.[44] Luckily an FRA patrol was in the area and soon arrived at the crash site and began looking for clues. Gunner Cain's SLR was missing and bizarrely, one of the bodies had obviously been mutilated after the crash.

Several weeks later a recce troop from Four Five Commando was in the area, going to the assistance of an ambushed RE convoy. They themselves came under attack from a cave sangar and the Troop Commander, Lieutenant Knott, threw a grenade into the cave to silence the opposition. He then went in and found a dead tribesman with a rifle containing parts from Gunner Cain's SLR rifle. Due to lack of evidence, the subsequent accident inquiry could not determine the reason for the helicopter crash. But the fact that rebel tribesmen had quickly arrived at the crash site and exacted their customary retribution on a fallen enemy indicated that they had probably shot down the aircraft.[45]

Another helicopter that saw useful service in South Arabia was the Westland Scout AH Mk 1. Apart from reconnaissance duties this machine was often used to airlift vital materials or supplies and in one case, to carry an unusual Blindicide screen. Major (later Brigadier) Joe Starling, Second-in-Command of 1 PARA was given the brief of reinforcing the tower of Sheikh Othman Police Station. This tower was one of the most vulnerable OP positions in the district and was subject to constant enemy attack. Starling devised a cunning scheme:

A device which had proved successful elsewhere was a Blindicide screen of rigid wire mesh, which exploded the rockets on impact so that the force of the explosion was dissipated and only the splinters hit the defences proper. The difficulty at OP4 was to fit such a screen over the fighting floor of the tower. To attempt to carry out the construction work involved – much of it being exposed to enemy fire – would have invited an unacceptable number of casualties. The obvious solution was to construct a screen on a frame and lower the whole thing over the tower by helicopter. 60 Field Squadron quickly produced a birdcage-like structure out of tubular scaffolding and wire mesh ... Then promptly at first light, the Scout helicopter appeared, flew over the surprised inhabitants of Sheikh Othman and hovered over the Police Station with the 'thing'. Those on the ground passed the word to the pilot to drop, and the 'thing' came to rest within a few inches of its designated position.

The 'thing' proved successful and although many more Blindicides were fired at the OP, no further casualties were suffered. Operation Big Lift was an excellent example of what can be achieved by inventive minds, skilful flying, good timing and plain old-fashioned guts.[46]

Such Observation Posts were invaluable to army foot patrols, which formed the core of internal security work. Major (later Major-General) Michael Tillotson was a senior Company Commander with 1 PWO and was well placed to observe the difficulties of street operations. Having previously served in Indo-China and Malaya, he came out to South Arabia in 1965 to command a Company comprising three rifle platoons and a support platoon. He found the main problem was a lack of continuity in operations:

Companies rotated every six days between static guard duties, operational duties in Crater, and reserve and training. But, if you were on operational duties, six days was hardly long enough to familiarise yourself with the place, or indeed to follow up on cordon and search, or patrol leads. When someone from the successive Company acted on your own carefully nurtured leads, your informant might take fright.

One of the challenges facing Company Commanders was to maintain a sense of purpose among the men. This meant constantly devising new operations to foil the terrorists. We would provide bait for the enemy, perhaps someone in a Landrover or a patrol, or a staged lorry breakdown, while two of our snipers would lie in wait for the enemy grenadiers, who often worked in pairs. Or a roadblock would be set up at a checkpoint, with a pre-arranged escape route, which would be cordoned off, out of sight, with concertina wire. Any vehicle refusing to stop at the main checkpoint, we knew was up to no good, but we'd catch them as they belted up the blind escape route. It certainly raised the men's morale, as routine checking of cars normally produced very little.[47]

Battalions rotated regularly and, as Major Tillotson points out, it was not always a beneficial policy. At a more senior level, commanders changed approximately every two years, and as 1966 drew to a close, Brigadier Hew Butler took over as the new CO of 24 Brigade, covering Little Aden and up-country. Butler, a veteran of the Western Desert in World War II and more recently Regimental Colonel of the Royal Green Jackets, had a positive start in his post. For the first three months he was fortunate to have the services of Major Andrew Myrtle as his Brigade Major – a great all-rounder – who had proved a competent regimental as well as staff officer.[48] There were also new battalions arriving for Aden Brigade, including the 3rd Battalion The Royal Anglian Regiment, which came in during October to take over responsibility for Sheikh Othman and al-Mansoura. Aden State was still the preserve of British Army units, as the FRA couldn't be relied upon to apply the principles of 'minimum force'. Brigadier Charles Dunbar of MEC was emphatic that the local Arab force could not be used:

> The Federal Forces could not act according to these principles as understood in Britain. The simplest illustration of what I mean is that if Lance Naik Ali Ahmed was ordered to fire one round at a man in a green turban and did so, inevitably a blood feud would begin. The principle which Federal Forces had to use was a considerable burst of fire, not all of it accurately aimed. This was unacceptable to HMG who would have found it difficult if not impossible to justify to world opinion.[49]

Yet despite Brigadier Dunbar's reservations about using inexperienced FRA troops, newly arrived British troops were sometimes pitched straight into riot situations. Facing a howling Adeni mob was a nerve-wracking experience and riot control could be an unpredictable operation. It was not made any easier by the clumsy equipment troops had to handle, as 'C' Company, 1st Battalion The Lancashire Regiment (Prince of Wales's Volunteers) discovered:

> We dispersed the rampaging crowds in Tawahi, with the aid of 204 gas grenades to say nothing of gas cartridges. We threw quite a lot when they burnt down the Marina Hotel, too. Perhaps we did overdo it a bit. The place stank of gas for days. We also had a dye truck which squirted green dye, but it was not an unqualified success as it was non-selective and squirted us as well as the rioters.[50]

In the coming year, British troops would face their toughest test, as mutiny and massacres threatened to plunge South Arabia into anarchy.

NOTES

1   Claude Deffarge's excellent account of the Civil War was published as *Yemen 62–69*, Robert Laffont, Paris 1969. Troeller made a number of documentary films about Yemen. The partnership later covered the fighting in Hué during the Tet Offensive in the Vietnam War. For McLean, see *Yemen 62–69*, p. 115.
2   Richard Beeston, *Looking for Trouble*, Brassey's, 1997, pp. 77–85.
3   Crouch, op. cit., p. 172. Also *Globe & Laurel*, October 1966 and PREM 11/4357, 4 March 1963, NA.
4   The role of the media and terrorism is explored by Maxwell Taylor in *The Terrorist*, Brassey's, 1988, pp. 67–70. See also Colin Beer, 'The Press and Revolutionary Warfare' in *On Revolutionary War*, Galago, 1990.
5   High Commission to Arabian Department, FO, 24 January 1967, DEFE 24/252, NA. Shamshir's terrorist contacts ranged from Taiz to Sheikh Othman, Crater and Little Aden. See High Commission to Arabian Department, FO, 28 September 1966, DEFE 24/252, NA.
6   Memorandum of meeting 28 September 1964, attended by Sir Kennedy Trevaskis and Sir Henry Hardman (MOD), CO 1027/701, NA.
7   C Roberts to L Monson, 1 October 1964, CO 1027/701, NA. Tony Ashworth was the Federation's Information Advisor.
8   Clare Hollingworth, op. cit., p. 210.
9   Ibid. Also Memorandum, C Roberts, 5 October 1964, CO 1027/701, NA.
10   *Life at War*, Time-Life Books, Time Inc., 1977, p. 294. Also *The Times*, 2 November 2001.
11   Major-General Tillotson to Author, 20 July 2002.
12   Their work featured as the main article in *The Observer* colour magazine, 11 June 1967.
13   High Commission to Foreign Office, 4 March 1967, FCO 8/425, NA. Despite the inaccuracy of the rumour, several German pilots serving in the South Arabian Air Force were quickly posted elsewhere.
14   1968 saw the first skyjacking by the Popular Front for the Liberation of Palestine. See Susan Caruthers, *The Media at War*, Macmillan, 2000, pp. 167–9. A recent study of media and the military is to be found in Stephen Badsey's 'Modern Military Operations and the Media', in *Strategic and Combat Studies Occasional Paper # 8*, 1994.
15   PREM 11/4357, 4 March 1963, NA.
16   See Hew Strachan, 'The British Way in Warfare' in David Chandler and Ian Beckett (eds), *The Oxford Illustrated History of the British Army*, OUP, 1994.
17   *Globe & Laurel*, October 1966. *Sunday Independent*, 21 August 1966. Also, Colonel McGarel-Groves to Author, 14 September 2001.
18   *Merip Report*, # 15, March 1973, AWDU.
19   The Aden Port Trust had been in operation since 1889. For a history, see *BP Visitors Guide to Aden*, BP Archives, UW.
20   Regular employees consisted of 300 British technicians and 1,800 Arabs.
21   However, most Arab countries had their own refining capacity. See Memo, D Mitchell to M Banks, 29 June 1966, File 65647, BP Archives, UW.
22   File 35449, BP Archives, UW.
23   Sir Humphrey Trevelyan was a non-exec. Director of BP, 1965–75. Memo, A

H Dutton to P Batterbury, 23 May 1967, File 28693, BP Archives, UW. Another experienced Middle East hand, who later joined BP as a director, was the ex-C-in-C, MEC, Sir Charles (later Lord) Elworthy, Marshal of the Royal Air Force.

24   Baby sharks could still enter the nets, where they could grow larger. A welcome diversion for BP families was to watch Royal Marines periodically blasting these threats out of the water with grenades; Ann Cuthbert to Author, 6 March 2004. For monthly statistics on BP employment, see Files 13225 and 65647, BP Archives, UW. Also James Bamberg, *British Petroleum and Global Oil 1950–1975*, CUP, 2000, p. 72. Shell Oil was based in 'Big Aden', and also had one Arab representative in Little Aden.

25   File 121912, BP Archives, UW.

26   When Major-General Philip Tower was being briefed before assuming command of MELF in 1967, no mention was made by HMG or Whitehall about plans for BP. See A H Dutton to P Batterbury, 8 May 1967, File 28693, BP Archives, UW.

27   Barbara Binns to Author, 18 April 2002. Her brother was a Captain in the Territorials, who also came out to Aden in 1963 to help train soldiers in techniques for resisting enemy interrogation.

28   Dr Mark Littlewood to Author, 20 May 2002.

29   Eddie Izzard, the entertainer was born at the hospital in 1962. His father, Harold, was an accountant at the Refinery while his mother was a nurse at the hospital.

30   Davina Daintree to Author, 11 September 2002. Also BP Memo, 19 January 1967, File 108, BP Archives, UW.

31   Ann Cuthbert correspondence, 28 January 1965.

32   Ibid., 15 March 1965.

33   Memo, 23 April 1967, File 108, BP Archives, UW.

34   *The Lancashire Lad*, November 1997.

35   Robert Douglas to Author, 7 March 2003.

36   Because of the increasing danger to British newsreaders, Ann Cuthbert was advised to leave her job with Aden Television in 1966.

37   Statement by 'secret military command of FLOSY', 10 April 1967, File 2/1, Dunbar Papers, LHCMA.

38   'Confidential Report', Aden, 30 October 1967, FCO 8/252, NA.

39   Abdul al-Fattah Ismail subsequently moved to a Marxist position, and during the first post-independent government in 1969, he overthrew al-Sha'abi. By 1972 the PDRY had become a full-blown Marxist state. Both Ismail and Ali Antar were killed during an attempted coup in 1986. See Tareq Ismail, *PDR Yemen*, Francis Pinter, 1986, pp. 25–9.

40   Major Goschen was Assistant Advisor to Wahidi. See report on 'Destruction of Aden Airways Aircraft', FCO 8/172, NA.

41   Robert Douglas to Author, 7 March 2003.

42   Barthorp, op. cit., p. 43. General Leng was later Commander Land Forces Northern Ireland (1973–75) and Director Military Operations MOD (1975–78).

43   Martin Forde to Author, 19 November 2002.

44   Ibid.

45   'Accident Report, Sioux XT 125 Helicopter', 6 December 1966, AVIA 101/680, NA. For an appreciation of the respected casualties, see *Royal Artillery Regimental News*, January 1967.

46   The Scout helicopter remained in service with the British Army until 1994.

Brigadier Joe Starling, *Soldier On! The Testament of a Tom*, Spellmount, 1992, pp. 54–6.

47 Major-General Tillotson to Author, 20 July 2002.
48 At the end of 1966 Major Myrtle moved to the BAOR and was succeeded by another sound administrator, Major John MacMillan; Colonel Leslie Hudson RM to Author, 3 September 2001.
49 It was the High Commissioner who was primarily responsible for law and order in Aden State and his political considerations were of paramount importance. Brigadier Charles Dunbar to Lieutenant-Colonel J Paget, 25 September 1968, File 2/6, Dunbar Papers, LHCMA.
50 'C' Company Notes, *The Regimental Magazine of The Lancashire Regiment*, autumn 1967.

CHAPTER XI

Panic in Whitehall

The beginning of 1967 saw a large increase in the number of security incidents. In the first quarter of the year there were over 300, mostly involving grenade attacks. The relentless assassination of Federation officials continued. During the afternoon of Tuesday 10 January, the Deputy Superintendent of Police, Niaz Husain, was shot dead and later that month, Mohammed Nagi, one of the most senior Arab Civil Servants, was machine-gunned to death in Crater.[1] It was also a punishing time for British troops, for while they only lost one soldier killed in the first quarter, they suffered eighty-five wounded against terrorist casualties of only ten.

In addition to these losses, a number of Yemenis were murdered by mobs in and around Aden, some connected with cross-border activities in the Yemen. In February 1967 a Yemeni royalist in close contact with one of the Federation sultans was spotted by the NLF in Sheikh Othman. A mob was soon organised and the unfortunate Yemeni courier was lynched. The police failed to save him and although in his dying words the Yemeni admitted the object of his mission – pro-royalist and pro-Federation – the police continued to insist he was an intimidator and left him to be murdered by the frenzied crowd.[2] Inside Yemen, the republican government took immediate action against those receiving British aid. In Liberation Square in Sana'a, five Yemenis were publicly executed by firing squad after being accused of receiving supplies parachuted in by the British.

If anyone thought that the indiscriminate killing would fall away as the British withdrawal approached, they were sadly mistaken. In February A H 'Barney' Dutton, ex-Aden Financial Secretary and now advisor to the BP Economic Relations Department, predicted the worst:

> The Egyptians and FLOSY wish to make the withdrawal of British forces from Aden appear not to be a voluntary act but a military victory. To this end, if for no other reason, it seems probable that acts of sabotage and violence will continue up to the last minute.[3]

On 11 February, the eighth anniversary of the foundation of the Federation, the terrorists mounted a violent campaign throughout the territory, which they branded 'The Day of the Volcano'. However, a massive show of force by Aden Brigade severely restricted the campaign's impact, although the inter-factional fighting that erupted between PORF (FLOSY's military wing) and the NLF soon overshadowed this security success. Egyptian Intelligence, which was always anxious to be seen to be controlling the direction of the nationalist revolt, was steering PORF into open conflict with the NLF. Nasser was still holding the NLF leader, Qahtan al-Sha'abi, under house arrest in Cairo but his organisation was still operating under the control of his more radical comrades. As PORF cadres singled out NLF fighters for execution, retaliation killings became the order of the day and easier targets were sought, including the families of nationalist supporters.[4]

During the evening of 27 February a bomb exploded at the home of the former Chief Minister for Aden and FLOSY leader, Abdul Mackawee. The device had been placed on a windowsill and Mackawee's three sons had come out of the house to investigate it. They were joined by three police officers and as the group unwisely stood around it, the bomb ignited, killing them all. The following day, a huge set-piece funeral parade for the casualties provided the excuse for another riot. The parade was organised by FLOSY but it became an excuse for all nationalists to protest against the British, and although the NLF were suspected of the Mackawee bombing, they too came to march and make political capital out of the killings. Surprisingly it was not the British who were attacked during the parade but representatives from the South Arabian League, the less radical but also less adept nationalist group who had recently returned to open offices in Aden.[5] The crowd, who were whipped into a frenzy, then chased two of the League's men into a mosque, where they were captured and thrown out of the minaret to the mob below. The hapless men were then savagely beaten to death in front of reporters and watching Aden Civil Policemen. The mob then assaulted the offices of the League, which led to more shooting and killings as the League's gunmen retaliated. The fight was only stopped by the arrival of British troops, who finally separated the warring factions.[6] But it was too late to prevent a collapse in confidence in British control, much to the frustration of the Chief of Staff MEC, Brigadier Charles Dunbar:

> The Mackawee bomb incident terrified all FLOSY supporters in Aden and upset those who were beginning to think that we could after all, maintain law and order. It is hard to magnify the effect of the murders. The complete change of atmosphere afterwards was something that we had the greatest difficulty in contending with.[7]

As the rioting in Crater finally subsided by late afternoon on 28 February, the NLF embarked on an operation to wipe out British Security chiefs. A cocktail party was being prepared at the flat of Foreign Office official Tony Ingledow and his wife, Monica. Caterers preparing for the drinks party were assisted by ***, the Ingledows' trusted houseboy. But unbeknown to them, the houseboy's mother had been captured by the NLF, who threatened to kill her unless her son planted a bomb in the flat. Complying with this threat, the houseboy was given a 'jumping-jack' bomb with a timing device, which he hid in a bookcase in the sitting room while the Ingledows were out of the flat. When they returned, Monica Ingledow rearranged the furniture, including the bookcase, and in doing so, the hidden bomb fell on its side. That evening the guests, including leading members of the Aden security community and their wives, gathered for the party.

At 9pm a huge explosion rocked the flat. The full force of the bomb, which was designed to spring up and explode at head height, blew outwards through the French windows but it still cut a devastating swathe through the party. Two women closest to the blast, Judy Stuart, wife of the MI5 representative (SLO) Sandy Stuart, and Ruth Wilkes, wife of a Major in the Intelligence Corps, were killed and ten others were wounded. Tony Ingledow received a chunk of shrapnel through his foot while his wife was thrown across the room, the blast bursting her eardrum.[8]

While the NLF continued its assault against the British administration and security apparatus, British military units continued their rotation in order to meet the threat. During the traumatic month of February, a battalion Commander from a famous Scottish Regiment arrived to assess the situation for his unit's forthcoming tour. Lieutenant-Colonel Colin Mitchell, whose father had been an officer in the Argyll and Sutherland Highlanders during the Great War, was a forthright and experienced Commander. He had wide-ranging regimental experience, serving at platoon, company and battalion level in a number of counter-insurgency campaigns, and could be dismissive of fellow officers and superiors who had not seen similar action.[9] His subsequent post as Middle East specialist with the Chief of the Defence Staff, had allowed him to make two previous visits to Aden, but this most recent week's exploration on behalf of the Argylls convinced him that the security situation had dramatically deteriorated.[10]

The terrorist outrages of February were followed in the second quarter of 1967 by an even sharper rise in both terrorist inter-factional fighting and attacks on British troops. During the period April to June, there were over 1,000 incidents, involving increasing numbers of small arms and Blindicide rocket launchers. But as this quarter started, British soldiers found they were also up against the forces of nature as well as their customary enemy.[11] On April Fool's Day, the day before a United Nations three-man Commission arrived, there was a tremendous rainstorm and six inches of rain fell on Aden and Jebel Shamsan. The downpour had rarely been seen before and the rocks and rubble from the mountain were washed down with the torrent of water that flooded the streets and alleys of Crater and Ma'alla.[12] As Jebel Shamsan turned green, British troops waded knee-deep into the wash to rescue trapped locals and there were reports that even terrorist snipers who got into difficulties requested help from the soldiers.

The following day, as the flood mess was being cleared up, the UN Mission arrived in Aden. From the start, the delegates clashed with the High Commission and refused to meet the Federal Authorities. Their appearance also fuelled five days of street riots during which, units from the 1st Battalion Northumberland Fusiliers and 3 Royal Anglians attempted to keep control of the streets, exercising extraordinary restraint in the face of grenade and sniper attacks. They did this with the help of armour from 1 QDG who expended over 6,000 rounds from their Browning machine-guns during crowd control and cordon and search operations.

While the UN Mission prevaricated, FLOSY tried to eliminate pockets of NLF resistance within Crater. At the same time, a bitter fight erupted in Sheikh Othman as the NLF cleared out FLOSY opponents, gunning them down in broad daylight. Tension was heightened by a General Strike and amid the chaos, the UN men announced that they had seen enough and decided to leave. The fiasco of the Mission's visit was highlighted when their broadcast, which was due to be heard on the local radio and television network, was blocked by the Federal Government, who instead proceeded to relay an episode of the cowboy serial *Rawhide*. The UN men were furious and stormed out of Aden. In the resulting press coverage Britain was lambasted but there was great relief in the High Commission and at Middle East Command that at least one excuse for violence had been removed from the scene.[13]

Indignation in the Arab world was no longer directed just at the British, for in April a number of Americans including CIA representatives were expelled from Yemen on charges of espionage.[14] This coincided with the collapse of relations between the US and Egypt, which had deteriorated since the withdrawal of American food aid several months earlier. Much to the dismay of the British, this food aid had continued for many years, with the US maintaining that it was their only way to continue dialogue as well as leverage with the Egyptian Government. Playing up to this sentiment, the Egyptians had reportedly undertaken to offer to mediate in America's war in Vietnam by contacting the Vietcong in the hope of opening channels for US/North Vietnamese talks. It had all come to nothing and relations soon fell apart. The US continued to 'sit on the fence' on many Middle East issues but in some areas this actually suited Britain, especially where the US side-stepped King Feisal's request for intervention in the old Buraimi oil dispute. Nonetheless, the US continued to withhold positive support for South Arabia, with Colbert Held of the US State Department stating that the US was 'absolutely not prepared' to assist a future Federation that it believed could not survive.[15]

However, the resolve of the British forces remained firm. Elements of 22 SAS continued to carry out reconnaissance operations in Radfan as well as in Aden. There had been rotations in command and Lieutenant-Colonel John (later Viscount) Slim, successor to Lieutenant-Colonel Mike Wingate-Gray and son of the famous Field-Marshal, was the new CO of the unit.[16] At least one member of The Regiment maintained cover as a political officer while other SAS men, including a young Captain in the Welsh Guards, Charles Guthrie, donned 'Hawaii' shirts to guard key figures in the EAP.[17]

Elsewhere in the hinterland, the NLF kept up the pressure on British troops. The 1st Battalion Irish Guards repulsed a number of assaults on their positions at Habilayn Camp, but information was sparse about which local individuals were leading these assaults, as an Intelligence Summary points out:

Attack on British Camp, political officer's house and FNG fort. Enemy strength about 20. Weapons included 61mm mortar and Blindicide. B2 sources state that attack was carried out by Hassan Mudlah. Five enemy were wounded, inflicted by our mortars. Own casualties nil. Mudlah was not known as a dissident leader and he worked for the local authorities in Habilayn until four months ago. Follow up showed 4 large bloodstains and items of equipment and numerous bloody rags.[18]

The Irish Guards were not always on the defensive and carried out constant patrols and prepared ambushes on known enemy trails. These patrols could last several days and each platoon went out well equipped. Each man wore denim trousers and KF shirt, DMS boots, puttees and a tropical camouflage hat. They also carried a clasp knife, 50-round bandolier, face veil, ID card and discs, as well as two water bottles, field dressings, cutlery and a sleeping bag. In addition to all these personal items, each man was armed with either an SLR or Armalite rifle and carried either .36 or .83 grenades. The platoon weapons included a GPMG, 2 inch mortar, trip flares and a Carl Gustav rocket launcher. They would then be re-supplied out in the mountains by a Wessex helicopter, which also dropped heavier supplies such as additional mortar rounds, wireless batteries for the A41 and A40 radios, rations, sandbags and shovels.[19] But despite their fire-power, patrols could be dangerously exposed. On 20 April 1967 an Irish Guards patrol was ambushed near Habilayn, and four Guardsmen were killed and one wounded, but in returned fire, four of the enemy were killed and six wounded.

British casualties always relied on a band of brave and reliable medics to tend to them and organise their evacuation. Lance Corporal Robert Carroll, a regimental medical orderly with the 1 Lancashire Regiment (PWV), saw his fair share of action. He had arrived with his battalion in February 1967 and initially spent time up-country, near Mukeiras, but found himself helping the local Arab population as well as combat casualties. He became known as *Hakeem* (doctor and wise man) for his treatment of malaria and tuberculosis among local babies and adults. Later on, down in Aden, the streets of Tawahi and al-Mansoura offered him a different challenge. Often on call for twenty-four hours, he would rush to the scene of a grenade explosion and while under sniper fire, tend army or civilian casualties. The Medical Corps brassard offered no protection, and he was sometimes subjected to a second grenade attack. On one occasion, a grenade rolled onto the ground only five feet away from him but luckily failed to explode.[20]

While the world press and the United Nations continued to batter HMG over the disastrous visit of the UN Mission, in London the Wilson Government tried desperately to seek some accommodation with FLOSY. Despite the NLF's continuing influence in both the hinterland and Aden, its nominal leader, al-Sha'abi, was a shadowy figure, and the NLF guerrilla leaders in the mountains and back streets of Aden were largely unknown and certainly had no international profile. Consequently the Foreign Office persisted in trying to forge a deal with the urban-based FLOSY. The Labour Party had established links with the ATUC and they could identify Mackawee and al-Asnag as the leaders of FLOSY, even though that leadership was exerted from Cairo and Taiz. In early April the Foreign Secretary, George Brown, taking heed of the UN criticism of the High Commission, appointed Lord Shackleton to head a new Mission for South Arabia. Shackleton was certainly well qualified for the job. The Life Peer and son of the famous Arctic explorer was a former Permanent Private Secretary to the Foreign Secretary and had recently spent nearly three years in the post of Minister of Defence for the RAF. However, his new appointment, although without title, was a clear signal from George Brown that HMG had little confidence in the High Commissioner, Sir Richard Turnbull. As Lord Shackleton prepared a small team for his visit to Aden, Turnbull remained tight-lipped about what many in the High Commission regarded as a betrayal by HMG.

The Foreign Office planned a dual operation to induce FLOSY to engage in talks. Lord Shackleton would publicly embody HMG's new policy of 'cooperation' while a secret emissary would 'sound-out' FLOSY to discuss their terms. The High Commission were unaware of this secret emissary until a political officer spotted the notorious Tom Driberg in a bar in Aden. It transpired that Driberg, MP for Barking, had flown out using the cover of a journalist for the *Evening Standard*. Once there, Driberg had resorted to type and started boasting of his connections with the intelligence services, proudly announcing to fellow journalist Eric Downton that he had been a friend of the now exposed double agent, Kim Philby, and 'could interview him in Moscow, any time he wished'. However, for now, Driberg's brief was confined to cajoling Arab nationalists and terrorists.[21]

Driberg's life had always been a complete contradiction. He had started out as 'William Hickey', the society columnist for *The Daily Express*, and during World War II became an MI5 informant as well as subsequent bouts as a KGB contact. He relished the company of both 'low-life' and establishment figures in Britain but politically remained on the extreme left-wing of the British Labour Party. As a highly promiscuous and reckless homosexual, his address book featured the great and the good, many of whom lived in fear of exposure. His behaviour was so outrageous that Winston Churchill had once remarked that Driberg was 'bringing sodomy into disrepute'.[22] But Driberg was a fervent networker and included among his old friends Lord Louis Mountbatten, who was Chief of the Defence Staff until 1965 and still retained considerable influence within the military sphere. With his left-wing credentials, the Labour MP had also cultivated links with guerrilla and nationalist movements in old colonial territories, including FLOSY and the ATUC, and this made him a useful instrument for HMG. The policy of the Wilson Government was now aimed at driving the warring NLF and FLOSY into talks with the Federalists, but with a visit by George Thomson, Joint Minister of State at the Foreign Office, failing to produce results, the FO looked at Driberg as a useful go-between.

Remaining in constant contact with Thomson and Lord Shackleton, on 11 April Driberg visited al-Asnag in Taiz. The FLOSY spokesman confirmed that the violence would only be stopped if HMG started talks directly with FLOSY, excluding both the Federal Government and the NLF. In an attempt to block out the High Commission in Aden, al-Asnag also confirmed that discussions on the future of the sultans could only be carried out via 'indirect channels'.[23] Driberg then visited Khalifa Abdullah Khalifa, the man who had attempted to kill Sir Kennedy Trevaskis at Khormaksar in 1963, and who was now the FLOSY representative in Khartoum. Driberg reported that Khalifa was receptive to the idea of a meeting with Lord Shackleton in Khartoum but inferred that neither al-Asnag nor Mackawee, the leading lights in FLOSY, would talk to HMG because of Egyptian pressure. This was confirmed several days later by reports that Mackawee had announced that 'anyone who deals with Lord Shackleton will be killed'.[24]

Still undeterred, Driberg flew to Aden and sounded out local FLOSY commanders about contacting Mackawee. With his usual disregard for caution, he was seen driving with them through numerous military checkpoints, apparently undetected. Driberg, who was still under a journalist's cover, found out that Mackawee was now in Taiz and so travelled back there on 17 April. Having met Mackawee, he tried to convince him of Lord Shackleton's sincerity and his ability to radically change HMG's policy in South Arabia. Mackawee was obviously aware that Driberg was acting for Lord Shackleton and sent him away with a message from the FLOSY Revolutionary Council that there would be no meetings with HMG or her representatives. However, despite Mackawee's indignation at the High Commission staff and his apparent thwarting by Tony Ashworth and IRD, it was probably pressure from the Egyptians that always kept FLOSY away from talks with the British.[25]

Meanwhile, Lord Shackleton arrived in Aden on 12 April. By 28 April he had completed his assessment of the situation but had conspicuously failed to draw FLOSY into talks, while the threat from the NLF was not even on the agenda. He returned to London, accompanied by Sir Richard Turnbull, ostensibly to discuss the UN role with the Foreign Secretary. But George Brown was still smarting over the refusal by the High Commissioner to broadcast the UN Mission's statement and had already decided to remove Turnbull.[26] A colonial servant to the core, Turnbull had nevertheless become rapidly disillusioned with his political masters, and even cynical about his mission, later confiding to Denis Healey that once the British Empire had ended, 'it would leave behind it only two monuments: one was the game of Association Football, the other was the expression "F*** off"'.[27]

A move to replace Turnbull with Sir Humphrey Trevelyan was already well advanced, but at a meeting at Dorneywood with George Brown on 6 May, Trevelyan made it clear that 'if there was no prospect of leaving a stable government behind in South Arabia, it would be better to carry on with Sir Richard Turnbull'.[28] At the meeting, Trevelyan repeatedly voiced reservations about accepting the job as the last High Commissioner. He asked for a commitment from the Foreign Secretary that no immediate public statement would be made regarding the lack of RAF or Carrier presence, post independence. George Brown was clearly taken aback by Trevelyan's stance, even commenting to him years later, 'do you remember how bloody rude you were to me at Dorneywood?' Nevertheless, Trevelyan was hastily pushed into his new position, with George Brown 'refusing to take no for an answer'.[29] One consolation was that Trevelyan was eminently suitable. He was an experienced diplomat who was recently HMG's ambassador in Moscow, but despite his undoubted qualities, there was much disquiet in the High Commission about Turnbull's summary dismissal. There was concern that Turnbull was removed not merely because he had presided over a deteriorating security situation but because Trevelyan was 'more friendly towards President Nasser'.[30]

Trouble was escalating throughout the Middle East. Furthermore,

Israeli Intelligence, which monitored Soviet political pressure in the region, attributed the increase in Soviet activity to the British announcement of a withdrawal from Aden. Russian military instructors and hardware were indeed pouring into both Egypt and Syria but the Arab home forces remained weak compared to the Israeli military. On 7 April, in an escalation of the border dispute with Syria, Israeli aircraft launched a devastating attack on Syrian artillery batteries and shot down six Syrian MiG fighters. It was a serious humiliation for the new leftist Syrian Ba'ath regime, compounded by the failure of any Arab government to come to its aid. As a result, Israeli confidence reached new heights. In mid-May Egyptian troop concentrations near the Israeli border failed to excite the Israeli government, primarily because they could not believe Egypt was capable of launching an attack against them while it had such a large military commitment in Yemen. Yet recent arms deals clinched with the Soviet Union had pushed the total Egyptian compliment of tanks to over 1,200 while its Air Force possessed 500 aircraft, including the latest MiG-21. This prompted Nasser to boast that 'Egypt's Soviet-made aircraft were more than a match for anything Israel possessed'.[31] Despite Nasser's public optimism, privately he was still concerned that should any Arab–Israeli conflict erupt, Britain would use her military bases in Libya, Cyprus and Aden to come to the aid of Israel. He therefore kept up his violent public denouncements of the British role in South Arabia.[32]

On 11 May Major-General Philip Tower flew into Khormaksar airport to take up his appointment both as the new GOC Middle East Land Forces (MELF), as well as Deputy to the Commander-in-Chief, Middle East Command. The retirement of Major-General Sir John Willoughby, who left Aden on the *Orsova* to the strains of 'Auld Lang Syne', was an unfortunate, though not an unsurprising move. Willoughby had carried out his two-year appointment as GOC with distinction and had even received the unusual accolade of a KBE whilst still commanding in Aden. But with only six months to go until the British withdrawal, it seemed to many a hasty action and that he should have been allowed to see the job through to the end.

The new GOC, Major-General Tower, was a 'gunner', who had fought in World War II at Arnhem and in Norway, and during the 1950s had commanded 'J' (Sidi Rezegh) Battery RHA, who had recently given sterling service in the 1964 Radfan Campaign. His subsequent command of 51 and 12 Infantry Brigades had been followed by a two-year appointment in 1965, as Director of Public Relations (Army); and it was this PR background that deemed him a suitable choice to handle the last months of British rule, even though he had not seen active service since World War II.[33] Furthermore, General Tower conceded that he had no great knowledge of the region, but during his two-week intensive briefing prior to taking up his new command, he impressed many with his grasp of the problems involved in the British withdrawal.[34]

Communiques were issued daily by the NLF containing an unrelenting list of assassinations. On 9 May they announced that 'NLF commandos executed the agent Sultan al-Haddar Salih of Upper Yafa, while driving in his car with his nephew'. Two days later they declared that they had 'shot and killed Mr Shantilal Pankhinia, a British Intelligence Officer in Tawahi' whom they described as 'heading a spy-ring and holding a senior post in the RAF but who always wore civilian clothes'.[35] This terrorist pressure was not only applied to the Western states of the Federation but also extended to the Eastern states still outside the Federation. On 15 May in Mukalla, Abdullah Qadhi, the religious head of the Shibam district, was shot dead but a burst of automatic fire failed to kill the Vice-Governor of Western Qu'aiti. Blindicide rockets were fired at the British Residency and there were reports that HMS *Brighton* lying offshore had received incoming rounds.[36] The failure of the state forces to follow up any of these incidents in the EAP made Jim Ellis, the Resident Advisor, realise the end had come. He sent off an urgent telegram to John Wilton, the Deputy High Commissioner in Aden:

> Monday night's incident and the lack of arrests since then have depressed the morale of the Europeans in Mukalla to an all-time low. The reason for the State Forces' inability to make arrests is their own distrust of our future intentions. If they have to make terms with the NLF or FLOSY, then they cannot afford to cross swords with them. The position has sunk in to my colleagues and their attitude is that if it looked as if they could accomplish something, they might be prepared to risk life and limb a little longer, but if we continue the way we are going, purpose is non-existent and the sooner we get out the better.[37]

However, morale remained high among British troops, and when 3 Royal Anglian Regiment left Aden for the last time on 24 May 1967, they left as proud members of a new regiment. They had suffered 174 casualties but an identity was forged out of their experiences in South Arabia. They handed over in Sheikh Othman to the 1st Battalion The Parachute Regiment (1 PARA), under the command of Lieutenant-Colonel (later Major-General) Mike Walsh, and it was not long before the Paras were in the thick of the action. On 1 June the NLF and FLOSY generated a General Strike to disrupt Aden but, as the Paras' CO remembered, it was not a case of peaceful demonstrations:

> I do not believe that many people, except those directly involved, really appreciated what a General Strike in Aden really meant in

terms of violence and bloodshed. Dye trucks, riot acts, and tear gas were now things of the past; this was open insurgency.

At 0200 hrs I deployed D Company with, under command, a platoon of C Company, into the heart of Sheikh Othman. This force, under the command of Major Geoffrey Brierley was to occupy eight OPs including the main Police Station. These OPs provided good positions from which to dominate the main thoroughfares, the principal Mosque (which was the centre of previous disturbances) and the main route to the North.

The first incident occurred when a patrol was grenaded outside the main Mosque. Immediately fire was returned from one of our OPs in the Eastern Bank building, killing two men running into the Mosque and a third who had taken refuge behind a plate glass window. In the meantime, the patrol captured a fourth member of the grenade party. This incident appeared to be a signal for battle to be joined, because immediately all OPs were engaged by accurate and sustained fire, in some cases from as close as 50 yards across the rooftops. This firefight went on continuously for nearly five hours, and in the course of it, a sniper killed one of our GPMG gunners and one man was wounded. Two troops of armoured cars patrolled the streets and engaged targets, indicated to them by tracer fire from the OPs.

At 1100 hrs the main Mosque began to broadcast what appeared to be instructions to the terrorists to change positions, since a lull in the battle followed for about 20 minutes. This was the moment that changed the course of the battle because it gave the Company Commander the chance to gain the initiative. All OPs were ordered to fire short bursts into all identified terrorist positions and into other rooftop positions. This had a marked effect on the terrorists who hereafter were forced to use positions up to 300 yards away from our own OPs.[38]

The fight continued until well after dark, by which time the Paras had resisted all terrorist attempts to eject them from Sheikh Othman. They accounted for eight terrorists killed and a significant number wounded, but their successful action gave them little respite. Together with other British troops, they would soon be on the receiving end of a furious Arab backlash. The 'Six-Day War' or as Arabs know it, 'The Setback', was about to begin.[39]

In Aden on 4 June, which was the eve of the Six-Day War, two elderly Jews were attacked and trampled to death by a mob in Crater. It was a foretaste of the impending Arab/Israeli hostilities, and arrangements were hastily made to move the remaining Jews out of Crater and into the Tawahi district. The hard-pressed 1 Lancashire Regiment (PWV) were given the task of protecting the Jews but, as the citation for a humanitarian award records, no area was safe for them:

A Jewish owned hotel and block of shops were burned down and looted, but although several attempts were made on their lives and property, The Lancashire Regiment prevented any casualties being inflicted on the Jewish community. They also recovered, at considerable risk to themselves, the property and belongings left behind by the Jews in Crater. Over a period of several days, the future of the Jews was uncertain. Eventually World Jewry produced aircraft and arranged for them to be evacuated to other countries.

During all this time, the 1st Battalion The Lancashire Regiment was responsible not only for protection, but for all other aspects of the life of this community of 141 persons. Their responsibilities included medical care, general welfare and the solving of domestic problems. But it was a far from pleasant task and by carrying it out they automatically increased the enmity of the local population. During the period, the Battalion had one man killed and suffered other casualties.[40]

Despite many attempts on their lives, the small Jewish community in Aden survived unscathed until evacuation, except for one unfortunate man who attempted to go back into Crater and was immediately beaten to death.

While the Jewish population remained 'corralled' in Aden, it was a different story in their homeland. The Israeli Defence Force (IDF) was poised to inflict huge losses on its Arab opponents. Despite the rhetoric, Egypt was not ready for war, and indeed, many commentators have maintained that her deployment of large forces in Sinai was not for offensive reasons but was designed to deter Israel from attacking Syria.[41] If so, it was a massive miscalculation. The IDF comprised twenty-five brigades, 175 fighter planes and over 1,000 tanks, easily capable of crushing any Arab army on any of its borders. At 7.45am on Monday 5 June 1967 the Israeli air force attacked the Egyptians, wiping out their air force on the ground. By the evening, the Jordanian air force was destroyed and the Syrians crippled. With complete air control, the Israeli armoured brigades turned on the Egyptian Army in Sinai and obliterated its fleeing troop columns. In four days, the Israelis had reached the Suez Canal, and by the end of the week, had stormed the Golan Heights. With the road open to Damascus, the Syrians sued for peace.

The scale of the Arab defeat was catastrophic. The Egyptian Army lost some 12,000 men, including 1,500 officers and forty valuable pilots, with a further 5,000 men missing in action. Over 85% of Egyptian military hardware was captured or destroyed. Against this, Israel suffered only 800 killed and by the end of the short war it had expanded its territory over three and a half times.[42] There is no doubt that the absence in Yemen of elite Egyptian troops depleted the Arab home defences and was also a consideration in the timing of the Israeli attack. However, even the presence of extra troops could have made little impact against an attacker who had achieved immediate air superiority. Conversely, the absence in Yemen of so many Egyptian units had saved them from certain destruction.[43]

The Six-Day War had wide repercussions and involved re-alignments in Middle East policies. Nasser's failure left him with no alternative but to attempt reconciliation with King Feisal, who in turn organised the oil-rich members of the Arab League to bail Egypt out financially, no doubt expecting to exert leverage on the issue of Egyptian troops in Yemen.[44] But while Feisal was careful not to rupture Saudi relations with the US, Nasser had no such inhibitions. He swiftly denounced the US for complicity in the Israeli attack and severed diplomatic relations. Yemen and five other radical Arab states swiftly followed Nasser's lead.

Miles Copeland, CIA Station Chief in Cairo, observed the different attitudes of Egyptian leaders after the disastrous defeat. Abdul Hakim Amer, Egyptian Chief of Staff, 'was holed up in his house, licking his wounds and smoking hashish', while Nasser went on air with Radio Cairo, played the *mea culpa* card and soon had the crowds weeping and chanting for him.[45] While his standing with the other Arab governments undoubtedly suffered from the Six-Day War, the Egyptian President still managed to pull back support among the people in the streets, by reviving that all-important 'face' that Arabs felt they had lost at the hands of the Israelis. For many Arabs, especially those in South Arabia waiting for independence, there was a refusal to believe that two million Jews could defeat 100 million Arabs and that someone must have helped the Israelis. What became known as 'The Big Lie' emanated from Radio Cairo and proclaimed that it was the Americans and British who ensured the Israeli victory. It was exactly what the emotive Arab crowds wanted to hear. It certainly gave a huge fillip to the terrorists in South Arabia who were demanding a 'spectacular' against the British in Aden. The Israeli victory also disturbed the Federation's Arab army and there were offers from FRA battalions to give up their pay to help their 'Arab comrades in the fight against Israel'.[46]

During the Six-Day War, Lieutenant-Colonel Mitchell, together with an advance party of 126 officers and men from the 1st Battalion Argyll and Sutherland Highlanders had landed in Aden and prepared the way for the main body of the battalion to arrive several weeks later. As they were to take over from 1 RNF, the Argylls' advance party shared the Fusiliers barracks at Waterloo Lines, beside Khormaksar airfield. Joint reconnaissance operations took place and although 1 RNF had been particularly successful in their operations against terrorists in Crater, Mitchell's previous experience convinced him that more resolute action was required:

I considered that the Aden Brigade policy was 'containment' in the classic manner, that is, it was neither truly offensive nor purely defensive – middle of the road stuff. But confident that the Argylls were tough, trained and full of fight, I was planning a vigorous military domination of Crater.[47]

Several days after his arrival, Lieutenant-Colonel Mitchell was interviewed by Aden Forces Radio and in reply to a question on the adequacy of the security arrangements, commented that Aden was 'the least buttoned-up place I know'.[48] The scene was inevitably set for a conflict between a battalion Commander and his GOC. Lieutenant-Colonel Mitchell's prime instincts were military imperatives within Crater and pride in a fine regiment, whereas Major-General Tower had to juggle his military resources between Aden and up-country. The GOC also had to consider the effect that any military action had on the political future of South Arabia. However, given the collapse in political will in London and the feebleness of the Federal Government, it was not difficult to understand the frustration of subordinate Commanders in the field.

Meanwhile, the Yemen adventure was another financial disaster facing Nasser. The Six-Day War had made him reliant on Saudi and Kuwaiti aid amounting to over £100m a year, but Sallal's increasingly corrupt administration was estimated to be costing the Egyptian Treasury £50m a year. In the light of these economic strictures the Soviet Union began to increase its direct economic and military aid to Yemen, the Russian language was being taught in the few schools, and many Russians and East Bloc military advisors were now openly seen in the streets of Hodeidah and Taiz.[49]

On the streets of Crater and Sheikh Othman, British Commanders were always instructed to apply only the minimum force necessary to achieve their military objectives or to restore order in riot situations. This was in stark contrast to the policy of other countries, such as France, who had faced insurgency wars in their colonies. In Algeria, where the local population had been so terrorised by the nationalist guerrillas that they supported them out of fear, the French security forces attempted to counter this terror with a similar brutal force and thereby frighten the locals into submitting to their authority. However, British military Commanders always understood that there was a limit, beyond which a local population would not react to violence and threats, and such intimidation would become counter-productive.[50] But while the vast majority of British troops adhered to this concept, there were instances where discipline broke down, as one military policeman recalled:

On the whole, the British lads behaved well under difficult circumstances. But there were exceptions, and you have to remember that all armies have their share of brutal soldiers. We once had to guard four young infantrymen who had been accused of murder. They were to be court-martialled but I was amazed at the conditions of the cells they were kept in – more like the 'Black Hole of Calcutta'. And we had another call to arrest an SAS man who had gone berserk and was firing off rounds into the WAF unit. When we arrived, there were still screams coming from the building, but when we found him, he was just sitting there with a 'Coke' in one hand and a rifle in the other, calm as you like. He refused to say anything to us, but after we put him in a cell, two SAS officers arrived and spirited him away.[51]

If HMG could not leave a stable political government behind, there was at least a desire to leave a semblance of a unified army. On 1 June 1967 a new South Arabian Army (SAA) was formed out of the merger of the old Arab FRA and part of FNG 1, and it was hoped that when the remaining Eastern States joined the Federation, the Hadhrami Bedouin League would also join the SAA.[52] But under the veneer of a unified army the old tribal rivalries simmered as before. While the FRA had to a large extent been 'detribalised', the men from FNG 1 were historically recruited from the hinterland where tribal influence was still strong. It was estimated that nearly 30% of the Arab officers in the new SAA were from the Aulaqi tribe but only 23% of the Other Ranks were Aulaqis. This imbalance was further exaggerated by the appointment of Colonel Nasser Bureiq, a prominent Aulaqi, as Deputy Commander of the SAA. He had close ties to the Federal Government, and despite his average ability and suspect financial arrangements, was the first choice for Commander of the SAA after independence, a prospect that alarmed the majority of the Army.[53]

Brigadier (later Major-General) Jack Dye,[54] the Commander of the old FRA, was appointed the first Commander of the new South Arabian Army, and was assisted by Lieutenant-Colonel (later General Sir Richard) Lawson as Chief of Staff. Colonel Lawson was no stranger to anarchic situations, having won the DSO several years earlier when serving with the UN peace-keeping force in the lawless Congo, by saving a Belgian priest from an 800-strong mob, armed only with a swagger-stick.[55] In South Arabia he would not be called upon to repeat such acts of bravery but his administrative skills would be sorely tested. The FRA had brought five battalions, and FNG 1 had brought four battalions to the merger, with the brief to nearly double the size of the new army. At the same time support weapons and a logistical organisation were to be added, which proved a great challenge. Colonel Lawson also faced serious problems over FRA loyalties. All Arab officers were promoted from the ranks and therefore had little or no vested interest in the old system of rulers. And although many of the Arab officers were bright, educated and had received their military schooling at Sandhurst, their loyalty could no longer be assumed. Inevitably, they realised that the British were about to leave and that they would soon have to serve under either an NLF or a FLOSY government. Consequently, no intelligence could be offered to the Chief of Staff's office for fear that any SAA soldier would pass it straight on to the enemy.[56]

Consequently, the British had little warning that a petition was to be delivered to the Federal Minister of Defence on 3 June, complaining about the favouritism shown in the Army towards the Aulaqi tribe. What was worrying was that the petition was signed by four out of the six SAA *Aqeeds* (Colonels) and seven out of the 15 *Quaids* (Lieutenant-Colonels). It was well prepared, for the scheme was co-ordinated by the Dathini tribe together with the most senior officer in the FNG 1, and it reflected a deep and entrenched hostility within the SAA to the favoured Aulaqis and their Federal sponsors.[57] Unfortunately, at the time the petition was presented, the SAA Commander, Brigadier Dye, was on leave in Malta and the matter was left to fester until his return on 16 June.

Concurrent with the re-organisation of the Army was the establishment of a new South Arabian Police (SAP) force. This was to be created from the merger of a part of the old FNG 2, the Aden Civil Police and the Aden Armed Police.[58] And again, it was a far from smooth marriage. As recently as April 1967 40% of Other Ranks in FNG 2 had no uniform and the tribal based force was poorly trained and badly equipped. This contrasted with the 350 men of the Aden Armed Police who, until the events of 20 June 1967, had an excellent record. However, unlike the new army formation, the police amalgamation never really materialised and the combined South Arabian Police force existed in name only. Meanwhile, the NLF heavily infiltrated the old separate police forces with policemen regularly acting as conduits for terrorist weapons, while others split their loyalties between the force and the terrorists, which produced major tensions.[59] The only way to combat this problem was for British troops to regularly search police cars, which in turn created ill will. As the police already held a grudge against the Army for taking away their role in internal security duties, the relationship was under great strain. Such was the sensitivity of policing RAF sites that only British police could be entrusted with the task and extra men had to be drafted in.[60] Acting Corporal Jim Finn was previously serving with RAF Police at Ballykelly in Northern Ireland:

> One day, while I was at home in Northern Ireland, there was a sharp rap on the front door. It was an RUC constable who instructed me to 'RTU [return to unit] immediately'. That night I found myself on the Belfast–Liverpool boat en route to London to join a BOAC VC10 planeload of servicemen bound for Aden. As we approached Aden at 0300 hours, the aircraft suddenly lurched upwards and the cultured voice of the pilot with typical English coolness, announced over the

intercom, 'I'm sorry about that sudden change of direction. We seem to have encountered some hostile enemy fire. I'm going to circle for a couple of minutes until the chaps on the ground clear the approach for us'.

When we eventually landed there was a small fleet of open top Landrovers waiting for us, all of which had a long metal pole welded to its front. Apparently there had been occasions when cheese cutter wire had been stretched across the road by terrorists hoping to lop off the heads of military personnel and these metal poles were supposed to combat this.[61]

When Brigadier Dye returned from leave on 16 June he was shown the petition against Aulaqi domination, which was by now two weeks old and subject to much heated debate within the SAA. The time lapse had also allowed the NLF to work on this disaffection. Dye discussed the issue with British officials in the Federal Ministry of Defence and on 18 June decided to officially suspend the four leading Arab Colonels pending an investigation. It was the Colonels' attempt to go direct to the Federal Government, rather than through the correct Army channels, that prompted their suspension, and it had dramatic consequences.

The four Arab Colonels were incensed, for they had lost the all-important 'face' and were determined to recover their pride. Battalions of SAA had, during the two weeks of Brigadier Dye's absence, organised a campaign of disobedience and demonstrations. There was evidence that this disruption would occur not only in Aden but also throughout the hinterland, which was garrisoned by largely non-Aulaqi FNG, who had spent their careers in isolated up-country forts. It was enough to edge the already nervous Arab security forces towards open mutiny and well-placed officials such as Donal McCarthy, Political Advisor to Admiral Michael Le Fanu, C-in-C MEC, were in no doubt as to where the blame lay:

> The mutinies of June 20 this year might not have happened had malcontents not been able to take advantage of the exasperation of senior officers with the Federal Ministers' failure to sack the senior Arab officer of the Army, Nasser Buraik, whom all admitted to be quite unsuitable for command. Muhammad Farid was the chief villain of the piece, for the narrowest factional Aulaqi reasons. But other Ministers went along readily enough with him, particularly the ineffable Sultan of Lahej as Minister for Defence. One reason was clear enough: to put the onus on us.[62]

NOTES

1   Paget, op. cit., pp. 176–7.
2   Brigadier Charles Dunbar to C-in-C MEC, 8 March 1967.
3   Memo, A H Dutton to Dr J Carruthers, 8 February 1967. File 28693, BP Archives, UW.
4   Little, *South Arabia*, op. cit., p. 151.
5   The South Arabian League had drifted to the sidelines and its leaders had made indirect contact with the British. They were largely financed by Saudi Arabia but they had little chance of gaining power after independence. For the Mackawee bomb and funeral incident, see A J Wilton to D McCarthy, 8 March 1967, FCO 8/205, NA. Also D McCarthy to Sir Denis Allen, 28 February 1967, FCO 8/205, NA.
6   *The Times*, 1 March 1967, Ledger, op. cit., pp. 75–9, and *The Economist*, 4 March 1967.
7   Brigadier Charles Dunbar to Lieutenant-Colonel J Paget, 25 September 1968, File 2/6, Dunbar Papers, LHCMA.
8   D McCarthy to Foreign Office, 1 March 1967. Also Foreign Office to High Commission, 3 March 1967, both FCO 8/206, NA. Also Monica Ingledow to Author, 15 May 2002 and *The Times*, 1 March 1967.
9   Lieutenant-Colonel Colin Mitchell, *Having Been A Soldier*, Hamish Hamilton, 1969, p. 156.
10 Lieutenant-Colonel Colin Mitchell, 'The Truth About Aden', *The Sunday Express*, 18 October 1968.
11 In the second quarter, British forces saw their casualties total thirty killed and 101 wounded, whereas the terrorists would lose sixty-one killed and wounded. See Provost & Security statistics, WO 305/3722, NA.
12 The last reported downpour in Aden had been in 1943.
13 Confidential source and Ledger, op. cit., pp. 114–17.
14 Dresch, op. cit., pp. 239–40.
15 N R Power to G Stockwell, 30 January 1967, File 28693, BP Archives, UW.
16 Colonel John Woodhouse had retired from active service in January 1965 and was replaced by Lieutenant-Colonel Mike Wingate-Gray. Woodhouse's subsequent fact-finding role in Yemen is well documented in Alan Hoe, *David Stirling*, Little Brown, 1992, pp. 371–80.
17 Captain Charles Guthrie later became General Sir Charles Guthrie, Chief of the Defence Staff in 1997. See also Crouch, op. cit., pp. 213–16.
18 Intelligence Summary, 1 Irish Guards, January 1967, WO 305/3219, NA.
19 Intelligence Summary, 1 Irish Guards, February 1967, WO 305/3219, NA.
20 *Ashton-Under-Lyne Reporter*, 31 March 1967. Robert Carroll received the C-in-C's Commendation for bravery. He later joined the Lancashire Constabulary and the Merseyside Police. Retiring early, he took a PhD, but the memories of terrorist incidents still haunt him.
21 Driberg had a number of meetings (always witnessed) with Sir Maurice Oldfield, head of SIS. See Richard Deacon, *'C': A Biography of Sir Maurice Oldfield*, MacDonald, 1984, p. 153. For South Arabia, see 'Visit of T Driberg', FCO 8/232, NA. Also Downton, op. cit., pp. 343–4.
22 Driberg's eventual elevation to the peerage as Lord Bradwell was reportedly as a result of pressure from Michael Foot because Driberg was going blind. For Driberg's relationships, see Francis Wheen, *Tom Driberg: His Life and Indiscretions*, Chatto & Windus, London, 1990.
23 Sir Richard Turnbull to Foreign Office, 14 April 1967, FCO 8/232, NA.
24 Driberg to Thomson, 15 April 1967, FCO 8/232, NA. Also Foreign Office to British Embassy, Khartoum, 15 April 1967, FCO 8/232, NA.

25 Mackawee had given several recent interviews to journalists, including one to David Holden. See Driberg to Foreign Office, 'Conversations with Mr Mackawee, 17–18 April 1967', FCO 8/232, NA. See also Ledger, op. cit., p. 120 and Bidwell, *Two Yemens*, op. cit., p. 180.
26 R F Eberle, Personal Secretary to Sir Richard Turnbull, Tape # 926, Oral History Archive, BECM, Bristol. See also 'Sir Richard Turnbull Obituary', *The Daily Telegraph*, 24 December 1998. Unlike his predecessor, Sir Kennedy Trevaskis and his successor, Sir Humphrey Trevelyan, Turnbull left no memoirs.
27 Denis Healey, *The Time of My Life*, Michael Joseph, 1989, p. 283.
28 'Record of a meeting between The Foreign Secretary and Sir Humphrey Trevelyan', 6 May 1967, FCO 8/250, NA. The meeting was attended by senior figures in the Foreign Office and High Commission, including Lord Caradon, Sir Dennis Allen, T F Brenchley, D McCarthy and A J Wilton. In his memoir, *In My Way*, George Brown skirted over the issue of South Arabia, merely commenting, 'I agreed with my colleagues that we should get out of the Middle East, but did not agree on the speed and timetable', p. 141.
29 Humphrey Trevelyan, *Public and Private*, Hamish Hamilton, 1980, p. 60–1.
30 PM's Personal and Political Secretary to B Giles, 18 May 1967, FCO 8/250, NA. Also 'A Change of Men', *The Times*, 11 May 1967. Trevelyan's reputation as a friend of Nasser originated during his time as Ambassador in Cairo in 1956 at the time of the Anglo–French landings in Suez.
31 Moshe Gat, *Britain and the Conflict in the Middle East 1964–1967*, Praeger, 2003, p. 23.
32 Moshe Gat, op. cit. pp. 69, 93, 151. It would be some time before the US could fill the vacuum in the Middle East, due to its huge commitment in South-East Asia.
33 Major-General Philip Tower to Author, 14 September 2001. He was appointed Commandant, RMA Sandhurst in 1968 and retired in 1972.
34 A H Dutton to P Batterbury, 8 May 1967, File 28693, BP Archives, UW.
35 'NLF *Communiqués*', 9 May 1967 and 17 May 1967, File 2/3, Dunbar Papers, LHCMA.
36 *The Financial Times*, 18 May 1967. See also 'Transcript of Radio Cairo Broadcast, 18 May 1967', FCO 8/252, NA.
37 Jim Ellis to John Wilton, 18 May 1967, FCO 8/252, NA.
38 Lieutenant-Colonel M J H Walsh, DSO, 'Everything under the Sun', in *RUSI Journal*, March 1969. The battalion's, Second-in-Command, Major (later Brigadier) Joe Starling, recounted his experiences in Aden in *Soldier On! The Testament of a Tom*, Spellmount, 1992.
39 Barthorp, op. cit., p. 48.
40 Citation for consideration of 'The Wilkinson Award', File 2/4, Dunbar Papers, LHCMA.
41 Commentators included the influential editor of the Egyptian newspaper, *al-Ahram*. See also Michael B Oren, *Six Days of War: June 1967 and the Making of the Modern Middle East*, OUP, 2002, p. 76.
42 For a recent analysis of the war and its effects, see Oren, op. cit., and for the origins and aftermath of the war, see Walter Laqueur, *The Road to War*, Weidenfeld & Nicolson, 1968. One unsolved mystery of the War was the extraordinary Israeli attack on the American spy ship, USS *Liberty*.
43 It is estimated that of Egypt's forces in Sinai, 40% were reservists and 60% regular or conscripted troops. See Ali Rahmy op. cit., p. 251.
44 Rahmy, op. cit., p. 142.
45 Miles Copeland, op. cit., pp. 237–8. Field-Marshal Amer was arrested after

the June disaster and several months later it was announced that he had 'committed suicide' in custody. See Anwar el-Sadat, op. cit., pp. 190–4.

46 Trevelyan to Foreign Office, 11 June 1967, FCO 8/252, NA.
47 Lieutenant-Colonel Colin Mitchell, *Having Been a Soldier*, Hamish Hamilton, 1969, p. 6. Also his article, 'The Truth about Aden', *The Sunday Express*, 18 October 1968.
48 Ibid.
49 Moshe Gat, op. cit., p.16. Also Wenner, op. cit., p. 145.
50 Major-General Sir John Willoughby, 'Problems of Counter-Insurgency in the Middle East', in *RUSI Journal*, May 1968.
51 Confidential source to Author, 11 July 2003.
52 Lord and Birtles, op. cit., p. 63.
53 Bureiq had also broken a 'golden rule' of service in the Arab Army, in that he had not retired after failing to gain promotion during the past three years. 'Notes on the Aden Mutiny 20 June 1967', Records of The Fusiliers Museum of Northumberland. See also Ledger, op. cit., pp. 134–7, and Paget, op. cit., pp. 212–13.
54 Brigadier Dye was CO 1st East Anglians during the Radfan Campaign and had been Brigadier CO, FRA since 1966. In 1971, as Major-General, he became Colonel Commandant of the new Queen's Division.
55 Colonel Lawson's extraordinary adventures in Congo (Zaire) are recalled in his book, *Strange Soldiering*, Hodder & Stoughton, 1963. As General, he later became Commander-in-Chief, Allied Forces Northern Europe 1982–4.
56 General Sir Richard Lawson to Author, 11 May 2001. Also Brigadier Dunbar, 'Notes for lecture on South Arabia 1967', File 2/5, Dunbar Papers, LHCMA.
57 The most senior officer was Lieutenant-Colonel Sharif Haidar, a nephew of the Sharif of Beihan. For a copy of the petition, see 'Report on the Mutinies', MEC, op. cit., DEFE 11/533, NA.
58 FNG 2 comprised units that only operated within individual state borders. FG I operated throughout the Federation. Neither Guard operated in Aden, the preserve of the Aden Civil Police supported by the Aden Armed Police. The intention was that the new SAP would also include The Lahej State Police.
59 'Notes on *Last Post*', in letter Brigadier C Dunbar to Lieutenant-Colonel J Paget, 25 September 1968, File 2/6, Dunbar Papers, LHCMA. Also 'The South Arabian Army and South Arabian Police', MEC, 26 October 1967, DEFE 11/533, NA.
60 'Lecture Notes II', File 2/5, Brigadier Dunbar Papers, LHCMA.
61 Jim Finn to Author, 30 June 2003.
62 Donal McCarthy to Arabian Department, FO, 13 October 1967, FCO 8/41, NA.

CHAPTER XII
Mutiny
(20 June 1967)

As ferment was quietly simmering within the SAA, events in London took a dramatic turn. In the House of Commons, George Brown announced that independence for South Arabia would be granted on 9 January 1968 but in a departure from the Government's policy of no military assistance, from that date a British force of Vulcan Bombers would be available to assist the Federation. To the jeers of his back-benchers the Foreign Secretary confirmed that the bombers, based on the nearby island of Masira, could offer conventional weapons support. They would be assisted by a strong British naval force, which would be stationed in South Arabian waters for six months after independence. This gesture to the Federation was too little, too late, but it staggered the Conservative Opposition who had always argued for such a commitment.[1]

Despite George Brown's gesture of support for the Federation, most British officials realised the Federal rulers were far too weak to combat the terrorists. One fundamental weakness was their complete lack of any independent intelligence network, either up-country or in Aden. This resulted in a lack of information about unrest within the SAA, exacerbated by NLF infiltration within its command structure. This infiltration was well advanced, with the 'NLF military liaison group' establishing firm contacts among the junior officers of the SAA. The Federal Government's prospects of maintaining future control looked slim indeed.

But snippets of information about the unrest did eventually reach the Federal Ministry of Defence. They were told that demonstrations were planned to start on 19 June but, apart from a doubling of the SAA guards at Bir Fuqum in Little Aden and also at Lake Lines, where the SAA maintained its training base, nothing was done. Stories of impending revolt were discounted as rumours, always endemic in life in South Arabia. However, on 19 June a plot to seize the armoury at Bir Fuqum was uncovered and it was only the swift actions of a loyal Arab officer, who removed the keys and sent them to 24 Brigade Headquarters, that prevented the arms falling into rebel hands. Yet this event went largely unreported. Incredibly, neither the British officials in the Federal

Government nor the SAA passed on official reports of the incident to either the High Commissioner or Headquarters MEC. The Federal Government made cursory enquiries about the stability of the SAA but Arab Commanders assured them that discipline would hold.[2]

Despite this, MEC was aware that trouble was brewing. Lieutenant-Colonel Mitchell was dining in Little Aden on the evening of 19 June, together with General Tower and other senior commanders and, according to Mitchell, the talk concerned unrest within the SAA. Specific threats were not discussed, but Colonel Mitchell sensed a sudden up-grading in the GOC's personal security.[3] At dawn on 20 June the NLF issued an ominous statement denouncing 'the attempts by Britain to hand over responsibilities for security to the Arab Army' and calling on 'all Arab officers and men to resist this dirty imperialist plot'.[4]

Then, at about 0800 hours on 20 June a commotion erupted in the main SAA base at Lake Lines, just outside Sheikh Othman. Arab army apprentices and trainees (but no serving ranks from the SAA) went on the rampage, shouting slogans in support of the suspended SAA officers and burning down huts. Shots were heard and an attempt was made to storm the armoury but order was eventually restored by loyal Arab officers and NCOs. In the meantime, the Federal Ministry of Internal Security heard about the incident and, without reference to any senior British or Arab officers, warned the South Arabian Police (then in barracks in nearby Champion Lines) to stand by in case their support was needed for riot control. Consequently, rumours spread rapidly through the South Arabian Police that the shots heard had come from British troops who were attacking Arab soldiers.[5]

By 0950 hours about 300 trainees from FNG 2, based at Champion Lines (who were in the process of integration into the South Arabian Police force), gathered inside the Northern Gate and barricaded it. The mutineers swiftly armed themselves and took up defensive positions inside Champion Lines, seizing an arms store and a lorry carrying .303 ammunition. Anticipating an attack from the British, the mutineers despatched a Bren machine-gunner to the minaret of the base mosque, who proceeded to spray the nearby airfield and adjacent British-occupied Radfan Camp. At about 1015 hours an Aden Police officer drove up to the gates of Champion Lines to investigate and, together with his driver, he was promptly shot dead. Hugh Alexander, a civilian member of the Public Works Department who was driving past the camp, was also shot and killed by the mutineers, who soon directed more of their fire towards the Radfan Camp.

In Radfan Camp, men from 13 Platoon D Company, 1 Lancashire Regiment (PWV) rushed to defensive positions and manned the stone sangars around the perimeter. Second-Lieutenant Angus Young, commanding the defence platoon, scuttled between the sangars, checking his men were accounted for and maintaining observation of the enemy. But in order to dampen down the situation, an order came through from Brigade that fire was not to be returned. As the 21-year-old subaltern raced between sangars to convey the order, he was shot dead.[6]

In the midst of the chaos, at 1030 hours, a 3-ton army lorry came into view of the minaret in Champion Lines. It was carrying nineteen men from 60 Squadron, Royal Corps of Transport (RCT) under the command of Captain Peter Godwin, returning from rifle practice at the nearby range. Second-Lieutenant Nick Beard was with his men in the back of the lorry and vividly remembered:

> We had gone out to the range for routine rifle practice in two 3-tonners. But one had become bogged-down in the nearby salt-pans, so for the return journey all 19 of us had to pile into one lorry. The driver was in his cab while the rest of us sat up in the open back with only one sentry with a loaded magazine. Every man had his weapon with him but it was unloaded, although there were bandoliers of ammunition in the box. As was the custom, we were not in radio communication for this routine trip.
>
> Suddenly, as we came within about 100 yards of the Champion Lines perimeter, incoming rounds started peppering the lorry. The driver slammed on the brakes – we were terribly exposed – and everyone baled out over the side, except for one man who must have been killed instantly. We tried to take cover where best we could but the fire was withering. Two men were killed beside me and one poor fellow was shot through the stomach. As he sank to his knees, he let out a ghastly cry and I remember Staff-Sergeant Butler, who couldn't see the man, bellowing at him to shut up so orders could be heard. We rallied the men as best we could, retrieved some ammunition and made for the only cover around, some hillocks 30 yards to our left, which turned out to be old graves. From a loudspeaker in the minaret there was a call for us to surrender. But then the firing increased and we were pinned down for three hours during which seven of our men were killed and six were wounded. One more died overnight. Among those killed were Staff Sergeant Butler, one of many brave men to die that day.[7]

The Federal Government, who were responsible for the South Arabian Police, were caught totally by surprise by the mutiny, and it was only at 1030 hours that they requested British troops to enter Champion Lines to restore order and protect loyal Arab soldiers. The Commander of the local duty battalion, 1 PARA, then sent in C Company, 1st Battalion The King's Own Royal Border Regiment (1 KOB) (on attachment) to quell the unrest.[8] But first, in order to assess the situation, the Company Commander went in with an infantry section mounted in an APC, together with two Saladin armoured cars and two Ferret Scout cars of 5th Troop, 'A' Squadron 1 QDG. They drove into the camp towards the guardroom, where they hoped to contact friendly troops and secure the armoury without engaging the opposition. The 1 KOB Company Commander, Major David Miller, together with his section of infantry, dismounted from their Saracen APC, but despite covering fire from 1 QDG, they were subjected to heavy small-arms fire. Fifteen minutes later support appeared in the form of two platoons of 1 KOB but as they arrived at the perimeter in 3-ton lorries, they were raked by the mutineers' gunfire and one soldier was killed and eleven others were wounded.[9]

During this mayhem, Reverend Robin Roe, Chaplain to the 1 Lancashire Regiment (PWV), was with his battalion in Radfan Camp. Always a man to be quickly on the scene to help any casualties, he 'gunned' his Landrover up and accelerated the 400 yards over open desert towards Champion Lines. But incoming gunfire sprayed his vehicle and a nearby officer turned him back. Reluctantly he returned to Radfan Camp, but soon set about helping medical orderlies with the local casualties until it was possible to retrieve the wounded from the main attack.[10]

Meanwhile, the arrival of 2nd Troop 1 QDG at Champion Lines provided the necessary armoured support and Major Miller moved forward to secure the guard-room area, while ordering his men not to return fire unless absolutely necessary. Inside the Lines, the mutineers' conduct was described as 'little short of berserk'. Nevertheless, volunteers from the RCT and 1 KOB went forward into the fire zone, advancing within range of the mutineers to recover British casualties. Eventually, by about 1330 hours, the armoury and guardroom were secured and the mutineer who had fired the machine-gun from the minaret lay dead. The mutiny in the camp had come to an end.[11] Control had been re-established only after a skilful and restrained operation by 1 KOB and 1 QDG, who, despite tremendous provocation, had stopped the situation in Champion Lines from escalating.[12] However, outside the camp, news and rumour had sparked further revolt.

In the Federal capital, al-Ittihad, it had been a quiet morning with Federal Ministers going about their business. But the small settlement had a garrison of South Arabian Police who heard the rumour that their men in Champion Lines were being attacked by British troops. Some time after 1130 hours the officers of the South Arabian Police disappeared and their ranks went on the rampage around the government buildings, smashing windows and breaking up the fixtures. Terrified officials barricaded themselves into their offices, while above them on the rooftops, the South Arabian Police mutineers took up positions and waited to repel British troops. In the meantime, the missing police officers were tracked down and sent back to al-Ittihad to persuade the mutineers to return to their barracks. This seemed to have the desired effect, and as no British troops had arrived to attack them, the rebellious policemen melted away.

Meanwhile, by 1100 hours news of the mutiny in Champion Lines had reached the Crater district and rumours started that the British were about to attack the Armed Police Barracks in Queen Arwa Road. Half an hour later, the Commander of 1 RNF, Lieutenant-Colonel R Blenkinsop, received notice in his Operations Room at Waterloo Lines, near Khormaksar that the Aden Armed Police were becoming restless. This branch of the police were controlled not by the Federal Government but by the British High Commission and consequently it was Aden Brigade HQ who gave the order that the Northumberland Fusiliers were not to enter the Armed Police Barracks.[13]

1 RNF were due to retire from South Arabia at the end of June 1967, after a nine-month tour.[14] On Tuesday 20 June 'Y' Company remained responsible for Internal Security duties in Crater while the rest of the battalion officially handed over to 1 Argyll and Sutherland Highlanders. At 1200 hours Lieutenant-Colonel Blenkinsop and the rest of his battalion lined up for a retirement inspection by the Commander-in-Chief, Admiral Sir Michael Le Fanu. As the C-in-C stepped out of his car, his duty officer told Blenkinsop that the state of alert had moved to 'red'. The 1 RNF Commander then ordered units of his stand-by 'Y' Company, operating out of the Supreme Court buildings on the edge of Crater, to occupy Main Pass and Marine Road and reconnoitre into Crater but he stressed that they were not allowed to enter the Armed Police barracks. At the same time, 2nd Lieutenant John Davis of 1 RNF was ordered to take part of his 8 Platoon into Queen Arwa Road to remove a barricade created by two hijacked buses, dangerously close to the Armed Police Barracks.[15] Although the patrol comprised mainly RNF men, they were joined by several 'Jocks' from the Argylls who were advance troops based at 'Y' Company HQ. At 1145 Davis was hurriedly packed off with only five men and no radio, but swiftly returned to gather eight men, another 2nd Lieutenant from the Argylls and this time, a radio. They moved off from the Supreme Court buildings, with Davis leading in an armoured 'Pig' followed by a Saracen APC, commanded by 2nd Lieutenant Campbell-Baldwin and headed up Queen Arwa Road. Davis soon noticed that the atmosphere on the streets had changed since his earlier patrol at 10.00 hours that morning. He reported back to base that now the shops had shut down, the streets were deserted and furniture had been piled up as barricades.[16] The patrol soon came across the roadblock and Davis ordered his men to dismount and assume covering fire positions, while he and one 'Geordie' moved the buses to a lay-by. At about 1200 hours Davis attempted to report back by radio to his Company HQ that he had successfully removed the roadblock but that Armed Police were

deploying around the perimeter of the barracks and threatening his patrol. At this point Major Moncur ordered Davis back to base, and although reception was intermittent, according to one officer at 'Y' Company HQ, Davis managed to radio 'I am returning to your location'. Shortly afterwards, Davis's patrol headed out of Crater and as they reached Main Pass, scattering rioters from the road, shots were fired at the patrol and soon after, the radio went completely dead.[17] Back at 'Y' Company HQ, the shots were heard and above their base at Supreme Court Buildings, the 1 RNF Observation Post came under heavy fire and had to be withdrawn.

Meanwhile, Lieutenant-Colonel Blenkinsop ordered a helicopter to take a 1 RNF party up to an OP above Temple Cliffs so that the situation at the Armed Police Barracks could be monitored. Down at the 'Y' Company base at Supreme Court Buildings, the Company Commander, Major John Moncur, was becoming concerned at the plight of Davis's party and sent out 9 Platoon under 2nd Lieutenant John Shaw to assess the situation. However, Shaw's patrol had only gone a short distance when Major Moncur suddenly recalled them.[18] The Platoon Commander remembered:

> We had travelled about 200 yards when I heard a radio report on the current situation in Champion Lines, which ended with the instruction that units were not to enter Crater. Immediately after this, my Company Commander came on the radio and ordered me to return to Supreme Court.[19]

Shaw's patrol returned to base and heard more shots coming from the Armed Police Barracks area, but no further radio contact was achieved with the Davis patrol and because of the failure of radio contact, Company HQ were unaware that Davis was taking the longer route back.

Within minutes, Major Moncur decided to see the situation for himself and called for two Landrovers to be 'saddled up'. As it was the handover period, Major Bryan Malcolm of the Argylls elected to accompany the 'recce', and after he arrived from Waterloo Lines, the party was ready to set off. At about 1245 hours the two Landrovers swung out through the gates of the base. The first vehicle carried Major Moncur, his batman, 18-year-old Fusilier Bernard Wyllie, and Company Sergeant-Major Warrant Officer Peter Hoare together with the driver, 23-year-old Fusilier George Hoult. The second Landrover contained Major Malcolm and two fellow 'Jocks', Private Johnny Moores and Private 'Pocus' Hunter, as well as Lance-Corporal Liddell and Fusilier John Storey of 1 RNF.[20] As they drove towards Queen Arwa Road they stopped briefly at the Chartered Bank to check its security.

Meanwhile, farther up Queen Arwa Road at the Armed Police Barracks, the situation was out of control. Inside the building mutineers had burst into the armoury. Sub-Inspector Fadhl Ali Aushabi was soon pushed aside in the rush to grab weapons:

> About 50 men, all in uniform rushed into the armoury and started taking their own rifles. They said there was trouble … some shooting started outside and those already in possession of arms, dispersed. Immediately, about 100–150 men rushed to the Armoury, pushed me to one side and helped themselves to arms. They were taking them one at a time. The men included Armed Police, Civil Police and MT drivers.[21]

The mutineers were now not only armed but also had access to over 15,000 rounds of .303 and 9mm ammunition. The senior police officers at the barracks, either through their support for the NLF or because of inertia, made little attempt to stop the rampaging policemen who quickly occupied all key OP posts around the barracks. The Assistant Commissioner of Police, Sayed Hadi, arrived at about 1230 hours with orders to calm the situation by addressing some 100 rioters. In his later testimony he stated that he stressed to the rioters that the British had not attacked Champion Lines and were certainly not going to assault the barracks. However, Hadi was secretly a senior figure in NLF circles and his 'help' may really have extended to involvement in the insurrection. Whatever the content of his discussion with the rioters, it was shortly followed by the eruption of gunfire from the perimeter near Queen Awra Road. Two British Army Landrovers were spotted approaching and the cry went up 'The British are coming'.[22]

Fusilier Storey was in the second Landrover as the recce party drove towards the area where 2nd Lieutenant Davis had cleared the buses. He vividly remembered:

> When the leading vehicle reached just short of the junction with Armed Police Road, the firing started. We jumped out of the Landrover, one stopping by the central island and one going on to the corner of the APB. I lay down in the middle of the road and fired some shots from my SMG at some Arabs who were firing at us from some flats on the right hand side of Arwa Road, but the heaviest fire was coming from the left hand side of us. I dived into the kerb of the island about five yards from the second vehicle. Both Landrovers caught fire. I saw one soldier with his clothes burning, rolling in the road, and also ***** ******* burning beside the Landrover nearest to me. I was creased by a bullet on my left side and shot through my left forearm. I got up and made a dash for the entrance of a blue painted block of flats. On the way I noticed ***** ****** in the road with a large bloodstain around his stomach. After I got into the flats, I ran to the first landing and put a handkerchief round my arm.

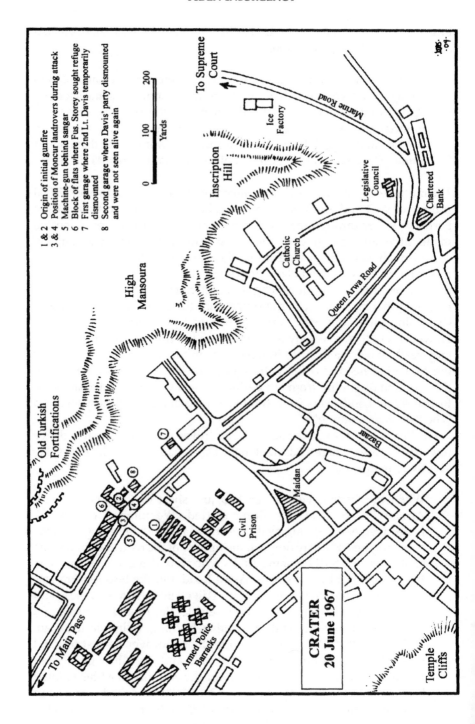

CRATER
20 June 1967

1 & 2 Origin of initial gunfire
3 & 4 Position of Moncur landrovers during attack
5 Machine-gun behind sangar
6 Block of flats where Fus. Storey sought refuge
7 First garage where 2nd Lt. Davis temporarily dismounted
8 Second garage where Davis' party dismounted and were not seen alive again

I then went up onto the roof and saw two Arabs in civilian clothes. One was holding a rifle up. I fired a burst at him from my SMG and think I hit him in the head as I saw him raise a hand to his head and fall backwards. I swung onto the second man but he ducked down behind a wall. I then rushed back downstairs.[23]

The massacre of the Moncur recce party at about 1245 hours had been swift and merciless. They were caught in intense cross-fire, which came from not only the ground-level sangars in the Armed Police Barracks but also from the five-storey buildings opposite, which had been occupied by NLF snipers. As Fusilier Storey sought refuge in the block of flats, his eight comrades lay dead in and around their burning Landrovers. Meanwhile, back at 'Y' Company HQ the gunfire from the slaughter could be clearly heard, as the base was barely half a mile away. At the time of the gunfire, radio contact with the Moncur party was lost. Then to everyone's surprise, 2nd Lieutenant Davis and his Platoon suddenly arrived back at the base. It was soon established that after running through the sporadic early gunfire and after repeated failure to contact his Company HQ by radio, Davis had decided to head back to base. He had continued up Main Pass, on towards Singapore Lines and back down Marine Road, a round trip of about five miles. When he arrived back, he was told by Lieutenant Riddick (who had taken over command in Major Moncur's absence) that Moncur had recently gone to look for the Davis party. Since then, the Company HQ had heard furious gunfire and also reports that a helicopter had been shot down near the Armed Police Barracks.[24] Radio contact with Moncur had been lost and no one knew what was happening – no one except the unfortunate helicopter pilot, who had witnessed the aftermath of the massacre from his aircraft.

Sergeant Pilot Martin Forde of 1 QDG often carried Commanders on their visits to units or carried men to Observation Posts. His orders on 20 June were therefore nothing out of the ordinary:

At 0600 hours I took a flight to Sheikh Othman for a Company Commander from the Paras. That morning Algeria had called for a general strike among Arab nations so we expected some activity. I then had to fly three Northumberland Fusiliers to a picquet post on Temple Cliffs, above Crater at 0700 hours. All was normal. I was then to collect them at 1200 hours if all was ok. At 12.00 I collected the men and their kit and as I flew them back towards the Argylls' HQ in Crater, I saw buses being lined up in the entrance to Crater. As I arrived at HQ, I was instructed to take the men back to the OP. As we flew back over Queen Awra Road, there was chaos. Near the Police Barracks there were two Landrovers and bodies all around. A mob was throwing one of the bodies onto a fire. Then we received incoming small arms fire from near the barracks. Ak . . . ak . . . ak . . . At first I thought it was the side straps of the Bell 47 flapping against the cockpit. Fusilier Duffy was inside with Corporal Jim Keightley lying on the litter outside the helicopter. Keightley, feeling somewhat exposed shouted 'it's not the straps. The bastards are firing at us'.

We were flying at 700ft and the cliff OP was now below us at 300ft. I started to approach the OP, slowing down in a circle. A terrorist was obviously waiting for us below the OP with a Kalashnikov and suddenly opened up. There was a huge bang as a bullet came up through the pedals and smashed my kneecap. Another round hit me in the right ankle and we started to go down. I needed the right pedal but my legs gave out and we started spiralling.

I quickly changed radio frequencies from 'tactical' to Khormaksar Air Traffic Control and shouted 'Mayday Mayday, Chopper Zulu 44 has been shot down'. With the cliffs only 50 ft below, I managed to pull the power lever out but we caught the edge of the ravine. Keightley fell off the litter and as the Sioux slid down the edge, it crushed his legs under the skids. Miraculously the helicopter came to rest upright at the bottom of the ravine but the engine-cooling fan exploded and hit me in the back. I shouted at Duffy to get out and help Keightley, but he dragged me out just as the machine was about to explode. He got his rifle and the radio out as well and 30 seconds later it burst into flames. A passing Sioux helicopter decided no one could have survived and went away. We were eventually rescued by the Marines and a Wessex.

After two operations, I was invalided home. On arrival in England, a Customs Officer insisted on taxing me for a cheap camera I'd bought in Aden.[25]

It was now approximately 1300 hours and at 'Y' Company HQ, Lieutenant Riddick ordered Davis and 2nd Lieutenant Campbell-Baldwin, together with nine men in two vehicles, back to Queen Arwa Road to assess the situation. Davis, in the leading armoured 'Pig', soon came under fire as the party passed the Chartered Bank at the bottom of Queen Arwa Road. Davis made one radio call to base as he neared the ambush site and about 200 yards short of the carnage, he dismounted to see if there were any survivors visible. He saw the bodies on the road and realised the only thing he could do was to stop the mutineers and terrorists from defiling them. He decided to take three men and a machine-gun, find a vantage point, and keep the enemy at bay until substantial help could arrive. He then climbed back into the 'Pig' and together with the accompanying Saracen APC accelerated ahead to the filling station, a site with cover and a view of the barracks opposite, just thirty yards short of the burning Landrovers.

The vehicles tore into the forecourt under a hail of bullets and again

Davis dismounted. As his Battalion Padre later commented, 'John must have known that he was going to his death as he could so easily have stayed in his armoured car'. He took with him Fusiliers Walter Crombie, 'Ed the Deb' Stewart and C Smythe. Smythe, a big burly Irishman, carried out the Platoon GPMG together with a belt of ammunition. The Fusiliers, armed with SLRs, returned fire as Campbell-Baldwin helped Davis and his men into a building next to the garage. Davis then ordered Campbell-Baldwin to take the rest of the men and report back to Company HQ at the Supreme Court.[26]

As Davis and his men engaged the assorted rebellious policemen and terrorists, Campbell-Baldwin reported back to his Company HQ and told Lieutenant Riddick that 'both Landrovers were blazing and the crews were all dead' but added that 2nd Lieutenant Davis and his men had dismounted to fire at the enemy to keep them away from the bodies. Riddick then ordered 2nd Lieutenant Shaw to take half his platoon in a 'Pig', together with a Saladin, to rescue Davis and his men. The Saladin, commanded by 2nd Lieutenant Nigel Stephens, 1 QDG, led the way but no sooner had it passed the Chartered Bank, than it came under automatic fire. The patrol was then subject to a hail of gunfire as it approached the ambush site. As Stephens' Saladin engaged the enemy, Shaw's 'Pig' swung into the petrol station where Davis had been left, but there was no sign of the missing Fusiliers. Through his periscope, Shaw could see:

> Six armed policemen with blue steel helmets in the sangar, at the perimeter of the barracks. I am certain that there were two machine-guns firing at us from the sangar. They had the slow thump of Bren guns as opposed to the rapid staccato of the GPMG. In addition the strike of the bullets on the vehicle made high-velocity cracks . . . my driver's periscope was then smashed by a bullet, which passed through it and finished up in Fusilier Straughan's thigh.[27]

Meanwhile, Stephens' Saladin was also in trouble. He recalled:

> Fire was so intense, my Browning machine gun was knocked out and I couldn't close the turret lid. Without cover from another Ferret we were pretty helpless. I asked permission to use my 76mm to knock out the Bren gun position on the police roof. The answer was negative, and we were forced to retire.[28]

The request to use the 76mm gun had been passed to Lieutenant-Colonel Blenkinsop in his operations room at Waterloo Lines, who in turn sought permission from Brigade to use either the Saladin gun or Carl Gustav rocket launchers, but permission was denied. The Saladin Commander was only allowed to use his machine-gun, but with this out of action, he had no alternative but to pull out. The two vehicles hurtled down Queen Arwa Road with Shaw's men returning fire through the roof hatches of their vehicle, and the subaltern noticed that 'at least 20 of the people firing at us were wearing khaki'.[29]

Another Saladin went in afterwards, but unable to use its 76mm gun, it was an easy target. The vehicle was lacerated by crossfire and had to retire, with its commander and radio operator wounded. While these rescue attempts were being made, 2nd Lieutenant Davis and his men bravely kept up a fusillade of fire from a flat roof, enforcing a cordon around the bodies of their dead comrades. At some stage they either ran out of ammunition or were overpowered by the terrorists closing in on them. At this point Davis may have been separated from his three Fusiliers, for one source reported that he was killed in a nearby alleyway and a subsequent post-mortem revealed that he was killed by a sharp blow to the head. His body was later secretly placed on the 3-ton lorry together with the eight dead from the Moncur ambush.[30] Davis's men were also probably killed sometime that afternoon but by a different mob, as their bodies were subjected to a mock trial, severely mutilated and dragged through the streets, eventually to be left outside a coffee shop in Maidan Square, some 300 yards from the ambush site.[31]

Whilst the mayhem carried on around Queen Arwa Road, Fusilier Storey had managed to remain alive inside a block of flats. He was then discovered by Armed Policeman Salah Salem Ali, who later testified:

At about 1500 hours, whilst on duty near the entrance of the Armed Police Barracks, I heard some civilians who were hanging around the entrance saying that there was one British soldier still alive and that he was hiding in a block of flats on the other side of Queen Arwa Road. I heard them planning to go and burn the flats in order to kill the soldier.

I immediately reported what I had heard to the Assistant Commissioner Abdul Hadi. He told me to take another man with me and go and find the soldier and bring him back. I went to the block of flats and in the entrance I saw blood. I followed the blood splashes to the door of a flat. I knocked on the door but there was no reply so I went to the roof and searched, but there was no one. I returned to the flat door and knocked and kicked at the door. This time it was opened. I was told by the occupants that a British soldier had been with them and that he was wounded and had jumped out of the window. From the window, I could see nothing.

I then went up on the roof and saw a person in British soldier's uniform hiding between the block of flats and the cliffs close by. I shouted to him in English, 'I'm a policeman. Stay there and I will take you back to the Armed Police Barracks'. I took his gun from him and then escorted the soldier to the roadway. And when we reached the roadway, a crowd of civilians gathered. They wanted to take the soldier from me and were shouting that they would kill him. I pointed the soldier's sub-machine gun at the crowd and told them I would shoot into them if they attacked me and tried to take the soldier. The crowd then moved away from me.

I escorted the soldier to the entrance of the barracks, where a crowd there also shouted that they wanted to kill him and started to try and take him away from me. I again shouted that I would fire into the crowd and at the same time, took the soldier up into a police truck standing in front of the barrack's entrance.[32]

Although relieved to be still alive, it was not the end of Fusilier Storey's ordeal. He personally takes up the account:

I was put in the front of this APB 3-tonner and we drove to the junction of Queen Arwa Road. There, the Armed Police with the aid of various civilians, started picking up the bodies on a stretcher and putting them in the back of the 3-tonner . . . We parked in the road whilst an argument went on between the police and some armed civilians who I understood wanted to kill me. One of the civilians had a GPMG, identical to British issue, and belts of ammunition around him. Many other Arabs in a crowd of about 20 were also armed. Then, there were a couple of explosions and some shooting from the direction of the Main Pass area, and the Arabs scattered and an Arab drove the 3-tonner back to the entrance to the APB.[33]

During the afternoon, negotiations were carried out between the British Commissioner of Police, Peter Owen and Mohammed Ibraham, the Commander of the Armed Police. A normally amenable man, the half Pakistani, half Arab Commander had become sullen but communication had to be kept open with him in order to exert pressure on his rebellious Armed Police. By 1600 hours an amnesty was agreed and an ambulance was called forward to go in and collect the British dead and wounded. In the meantime, the bodies of six of the British soldiers killed in the ambush had been placed in a 3-ton lorry opposite the police barracks, and the CO of 1 RNF pressured Commissioner Owen to obtain their release from Crater. So at about 1700 hours Flight Lieutenant Scott Martin, a Medical Officer from RAF Khormaksar found himself on an extraordinary mission but curiously he was offered little help and was clearly expecting to collect more wounded than dead:

On arrival at Main Pass, an Army officer informed me that a number of dead and wounded soldiers were still in Crater. He did not know how we could get them out as we had lost control in the area. I set off in the ambulance with three nursing attendants, a driver and an RAF Police Corporal. A police Landrover with a loudhailer met us about 200 yards down Queen Arwa Road from Main Pass and led us to the entrance to the Armed Police Barracks. During the journey announcements were made over the loudhailer in English and Arabic calling on people collected on roofs, balconies and at windows, not to shoot. People with rifles were at windows and on the roofs of flats opposite the Armed Police Barracks. In Armed Police Road I saw a large number of persons in civilian clothes, armed with rifles and pistols. The entrance to the APB was virtually blocked by a lorry with five or six dead bodies in the back. Some of the bodies were burned.[34]

Forcing his way through the angry crowd, Flight Lieutenant Martin then went into the barracks to collect any wounded and found Fusilier Storey in a shocked state. He collected Storey and was then asked by the police if he would also take the bodies. The Medical Officer continues:

As I had already been told that some [bodies] were still in Queen Arwa Road, I said I would send back another ambulance and asked them to get all the bodies together. The Police Officer refused to collect the other bodies from Queen Arwa Road. At this time a crowd of 200–300 people in civilian clothes had gathered around us and some were flicking their cigarette ends onto the bodies in the back of the lorry. They appeared to be very hostile. I explained to the Police Officer that I could not take the bodies with me as I had a wounded soldier and in any case did not have sufficient room . . . I asked for an escort and an officer said he would not accept orders from the British, but after a few minutes a Landrover with a loudhailer escorted us back to Main Pass.[35]

Martin then reported back in order to arrange recovery of all the bodies, but quite why the lorry containing six of the dead could not have been driven back by one of his party remains uncertain. Subsequently the mutineers moved the lorry out towards Queen Arwa Road and picked up the two remaining burned bodies from underneath the Landrovers. They then moved the lorry containing the eight bodies 500 yards down Queen Arwa Road and left it outside the Roman Catholic School. Fearing an ambush, a party of Fusiliers approached the lorry only when darkness fell but they soon came under attack from rocket-launcher and small arms fire and had to withdraw.[36]

At 1630 hours the CO of 1 RNF was ordered not to enter Crater again. Although this critical order came from Brigade, it emanated from MEC following a tense emergency meeting of the Commander-in-Chief's

Council, hurriedly convened to discuss the level of force to be used. After news of the mutinies had reached MEC a conference was called to thrash out 'the corporate military advice' to be given immediately to the High Commissioner. In the absence of Admiral Le Fanu, the chairman of the meeting was the acting C-in-C and Commander of the RAF, Air Vice Marshal Andrew Humphrey. The GOC, MELF, General Tower, who had arrived from his temporary HQ at Seedaseer Lines, Khormaksar, took the line that re-entry should not take place immediately. This view was supported by the Senior Air Staff Officer at MEC, Air Commodore (later Air Marshal Sir Freddie) Sowrey, while the Naval representative was undecided.[37] In arriving at their decision, the meeting took Brigadier Dunbar's advice. He was, after all, Brigadier General Staff MEC and was responsible for all Army operations and plans within Middle East Command. Consequently, he held himself fully accountable for that advice:

> The advice to halt the operation came not from the High Com-missioner but mainly from me and if this decision was wrong, then I should be the person pilloried. I did not enjoy giving the advice, but discussions with senior Arab Officers, the fact that we had lost control of our Arab forces, knowledge of the degree of force we would have had to use, convinced me that the operation would be disastrous if carried out on, or in the days immediately following the 20th.
>
> I was able to convince the GOC, the AOC (who was acting C in C) and we all finally convinced the High Commissioner of this and the decision was unanimous and a joint one. The stuff in the papers was a tissue of mischievous lies. It is important in all this to remember that we were not trying to hold on to Aden, but to hand it over as a going concern. Had we merely wanted to hold on to it, we would have gone straight into Crater, disbanded the Army and Federal Guard and started again. We would first have had to withdraw our people up country. Had we done so in circumstances of our aim to hand over, this would have been regarded as a sign that we intended to attack. Tom Lehrer has a word for the way we lived for two or three weeks – 'Sliding down the razor blade of life'.[38]

As Brigadier Dunbar stressed, one of the main considerations of those advocating restraint was the presence up-country of 150 British advisors and technicians, officially the responsibility of the SAA. They were spread across the hinterland, teaching their successors about well digging and agriculture as well as elements of military science. The overriding concern was that should the false rumours of a British attack on the SAA at Champion Lines spread through the SAA up-country, they might turn on their British charges. Consequently, during the afternoon of 20 June there were frantic efforts by Brigadier Dye, Commander of the SAA to contact his senior Arab commanders to allay their fears. A delegation arrived at the important RAF radar post at Mukeiras, just in time to prevent the local SAA battalion from attacking the RAF personnel. At 1500 hours an aircraft from the Army Air Corps operating in the hinterland had observed the Lahej Company of the SAA moving without authority from their base at Al Anad towards Aden. The Lahej men had heard the rumours that the British were attacking their SAA comrades in Champion Lines, and it was only the intervention of senior Arab officers that later persuaded them to return to their base.[39]

However, it was by no means certain that events in the hinterland would automatically follow what happened in Aden and the military commanders at MEC weighed up the probabilities.[40] In his earlier study of South Arabian military operations, *Last Post: Aden 1964–1967*, Lieutenant-Colonel Julian Paget pointed out that the events surrounding Crater highlighted the difficulties of subordinating 'military necessity to broader political aims'.[41] Certainly battalion commanders at the time felt that more could have been done to inform the troops about how the changing political situation affected military operations on the ground.[42]

It was a sufficient tragedy that Major Moncur and his patrol had been massacred, but the issue of leaving behind 2nd Lieutenant Davis and his three Fusiliers angered their comrades. The embargo on the use of anything larger than a machine-gun ruled out the possibility of knocking out the mutineers' strong points. Even bearing in mind the policy of mitigating the death toll, it is conceivable that Flight Lieutenant Martin, who was initially sent in to retrieve the casualties, could have been given more support, or at least a larger vehicle. He had, after all, gained access to the Armed Police Barracks and had even received a police escort through the ambush site. He had negotiated with the police but only from a weak numerical position. A larger escort could possibly have cordoned the area and delivered the missing Fusiliers.[43]

Two British correspondents inside Crater had witnessed the fate of Davis's men and the British press ran lurid stories about the incident. Because of security, the men's families were prohibited from attending the funerals and attempts by relatives to discover what had happened remained frustrated.[44] All strands of military command were caught unawares by the tragic events of 20 June and the shortage of information caused Middle East Command to react in the most cautious way. The failure of radio communication remains a contributing factor and the condition of some of the wireless sets was cause for concern, though the massive wall of rock surrounding Crater can even defeat modern wireless systems.

Although the uprising by the Armed Police appeared to have been a spontaneous reaction to events at Champion Lines, there were indications that the mutiny was NLF inspired. The original bus barricade was arranged near the AP barracks and could be covered by the OP sangar at the barracks perimeter. The Civil Prison adjacent to the barracks was opened up by the rioters and no doubt many of the escaping prisoners joined other armed civilian insurgents in taking up prime sniping positions around Queen Arwa Road. There were numerous witnesses who also confirmed seeing khaki-clad insurgents on the surrounding flat roofs.

There was some consolation that no actual members of the SAA had taken part in the mutiny, which was confined to the South Arabian Police and the Aden Armed Police. In that respect, the major concern at Middle East Command that the SAA would fall apart was not realised. In fact, some hoped that the part played by many Arab NCOs in restoring order, indicated a promising future for the Arab army. But it was a forlorn hope.[45]

Events had moved fast, and because there had been so little effective warning of the mutinies, decision-making had to be quick and decisive. But the sheer complexity of command structures in the Federation made this difficult. For the two rebellious police units, the South Arabian Police and the Aden Armed Police, were responsible to two different administrations, which hardly helped decisive action.[46] The effects of Nasser's 'Big Lie' cannot be overestimated, for it reached many semi-literate Arabs, including police trainees, who could not be reached by the more sophisticated counter-propaganda from the West. Another serious problem, which could never have been addressed in the time allowed, was the issue of tribal rivalries within the SAA, which had ignited the whole affair in the first place.

At midnight on 20 June the bulk of 1 RNF were deployed to contain Crater by blocking Main Pass, Marine Road and the main path over Jebel Shamsan. In an attempt to completely seal off the town, the water supply was then cut off. Meanwhile inside Crater, mobs rampaged through the Legislative Council building and a nearby school and banks were ransacked. As the day ended, the terrorists were in complete control of the town, while British forces had suffered ten killed and twenty-two wounded in the uprising in Champion Lines and twelve killed and five wounded in the Crater massacres.[47] And the setback was compounded by other events that day. Up-country, the NLF had enjoyed striking success in Dhala, when their local commander, Ali Antar, together with his gang, forced out the two British political officers and raised the NLF flag over the market place. Some of the ranks from the SAA joined in the revolt while the bulk of the Army stood by. The ease with which the NLF took over Dhala was an ominous pointer to the fate of the other Federal States.

If the tragic events of 20 June proved anything, it was that the Federal Government had no grip over its security forces and its intelligence network was woefully inadequate to fend off the terrorist challenge, both in Aden and the hinterland.

NOTES

1 *The Times*, 20 June 1967.
2 'Events of 17–20 June', 16 October 1967, MEC, DEFE 11/533, NA. Also Mitchell op. cit., p. 3.
3 Mitchell, op. cit., p. 3.
4 'NLF *Communiqué*, 20 June 1967', File 2/3, Dunbar Papers, LHCMA.
5 It should be remembered that since the Arab–Israeli Six-Day War, Nasser had accused British troops of being 'agents of Zionism'. This, no doubt, was still in the minds of many Arabs throughout South Arabia. See 'MEC Staff Notes – Facts on the 20 June Mutiny', File 2/4, Dunbar Papers, LHCMA.
6 *The Regimental Magazine of The Lancashire Regiment*, autumn 1967 and spring 1968.
7 Nick Beard to Author, 11 May 2004. He still has a bullet, which passed through his field dressing and ricocheted off his belt ring. For further comment on the RCT massacre, see Brigadier Charles Dunbar to A G Fraser, 27 June 1970, File 2/6 and 'MEC Staff Notes', File 2/4, both Dunbar Papers, LHCMA. The RCT killed were Staff Sergeant E Butler, Sergeant R Garth, Driver N Fraser, Driver M Geall, Driver F Pouton, Driver J Trevendale, Driver M West, Driver R Goldsworthy. See also 'Events of 17–20 June', MEC Report, 26 October 1967, DEFE 11/533, NA.
8 The King's Own Royal Border Regiment was based in Bahrain, but one company was detached for service in Aden under 1 PARA. Other single Companies to serve in Aden came from 2 PARA, The Gloucestershire Regiment and the Royal Irish Fusiliers.
9 *The Lion and the Dragon*, summer 1967.
10 Appreciation in *The Regimental Magazine of The Lancashire Regiment*, April 1968. The Rev. Roe received the Military Cross for his courage and compassion during his battalion's nine-month tour, sharing the battalion's most dangerous moments in Tawahi and al-Mansoura.
11 *The Regimental History of 1st The Queen's Dragoon Guards*, p. 498. I am also indebted to Charles Russell, who provided extracts from 'sitreps' of the 1 QDG. Also *Pegasus*, File 2/1 and 'King's Own Royal Border Regiment – Newsletter June 1967', File 2/1, Dunbar Papers, LHCMA. Also Trevelyan to Foreign Office, 25 June 1967, FCO 8/257, NA.
12 Major Miller was awarded the Military Cross for this action. Because of the breakdown in communications, the survivors of the RCT massacre were not rescued until 1340 hours. 'Events of 17–20 June 1967', MEC Report, 26 October 1967, DEFE 11/533, NA.
13 Notes by Lieutenant-Colonel Blenkinsop on the 'Aden Mutiny 20 June 1967', FMN.
14 In correspondence between The Army Historical Branch, Ministry of Defence and Mrs Pamela Davis, the MOD could not initially locate any surviving Unit Historical Record (UHR) for the 1 RNF during the crisis in Crater. It was later located, but records covering the events of 20 June are often sketchy and inconsistent.
15 According to another Platoon Commander, 2nd Lieutenant John Shaw, at about 1100 hours 'Y' Company HQ received a radio message from an RNF OP post on Inscription Hill, overlooking the sector. The message reportedly

said that two civilian buses had been moved to block Queen Arwa Road at
grid ref. 0382 1296, about 100 yards below the Armed Police Barracks. Shaw
Testimony, July 1967, FCO 8/438, NA. However, a member of Davis's patrol
recalled that by the time they arrived at the barricade, there were fifteen buses
to move. Correspondence and testimonies, Davis Papers.
16   According to 2nd Lieutenant Campbell-Baldwin, the reply from base to
     Davis's report was that this situation 'was usual at this time of day';
     Campbell-Baldwin to Colonel and Mrs Davis, 22 August 1967, Davis Papers.
17   There were reports that the battery for the patrol radio was nearly flat, but
     this was not confirmed. The high mountains surrounding Crater were also
     known to cause transmission problems. See Dunbar to Paget, 26 September
     1968, File 2/6 Dunbar Papers, LHCMA. Also correspondence and
     testimonies, Davis Papers.
18   Major Moncur was an experienced soldier having served with the 1 RNF in
     Korea, Kenya and recently in the emergency in British Guiana. Quite why the
     first recce party was recalled remains uncertain. The MEC report surmises
     that Moncur had received orders not to venture near the Police barracks but
     Davis had already been sent to the area. Most testimonies from soldiers on
     duty that morning state that the first order only prohibited entry to 'any
     police barracks', but later orders prohibited entry to Crater. See 'Events of
     17–20 June', MEC Report, 26 October 1967, DEFE 11/533, NA. Also
     Testimony of Second Lieutenant John Shaw, July 1967, FCO 8/438, NA.
19   Ibid.
20   Fusilier Hoult was a skilful driver, having driven Saracen APCs and the
     Fighting Vehicle FV 432, before being selected to drive for Major John
     Moncur. In fact, most of the recce party were experienced soldiers. See
     Testimony, Fusilier John Storey, July 1967, FCO 8/438, NA. Also 'Obituaries',
     St George's Gazette, 30 September 1967.
21   Testimony, Fadhl Ali Aushabi, July 1967, FCO 8/438, NA. According to the
     Armourer, 323 rifles of .303 calibre were taken together with twenty-seven
     Sterling Sub-Machine Guns.
22   Testimony, Assistant Commissioner of Police Abdul Hadi, July 1967, FCO
     8/438, NA. See also Dunbar to Paget, 25 September 1968, File 2/6, Dunbar
     Papers, LHCMA. Hadi almost certainly knew that British Intelligence
     realised that he had contact with the NLF. See B L Crowe to J E Pestell, 17 July
     1968, FCO 8/257, NA.
23   Testimony, Fusilier John Storey, July 1967, FCO 8/438, NA. In the testimony
     of ACP Abdul Hadi, he states that from the barracks, he saw 'a British soldier
     crawling towards a heap of sand near a newly built block of flats. I saw bullets
     striking the ground around him. I also saw the soldier fire once or twice
     across the road in return'. This soldier was probably Fusilier Storey.
     Testimony dated July 1967, FCO 8/438, NA.
24   Testimony, 2nd Lieutenant John Shaw, 25 June 1967, FCO 8/438, NA. Also
     correspondence, Davis Papers.
25   Martin Forde to Author, 19 November 2002. Fusilier Duffey was awarded the
     DCM for his gallantry. The artist, Terence Cuneo, later captured the dramatic
     incident in a well-known painting.
26   Correspondence, Davis Papers.
27   Testimony, 2nd Lieutenant Shaw, op. cit.
28   Lieutenant Stephens quoted in Michael Mann, The Regimental History of 1st
     The Queen's Dragoon Guards, Michael Russell Publishing, 1993, p. 500.
29   'Notes on Aden Mutiny', op. cit., FMN. Also testimony, 2nd Lieutenant
     Shaw, 25 June 1967, FCO 8/438, NA.

30 2nd Lieutenant Davis was the only casualty for whom the Pathologist could give an exact cause of death – 'that of a severe blow to the head with no other injuries apparent'. Flight-Lieutenant Barry Corke, Pathologist Report, 30 June 1967, FCO 8/438, NA. Also Pamela Davis to Author.

31 Trevelyan to Foreign Office, 22 June 1967, FCO 8/257, NA.

32 Testimony, Salah Salem Ali, July 1967, FCO 8/438, NA. Also testimony, Abdulla Audhali, 26 June 1967, FCO 8/438, NA.

33 Testimony, Fusilier John Storey, 23 June 1967, FCO 8/438, NA. The GPMG carried by a civilian in the mob may have been the machine-gun taken from the Davis party after their deaths. This would mean that they were killed before 1600 hours.

34 Flight Lieutenant Scott Martin, Testimony, 27 June 1967, FCO 8/438, NA.

35 Ibid.

36 Notes on 'Aden Mutiny 20 June 1967', Records of FMN.

37 Air Commodore F Sowrey to Brigadier Dunbar, 28 February 1969, File 2/6, Dunbar Papers, LHCMA. According to Brigadier Dunbar, the decision not to re-enter Crater immediately was also agreed by the Commander of Aden Brigade, Federal representatives, Brigadier Dye and Commissioner Owen.

38 'Staff-in-Confidence. Some random facts about the South Arabian Army and Arab Police Mutiny 20 June 1967', File 2/4, Dunbar Papers, LHCMA. As the senior Brigadier at MEC in 1967, Dunbar acted for the GOC, MELF in his absence, both as Army Commander and Security Commander in Aden. The decision not to re-enter Crater immediately was endorsed by Air Commodore Freddie Sowrey as well as the CO of the 1 RNF.

39 'Annex D' to MEC report on 'Diary of Events 19–20 June', DEFE 11/533, NA. The Company, which had reached Bir Nasir, were eventually persuaded to return to their base at 1800 hours. See also Brigadier Charles Dunbar to Lieutenant-Colonel Julian Paget, 25 September 1968, File 2/6, Dunbar Papers, LHCMA.

40 The CO of 1 Argyll and Sutherland Highlanders, Lieutenant-Colonel Mitchell, did not agree with the premise that the rest of South Arabia would follow Aden's path. See Lieutenant-Colonel Colin Mitchell, *Having Been a Soldier*, Hamish Hamilton, 1969, p. 170.

41 Paget, op. cit., p. 222.

42 Notes on 'Aden Mutiny 20 June 1967', FMN.

43 However, a larger escort might not have been allowed in without a serious fight, a situation MEC were determined to avoid.

44 Regimental Depots did try to help, but there was a dearth of official information available. There were also a number of conflicting reports.

45 'Report on the Mutinies within the South Arabian Forces', HQ MEC, 26 October 1967, DEFE 11/533, NA.

46 The SAP were responsible to the Federal Government and the Aden Armed Police to the British High Commission.

47 For a detailed breakdown of all the casualties, see 'Casualty List – Annexe A', MEC report into the Mutinies, DEFE 11/533, NA.

CHAPTER XIII
Who's to Pay the Piper?

The day after the Mutiny the terrorists established their grip on Crater completely unhindered by, and in some cases with the active support of, the Armed Police. At the same time, the British positions surrounding Crater came under fire from the Armed Police Barracks and rebel sniper positions inside Crater. The terrorists were attempting to hit OPs manned by Four Five Commando and 1 RNF in the surrounding hillsides, and in several cases they were successful.[1] But the remaining terrorist strongpoint in the old Turkish fort commanding Main Pass continued to hold up British control of the heights above Crater and permission was sought to destroy the position. MEC allowed a Saladin armoured car to use only one round against the fort and the Saladin gunner made sure his round found its mark. As the shell slammed into the fort, four men ran out and were cut down by supporting fire. Four Five, who took part in securing the heights, were also allowed to clear a sniper's den with a Carl Gustav rocket launcher, and these few offensive gestures raised morale among British troops.[2]

Elsewhere on 21 June, it was a day of fevered negotiations over recovery of the British dead. Peter Owen, the British Commissioner of Police, and Commander Ibraham of the Armed Police were in contact but trust had collapsed and any arrangements made to collect the bodies might be subject to further ambush. However, later that night under a cease-fire, British forces finally retrieved the lorry containing the eight bodies of the Major Moncur party together with 2nd Lieutenant Davis.[3]

It was not the end of the sorry story. At 2300 hours on 21 June the Assistant Commissioner of Police, Abdul Hadi, confirmed that he heard that there were the remains of three more British soldiers outside the 'Zakku' Coffee Shop in Maidan Square, Crater. According to Hadi, his order for the bodies to be collected at dawn the following day was not complied with. Consequently, Inspector Abdulla Yafai then went to the Square and discovered a mob of forty men surrounding the burning remains of the Fusiliers. Pushing back the threatening crowd, he retrieved the remains and at 0715 hours on 22 June they were returned to the RAF Hospital at Steamer Point. At last, all the missing were accounted for but

Lieutenant-Colonels Blenkinsop and Mitchell still had the task of identifying the bodies. For both Commanders, it was a harrowing task and the barbaric acts inflicted on some of the bodies persuaded the CO of the Argylls that firm, tough action in Crater was the only solution.[4]

Inside Crater, all shops, offices and banks were closed and only a few taxis or buses were running. Consequently, food prices soared, and as there were no 'sweepers' to be seen, rubbish littered the streets. Many of the 75,000 Arabs, Hindus and Somalis who populated Crater, stayed indoors while the remaining British families barricaded themselves in their houses. Egyptian, Syrian and Lebanese flags were raised, and even the Mayor of Aden, Fuad Khalifa, came out openly in support of FLOSY and hoisted a red flag, proclaiming the 'People's Democratic Republic of Crater'.

Meanwhile in London, stories were circulating about the massacres and how British troops were stopped from retaliating. The House of Commons engaged in a heated debate on the issue. A Government MP blamed the violence in Crater on 'the hopelessness of the Sandys constitution', to which there were retorts of 'murderer' from the opposition benches.[5] But the controversy had at least prompted legislation declaring that troops in South Arabia were at last 'on active service'. For previously this description was only applied to service 'in a foreign country', and Aden and the Protectorates were deemed to be British possessions. Brigadier Dick Jefferies, Commander of Aden Brigade, had lobbied long and hard for this change, and it was a great morale boost to the troops, not least because military rather than civilian awards could be now be made for gallantry.[6]

The newspapers and television news in Britain led with the story of the mutiny and massacre and the more sensational papers were full of accounts of the atrocities carried out against the three dead RNF soldiers. Several journalists had seen the remains of the soldiers in Maidan Square and showed little restraint in reporting the details. Official Army sources were tight-lipped but many junior officers and men were outraged at the decision not to re-enter Crater straightaway to retrieve the bodies.[7] To the Egyptian press, still keen to promote FLOSY as the main protagonists in South Arabia, it was a licence to publish outlandish accounts of the mutiny claiming that the 'popular resistance' had occupied Aden and British troops had lost 120 dead and 300 wounded in the fighting.

There remained the question of funerals for the fallen soldiers. Since March 1967 it was possible for the next-of-kin to ask for repatriation of a dead serviceman, but the delay in retrieval of the casualties made swift burials a necessity. So, on Sunday 25 June a brief and poignant funeral ceremony with full military honours was held at the stark Silent Valley Cemetery in Little Aden. The twenty-four servicemen and one civilian were laid to rest, with Union flags draped over each grave, and as there were no flowers in Aden, wreaths were placed at each gravestone. There were buglers and a Firing Party from the 1 Irish Guards while an Argyll Piper played the Lament.[8] The photo-journalist, Terry Fincher, recorded the sorrow of the day, with a photograph of a Northumberland Fusilier biting his lip as he stood to attention beside a comrade's grave. The image was flashed across the world and graphically showed the cost of Britain's disengagement from South Arabia.

Sporadic terrorist attacks continued, with rocket assaults on military OPs and bomb attacks against fuel installations, resulting in 17,000 tons of diesel oil flooding the road to Ma'alla. But despite these provocations, High Command still took an extremely cautious line. On 23 June Major-General Tower, who as GOC MELF was also Security Commander in Aden, stated 'It is a deliberate decision by me that we are not going in at the moment, because I do not want to disturb the hot pot – but we intend to go in at some time'.[9] And there were similar sentiments at the British High Commission, with Sir Humphrey Trevelyan confirming that 'if the army moved in now, there would be a large number of Arab casualties. The South Arabian forces would probably mutiny, which would be the end of the Federal Government and would reduce the old Protectorate to chaos'.[10] Nigel Pusineli, Director of Establishments, summed up their concerns:

> We were concerned that the FRA would march down from the hinterland and engage the British Army, who were much smaller. We wanted to play withdrawal quietly, but Mitchell risked stirring it up. It was terribly delicate for 48 hours, whether the FRA would turn against us.[11]

Lieutenant-Colonel Colin Mitchell was not concerned that he might be accused of 'stirring it up'. He would be given the responsibility of IS duties in Crater from 26 June and realised that most Adenis saw the withdrawal of forces from the township on 20 June as a defeat for the British and the Federal Government. Mitchell, despite his reputation as a 'showman and self-publicist', considered that the only way to shore up the Federal writ was a speedy re-occupation of Crater. To enable him to do this, he knew that he had a resilient battalion under him, who had plenty of experience of insurgency warfare as well as major conflicts. The Argylls had seen action in Palestine, Korea, Cyprus and most recently in Borneo, which had proved an excellent training-ground for junior leaders and where Lieutenant David Thomson had won the Military Cross and Lieutenant (then Sergeant) Brian Baty had gained the Military Medal.[12] And the battalion were well prepared for service in Crater. Prior to leaving the UK they had been made familiar with the landmarks of the township and had trained in cordon and search techniques, even learning some basic Arabic, though the most fluent linguist remained Major Nigel Crowe, Mitchell's second-in-command and ex-GSO2 in the FRA.

Even Mitchell's detractors had to admire his enormous energy, which was soon channelled into devising an occupation plan. This plan was discussed and approved, with modifications, by Brigadier Dick Jefferies but the next more difficult step was to gain the approval of Major-General Tower and his Brigadier General Staff, Brigadier Charles Dunbar. Both were anticipating a re-entry into Crater but were mindful of political considerations as well as the progress of discussions with Arab police and army officers inside Crater. Together with the High Commission, MEC's policy continued to be one of strict caution.[13]

In the meantime, Brigadier Dunbar had been co-ordinating efforts to negotiate not only with senior FRA and police officers but also through certain of their officers, with the terrorists inside Crater. One of these officers, Abdul Hadi, a senior Arab policeman, was known by the British to be an NLF conduit, and he was almost certainly aware that his activities were monitored. The Crater discussions were an extremely sensitive issue but, according to Foreign Office sources, Lieutenant-Colonel Mitchell was unaware that these discussions were taking place.[14] However, while the British Army could not be seen to be in direct negotiations with the terrorist group, it was privately understood that any agreement with the Armed Police about safe re-entry, 'would in effect be underwritten by the NLF'.[15] No doubt the NLF realised that in any battle with British forces they would suffer high casualties among their cadres and this would jeopardise their future chances of destroying FLOSY.

However, Brigadier Dunbar was resolute in his determination to save even small numbers of casualties, later asserting 'we still kept coming up against the same stumbling block that whatever we did, if it caused casualties, the Arab Forces would re-mutiny. We had to find a way into Crater without having a battle'.[16] One way was to make both the Arab Security Forces and the terrorists realise that British troops were the only force capable of restoring order in Crater, at least in the short term. One questionable decision was to pardon the Armed Police even though, according to eyewitnesses, many were in direct collusion with the terrorist gunmen on 20 June. Sir Humphrey Trevelyan cabled the Foreign Office, confirming:

> Owen, Commissioner of Police, went into Crater this morning, for the first time since 20 June. He visited the Armed Police Barracks and spoke to the officers and men. He told them that it appeared from the enquiry still in progress that they were exonerated from the charge of killing British soldiers, but they had clearly misbehaved and he would have to consider how to deal with them.[17]

British troops would see the term 'misbehaviour' as an understatement but Trevelyan clearly felt that 'the available evidence did not allow the blame to be put fairly and squarely on the Armed Police', and for 'tactical reasons' he wished to avoid any emphasis on their involvement.[18] Even Commissioner Owen concluded from his talks with the mutineers that they had acted in panic. But while there was spontaneous excitement among the Armed Police about an attack, several armoured vehicles and two Landrovers hardly amounted to an assault on their barracks; and panic did not grip them to the extent that strategic sangars could not be manned and fire directed in a quick and devastating way. The BBC ran a story about a British demand for those policemen involved in the killings to be handed over. But no demand came from either the British Army or the Federal Government, who feared that the dismissal of over 120 Armed Police would cripple the South Arabian Security Forces. There was talk of an inquiry into 'Bloody Tuesday' to be conducted by Sir Richard le Gallais, the Chief Justice of Aden, but nothing materialised.[19]

During negotiations between MEC and senior Arab Police and SAA officers, the latter had given tacit consent to a British re-entry into Crater. However, while these officers implied they would not oppose re-entry, their terrorist contacts were less predictable. The terrorists were a disparate band, with PORF, the armed wing of FLOSY, assuming the upper hand over the NLF in Crater. The town was traditionally a FLOSY stronghold with local officials known to be supporters, but many of the prime agitators on 20 June were actually NLF cadres. To make matters worse, British negotiators were not always sure which terrorist organisation senior FRA or Police officers were reporting to.[20] It was known that the senior Police officer, Abdul Hadi, who on 20 June had played such a significant role, was an NLF supporter, but it was entirely possible that FLOSY would spoil any NLF deal with the British and resist re-entry.[21]

There is no doubt that MEC's decision to play for time while secret negotiations were carried on also suited the terrorists who saw their occupation of Crater as a huge propaganda victory. Abdul Fattah Ismail, a former schoolteacher and the main NLF military commander in Aden, was jubilant:

> The crowning episode was the occupation of Crater. We held the area for more than a fortnight and this represented a turning-point in the whole armed struggle: it served to mobilise the masses in the rural areas who seized power in place after place, overthrowing the sultans who had ruled there. The Crater occupation took place within the context of the Arab world as a whole at that time – Israel had just defeated the Arab states . . . The British tried in various ways to regain control. They were of course, militarily far more powerful than us,

but we were not trying to retain control of Crater, since we had won the political victory that we had set out to achieve.[22]

Even allowing for revolutionary rhetoric, it was clear that many Arabs saw the Crater occupation as retribution for the crushing defeat of Arab armies in the Six-Day War only two weeks before. Nasser had famously linked Britain to the Israeli cause and the NLF duly capitalised on Arab desires to see 'face' restored. To this end, the NLF used the occasion of Friday Prayers at the al-Asqualani Mosque, in Crater to reach large numbers of Adenis. In one speech, delivered by an NLF spokesman after prayers, the movement claimed credit for the '20 June Uprising', declaring:

> The Colonialists believed that the relapse which the Arab nation has suffered in the land of Palestine would affect the struggle of our people in the Occupied South Yemen. The recent upsurge in violence has shown the contrary.[23]

With the interior of Crater firmly under their control, the terrorists lost no time in settling old scores and with over 200 criminals released from prison there was no shortage of foot-soldiers. One of the NLF leaders, Abdul Nabi Madram, was gunned down by PORF assassins while sitting in a café in Maidan Square and his body dragged through the streets. Groups of self-styled 'NLF Commandos', such as the 'Haras al-Futuwa' unit, roamed the back alleys stalking their opposite numbers in PORF. Targets were duly despatched and even the FLOSY-supporting Mayor Khalifa was kidnapped.[24]

The day after the Argylls took over in Aden, 'X' and 'Y' Companies, 1 RNF together with their HQ, finally left Aden. On their arrival in the UK they were besieged by the press, hoping for controversial comments about the events of 20 June but the Fusiliers remained tight-lipped. Such restraint must have been difficult, for the regiment had suffered nine killed and thirty-five wounded during the nine months of their service in Aden. Nonetheless, they had been extremely successful in their IS duties, and while operating in the heart of enemy territory, had contended with a total of 308 shootings and 212 grenade incidents. Despite continuous provocation they had managed to contain the insurgents with a minimum of force, killing fifteen and wounding thirty others.[25]

During the next two weeks, the NLF and some elements of FLOSY co-ordinated their occupation of Crater. British troops, in their positions in the surrounding hills, were only officially allowed an observation role, but if armed terrorists presented themselves, they could be shot. This was played down, as was the presence of 'G' Squadron, 22 SAS, who maintained OPs on the Jebel Shamsan. There were reports that as soon as it became dark, squads of SAS would slip down the mountain and quietly move into Crater to carry out recce and elimination operations against known gunmen. During the day, British units also took opportunities to dispatch terrorists. One Royal Marine sniper took up positions in the old Turkish fortifications overlooking Queen Arwa Road and one day fired three shots, killing two terrorists and wounding one. He was pleased to carry out some retribution for 20 June, commenting 'one of them had a British rifle that could only have been captured in last week's ambush. I felt good when I saw him fall to my shot'. There are no figures for terrorist casualties during this period but in this highly charged atmosphere, it is likely that considerable numbers were shot.[26]

As the wives and children of BP employees were being evacuated on 29 June, the GOC and Brigadier Dunbar were finalising the outline plan for the re-occupation of Crater. There were to be three distinct phases:

A) 1 Argyll and Sutherland Highlanders to enter by Marine Road and establish, by phases, a presence in the business and banking sector.

B) To exploit to the Police Station and control the centre and southern parts of the town.

C) To move towards the Armed Police Barracks, but to avoid close contact with it.

Lieutenant-Colonel Mitchell also had at his disposal 'A' Squadron, 1 QDG, and a troop from 60 Squadron Royal Engineers together with a helicopter from 47 Light Regiment Royal Artillery. But Brigadier Dunbar stressed that there were 'certain report lines and Colin Mitchell was told that if there was no opposition, he could carry on over the first report line, when he would get further orders'. These orders would normally have come via Aden Brigade, but on 29 June their Brigade Commander, Brigadier Dick Jefferies went on leave and handed over temporary command to the capable Lieutenant-Colonel Peter Downward of the 1 Lancashire Regiment (PWV), the senior battalion Commander but still an officer of the same rank as Mitchell.[27]

The operation for re-entry was finally set for the evening of 3 July. During the late afternoon Mitchell assembled the bulk of the battalion together with the Saladin armoured cars of 'A' Squadron 1 QDG, commanded by Major Tony Shewan, in a quarry beside Marine Road but out of sight of Crater.[28] Across the town, on Ras Marshag, two platoons of 'Jocks' had been dropped earlier by helicopter in order to cover the seaward flank. Further cover for the main Marine Road assault was provided by a platoon holding Aidrus Hill, south-west of the town.

At dusk, as the Argylls prepared for their assault, pressmen and photographers responding to a tip-off that 'something big' was about to happen arrived at the quarry. They were greeted by the sight of two Companies of Argylls in their distinctive glengarries, lined up with pipers and armoured support. Lieutenant-Colonel Mitchell discussed last-minute details with his Intelligence Officer, Lieutenant David Thomson, and Major Ian Mackay who would carry the late Major Bryan Malcolm's cromach back into Crater.[29] As darkness fell, the engines of the Saladins started up, Pipe Major Kenneth Robson sounded the Regimental Charge, 'Monymusk', and the men advanced in single file out into Marine Road towards Crater.[30]

As soon as the Argylls' assault party came into view, shots rang out from the waterfront palace of the Sultan of Lahej while sniper fire came from the commercial district. As the Pipe Major played on oblivious to incoming rounds, Mitchell ordered his Saladins to 'brass up' the opposition, and after they had put some limited but well directed fire into the enemy positions, the shooting subsided. Mitchell soon managed to establish OPs in the Chartered Bank and in the old Legislative Council building, a former church but now a shell, which had been burnt out by the rioters some weeks before. The Argylls then fanned out in a text-book operation, occupying nearby Sirah Island where they raised the regimental flag, while Captain Robin Buchanan's unit moved in from Ras Marshag on the far side of Crater. It was here, outside the cinema on the edge of the old Turkish fortifications that the only casualty of the night occurred, when a suspect was challenged and shot dead.

A strategic building still had to be secured. The Treasury, which stood near the site where Sir Arthur Charles had been assassinated, contained the whole of the currency reserve for South Arabia and was guarded by the Armed Police. Mitchell's second-in-command, Major Nigel Crowe, went in and tackled negotiations in Arabic with a wary police force. The normally tough, acerbic Crowe bravely stood out in the street with his 'Jocks' and persuaded the police to open up and allow the Argylls to occupy the Treasury. With the currency reserves for the whole of South Arabia now under British control, Mitchell was determined to press on, maintaining the momentum and tremendous morale that had seen his men through the first four hours of the action. Although they had reached as far as Banin Street, permission was sought from and approved by, Brigadier Dunbar for an advance as far as the civil Police Station, some 300 yards farther on.[31] This was achieved by a mixed infantry and armoured force by 0045 hours on 4 July, while Lieutenant-Colonel Mitchell set up a temporary HQ in the Aden Commercial Institute in Maarif Road. In the typical upbeat style of the Argylls, it was named 'Stirling Castle' in large letters across the front of the building.[32]

Secrecy surrounding the operation had been impressive. The Federal Government were only advised shortly before the re-entry started and the residents awoke on 4 July to the sound of a 'Long Reveille' by the

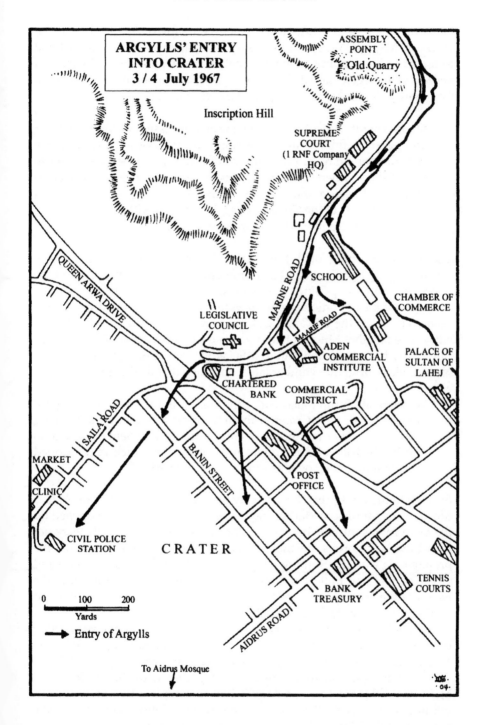

ARGYLLS' ENTRY
INTO CRATER
3 / 4 July 1967

ASSEMBLY
POINT
Old Quarry

Inscription Hill

SUPREME
COURT
(1 RNF Company
HQ)

SCHOOL

CHAMBER OF
COMMERCE

MARINE ROAD

QUEEN ARWA DRIVE

LEGISLATIVE
COUNCIL

MAARIF ROAD

ADEN
COMMERCIAL
INSTITUTE

PALACE OF
SULTAN OF
LAHEJ

CHARTERED
BANK

COMMERCIAL
DISTRICT

SAILA ROAD

MARKET

CLINIC

BANIN STREET

POST
OFFICE

CIVIL POLICE
STATION

CRATER

0   100   200
Yards

Entry of Argylls

BANK
TREASURY

TENNIS
COURTS

AIDRUS ROAD

To Aidrus Mosque

battalion's pipes and drums wafting across the town. At 1000 hours that morning, Major P Wade, commanding 'B' Company 1 PWO, was ordered to report to Lieutenant-Colonel Mitchell at the Argylls' HQ.[33] Wade had answered an urgent signal about a new task, and when he arrived at the Commercial Institute, he was uplifted by what he saw:

> My first sight of the Argylls gave me an impression of controlled and organised confidence: an impression of an exercise at Aldershot on a hot summer's day: of photographs of training at Peshawar in those far off days, when India and Pakistan were the fields of Victorian military education and practice. Outside their HQ were armoured cars and ferrets of the Queen's Dragoon Guards with pennants flying and RNF hackles pinned to their radio aerials.[34]

During the morning of 4 July Major-General Tower visited Colonel Mitchell and held a Commanders Conference to plan the final phase of the re-occupation, comprising a sweep through the remaining sectors. Throughout the operation the press were keen to report any difference of opinion between the GOC and Colonel Mitchell over the speed of the re-entry. The fact that Mitchell had organised press coverage of the re-entry can hardly have endeared him to MEC who were pursuing a low profile. Nevertheless, Brigadier Dunbar later confirmed that during the operation:

> We were all in full touch with progress ... In the event, the Argylls, very ably led, took Crater without, or almost without a shot being fired ... however I cannot over-emphasise the excellent organisation and battle drills of the Argylls and the way in which they gripped each area they took over as soon as they entered it.[35]

By 1900 hours on 4 July 'D' Company had secured the notorious Aidrus Mosque, the Municipal Market and the Bayoumi Clinic, which opened up the main routes into the heart of Crater. Although the terrorists were not launching a vigorous defence of Crater, they certainly kept up the propaganda war, distributing lengthy tracts about the re-occupation and swearing that 'our bullets and grenades will continue to cause fear in the hearts of the Scottish red rats'.[36] But there was little fear among the 'red rats' – only resolve to finish the job.

Equally important to the success of the operation were the supporting units, such as the 1 PWO. Major Wade of 1 PWO had been briefed by Mitchell and warned for 5 July to organise his men to occupy the OPs on the volcanic peaks surrounding Crater, together with the roadblock in Main Pass.[37] Meanwhile, the Argylls had to complete two very difficult but important tasks – the entry into the Armed Police Barracks and the recovery of the Moncur Landrover wrecks. Major Wade continues:

The first was achieved single-handed and publicised by a dramatic radio monologue by Colonel Mitchell as he drove up to and entered the Armed Police Barracks. He reported that Mohammed Ibrahim, the Commander of the AP, was waiting for him and that all was quiet and friendly. The second was executed in a very slick armour/infantry combined operation, when a platoon of the Argylls and a troop of the QDG re-entered Crater through Main Pass and gave protection to an APC, which dragged the squealing and protesting wheel-less hulks up the road and out of Crater.[38]

By nightfall on 5 July the re-occupation was complete. However, it was only the beginning of the Argylls' presence in Crater and they were determined to keep a tight grip on the streets. Meanwhile, on 13 July the GOC, realising that he would have to work with the Armed Police, attempted reconciliation by taking part in a ceremonial parade at their barracks. General Tower took the salute, and although the Argylls were required to attend, they did so under sufferance. Such events just reinforced Colonel Mitchell's disregard for the Armed Police, while strengthening his determination to 'dominate and pacify Crater'.

The application of 'Argyll Law' was proving an embarrassment to MEC, who were landed with the policy of co-operation with the local police and low-profile security enforcement. Whatever indications had been given to senior Arab Police officers during the 'Crater discussions' about the future level of this security enforcement, Mitchell's methods of rigorous house searches and the interrogation of terrorist suspects were clearly going against the political flow. Yet during this period in early July, many Yemenis still left their anarchic homeland to seek sanctuary in Aden, an indication that life for most Arabs in Crater was untroubled by the firm tactics of the Argylls. Nevertheless, on 18 July Major-General Tower ordered the Commander of the Argylls to 'throttle back forthwith'.[39]

This proved too much for Lieutenant-Colonel Mitchell. He distributed a Part 1 Order to his men, which he claimed was to re-affirm General Tower's policy for policing Crater. However, although Mitchell praised his men for the way they had pacified the rebellious township, he also made implied criticisms of the policies his superior Commanders were required to adopt. When Major-General Tower read the order, he decided that the time had come to take issue with his junior commander.[40]

While the GOC was considering what retribution to exact, the tension on the streets showed no sign of abating. During the days following the distribution of Mitchell's Part 1 Order, a terrorist was shot dead by the Argylls, while on 21 July Lance Corporal Willie Orr, a veteran of the Cyprus Emergency, was killed as he inspected an OP in the market place. In the follow-up, another terrorist suspect was shot dead breaking out of a cordon. As far as MEC was concerned, such events were ample evidence that Mitchell was not 'throttling back'. His cavalier role as 'Mad Mitch' was providing excellent copy for Fleet Street journalists, but it was his Part 1 Order that finally brought him before the Commander-in-Chief, Admiral Le Fanu. The C-in-C proceeded to rebuke him for 'issuing a disloyal Part I order to his battalion'. However, as there was no formal procedure for reprimanding a Lieutenant-Colonel short of a court-martial, Colonel Mitchell was never 'formally' reprimanded.[41]

Thus chastened but not perturbed, Mitchell led his battalion through the next few difficult months of service in Crater. From their new HQ in the Chartered Bank building, the 'Jocks' relentlessly pursued the terrorist gunmen and grenadiers through the back alleys. Though they were sometimes thwarted by the ban on entering Mosques, where weapons and explosives were often hidden, the message from the Scots was clear and uncompromising – 'any man who appears on the streets with a weapon will be shot dead'.[42] It was no idle bluff, and when during August 1967 both NLF and FLOSY launched concerted grenade, mortar and rocket attacks against the Argylls, the terrorists suffered casualties of twenty killed and five wounded. Such tough action, which was more a military operation than a security exercise, had also come at a price for the Argylls, who had lost five killed and thirteen wounded in 117 incidents by the end of August.[43]

Meanwhile, the Federal Government was unravelling. Such intelligence apparatus as the Federation possessed was dealt a fatal blow when their administrative officer, Captain Jefferson, was machine-gunned to death. Air Force personnel were also singled out for execution. Quartermaster Sergeant Brian Hughes of 84 Squadron had recently waved goodbye to his wife and twins, departing on a flight back to Britain, and was about to put his car onto a boat for transporting home. He called at Ma'alla's Esso garage on the way to the waterfront and, within seconds, was shot dead.[44] At the same time, two other RAF men in a nearby garage were shot dead, probably by the same gunman.

During this period the High Commissioner had to delegate most of the day-to-day running of Aden to his Deputy, Tom Oates, while he concentrated on keeping watch over the ever changing political scene. The Federation rulers were becoming desperate and their ruling body, the Supreme Council, appointed Hussain Bayoumi as Prime Minister in July, with the hope that he could deliver a broader based government. Bayoumi was the brother of one of the pioneers of the Federation, and although he lacked his late brother's political acumen, he claimed he had access to both FLOSY and the NLF and would bring their representatives into government. His attempts soon turned into farce, with the terrorist groups threatening to kill anyone who co-operated with him:

The Front warns any person, man or woman, from trying to cooperate with Ashworth and his gang, or who agrees to work at the TV and broadcasting station. Bayoumi is a traitor to Arabism and Islam, who will face the just sentence of the people.[45]

The threats were real, as PORF gunmen had recently embarked on the systematic elimination of Yemenis who worked as announcers for Aden Television and Radio Services.[46] There were few British announcers left to fill their places, as most had departed with the families of servicemen and Service-sponsored civilians between June and July. Even the MEC sponsored services newspaper, *The Dhow*, ceased publication in July, as few journalists were prepared to work after threats and thirteen nationalist inspired strikes.

The NLF began attacking military HQs and even Government House, using 2 inch and 81mm mortars. Less dramatic, but more deadly was the emergence of a number of 'pistol assassins' in Tawahi, who targeted unarmed white civilians. The IS Company of 1 PWO also faced a number of terrorist traps in this area, which involved a pistol shot to draw in soldiers, followed by a grenade, or, as they had so many '36' grenades, two or three would be thrown in succession.[47] Guarding strategic buildings was also part of the Yorkshiremen's brief, but there was some irritation at the formalities involved in protecting Command Hill, where the residences of the Service Chiefs had to be guarded in 'starched shirts and shorts, hosetops and puttees of a bygone age, and totally unsuited to protection duties'.[48] Meanwhile, in the less salubrious surroundings of Sheikh Othman, the regular round of house searches went on. One morning in July, soldiers from 'C' Company, 1 KOB heard shots fired inside a house and burst in to investigate. They found four local men bound and gagged. Two had already been executed, but the two terrified survivors were released while Lieutenant Higgins shot and killed an armed suspect running from the scene.[49]

By 30 June British forces had handed over responsibility for up-country security to the SAA, while all British units were recalled to Little Aden and Aden State and some units, like 1 QDG, left for the UK.[50] It was then that the revolution started in earnest. It was no coincidence that many of the Federal rulers were away from their seats in Europe or the Middle East, trying to patch together a last-minute deal. The states of Audhali and Lower Yafa soon fell to the NLF and on 13 August they captured the ruler of the Muflahi Sheikhdom. The following day Dathina was taken over, followed swiftly by the Fadhli Sultanate. As the collapse continued there was surprisingly little bloodshed, and despite the sultans' claims that they had good intelligence, the rulers themselves were surprised by the speed and efficiency of the NLF coups. Even the rulers' personal retainers failed to stand in the way of the terrorist cadres, who swiftly set up ruling councils.

But these NLF takeovers were not always what they seemed, as 'Barney' Dutton, of BP, observed:

> Another view of the scene is that there is increasing disintegration into tribal warfare; no real control or authoritative administration in place of the former Rulers; groups may raise an NLF (or FLOSY) flag without having any idea what the party stands for and without accepting direction from the so-called political leaders; and military units in the field operate according to the tribal or ideological sympathies of the local commander.[51]

Nor were all the coups bloodless. In Wahidi, the only eastern state to join the Federation, the ruler returned from Beirut on 3 September to try to quell the unrest. He was provided with a British escort, in this case Major Peter Gooch, who was still serving with the SAA, as well as an Army Air Corps pilot. As the party landed in Wahidi, there was a disturbance and Major Gooch and his pilot were both raked with machine-gun fire as they attempted to lift off, the helicopter crashing and killing them both. The NLF, desperate not to risk RAF retaliation, swiftly used a bulldozer to bury the evidence.

Elsewhere, the British forces were reluctant to intervene. In Beihan state, one of the key states of the Federation and nominally controlled by the enigmatic Sharif, terrorist gangs made unexpected advances. Then on 3 September, in the face of this rather weak opposition, the Sharif inexplicably left for Saudi Arabia. There was talk that he had gone to seek Saudi help to annexe the state of Beihan but there seemed little reason for the Sharif to have left his state in the hands of an inexperienced nephew who was no match for the NLF. When the NLF brushed the nephew aside and assumed power with the help of the SAA, the Sharif threatened to regain control of his state. But he was now warned that if he attempted to re-enter Beihan, the RAF would attack him. The absurdity of the situation was not lost on Sir Humphrey Trevelyan, who was saddened 'to threaten the use of British aircraft against an attempt by a man who was still nominally under British protection, to recover his State'.[52]

The Federal rulers had hardly helped their own cause, with too many of them spending time away from their 'seats' at a critical period. They had further jeopardised their position by attempting a last minute 'UDI', which soon collapsed through lack of SAA support. Their demise was in stark contrast to the sheikhs and tribal rulers across the border in Yemen, who, through deft political manoeuvres and close contact with their tribes, had held onto their local power bases despite a republican revolution. By the end of August, the NLF had driven out most of the rulers of the western states of the Federation, though in Beihan and the Aulaqi states there was a contest for power with FLOSY. Most SAA officers realised that the NLF was going to win but thought its organisation was weak and it would be possible for the Army to dominate it in the future. Few officers supported the left wing of the NLF but within their ranks there was considerable support for leftist policies and this shifted the Army as a whole away from FLOSY.[53]

The ease with which the Federal rulers capitulated appalled many who had endeavoured to make the Federation work. Donal McCarthy, Political Advisor to the C-in-C, MEC, was unequivocal about the final 'own goal' by Federal Ministers. They, like everyone else, had succumbed to intriguing with the opposition:

> The ultimate collapse owed much to the fact that the whole Federal team insisted on going to Geneva to see the Mission, whereas the High Commissioner wanted the team kept down to six. And their actions were entirely characteristic when the crisis came. The most recent Fadhli Sultan's last action before going to Geneva, when threatened with trouble, was to open his jail and let out, among others, the most dangerous NLF killer we had ever captured. Safely in Geneva, he [the Sultan] was the first, however, to demand that the British Army and a British Air Strike should be used against the dissidents in his own State.
>
> Even the Audhalis are not free of this. Sultan Saleh had agreed with Naib Nasser not to use tribesmen against the villagers to put down the revolt and thus start generations of feuding ... A couple of days earlier, Naib Nasser had pressed the High Commissioner to use the RAF against Lodar town. Again it was all right if it was our responsibility and not theirs.[54]

Much of the disheartening news up-country was kept from the residents of Aden. As the Federation crumbled all around them, South Arabian Television issued increasingly frequent news bulletins, but kept up attempts at normality. It continued its usual diet of *Robin Hood* and *The Saint*, but the few cinema-goers that visited 'The Globe' could hardly be accused of 'escapism', having to sit through repeats of Stanley Baker in *The Sands of Kalahari*.

On 2 September Qahtan al-Sha'abi, leader of the NLF and until now a virtually unknown figure in the West, gave a press conference proclaiming that the Federation had collapsed but that the NLF were ready to work with the South Arabian Army. They were categorically not prepared to work with FLOSY, who were making overtures about a coalition government. FLOSY's association with Egypt no longer held an automatic *cachet* in the Arab World and they were desperate to find a way into a future government.

By 5 September 1967 Sir Humphrey Trevelyan had to publicly admit

273

that the Federation had disintegrated and that the Nationalist forces had to be recognised. Talks were offered to all parties but al-Sha'abi demanded exclusive recognition of the NLF and refused to talk, a position that he maintained for the next two months. This was a holding tactic while NLF cadres set about destroying FLOSY and its military arm, PORF. The scene for this bitter duel in early September was 'Area North'. This was territory that had been jointly controlled by 1 PARA and the 1 Lancashire Regiment (PWV) since 25 May. The 'Toms' from 1 PARA operated largely in Sheikh Othman where they had a Company permanently based in the old Mission, re-branded as 'Fort Walsh', as well as another based near the unstable town of Dar Saad.[55] Meanwhile, 1 Lancashire Regiment (PWV) were responsible for the troublesome area surrounding al-Mansoura.[56] On 6 September bitter fighting erupted in Sheikh Othman and Dar Saad between heavily armed NLF and PORF fighters. For five days they slaughtered each other, employing the usual terrorist arsenals including Blindicides, mortars and semi-automatics. For 1 PARA to intervene would have resulted in unifying the terrorists against British and SAA forces, so resources were committed to trying to negotiate a cease-fire. Even the Egyptian President tried to exert pressure on the terrorists, and when an SAA sponsored peace-treaty was finally agreed, hundreds of gunman lay dead or wounded on the rooftops and in the back streets of Sheikh Othman. At the same time, fighting erupted around al-Mansoura and patrols of 1 Lancashire Regiment (PWV) found themselves subject to persistent attacks. Their guards around the Detention Centre came under sniper fire, and on 8 September Corporal J Blenkharn was shot and killed in his Ferret Scout Car while coming to the aid of a patrol, pinned down by enemy fire.[57]

While the NLF paused for breath in Aden, they were hard at work in the eastern states of South Arabia. September saw the Sultanates of Kathiri and Qu'aiti fall to their cadres, who had invested in a policy of establishing branches throughout the Wadi Hadhramaut. Although this was the most conservative area of South Arabia, with stricter caste divisions in its society, paradoxically it seemed to foster the most radical and left-wing elements of the NLF movement. British vessels off the coast near Mukalla suddenly found themselves subject to random and aggressive searches. A cargo skipper recalled:

> At 1530 six members of the NLF boarded the vessel, all armed with automatic weapons, pockets bulging with ammunition and hand grenades. They came to my cabin and while two stationed themselves outside, the others came in, helping themselves to my cigarettes. I was told that myself and my deputy were to go ashore for political questioning About another dozen guerrillas joined the party, some in Arab dress, others in an assortment of ragged clothing, but all were

heavily armed and liberally draped with two or three hundred rounds of ammunition.[58]

The rulers of the eastern states had also left their home territories at a critical moment, and although they went to abortive talks in Geneva at the behest of the British High Commission, they travelled via Beirut and Cairo, adding weeks to their journey.[59] And the British-raised HBL, the only military instrument that could be used against the NLF or marauding gangs, could now expect little help from British Forces. Despite pleas for RAF cover, they were told that unlike the agreement with the SAA, there was no longer any undertaking to provide air support for the HBL.[60] The NLF advance in the eastern states, as in the west, was so swift because they faced little opposition from other nationalist groups in the hinterland. FLOSY had no material organisation or support structure outside Aden, although they did manage to temporarily oppose the NLF in Wahidi and Aulaqi. However, Sir Humphrey Trevelyan reported that the FLOSY leader, al-Asnag, was very much in the dark on hinterland affairs and 'there was not one clan whose name he knew, let alone one whose support he could claim'.[61]

As the situation deteriorated, so did the assessments of George Brown, the Foreign Secretary. His pronouncements were increasingly erratic and bizarrely he opened a meeting in London on 21 September by announcing that 'the situation in South Arabia seems to be improving'.[62]

Regardless of announcements from London, the withdrawal plan was underway. After the hand over to the SAA up-country, British troops could only intervene in the hinterland at the request of the Federal Government, but the RAF was still expected to provide air cover for the SAA. Over 150 Hawker Hunter sorties were flown per month, though most were in support of supply operations on the ground. 84 Squadron were still busy airlifting troops and supplies back from the hinterland when one of their Beverleys hit a landmine on Thumier airfield and had to be destroyed. 208 Squadron, who had provided excellent air support during the Radfan campaign, had already moved to the Gulf, but 8 and 43(F) Squadrons continued to operate out of Khormaksar.[63] The bulk of MEC was closing down in Aden, though a skeleton command would reside at Khormaksar until independence. In its place, responsibilities were taken up by the new Commander, British Forces Gulf (CBFG), appointed on 1 September and operating from Bahrain. The three single Service HQs from Aden would be transferred to Bahrain from the beginning of October.[64]

Ironically, while any sort of accommodation between the warring parties in South Arabia seemed impossible, in Yemen a peace deal was looking viable. July and August had seen demonstrations against the Egyptian presence and thirty of her soldiers were killed by a mob.

Egyptian troops were already starting to withdraw, but the royalists failed to capitalise on the situation, much to the exasperation of the Saudis. Al-Badr had few excuses, but his weak leadership was exacerbated by the rivalries within his family and supporting tribes, though he still had help from the European mercenaries who remained in the front line. Still under the command of Colonel David Smiley, the band continued to suffer casualties in Yemen. Smiley recalled an ambush in August 1967:

> I was visiting the British radio operators in their cave one evening, when a signal came in from al-Hassan to say a truck had just arrived with the bodies of three British soldiers. The following afternoon, the full story emerged. They had left Amara on a four-hour drive to al-Hassan's base, taking with them, Ali, the young Yemeni boy who made the tea in the British cave. Their Landrover had been stopped near a village by a roadblock manned by, whom they thought at first, were royalist tribesmen. Since they had been expecting no trouble, the Englishmen had brought only one rifle between them. While two of the tribesmen kept the vehicle covered, the third approached and questioned them in English, for about 20 minutes. Finally he asked for money to let them through, which they gave him, and then he demanded their rifle. Ali whispered, 'do not give him your gun'. But the Englishmen innocently handed over the rifle, whereupon the tribesman opened fire, killing one of them instantly and wounding the others.
>
> Although hit in the leg, Ali managed to crawl behind a rock, but the two remaining British soldiers tried to shelter by their car, where a grenade finished them off.[65]

The loss of comrades was always a blow to Colonel Smiley, especially when one, in his own words, 'had been a good friend of mine who had served in the SAS under me in Oman'. Their operations had certainly hindered Nasser's adventure in Yemen, and thereby his designs on the Arabian Peninsula. The republican government had increasingly come to be seen as a 'stooge' of Egypt and disillusioned republicans soon flocked into South Arabia. King Feisal of Saudi Arabia sensed the financially crippled Nasser was at last ready for a deal. And on 29 August in Khartoum, Feisal agreed to bail out Nasser in the sum of £50 million a year, in return for an Egyptian pullout from Yemen.[66]

By mid-October the Egyptian troops had withdrawn from Sana'a to the coast and within weeks had left the country. Several weeks later, President Sallal, now without any foreign force to shore him up, left for Moscow. While he was away, a bloodless coup headed by Qadi al-Iryani ousted him from power.[67]

Meanwhile, political manoeuvring on South Arabia was not just confined to Arab states. Julian Amery, Sir Kennedy Trevaskis and Billy McLean reportedly made last-ditch attempts in New York to seek outside economic aid for the Federation. Optimistically they hoped that a financial package, supported by countries like Japan, could be used to expand the port and Refinery and thereby stabilise the Federation. It was all too late. And in October, as if to reinforce the message, the terrorists embarked on a further ruthless assassination campaign.

Responsibility for Sheikh Othman and al-Mansoura was transferred by 1 PARA and 1 Lancashire Regiment (PWV) to the SAA on 24 September. Now there were no further British personnel in those areas, the terrorist gunmen had to look for targets in the Tawahi and Steamer Point areas.[68] They found them among the officials of the High Commission and Foreign Office, who at this late stage were making plans for their careers after independence. Two young Arabists who shared a flat looked forward to a promising future; David Ledger, who would later write an account of the troubles in *Shifting Sands*, hoped to work as Personal Advisor to one of the Emirs in the Gulf, while his flatmate, Derek Rose, assistant to Tony Ashworth in the Information Department, was expecting to secure a job with the British Council in Switzerland. However, Rose first had to wind up his duties in Aden. On 20 October he visited Francis Rais of the Red Cross at the Crescent Hotel and then drove back to his office. On the way he stopped in Tawahi, parked his car near the waterfront and went into a shop to buy a film. He soon came out, climbed into his borrowed sports car, and as he started the engine, a young NLF 'commando' came alongside the vehicle. Derek Rose had no time to draw his automatic pistol before he was shot twice in the back of the head. He slumped forward, his foot hitting the accelerator and the car smashed into the pier wall, almost within view of Tawahi Police Station.[69]

The senseless killing of this likeable and talented young official was carried out by one of a small number of assassins who operated alone in the Steamer Point area. Although some of Derek Rose's work for IRD had been of a sensitive and secret nature, it is quite likely he was killed randomly as a representative of the High Commission. Despite the NLF immediately claiming responsibility, it could just as easily have been the work of a PORF gunman. Sadly it was not an isolated incident, for some days later a Danish Sea Captain, Johanne Theison, was shot in the back and killed. Michael Booth, an accountant at the British Bank of the Middle East, was shot through the neck, while on 29 October it was again the turn of a British colonial servant. Allan Macdonald had just finished dinner at the Crescent Hotel and was walking back to his accommodation in the annexe, when a lone gunman walked up to him. Macdonald managed to grapple with the terrorist but was shot in the stomach, and staggered into the annexe groaning 'the bastards have put one in me. Get the police and an ambulance'.[70]

Carrying discreet pistols in shoulder holsters offered little protection as Walter Mechtel, a German TV reporter, found to his cost. Posting a letter near the Crescent Hotel, Mechtel was shot twice in the back of the head before he had time to draw his weapon. These grim statistics brought civilian casualties for the four months up to 31 October, to fifty-one killed killed and 132 wounded, many of whom were casualties in incidents watched by an inactive police force.

While some of these assassins may have been 'mavericks', their agenda was shared with the NLF whose spokesman stated, 'some may ask, why fight for independence when the British will grant it freely? Comrades, true independence is not given away, but taken'.[71] It was this cruel rationale that the NLF applied right to the end, to show the world that it was they who were evicting the British rather than the British themselves electing to withdraw.

Although the preparations for the withdrawal were well advanced, the final date still had to be flexible. Brigadier Dunbar had to allow for unforeseen circumstances:

> We planned for months to have sufficient flexibility to come and go as the political situation demanded and to this end had secured a large and formidable Naval Task Force. From this we could be rationed, supplied with ammunition, helicopters and air protection of various sorts from a carrier. We could also be supplied with soldiery in the form of a carrier-born Commando, so it was therefore easy for us to withdraw under any conceivable circumstances.[72]

On 2 November the Foreign Secretary finally confirmed the withdrawal date for the end of November. The NLF and FLOSY together with their supporters within the SAA now had a firm timetable. Whatever the intent of the terrorist leadership, there were enough roaming gunmen with personal and clan vendettas to upset any subtle planning. So during the afternoon of 3 November a grenade exchange between rival gangs re-ignited a full-scale conflict between the NLF and PORF in Sheikh Othman. The indiscriminate fighting soon spread to Dar Saad and al-Mansoura, but as soon as the PORF gunmen appeared to be coming out on top, the SAA moved to separate the warring factions. It was not long before the SAA were openly siding with the NLF gunmen in hunting down PORF and FLOSY members, but the wild nature of the shooting ensured that many innocent civilians were killed. As NLF cadres burst into their rivals' houses, there were appalling scenes of brutality with few prisoners taken. In a week of fierce fighting over 300 perished and many times that figure were wounded before FLOSY and its military wing were, quite simply, extinguished. The SAA then formally declared for the NLF on 7 November.[73]

On 13 November HMG had to formally recognise the NLF as the successor government and called for talks in Geneva. After tactical delays, the NLF delegation lead by Qahtan al-Sha'abi eventually arrived in Geneva. Apart from al-Sha'abi, the other NLF representatives were shadowy figures and most were a generation younger than their leader. Nevertheless, in the ensuing bargaining the 'inexperienced' NLF team extracted £12 million from HMG for a future aid package.

The huge British base at Little Aden was the first part of Aden state to be handed over to the SAA. Recently finished at an estimated cost of £18 million, the base had been home not only to the Royal Marines and other units but also HQ 24 Brigade. In the event all fixtures and contents were also to be handed over – an exercise that appalled Captain Leslie Hudson, a Royal Marine on the Staff of 24 Brigade. It was British officialdom at its worst, he recalled:

> When we had to finally leave our quarters in Little Aden, we knew that they were to be handed over to the terrorist regime. Just before we left, the Property Services Agency arrived. We couldn't believe it. They went around, armed with clipboards, making notes of any defects in the houses so that the officers who had occupied them could be duly charged – and they were all being given away anyway. As the Brigade Staff pulled out of Little Aden, so they passed a stream of lorries, driven by locals, going in to strip the houses of anything serviceable.[74]

Because the talks in Geneva were only settled at the last minute, MEC didn't know whether they would be faced with a fighting withdrawal. The provision of a Naval Task Force was to satisfy the need for flexibility. This force included the aircraft carriers, HMS *Eagle* and HMS *Hermes*, holding Sea Vixen aircraft for ground attack and Buccaneers for a strike capability, so that the number of RAF fighter planes onshore could be reduced to an absolute minimum. Supply ships would also hold stores and equipment for any eventuality.[75] There was also the commando carrier, HMS *Bulwark* with an embarked commando, using helicopters that could also be employed instead of trucks. Naval Hospital facilities were at hand should casualties be incurred in any fighting breakout. There would still be a need for two infantry battalions to hold Khormaksar until the last minute; both to guard the vast ammunition dump near the southern perimeter and to secure the airfield as an embarkation point. If there was a total collapse of law and order at the end, then the preferred option of airlifting troops out from Khormaksar might not be safe and the Naval Task Force would be utilised.[76]

In the event, the withdrawal went extremely smoothly. The troops were moved out in shuttles using Hercules transport planes, which shifted nearly 4,000 men and supplies from Aden to Bahrain or Muharraq in the Gulf, for onward transfer to the UK. 1 PARA and 42 Commando together with Four Five Commando covered the evacuation as Government House was handed over, and the last of the military strong-points were vacated without casualties. Acting Corporal Jim Finn, pleased to be leaving without a scratch, was on one of the RAF coaches leaving Steamer Point and bound for Khormaksar and the airlift. As the coach sped along Ma'alla Strait, a grenade hit the wire mesh covering the vehicle windows alongside Finn, but luckily failed to explode. The remaining High Commission staff hastily evacuated sensitive documents, and in a burst of patriotic defiance, piled them up on an Aden beach in the shape of 'WAP' before setting them on fire.

On 29 November Lieutenant-Colonel Dai Morgan, Commander of 42 Commando Group, was the last British soldier to leave Aden.[77] The People's Republic of Southern Yemen was born. But this nationalist government was to be no guarantor of peace.

NOTES

1   One casualty was a Fusilier, Corporal Beal, who was wounded in the head by a sniper's bullet.
2   *Globe & Laurel*, October 1967, and Trevelyan to Foreign Office, 22 June 1967, FCO 8/257, NA.
3   Notes on 'Aden Mutiny 20 June 1967', FMN. Also Pathology Report by Flight-Lieutenant Barry Corke, 30 June 1967, FCO 8/438, NA.
4   Testimony, ACP Abdul Hadi, and Chief Inspector Abdulla Yafai, 30 June 1967, FCO 8/438, NA. The Pathology Report, 30 June 1967 makes disturbing reading, FCO 8/438, NA. Also Mitchell, op. cit., p. 170.
5   *The Daily Telegraph*, 22 June 1967.
6   Traditionally, gallantry awards were allowed for soldiers 'on active service' and in 'the presence of the enemy'. However, the trend since World War II has seen a percolation of civilian decorations into awards for valour in the field. The Campaign Service Medal was available to all the Services, awarded for 'Radfan' (23 April–31 July 1964), and 'South Arabia' (1 August 1964–30 November 1967). Until 1993, Officers were awarded the Military Cross, and ORs, the Military Medal. Since 1993, the Military Cross is available to both.
7   The account of the massacres was the lead story in all national papers and news bulletins. *The Daily Express* and *The Daily Sketch* carried more stories on the massacres on successive days.
8   Apart from the eight members of RCT, those buried included the casualties of 20 June – nine from 1 RNF, three from 1 Argyll and Sutherland Highlanders, 2nd Lieutenant R Young of 1 Lancashire Regiment (PWV), Private A Ferguson of 1 King's Own Border Regiment, as well as H Alexander of the Public Works Department. In addition, Sergeant J Webb, REME who was killed in Crater on 16 June, and Private J MacIntosh, 1 PARA, who was shot by a sniper on 18 June, were also buried.
9   *The Times*, 24 June 1967.

10   Trevelyan to Foreign Office, 21 June 1967, FCO 8/257, NA.

11   Nigel Pusineli, Tape 652, Oral History Archive, BECM, Bristol.

12   *The Dhow*, 29 June 1967. The Services' newspaper, which covered the Middle East, produced its last issue in July 1967. Major-General Thomson, CB, CBE, MC, was subsequently Colonel of the Argyll and Sutherland Highlanders.

13   'Draft Answer to Parliamentary Questions', undated 1968, FCO 8/257. In post draft margin notes, the British Government were at pains to point out that there was no political pressure applied to MEC or the HC.

14   'Draft Answer to Parliamentary Questions', undated 1968, FCO 8/257. Mitchell would probably have suspected that discussions with the terrorists were taking place.

15   J E Pestell to B L Crowe, 17 July 1968, and B L Crowe to J E Pestell, 17 July 1968, both FCO 8/257, NA. Also J E Pestell to B L Crowe, 19 July 1968, FCO 8/257, NA.

16   Dunbar to Paget, 25 September 1968, File 2/6, Dunbar Papers, LHCMA. Also 'Report on the Mutinies', MEC, 26 October 1967, DEFE 11/533, NA.

17   Trevelyan to Foreign Office, 24 June 1967, FCO 8/257, NA.

18   Trevelyan to Foreign Office, 25 June 1967, FCO 8/257, NA.

19   Trevelyan to George Thomson, 5 July 1967, FCO 8/257, NA. Also *The Sunday Express*, 24 June 1967.

20   'Report on the Mutinies', MEC, 26 October 1967, DEFE 11/533, NA. Also B L Crowe to J E Pestell, 22 July 1968, FCO 8/257, NA.

21   In the light of PORF's superiority in Crater, Hadi probably thought it worth repairing fences with the British. See also Trevelyan to Foreign Office, 21 June 1967, FCO 8/257, NA.

22   Abdul Fattah Ismail, 'How we liberated Aden', in *Armed Struggle in Arabia*, File Omn.3a, AWDU. Upon the removal of al-Sha'abi in 1969, Ismail became General Secretary of the NLF and a leading Marxist in the Government.

23   'NLF Crater Daily Bulletin', undated, File 2/3, Dunbar Papers, LHCMA.

24   The Mayor was a relative of Khalifa the grenadier, who had attempted to assassinate Sir Kennedy Trevaskis. See Trevelyan to Foreign Office, 28 June 1967, FCO 8/257, NA.

25   For details of all the incidents in which Fusiliers were wounded, see *St George's Gazette*, 30 September 1967. Also Unit Historical Record of 1 RNF, Army Historical Branch, MOD. Also Davis Papers.

26   The targeting of terrorist gunmen may have been selective. To allow widespread and indiscriminate shooting of terrorists would have risked upsetting negotiations for a peaceful re-entry to Crater.

27   In the absence of Brigadier Jefferies, Lieutenant-Colonel Downward assumed temporary command of Aden Brigade for four weeks.

28   Major Shewan was mentioned in Despatches.

29   Lieutenant David Thomson became the battalion Adjutant in August 1967. Lieutenant Brian Baty became Intelligence Officer in his place.

30   This scene was immortalised in Peter Archer's painting, 'Argylls' entry into Crater', which hangs in the Regimental Headquarters at Stirling Castle.

31   'The Re-taking of Crater', MEC Report, 26 October 1967, DEFE 11/533, NA. Also Dunbar to Paget, 25 September 1968, File 2/6, Dunbar Papers, LHCMA.

32   Good descriptions of the re-entry into Crater are contained in Colonel Mitchell's book, *Having Been A Soldier*, op. cit., pp. 176–87. Also Stephen Harper, *Last Sunset*, op. cit., pp. 104–15. Harper was a journalist for *The Daily Express* and eyewitness to the operation.

33   1 PWO was commanded by Lieutenant-Colonel Bill Todd, the last serving

officer in the battalion to have had combat experience in World War II. See Tillotson, op. cit., p. 42.

34 *The White Rose* (Regimental Journal of the Prince of Wales's Own Regiment of Yorkshire), Vol. 9, October 1967, pp. 131–3. The 1 RNF, now back in the UK, received the heartening message that their distinctive red and white hackles were now seen again in Crater.

35 Dunbar to Paget, 25 September 1968, op. cit.

36 'The Blazing Hills', NLF newsletter, 5 July 1967, Dunbar Papers, LHCMA.

37 During their third tour of Aden, 1 PWO suffered twenty-nine casualties, including two dead (Lance-Corporal Leslie Roberts and Lance-Corporal Trevor Holmes) and five seriously injured. Corporal R Bradley and Private P Davison received the Military Medal for gallantry.

38 *The White Rose*, October 1967, op. cit.

39 Colin Beer, op. cit., p. 83.

40 For the detailed content of the Part 1 Order, see Mitchell, *Having Been a Soldier*, op. cit., pp. 199–200 and also his article 'Before the C-in-C', *The Sunday Express*, 20 October 1968.

41 'Draft Answers to Parliamentary Questions', undated 1968, FCO 8/257, NA.

42 Colonel Mitchell, op. cit., p. 226. Otto Heilbrunn discusses military tactics employed against terrorists in various emergencies in 'When the Counter-Insurgents Cannot Win', *RUSI Journal*, March 1969.

43 'Comparative British Unit Casualties in Aden State: April–August 1967', MEC, File 2/4, Dunbar Papers, LHCMA. In addition to the three deaths on 20 June and Lance-Corporal Orr, the Argylls suffered another fatality on 4 August when Pipe-Corporal Jimmy Scott was hit by a mortar round.

44 Robert Douglas to Author, 7 March 2003.

45 'Statement by FLOSY on the General Strike', File 2/3, Dunbar Papers, LHCMA.

46 According to David Ledger, PORF gunmen killed twenty-four announcers, between May and July 1967. See Ledger, op. cit., pp. 155–7.

47 *The White Rose*, spring 1968.

48 Tillotson, op. cit., p. 31.

49 'Newsletter, July 1967, '1st Battalion, The King's Own Royal Border Regiment', File 2/1, Dunbar Papers, LHCMA.

50 1 QDG went on to successful tours of Berlin, Northern Ireland, Beirut and were involved in the First Gulf War.

51 A H Dutton to J Macwilliam, 9 October 1967, File 28693, BP Archives, UW. Examples of pure 'banditry' are quoted in Lord Caradon to Foreign Office, 28 October 1967, and Trevelyan to Foreign Office, 19 October 1967, both FCO 8/252, NA.

52 Sir Humphrey Trevelyan, *Middle East*, op. cit., p. 253.

53 Lackner, op. cit., p. 102.

54 Donal McCarthy to Arabian Department, FO, 13 October 1967, FCO 8/41, NA.

55 1 PARA continued their operation until 27 November 1967, when they handed over a much-reduced area to 42 Commando, for the final pullout. 'Fort Walsh' was the old Mission Hospital. For an account of 1 PARA activities, see Lieutenant-Colonel Mike Walsh, DSO, 'Everything Under the Sun', in *RUSI Journal*, March 1969.

56 During their tour of Aden, 1 Lancashire Regiment (PWV) suffered four killed and thirty-nine wounded.

57 *The Regimental Magazine of the Lancashire Regiment*, autumn 1967.

58   'Report on Mukalla Bay', 17 October 1967, FCO 8/252, NA.
59   Lord Caradon to Foreign Office, 28 October 1967, FCO 8/252, NA. These meetings in Arab capitals were attended by NLF and FLOSY representatives but came to nothing.
60   HBL forts were coming under attack from the Yemen at the same time. In the past, there were numerous instances of RAF bombing sorties in support of the HBL. Trevelyan to Foreign Office, 24 September 1967, FCO 8/252, NA.
61   Trevaskis, *Shades*, op. cit., p. 172. For a sober assessment of the NLF takeover in the eastern states, see Jim Ellis to High Commission, 5 October 1967, FCO 8/252, NA. Also Lackner, *PDR Yemen*, op. cit., pp. 44–7.
62   Memorandum of meeting between George Brown and Kuwaiti Foreign Minister, 21 September 1967, FCO 8/41, NA. Those attending meetings with the Foreign Secretary observed a more consistent attitude first thing in the morning. After 'refreshments', things began to slide.
63   No. 8 Squadron moved to Muharraq, in the Gulf, before independence, but 43(F) Squadron remained until November, when it was finally disbanded.
64   Air Chief Marshal Sir David Lee, op. cit., p. 243–4.
65   David Smiley, *Arabian Assignment*, op. cit., p. 222. The SAS Regiment's memorial clock at their Hereford base records the death of two SAS men in South Arabia during 1967 – Trooper G F F Iles, and Lance Corporal A G Brown. See 'Appendix A', Geraghty, op. cit.
66   Page, op. cit., p. 108.
67   Sallal subsequently sought sanctuary in Baghdad, where the Iraqi Government provided him with a pension. See Dresch, op. cit., p. 114.
68   After four months in Sheikh Othman, 1 PARA had lost three killed and twenty-two wounded.
69   Sir Humphrey Trevelyan to Foreign Office, 21 October 1967, FCO 8/206, NA. Also *The Times*, 21 October 1967. Also B Crowe to D McCarthy, 20 October 1967, FCO 8/206, NA.
70   Sir Humphrey Trevelyan to Foreign Office, Telegrams 808 and 809, 30 October 1967, FCO 8/206, NA. Also *The Daily Mail*, 30 October 1967. Fortunately Allan Macdonald survived.
71   Quoted in Dresch, op. cit., p. 110.
72   Brigadier Dunbar, 'Speech for Rotary Luncheon, 28 November 1968', File 2/5, Dunbar Papers, LHCMA.
73   Parliamentary Question, 8 November 1967, FCO 8/206, NA. Also Ledger, op. cit., pp. 206–9, and Downton, op. cit., pp. 256–7.
74   Colonel Leslie Hudson to Author, 3 September 2001. After distinguished service in Northern Ireland, Colonel Hudson went on to be Commandant of the Royal Marines Training Camp, Lympstone, Devon.
75   Sea Vixens were provided by 892 and 899 Naval Air Service (NAS), while 800 NAS flew Buccaneers.
76   'Lecture Notes on South Arabia', File 2/5, Dunbar Papers, LHCMA.
77   Although 42 Commando were the last to leave, it was Four Five Commando who, for seven years, had been the longest serving unit in Aden. In that time they suffered six killed and sixty-two wounded, and were awarded three MBEs, three MCs, four MMs and fourteen Mentioned in Despatches.

CHAPTER XIV

Epilogue

'It is someone else's turn now.'

*Sir Winston Churchill, after Britain's
withdrawal from Palestine, 1948.*

Total casualties for the conflict in South Arabia were among the lowest of any of Britain's 'small wars' at the end of Empire. Estimates vary depending on the years subjected to study. Julian Paget calculated that fifty-seven British Servicemen were killed and 651 wounded during the four years of the official 'Emergency'. This only relates to 'Aden State' casualties, for which Middle East Command maintained records and would not include the large number of 'lightly wounded:[1] for the war in the hinterland and the unofficial conflict in Yemen, records are incomplete, partly because those men killed or wounded up until 1967 were not officially casualties 'on active service'. When Royal Marine, RAF and Special Forces are added to army regimental casualties, the number of those killed in South Arabia between 1962 and 1967 approaches 200.

Due to the nature and conditions of low-intensity warfare in the 1960s, the ratio of wounded to fatalities was much higher than in larger conflicts and a total of over 1,500 wounded may have been suffered during this six-year period.[2] Some of those killed rest in Ma'alla Cemetery, while others are buried out in the hinterland. Post-1965 casualties lie in the stark, but well maintained, Silent Valley Cemetery.

Attitudes at the time towards casualties in Britain's 'End of Empire' campaigns had not changed much since the Second World War. By and large the losses were met with resignation – treated as a tragic part of the cost of the withdrawal from Empire. After the Aden Insurgency, there was bitterness among some of the next-of-kin that their men had died in vain. This was particularly evident concerning those killed on 20 June 1967 when some felt the Army at best was betrayed by its political masters or at worst conceded too much ground to political needs. The many assassinations robbed other relatives of the prop that their men had been killed in combat, in a fair fight against a respected enemy. Yet despite the grief and sorrow, there was still a pride that British troops had carried out their duties professionally and, when called upon, with great bravery. Even the sensitive issue of death by friendly fire was met with stoic acceptance.[3] Brigadier David Baines, who had commanded 1 RHA throughout its tour of South Arabia, later compared these attitudes with present-day reactions:

> My generation, who were in the Second World War or the colonial conflicts that followed, felt that if someone was killed by 'friendly-fire', it was a tragedy but part of the risk that we all accepted – the press and the public took the same view. Today, with television cameras everywhere, any such incident hits the headlines and the resulting pressures on Commanding Officers are appalling. We also felt that 'friendly fire' was an absolute fact of life. It occurred frequently in the Army, and most soldiers with combat experience have, at some time, been shelled or shot at, by their own side. It is now looked at as an absolute horror, and commanders are so worried by media reaction that initiative can be destroyed.[4]

When the British Government announced a complete withdrawal, the cause of the Federal Government was hopelessly lost. It had never enjoyed widespread support, but once it was clear that it would receive no further military aid or continue to enjoy economic support derived from the British base, it was helpless before an organised and committed terrorist campaign.[5] And if strident external forces fuelled this opposition, the collapse of the Federation was a *fait accompli*.

There had been no consistent, tough political figure, who could weld together the disparate forces within the Federation. If Hassan Ali Bayoumi, Aden's Chief Minister, had not died prematurely in April 1963, conciliation might have been possible. He was, after all, about the only Adeni politician whom the Federal Leaders could respect. His succession by the ineffective Zein Baharoon, followed by the openly hostile Abdul Mackawee, sealed the fate of the Federal Government.[6] Any successive candidates were assassinated or succumbed to pressure to withdraw from the political arena.

From the outset, the British government was faced with a uniquely difficult task in the hinterland. The sheer number and diversion of clans and tribes meant that any idea of 'federalising' them would always be an immense and time-consuming task. Furthermore, the pressures within Britain to de-colonise, combined with the surge in Arab nationalism, meant there would never be enough time available. To compound these difficulties, the removal of proscription bombing towards the end of the British presence destroyed the one means of keeping the myriad of warring tribes in check.

South Arabia had suffered from decades of political inertia. Unlike other regions in Britain's mesh of Condominiums, Mandates and Treaties, there was a singular lack of investment and development in South Arabia, and in the end, no administrative legacy. Although medical services brought welcome relief both in the hinterland and Aden, developments such as the Abyan Cotton Scheme were the exception rather than the rule. Ultimately, there was no evangelical spirit, no desire to improve or educate the region to go hand in hand with strategic and economic gain.[7] If pre-war British governments had adopted a forward-looking policy for the old Protectorates, events might have moved more smoothly. Post-war Conservative governments similarly failed to grasp opportunities. The 1964 Labour Government certainly had a policy on South Arabia but it was one of scuttling from the scene as soon as possible. The Wilson Government's announcement that withdrawal would take place no later than January 1968 was designed to bring the opposing parties together around the conference table. Authorities have suggested that Wilson was trying to repeat the Attlee policy surrounding Indian independence. However, in South Arabia neither of the main nationalist groups was prepared to share power, and HMG's policy merely enabled the NLF and FLOSY to work to a revised timetable of terror and intimidation.[8]

Once the local population knew when British control was to cease, there was a rapid re-alignment of loyalties among those who would be left behind. This made the Aden Insurgency uniquely difficult for Security Forces, as even local military units had no confidence in British intentions. Local policing and arrests were always carried out with one eye on the future political masters, resulting in a pathetic tally of prosecutions. As both the NLF and FLOSY made abundantly clear through their series of public assassinations, everyone's actions were being watched.[9]

As trust haemorrhaged, the little intelligence available was lost. Consequently, when the mutinies and massacres occurred on 20 June 1967, both British Middle East Command and the Federal Government were caught off balance. MEC later blamed the Federal Government for this lack of forewarning but the responsibility also lay with those commanding the British Security Forces. To be successful, intelligence has to be organised and co-ordinated before an insurgency starts, so that the sources can be protected both before and during that insurgency. That patently failed to happen in South Arabia and the early growth of numerous intelligence agencies, together with the failure to appoint a single Director of Intelligence before 1965, stands as a major defect in British policy.[10] There were intelligence successes in South Arabia, particularly during 1966 and 1967 but by their very nature, much of their detail still remains secret. However, despite the successes of individual intelligence officers, the extent of the NLF structure and infiltration was not discovered until it was too late. The source of funding for the terrorist group also remained a mystery. While their highly efficient system of 'subscription' collection was supplemented by bank raids and extortion, it could hardly have provided the funds to finance such a well-organised movement. Individuals in Kuwait were identified as possible backers, as were sources in the Eastern Bloc, but it appears that little progress was made in cutting off the NLF's financial support.[11]

The fixation of the Wilson Government with FLOSY, as the main contender for power in South Arabia, also allowed the NLF to go unchecked. Their old contacts with the Aden Trades Unions persuaded the Government to be blinkered by FLOSY's own exaggerated statements. Though in the end it seemed to matter little to HMG whether or not the Federal Government survived, and indeed, which terrorist group seized power in South Arabia after withdrawal. Their professed ideals about allowing nationalists to control their own destinies was selective, especially in the Gulf region, where Britain would continue to cling to her remaining areas of economic interest. By September 1967 George Brown had clearly washed his hands of the South Arabian commitment, confiding 'it can't be helped – anyway, we want to be out of the whole of the Middle East as far and as fast as we possibly can'.[12] And there were many influential members of the Wilson Government who were delighted when the Federation collapsed. Richard Crossman, Brown's fellow Cabinet Minister and Leader of the House of Commons, gleefully greeted the news, noting in his diary, 'that the regime that he [George Brown] backed should have been overthrown by terrorists and has forced our speedy withdrawal, is nothing but good fortune'.[13] With such sentiments it was hard for either Middle East Command or the High Commission to salvage anything from the wreckage, save an orderly and casualty-free evacuation.

The outcome of the Aden Insurgency is often compared unfavourably with other wars at the end of Empire, notably Malaya. Yet South Arabia's proximity to the important rebel sanctuary of Yemen gave the insurgents a huge advantage that was never available to the more geographically isolated guerrillas in Malaya. Furthermore, insurgencies like Palestine, Cyprus and Aden that included a significant urban element have never proved as successful for British military forces as rural or jungle wars. Depressingly, little of the experience that British forces had previously gained in Cyprus, Malaya or Borneo was ever applied to South Arabia. Though this problem was not just confined to the British: the Americans found that they were encountering the same problems in Vietnam in the 1960s that the French had faced ten years earlier.[14] With the notable exception of Four Five Commando, who used trickle drafting to ensure continuity of experience, most infantry units arrived for a six-month tour and left together, taking their knowledge of the desert, mountains or back-streets with them: there were 'hand-over' periods but these were inevitably short.

There has been much discussion in previous histories of the region concerning the diverse and rebellious nature of the tribes in South Arabia. Certainly South Arabia's vast mix of warring clans was probably unparalleled in the Arab World, but Britain has often been criticised for trying to weld together these hinterland tribes at the same time as tying them into a union with the more sophisticated and urban Adenis. Yet Ibn Saud created the country of Saudi Arabia despite the diversity of her tribes, and the most recent government in Yemen has achieved the semblance of a country incorporating the very tribal rivalries that so dismayed the British. Importantly, the fact that they were welded together by tough Arab regimes rather than a foreign power may have had a bearing.[15]

There is no doubt that the Aden Insurgency was fuelled by external sources and it is no accident that it erupted at the very time that Arab nationalism was at its most volatile. The Middle East, with its oil wealth and strategic geographical position, had become a region hotly disputed by the superpowers, while the revolution in neighbouring Yemen had a huge impact on events in the Arabian Peninsula. However, although the British could have better exploited the divisions among Yemeni republicans over the Egyptian occupation in the early 1960s, by the time of the Six-Day War in 1967, Arab passions had created a heightened desire for revenge against Britain, the local colonial power.[16] And the stakes were often raised by the presence of 'Face', that vital intangible ingredient in the Arab psyche that had to be preserved, not only in tribal warfare but also in the complex rivalry between Arab nationalist groups.

While the British political process may have lacked unity of purpose during periods of the Aden Insurgency, this was not true of the military command. Although their grasp of public relations left much to be desired, Middle East Command was faced with the almost impossible task of implementing the will of political masters whose position was constantly shifting. To their credit, MEC, particularly towards the end, managed to maintain unanimity between their Command and the officials from the High Commission in Aden. Much of the credit for that lay with Admiral Sir Michael Le Fanu, the personable but highly motivated C-in-C.[17] However, the Deputy and Assistant High Commissioners, together with their political officers, also played their part and through all the turmoil and uncertainty, Donal McCarthy, as Political Advisor to the C-in-C, maintained a steady hand on the administrative tiller.

Brigadier Charles Dunbar, Brigadier General Staff, MEC, was under no illusions about the huge difficulties of mounting military operations in South Arabia:

We had to contend with greatly increased terrorism of all descriptions, ranging from assassination to intimidation. We had to

contend with strikes. We had the effects of the Arab–Israeli War which led directly to mutiny in June 1967, and which touched off the revolution throughout the country, as a result of which the NLF came to power. We had at all times to compete with tribalism and the wider struggle between Egypt and Saudi Arabia.

In all our dealings we had to be mindful of the effect of what we did on other Arab countries, notably the Gulf countries where so much of our oil comes from and we had to be sensitive to world opinion as expressed in the United Nations. In short we were involved in a politico-military operation of the first magnitude.[18]

Despite these problems, there were some military lessons learned. South Arabia proved to be a training ground for insurgency conflicts to come, and discoveries were made about how the terrorist operated – his preferred weapons, tactics and support structure, as well as how cells worked. The Radfan Campaign provided invaluable experience for the SAS in the coming conflict in Oman, as well as for Rhodesian units in their own impending insurgency. But it would take another fifteen years before Britain was again involved in the serious application of air power during the Falklands War. By then, technology had dramatically changed the hardware and, in this later conflict, British pilots had to contend with a tough and experienced enemy air force, an element not present in South Arabia. However, the importance of Forward Air Controllers and good ground intelligence was still of vital importance. In Aden, street fighting skills were honed which would soon be required in Northern Ireland. The importance of positioning good OPs, with the elimination of blind spots and allowance for cross-cover with other posts; the value of re-supply by helicopters and the use of armoured cars and APCs in urban riot control, were all lessons put to good effect later in Northern Ireland.[19]

Unfortunately there were other, unwelcome, parallels with Northern Ireland. The issue of 'no-go areas' in Crater would again surface in Londonderry in 1972, while events like the isolation and brutal killings of the Davis Patrol in Crater would be compared with the later murder of two Royal Signals Corporals as they drove into a republican funeral procession in Belfast in 1988, and failed to be rescued.[20]

Another side to the conflict in South Arabia was that it provided excitement to many young soldiers on their first tours of duty. Some were under 18 years of age, and when in 1963 the last of the National Servicemen had left, it became a regulars' war. Although the insurgency erupted in a part of the world most would not relish, it still provided the action that most young soldiers craved. One subaltern recalled the extraordinary sense of freedom, at least up-country, that soldiering in South Arabia allowed, 'the general atmosphere in which we lived and worked was a far cry from what would now be called politically correct. We'd just be British. There is no intention to criticise or confess in this. It was just the way it was'.[21]

As soon as the Federation crumbled, the state rulers made for Saudi Arabia or the United Arab Emirates. Despite the fact that many were now penniless, their new hosts funded their families, but from the country that had encouraged the creation of their Federation, there was no such hospitality.[22] Some months after the British withdrawal, there were a series of show trials and six Federal figures were condemned to death *in absentia*. The Army and Police were purged but many who had assisted the NLF to achieve power now found themselves ousted by jealousy or suspicion. Random killings and vendettas took place including the killing of three of Godfrey Meynell's former Arab political assistants in the Radfan.[23] Although most of the old Federation rulers were by now beyond the reach of the new regime, the young Yafai sultan unwisely believed he could make his peace with them. When he, his brother and their retinue came down from the mountains, they were all promptly imprisoned.

Meanwhile the splits between the left and right within the new NLF regime almost ruptured the party. Qahtan al-Sha'abi maintained the dominance of the right in the first government, broadly following Nasserite policies and using many of the old Federal institutions and Army structures.[24] But the NLF Fourth Congress in March 1968 saw a victory for the left and the country quickly lurched from a broadly Nasserite state to one which embraced 'Marxism-Leninism'. This was cemented in June 1969 when, following the pattern of most revolutions, the original architects, Qahtan al-Sha'abi and his cousin Faisal al-Sha'abi, were evicted from office by the emerging radical group under Abdul Fatah Ismail. Feisal was killed the following year 'trying to escape', while Qahtan later died under house arrest in 1976.[25] The new leaders feared that the imprisoned ruling family of Yafa, one of the most ancient in Yemen, could still pose a threat. The young sultan and his family were driven out of prison in a truck and taken into the desert. There they were machine-gunned to death. In November 1970 South Arabia was renamed The People's Democratic Republic of Yemen (PDRY) and, as the first and only Arab communist state, it was soon subject to widespread nationalisation programmes together with repeated purges of the Army and Civil Service.

The major concern for remaining British interests in the Gulf region was that it appeared that traditional rulers in South Arabia were thrown overboard in the rush to independence. This hardly reassured the sheikhs and sultans in the British-protected states of the Persian Gulf, such as Bahrain, Qatar and the Trucial States, and British political agents worked at convincing them that the South Arabian Federal rulers had not helped themselves.

291

> We have given every possible encouragement and backing to the Federal Rulers in the hope that they would prove capable of establishing a viable successor government. Their failure to get to grips with the problem and collaborate effectively – culminating in the Bayoumi fiasco – is no fault of ours.[26]

Attitudes at the Foreign Office Arabian Department became defensive and antagonistic towards the deposed Federal rulers. Clearly months of frustration had hardened these attitudes but it was ironic that the FO felt that they were now the injured party:

> When the recent troubles began in the up-country states, not one of the rulers then in Geneva and later in Beirut returned to South Arabia to deal with the trouble and most of those still in South Arabia seem to have thrown in the towel without a fight ... The rulers brought about their own downfall by failing to behave in a responsible or enlightened manner. The fact is that they have deserted us rather than we them.[27]

Meanwhile, the US took a pragmatic view of the collapse in South Arabia. Many in the State Department claimed that it was inevitable and although no US troops would be committed to the Gulf because of commitments in Vietnam, it was decided that the Shah of Iran was quite capable of looking after US interests during the next decade.[28]

The period immediately after withdrawal saw an accelerating British retreat from her remaining commitments around the world. The Arab oil embargo and the Nigerian Civil War caused severe economic problems for Britain and her remaining military presence in South-East Asia was scheduled to cease by 1971 while at the same time commitments to the Gulf would be reduced. All this would put further pressure on the concept of a Strategic Reserve.[29]

Major-General Sir John Willoughby, who had retired after his term as GOC, MELF in May 1967, was recalled to the active list in 1968. He always maintained that after five years of the Aden Insurgency 'there were virtually no new lessons; they were all old ones'. Nevertheless, he used his considerable local experience to great effect as the new Defence Advisor to the United Arab Emirates, and worked tirelessly to enforce a better security organisation for the Gulf region, including the strengthening of the Air Forces of Kuwait, Oman and Abu Dhabi.[30]

Attention was also paid to developing the local Gulf defence force, the small British-commanded Trucial Oman Scouts. There had been alarm at the ease with which the Federal Regular Army of South Arabia went over so effortlessly to a radical terrorist movement, and there was concern in Whitehall as to the reliability of the Trucial Scouts. This point was not lost on the governments in Sana'a or Cairo who were quick to bracket British involvement in South Arabia and her influence in the Gulf. But this parallel was misleading, for in the Gulf States the rulers exercised effective authority in their sheikhdoms, aided by the fact that there was no tradition of continual tribal warfare on the scale of South Arabia.[31]

The Gulf States certainly benefited from the South Arabian experience in the field of intelligence. The security apparatus that was used in South Arabia, which had been co-ordinated and strengthened by Sir John Prendergast, was put to good use. Documentation of terrorist tactics and techniques were passed on to Special Branch in the Lower Gulf in early 1967, where there were regular meetings of the Gulf counter-subversion group. Attempts were made to keep British troops 'out of the internal security scene' in the region, and in this, they were successful. Some of the best officers who survived from Aden Special Branch were moved from South Arabia to the Lower Gulf and this undoubtedly helped their security operations.[32]

A few British personnel, mainly medics and nurses, witnessed the aftermath of withdrawal. Barbara Binns, the ex-nurse who had seen her houseboy become a terrorist, had an unwelcome encounter:

> After the withdrawal, I still had to finish my work with the local children at the hospital and was travelling home at Christmas when I caught sight of our old houseboy ***** at the airport – he was staring straight at us and I didn't want to acknowledge him so I moved on quickly. I knew he was a hero in the eyes of the victors but I could never forget the bloodshed amongst our compatriots.[33]

For the fifty corps and regiments that had served in the conflict between 1962 and 1967, it was the last time that they would operate together under the 'Brigade' structure. On 1 July 1968 the British Army was restructured and the fifteen infantry brigades disappeared. The 'Brigade' system had only been introduced in 1948 as an organisational entity for training and there was little emotional attachment to it – to soldiers, the regimental cap badge remained the real source of pride. The new system saw a divisional structure of just six divisions, comprising the Guards, Scottish, Queen's, King's, Prince of Wales's, and Light Division.[34] The Scottish Division was created out of the Lowland and Highland Brigades, but one notable casualty was the Cameronians (Scottish Rifles) who, despite their excellent service in South Arabia, were disbanded in May 1968.

Fiscal restraints also affected the future of The Royal Northumberland Fusiliers, who had similarly given good account of themselves in South Arabia. Despite their lineage, which could be traced back to 1674, they were amalgamated with The Royal Warwickshire Fusiliers, The Royal Fusiliers and The Lancashire Fusiliers to form The Royal Regiment of Fusiliers.[35]

The other regiment in line for abolition was the Argyll and Sutherland Highlanders but they had no intention of going quietly and neither did their commanding officer, Lieutenant-Colonel Colin Mitchell. One excuse put forward for their disbandment was that they were the most junior of the Highland Regiments, being formed from the 91st (Argyllshire Highlanders) Foot (1794) and the 93rd (Sutherland Highlanders) Foot (1799).[36] Lieutenant-Colonel Mitchell embarked on a vigorous 'Save the Argylls' campaign, taking his whole battalion back to their regimental territory and embarking on a widely publicised recruiting campaign. Senior Argyll Commanders, including General Sir Gordon MacMillan, weighed in and eventually a reprieve was won for the regiment. And although in 1971 they were reduced to one regular 'Balaklava' Company, when the Conservatives returned to power in 1972 the 1st Battalion was restored to full strength.[37]

Although the Argylls' profile was rising, during the early months of 1968 Mitchell's personal career stalled. He would not be promoted to full Colonel and the only position on offer from the Military Secretary's Branch appeared to be a return to Staff duties.[38] Although Mentioned in Despatches, unlike most of his fellow COs he did not receive the Distinguished Service Order (DSO) for his actions in Aden. A future political career was mooted and this was sufficient excuse for the Government to announce his retirement from the Army, and in August 1968 a government spokesman notified the House of Commons:

Colonel Mitchell has requested that he be allowed to retire from the Army on 30 September for personal reasons and this request has been granted. He has recently announced that he will be a Conservative candidate in a Parliamentary by-election in the near future. We cannot possibly allow an announced Parliamentary candidate to hold an active military post, and I have therefore decided that Colonel Mitchell should go on leave until the date of his retirement. The Army needs 'Mad Mitches', but too many of them would be an embarrassment.[39]

Although there were precedents for serving army officers to also serve as MPs[40], it was Mitchell's penchant for publicity that really ensured his departure from the Services. The Government spokesman added almost as a footnote, 'Army regulations, which restrict access to the press by serving officers, were designed as much to protect the officer himself, as for any other reason'.[41]

In October 1968, in advance of the publication of his book, Lieutenant-Colonel Colin Mitchell wrote a series of sensational articles in *The Sunday Express*, castigating the decisions and policies of his senior commanders during the Crater crisis in June 1967. The furore was further stoked up when his book, *Having Been a Soldier*, was published in April 1969, predictably upsetting many from MEC who had played a part in the decisions of 20 June 1967. Major-General Philip Tower, who was now Commandant at Sandhurst, was guarded in his comments but admitted to his former Brigadier General Staff that the book 'while not libellous, is thoroughly unpleasant to many people including myself'.[42] Nonetheless, the book did strike a chord, with many reviewers applauding Colonel Mitchell's stand, maintaining tough measures in Crater. However it was on the issue of media handling that Mitchell showed a surer touch, though this hardly endeared him to his superiors. He understood that news media and journalists could be controlled and channelled whilst in operational theatres. Discounting the public relations mistakes of the Radfan Campaign, he knew the importance of public support for the morale of his troops in Aden as well as for his subsequent campaign to 'Save the Argylls'.[43] More sanguine observers felt that while South Arabia had the space for a showman, the next insurgency war Britain had to face in Northern Ireland would not be so conducive.

In July 1968 the Labour MP Tam Dalyell tackled the Defence Minister, Denis Healey, over the issue of Lieutenant-Colonel Mitchell and the occupation of Crater. He subsequently pursued the Minister of Defence for Administration over accusations that the Argylls' Commander had disobeyed administrative and operational orders, and particularly 'the time schedule of his orders to re-enter Crater, which had not been controlled by British troops for two weeks'.[44] A retort from the Government Minister was followed by a rebuttal and full explanation of the circumstances from Major-General F C C Graham, Colonel of the Argylls. But the press continued to pursue the story, especially as the issue of the disbandment of the regiment was proving a hot debate. The allegations were widened to include the incorrect assertion that Middle East Command had not informed the British High Commission of the decision to send the Argylls into Crater.[45]

In August 1968 the Government finally released an account of the mutiny and massacres of 20 June 1967 but the issue of the radio failures was omitted. It was an issue that continued to be pursued by the Conservative MP Teddy Taylor, as well as influential correspondents such as Charles Douglas-Home.[46] The Ministry of Defence, through its Public Relations Department, continued to stress that the decision not to re-enter Crater straightaway on 20 June had resulted from a policy of minimum force and the avoidance of large-scale bloodshed.[47]

Some of the relatives of those killed on 20 June visited Aden in November 1969. The party, which included Brigadier Derek Davis and his wife Pamela, parents of 2nd Lieutenant John Davis, were closely escorted, as it was a time of great political upheaval in the country. The group visited Silent Valley Cemetery and a number of restricted sites around

Aden but later the Davis's made their own way into Crater to investigate the circumstances of their son's death. Although there was a charged atmosphere in the town, they mapped and photographed the ambush site and later spoke to local people, hoping to glean more information. Despite their exhaustive searches nothing conclusive was found.[48] For some of the relatives it was a cathartic experience, but blighted by news that the new regime annually celebrated 20 June as 'the day they defeated the British Army'. In a macabre gesture, the PDRY politburo had apparently even invited the British Ambassador to attend the previous celebration.

Across the northern border in the Yemen Arab Republic, the civil war spluttered on until May 1970 when the royalists were finally reconciled to the republicans and a national government was formed. With this accord, Saudi Arabia and Britain finally recognised the YAR. There followed some tumultuous years in the YAR during the 1970s when two Prime Ministers were assassinated but it was in the southern Marxist state of the PDRY where the blood-letting was most prolific. Soviet and Chinese aid propped up the regime, while the Soviet Fleet used Aden as its area base, particularly useful when it assisted a brutal Marxist regime to take power in Ethiopia in 1974. The PDRY also played host to some of the most notorious terrorist groups in Europe, including Baader-Meinhof, the Japanese Red Army and the Popular Front for the Liberation of Palestine.[49] Although the country had become a safe sanctuary for these terrorist groups, it was itself riddled with factions. In 1979 fierce fighting erupted and the leading radical, Abdul Ismail, was forced into exile. He eventually returned in 1985 and was temporarily reconciled to the new President of the PDRY, Ali Nasir, and allowed back into the Politburo. Then on the morning of 13 January 1986, as the ruling group was taking tea, one of Ali Nasir's bodyguards dropped the Samsonite case he was carrying and produced a Skorpion machine pistol. On the orders of Ali Nasir, he then raked the room with gunfire, killing Ismail as well as Ali Antar, the old guerrilla leader from the Radfan Campaign.[50] This signalled another violent civil war and after six months of fighting, it was estimated over 10,000 people were killed. The voices that so roundly condemned British security operations in the 1960s were silent when confronted with the worst excesses of the PDRY Marxist regime.

Remarkably, four years later in 1990, the PDRY united with its northern neighbour, the YAR, and formed the new country of the Yemen Republic. Although there was a violent southern revolt in 1994, the new country of Yemen settled down to relative peace.[51] It was enough to allow a British party of mainly military veterans to return in November 1997, thirty years after the withdrawal. The forty-four-strong group, led by Brigadier David Baines, contained representatives from many of the regiments and corps who served during the insurgency, as well as the ex-political officers, Stephen Day and Godfrey Meynell. They visited Little Aden and found much of the old Falaise and BP camps bulldozed flat, while the BP oil refinery was still working, but under reduced capacity. They were pleased to find the nearby British Military Cemetery in Silent Valley in good order, with the graves of those who died between 1965 and 1967 still in good repair. Moving into the hinterland, the party discovered that the large military camp and airstrip at Habilayn had disappeared, to be replaced with a new town. They travelled on to Dhala, where Godfrey Meynell, the political officer who had become something of a legend in Radfan, was surrounded and cheered by locals who remembered the splendid work he had done there during the 1960s.[52] Although current Foreign Office advice deters trips to Yemen because of security, those who know the country well still return. The British–Yemeni Society make regular visits to Yemen, continuing their brief of building links between the two countries as well as fostering Yemen's rich cultural heritage. Even Colonel David Smiley, veteran of the long and bitter Yemen civil war, returned in February 2003. The sprightly 87-year-old had come back, after an absence of thirty-five years, to help the Yemeni government with their official history of the conflict.[53] Meanwhile in the UK, the recently formed Aden Veterans Association does much to preserve the memory of those Servicemen who did not return from South Arabia and has successfully lobbied to be included in recent Remembrance Day ceremonies.

Despite the efforts of the current President Hadi and his more enlightened government, Yemen finds itself in the front line of the fundamentalist assault against the West. Osama bin-Laden, former leader of the al-Queda movement, had family connections there – his father, Mohammed, was born in Yemen and bin-Laden's youngest wife is the daughter of a tribal patriarch from the Yemen highlands. Some of bin-Laden's closest aides, including his Chief of Operations for the Gulf, Abu al-Shair, have been identified as Yemenis by US Intelligence.[54] It is therefore not surprising that the country has been the scene of recent serious terrorist incidents. In October 2000 an explosive-laden boat rammed the USS *Cole* in Aden Harbour, killing seventeen US sailors and in the same year the French super tanker *Limburg* was attacked. Retaliation against al-Queda contacts in Yemen was inevitable. In November 2002 an unmanned American Predator aircraft spotted a Land Cruiser known to be carrying six al-Queda members, travelling up a track in Marib province. The 27-ft drone was then guided down and its missile smashed into the vehicle, killing all the occupants, including one known as Abu Ali, a suspect wanted for the attack on the USS *Cole*.[55]

Attacks by extremists, linked to al-Queda, against Western individuals or interests have continued.[56] In September 2003 a plot to destroy the British Embassy in Sana'a with a massive truck bomb was foiled when militants were caught filming the building prior to the operation. Yet Yemen is attempting to cooperate in the 'global war on terrorism' and

Yemeni forces have clashed with al-Queda sympathisers in the mountains. US Special Forces have even been allowed to operate in Yemen in pursuit of this goal, and during 2004 joint military manoeuvres took place involving US and Yemeni forces.[57] President Hadi is walking a tightrope. While encouraging better ties with Washington, he may well upset the militant tribes, whose support he needs, should there be any encroachment by American Special Forces into tribal lands. The Yemeni government is trying to shed the country's lawless image, and some strides have been made against the extremists with a 'carrot and stick' approach.[58] But it has a long way to go.

While Britain has largely disappeared from the political and military scene, there are reminders. Glencairn Balfour-Paul, who had spent a lifetime in the Middle East, travelled through South Arabia some years after independence. His taxi driver, the normal fount of all knowledge, announced that local Adenis sometimes missed the British presence and customs, especially 'the walking on the pavement and the pressing of trousers'.[59] Such an innocuous legacy could never have been left behind after an Algerian or Vietnam war of independence. In a curious way, this absence of bitterness was a fitting tribute to the professionalism of the British Armed Forces.

NOTES

1   Julian Paget, *Last Post* op. cit., p. 264. His figures match those contained in 'Casualties – Aden State 1964–1967', File 2/4, Dunbar Papers, LHCMA. Also Major-General David Thomson to Author, 16 April 2004. The Royal Garrison Church of All Saints in Aldershot contains an Aden Book of Remembrance, holding the names of 519 Servicemen who died in Aden between 1839 and 1967. The book, bound in red leather and inscribed with the Aden formation sign of the Arab dhow, only includes army personnel and may be incomplete.
2   In part due to the fact that conventional forces encountered very little enemy artillery or air to ground contact. Also medical services, even in Radfan, were reasonably accessible. However, the widespread availability of devastating explosives, as seen in modern insurgencies, has changed this ratio.
3   Confidential sources to Author, 14 August 2003, 29 August 2003.
4   Brigadier David Baines to Author. Also his Memoir, Ref. 20062/5, Imperial War Museum Sound Archive, London.
5   John Newsinger, *British Counterinsurgency from Palestine to Northern Ireland*, Palgrave, 2002, p. 130. Also Lackner, *PDR Yemen*, op. cit., p. 47.
6   'Confidential Political Situation Report', Hargroves Papers.
7   Yemen remains an undeveloped country with a population of nearly 18 million, a literacy rate of only 45% and a life expectancy of fifty years.
8   General Sir William Jackson, *Withdrawal from Empire*, op. cit., p. 236.
9   Jim Ellis to High Commission, 18 May 1967, FCO 8/252, NA.
10 See 'Part V – Conclusions' in 'Report of the Mutinies', MEC, 26 October 1967, DEFE 11/533, NA.

11   Unsourced Intelligence assessment, 30 October 1967, FCO 8/252, NA.
12   Quoted by Richard Crossman, 5 September 1967, *The Diaries of a Cabinet Minister, Volume Two,* Hamish Hamilton, 1976.
13   Ibid., 30 October 1967.
14   For interesting comparisons between insurgency wars, see Captain D M O Miller, 'The Theory and Practice of Contemporary Insurgencies' (two parts), in *Army Quarterly,* January and April 1966. Although the *Army Quarterly* published a number of articles in the late 1960s and early 1970s on guerrilla and insurgency campaigns, there is little detailed reference to the war in South Arabia, probably because of Britain's continued and sensitive interest in the Gulf.
15   These Arab regimes also had little notion of democratic ideals.
16   John Malcolm to Author, 8 May 2004.
17   He remained in his post until 1968, when he became First Sea Lord. His distinguished career was cut short by his premature death in 1970.
18   Lecture given by Brigadier Charles Dunbar, 28 November 1968, File 2/5, Dunbar Papers, LHCMA.
19   Brigadier R Jefferies, 'Operations in Aden – Some Infantry Lessons', in *RUSI Journal,* March 1969.
20   However, in the case of the Belfast murders, the Army were unable to identify their men until it was too late.
21   Simon Mort to Author, 15 March 2004.
22   For details of what happened to the sultans after independence, see Stephen Day, 'Envoi' in *Sultans of Aden,* op. cit.
23   Memorandum, Foreign Secretary, 1 February 1968, FCO 8/477, NA.
24   Al-Sha'abi's first government contained, for the most part, Arab Nasserite socialists. There was probably only one Marxist, Abdul Fattah Ismail. Over the border in Yemen, in 1968 Soviet pilots flew combat missions on behalf of the republican regime; see Stephen Page, op. cit. p. 108.
25   J Bowyer Bell, 'South Arabia: Violence and Revolt', in *Conflict Studies,* No. 40, Nov. 1973.
26   British Residency, Bahrain, to Arabian Department, FO, 1 September 1967, FCO 8/41, NA.
27   Arabian Department, FO, to Bahrain Residency, 7 September 1967, FCO 8/41, NA.
28   The US also relied on a Rapid Deployment Force (RDF) to defend her interests in the Middle East. See Keith Wilson (ed.), *Imperialism and Nationalism in the Middle East,* Mansell, 1983, pp. 154–5.
29   General Sir William Jackson, op. cit., 242–3.
30   Quoted by Major-General Sir John Willoughby at a lecture at RUSI on 15 November 1967. He finally retired in 1972. He died on 23 February 1991. See Obituary, *The Times,* 8 March 1991.
31   FO 'Guidance notes on South Arabia and the Persian Gulf', 21 September 1967, FCO 8/41, NA. See also Anthony Verrier, 'British Military Policy on Arabia', *RUSI Journal,* November 1967. The difference in circumstances between South Arabia and the Gulf States is discussed in Glen Balfour-Paul, op. cit., pp. 134–6.
32   British Residency, Bahrain to Arabian Department, FO, 15 April 1967, FCO 8/41, NA.
33   Barbara Binns to Author, 18 April 2002.
34   Major-General David Thomson to Author, 16 April 2004. The Parachute Regiment and the Brigade of Ghurkhas were outside the divisional structure.

35 The RNF were taken on the regular establishment at the accession of William of Orange. In 1751 they were designated 5th Foot.

36 However, they could trace their origins back to the Earl of Argyll's Regiment formed in 1689.

37 P Mileham, *The Scottish Regiments 1633–1996*, Spellmount, 1996, p. 295. Also Obituary for Lieutenant-Colonel Mitchell, *The Daily Telegraph*, 24 July 1996.

38 Having served as a Brevet Colonel for the required four years, Mitchell could have expected promotion to Colonel.

39 'Draft Answer to Parliamentary Questions', undated 1968, FCO 8/257, NA.

40 One shining example was Sir Fitzroy MacLean, who served as MP for Lancaster from 1941 to 1959, while also serving in the wartime SAS.

41 'Draft Answer', op. cit.

42 Major-General Philip Tower to Brigadier Charles Dunbar, 31 March 1969, File 2/6, Dunbar Papers, LHCMA. Brigadier Dunbar subsequently became Director of Infantry, MOD, before retiring in 1973. He died in 1981.

43 Mockaitis, op. cit., p. 65.

44 *The Times*, 9 August 1968, and 'News Diary' extract, File 2/1, Dunbar Papers, LHCMA. Also B Crowe to J Pestell, 22 July 1968, FCO 8/257, NA.

45 A Ashworth to D McCarthy, 19 July 1968, FCO 8/257, NA.

46 *The Times*, 9 August 1968. Charles Douglas-Home was Defence Correspondent and later Editor of *The Times*.

47 MOD Press Release, 7 August 1968.

48 In the quest to get answers, Pamela Davis spoke to some Europeans who had remained in Aden after withdrawal. One BP employee alleged that a Roman Catholic priest had sheltered 2nd Lieutenant Davis for a time but this was never confirmed.

49 Through the PFLP, the regime was able to reactivate its old ties with George Habash.

50 *The New York Times*, 30 January 1986.

51 It remains an undeveloped country.

52 *Gunner*, Issue 327, February 1998.

53 For an account of Colonel Smiley's visit, see David Smiley, 'Return to Yemen', in the *British–Yemeni Society Journal*, Vol. 11. 2003.

54 *The Times*, 3 October 2003

55 *The Sunday Times*, 10 November 2002.

56 On 30 December 2002 three Americans were shot dead in the Jiblah Baptist hospital, by an extremist, while the following year, oil drilling was suspended 'for the foreseeable future' when an American and a Canadian were murdered in Marib province. Some of the attacks against Westerners are by individuals acting alone or as a result of general lawlessness, especially in the Marib province.

57 Aljazeera.net, 20 February 2004.

58 A Judge had recently been appointed, who has had some success in turning militants away from murder, through a better understanding of the Koran.

59 Glencairn Balfour-Paul to Author, 2 March 2004.

Appendix

The Tribes and States of South Arabia

Tribe	State	Original Protectorate	Date of joining Federation
Abdali	Lahej, Sultanate	WAP	1959
Amiri	Dhala, Amirate	WAP	1959
Audhali	Audhali, Sultanate	WAP	1959
Aulaqi	Upper Aulaqi, Sheikhdom	WAP	1959
Beihan	Beihan, Habili Hashimi, Amirate	WAP	1959
Fadhli	Fadhli, Sultanate	WAP	1959
Yafa	Lower Yafa, Sultanate	WAP	1959
Aqrabi	Aqrabi, Sheikhdom	WAP	1960
Aulaqi	Lower Aulaqi, Sultanate	WAP	1960
Dathina	State of Dathina	WAP	1960
Balhaf	Wahidi, Sultanate	EAP	1962
Haushabi	Haushabi, Sultanate	WAP	1963
Sha'ib	Sheikhdom of Sha'ib	WAP	1963
Alawi	Alawi, Sheikhdom	WAP	1965
Muflahi	Muflahi, Sheikhdom	WAP	1965
Aulaqi	Upper Aulaqi, Sultanate	WAP	1965
Yafa	Upper Yafa, Sultanate	WAP	Never joined
Kathiri	Kathiri, Sultanate	EAP	Never joined
Mahra	Qishn and Socotra, Sultanate	EAP	Never joined
Qu'aiti	Shihr and Mukalla, Sultanate	EAP	Never joined

Glossary of Terms and Abbreviations

ADC	Aide-de-camp. A commissioned officer in personal attendance on a GOC or high-ranking diplomat
Aden	Peninsula containing townships of Crater, Ma'alla, Tawahi, Sheikh Othman, etc. Originally a Crown Colony and then a State within the Federation
AFME	Air Forces, Middle East
AIC	Aden Intelligence Centre
Amir	Tribal leader. There is no logical distinction between Amir, Sultan and Sheikh
ANA	Arab News Agency
ANM	Arab National Movement
APB	Armed Police Barracks, Crater
APC	Armoured Personnel Carrier
AP	Aden Police (Civil)
APL	Aden Protectorate Levies. Forerunner of the FRA
ARAMCO	Arabian American Oil Company
ATUC	Aden Trades Union Congress
BASO	Brigade Air Support Officer
Bedu	Nomadic tribesmen. Becoming increasingly settled
Blindicide	Belgian-made rocket launcher, popular with terrorists
BP	British Petroleum Limited
CIA	Central Intelligence Agency
Chador	All-enveloping black female garment
Dissidents	Known to British troops as 'dizzies'. Originally applied to Radfan rebels in 1950s and early 1960s. As dissent became more violent and organised after the State of Emergency in 1963, the word 'terrorist' increasingly appears in contemporary documents, and is therefore the term applied in this study
DLF	Dhofar Liberation Front. Omani terrorist movement
DZ	Dropping Zone
EAP	Eastern Aden Protectorate
FAC	Forward Air Controller. Ground based spotter for aircraft

FAP	Federal Armed Police
Fedayeen	Arab guerrillas
FLOSY	Front for the Liberation of South Yemen
FNG	Federal National Guard. Comprised two sections, FNG 1 and FNG 2
FO	British Foreign Office
FOO	Forward Observation Officer; artillery spotter
FOME	Flag Officer, Middle East. Naval Command
FRA	Federal Regular Army. Arab army, successor to APL
Futa	Men's skirt or kilt
GCHQ	Government Communications Headquarters
GOC	General Officer Commanding
GPMG	General Purpose Heavy Machine-Gun.
Grenadier	Terrorist grenade thrower
GSO1	General Staff Officer Grade 1
HBL	Hadhrami Bedouin Legion
HMG	Her Majesty's Government
Jambiya	Ceremonial curved dagger, worn by men at their waist
Jebel	Mountain
IDF	Israeli Defence Force
Imam	Leader of the Zaydi sect, a moderate branch of the Shi'ah form of Islam. In common with most chieftains in South-West Arabia, the position was never purely hereditary but the Imam was chosen from an hereditary group
IRD	Information Research Department
IS	Internal Security. Usually in reference to military operations in Aden
LMG	Bren Light Machine-Gun
MEC	Middle East Command. Controlled all three service commands, MELF, AFME and FOME
MECAS	Middle East Centre for Arabic Studies
MELF	Middle East Land Forces. Army Command
MI5	British Security Service
Maftuh	Open or clear for anyone to see
Naib	Deputy Ruler
NLF	National Liberation Front
NSA	National Security Agency. US intelligence bureau
OLOS	Organisation for the Liberation of the Occupied South. Brief political group, merged into FLOSY
OP	Observation Post
PDRY	People's Democratic Republic of Yemen. First post-independence regime in South Arabia
Pig	3-ton armoured vehicle for transporting infantry

PORF	Popular Organisation of Revolutionary Forces. Military wing of FLOSY
PSP	People's Socialist Party (political arm of the ATUC)
Qat	Mildly narcotic leaf. Chewed in company throughout South Arabia
SAA	South Arabian Army. Successor to FRA
Sangar	Small defensive position consisting usually of a semi-circle of dry stone walling. Built above ground where the soil is unsuitable for excavation
SAP	South Arabian Police (Civil)
SAS	Special Air Service
SB	Police Special Branch
Sharif	A leader who had proven descent from the Prophet Mohammed
Sheikh	Literally 'old man'. Head of a tribal group. In South Arabia, it also denoted membership of an hereditary religious family
SIS	British Secret Intelligence Service. Also known as MI6
SLR	Self-loading Rifle. Standard issue British infantry rifle
SMG	Sterling Machine-Gun
South Arabia	Region covering the old Colony of Aden together with the Western and Eastern Protectorates. Later became the Federation of South Arabia
South Arabian League	Nationalist organisation supported initially by Egypt and latterly by Saudi Arabia. Lost out to both NLF and FLOSY
UAR	United Arab Republic. Brief union between Egypt, Syria and Yemen
UN	United Nations
Wadi	Dried river bed
WAP	Western Aden Protectorate
YAR	Yemen Arab Republic. Post-1962 republican regime
Yemen	The Immamate, pre-1962 (the kingdom of North Yemen) and the Yemen Arab Republic, post-1962. As Manfred Wenner has pointed out, because the name Yemen appears in Arabic with an article, ie., *al-Yaman*, some European writers refer to 'the Yemen'. But this usage is no more logical than referring to 'the France', because in French it is *la France*

The spelling of Arabic words conforms to common usage.

Select Bibliography

I UNPUBLISHED SOURCES

1 *National Archives & Kew, London. (NA)*

Files covering the military, political, intelligence police activities in Aden and the Federation of South Arabia 1962–7.

FO 93/371/372/800/953/961/1016 series: Records created & inherited by the Foreign Office.

FCO 8/46/49/53/60/73/77 series: Records of the Foreign & Commonwealth Office.

CO 725/853/858/859/936/968/1015/1025/1026/1027/1032/1037/1038/1045/1055 series: Records of the Colonial Office.

DEFE 7/11/13/24/25/28/31 series: Records of the Ministry of Defence.

PREM 11/13 series: Records of the Prime Minister's Office.

WO 32/181/305/373/386 series: Records created or inherited by the War Office.

DT 18/43 series: records of the General Nursing Council.

AIR 2/10/19/20/23/28/2964 series: Records created or inherited by the Air Ministry.

T225/317 series: Records created or inherited by HM Treasury.

OD 8 series: Records created and inherited by Overseas Development bodies.

CAB 130/164/165 series: Records of the Cabinet Office.

DO 174 series: Records created or inherited by the Dominions Office.

HO 213/325: records created or inherited by the Home Office.

CAOG 13/15 series: Records created or inherited by the Crown Agents for Overseas Development.

ADM 1/202 series: Records of the Admiralty & Royal Marines.

MEPO 38 series: Records of the Metropolitan Police – Special Branch. Registered Files.

2 *Liddell Hart Centre for
   Military Archives,
   King's College, London.* Lord Julian Amery Papers.
   (LHCMA)   Air Chief Marshal Sir Denis Barnett Papers.
                         Major-General Charles Dunbar Papers.
                         Sir Charles Johnston Papers.
                         Major-General James Lunt Papers.
                         Air Vice Marshal Brian Yarde Papers.

3 *Arab World
   Documentation Unit,
   University of Exeter.* Conference Papers, Exeter 1998, 'Yemen: the
   (AWDU)   Challenge of Social & Economic Development'.
                         CAABU Collection.
                         Unpublished and published articles and
                         journals relating to Yemen & South Arabia.

4 *University of Warwick,*
   Special Collections.   Archive of British Petroleum Limited.
   (UW)

5 *British Empire &*   Oral testimonies & transcriptions from the
   Commonwealth   following:
   Museum, Bristol.   F N Pusinelli CMG, OBE, MC (Financial
                                 Secretary, Assist. High Commissioner *(BECM)*
                                 1958–67)
                             R F Eberlie (Secretary to High Commission
                                 1957–67)
                             Jim Ellis OBE, DSM (Political Officer, British
                                 Resident EAP 1951–67)
                             Susan de Heveningham Baekeland (British High
                                 Commission)

                             Moving Image Database (VHS film)
                             Michael Crouch (Political Officer, Resident
                                 Advisor, EAP)
                             Peter Hinchcliffe CMG (Political Officer,
                                 1961–7, Acting Deputy High Commissioner,
                                 1967).

6 *University of*
   Southampton,
   Special Collections.   Lord Mountbatten Papers.

7 *St Anthony's College*
   Oxford University.   PhD, DJ Clark: 'The Colonial Police & Anti-
                             terrorism'.

8 *Cambridge University.*   NJ Ashton: 'British Strategy and Anglo-
                             American Relations in the Middle East, January
                             1955–March 1959' (January 1992).

                             PhD, P Melshen: 'Pseudo Operations – The Use
                             by British & American Armed Forces of
                             Deception in Counter-Insurgency 1945–73'.

9 *Bodleian Library*   Macmillan Diaries.
  Special Collections,
  Oxford University.

10 *Private Papers.*   Brigadier David Baines Papers.
  Rev. Dr Robert Carroll Papers.
  Harry Cockerill Papers.
  Anne Cuthbert Papers.
  Pamela Davis Papers.
  Brigadier Sir Louis Hargroves Papers.
  John Malcolm Papers.
  Derek Rose Papers.
  Major-General WB 'Sandy' Thomas Chronicle.

II PUBLISHED SOURCES

1. Journals & Articles   *Aerospace Power Journal*
  Al-Ahram
  Army Quarterly
  Arab Journal
  Brassey's Annual 1957
  British-Yemeni Society Journal
  Conflict Studies
  Electronic Journal of International History
  Intelligence & National Security
  Gulf Studies
  Hansard
  Journal of Contemporary History
  Journal of Imperial & Commonwealth History
  Journal of the Royal Central Asian Society
  Middle East Affairs
  Middle East International
  Middle East Journal
  Middle Eastern Studies
  Middle Eastern Research & Information Project
  The Dhow (Middle East Forces Newspaper)
  The New Statesman
  The Observer
  RAF Quarterly

Review of International Studies
Royal Institute of International Affairs
RUSI Journal
Small Wars & Insurgencies
*Strategic and Combat Studies Inst. Occasional
    Papers*
Survival
*The Mideast Mirror (Regional News Services),
    Beirut.*
The Times
Twentieth Century British History
The US Army Professional Writing Collection
Yemen Times
War in History
World Today

2. Regimental Journals
& Magazines

The Coldstream Gazette (Coldstream Guards)
The Castle (Royal Anglian Regiment)
The Covenanter (Cameronians)
The Guards Magazine (Scots, Irish, Welsh Guards)
St George's Gazette (Royal Northumberland
    Fusiliers)
Globe & Laurel (Royal Marines)
Gunner (Royal Regiment of Artillery)
The Household Brigade Magazine (Life Guards,
    Royal Horse Guards, Grenadier Guards,
    Coldstream Guards, Scots Guards, Irish
    Guards, Welsh Guards)
The Lancashire Lad (The Queen's Lancashire
    Regiment)
*The Regimental Magazine of The Lancashire
    Regiment (Prince of Wales's Volunteers)*
The Lion and the Dragon (The King's Own Royal
    Border Regiment)
Pegasus (Parachute Regiment)
The Journal of the Royal Artillery
The Journal of the South Wales Borderers
The Thin Red Line (Argyll and Sutherland
    Highlanders)
The Tank (Royal Tank Regiment)
The Journal of the 4th/7th Royal Dragoon Guards

311

Regimental Journal of 1st The Queen's Dragoon Guards
The White Rose (The Prince of Wales's Own Regiment of Yorkshire)
The Wire (Royal Corps of Signals)

3. Unit Histories

Barthorp, Michael, *Crater to the Creggan – The History of The Royal Anglian Regiment 1964–74* (Leo Cooper, London 1976).
Beedle, Jimmy, *43(F) Squadron: 'The Fighting Cocks'* (Beaumont Aviation, London 1985).
Clayton, Anthony, *Forearmed – A History of the Intelligence Corps* (Brassey's, London 1993).
Forty, George, *The Royal Tank Regiment* (Spellmount, Staplehurst 1989).
Institution of Royal Engineers, *The History of the Corps of Royal Engineers, Vol. XI* (Chatham 1993).
Ladd, James, *By Sea, By Land: The Royal Marines 1919–1997* (HarperCollins, London 1998).
Lee, Air Chief Marshal Sir David, *Flight from the Middle East – A History of the Royal Air Force in the Middle East* (HMSO, London 1980).
Mann, Michael, *The Regimental History of 1st The Queen's Dragoon Guards* (Michael Russell Publishing, Norwich 1993).
Mileham, Patrick, *The Scottish Regiments 1633–1996* (Spellmount, Staplehurst 1996).
Paget, Julian (ed.), *Second to None: The Coldstream Guards 1650–2000* (Leo Cooper, London 2000).
Tillotson, Major-General Michael, *With the Prince of Wales's Own 1958–1994* (Michael Russell, Norwich 1995).
Young, David, *Four Five – The Story of 45 Commando, Royal Marines, 1943–1971* (Leo Cooper, London 1972).

4. Surveys, Census & Government Publications

Arabia: when Britain goes (Fabian Research Series 259, London 1967).
Aden and South Arabia (Central Office of Information, London 1966).
Federation of South Arabia, Conference Report 1964 (HMSO, London 1964).

Port of Aden Annual 1965–66 (Aden Port Trust 1965).

1955 Census Report (Government Press, Aden 1956).

A Survey of Social and Economic Conditions in the Aden Protectorate (Doreen Ingrams, 1946).

Welcome to Aden (Guides & Handbooks of Africa Publishing, Nairobi 1962).

Procedures for the Arrest, Interrogation and Detention of Suspected Terrorists in Aden (HMSO, November 1966).

5. Printed Books

Aldrich, Richard, *The Hidden Hand – Britain, America and Cold War Secret Intelligence* (John Murray, London 2001).

Balfour-Paul, Glen, *The End of Empire in the Middle East* (CUP, Cambridge 1991).

Barer, Shlomo, *The Magic Carpet* (Harper, New York 1952).

Beer, Colin, *On Revolutionary War* (Galago, Bromley 1990).

Beeston, Richard, *Looking for Trouble* (Brassey's, London 1997).

Belhaven, Lord, (as Master of Belhaven), *The Kingdom of Melchior* (John Murray, London 1949).

_____*The Uneven Road* (John Murray, London 1955).

Bell, Sir Gawain, *An Imperial Twilight* (Lester Crook, London 1989).

Bidwell, Robin, *Travellers in Arabia* (Hamlyn, London 1976).

_____*The Two Yemens* (Longman, Harlow 1983).

de la Billière, Sir Peter, *Looking for Trouble* (HarperCollins, London 1994).

Bloch, Jonathan, (and Patrick Fitzgerald), *British Intelligence & Covert Action – Africa, Middle East and Europe since 1945* (Junction, London 1983).

Bower, Tom, *The Perfect English Spy* (Heinemann, London 1995).

Brent, Peter, *Far Arabia – Explorers of the Myth* (Weidenfeld & Nicolson, London 1977).

Broadbent, Sir Ewen, *The Military and Government, from Macmillan to Heseltine* (Macmillan, London 1988).

Brown, Anthony Cave, *Treason in the Blood – H. St. John Philby, Kim Philby and the Spy Case of the Century* (Robert Hale, London 1995).

Brown, George, *In My Way* (Victor Gollancz, London 1971).

Cain, P J, (and A G Hopkins), *British Imperialism: Crisis and Deconstruction 1914–1990* (Longman, London 1993).

313

Carruthers, Susan, *The Media at War: Communications & Conflict in the 20ᵗʰ Century* (Macmillan, London 2000).

Carver, Michael, *War Since 1945* (Weidenfeld & Nicolson, London 1980).

_____ *The Seven Ages of the British Army* (Weidenfeld & Nicolson, London 1984).

Cavendish, Anthony, *Inside Intelligence – The Revelations of an MI6 Officer* (HarperCollins, London 1990).

Charters, David, ed. (and M Tugwell), *Deception Operations. Studies in the East-West Context* (Brassey's, London 1990).

Cookridge, E H, *Shadow of a Spy: The Complete Dossier on George Blake* (Leslie Frewin, London 1967).

Cooper, Johnny, *One of the Originals* (Pan Books, London 1991).

Copeland, Miles, *The Game Player* (Aurum Press, London 1989).

Cradock, Percy, *Know Your Enemy – How the Joint Intelligence Committee Saw the World* (John Murray, London 2002).

Crook, Brig. Paul, *Came the Dawn – 50 Years an Army Officer* (Spellmount, Tunbridge Wells 1989).

Crouch, Michael, *An Element of Luck – To South Arabia and Beyond* (Radcliffe Press, London 1993).

Crossman, Richard, *The Diaries of a Cabinet Minister, Vol. I* (Hamish Hamilton, London 1975).

_____*Vol. II* (Hamish Hamilton, London 1976).

Darby, Phillip, *British Defence Policy, East of Suez, 1947–68* (OUP, London 1973).

Davies, Philip, *MI6 and the Machinery of Spying* (Frank Cass, London 2003).

Deacon, Richard, *'C': A Biography of Sir Maurice Oldfield* (Macdonald, London 1984).

Deffarge, Claude (and G Troeller), *Yemen 62–69: De la révolution (sauvage) à la trêve des guerriers* (Robert Laffont, Paris 1971).

Dickie, John, *Inside the Foreign Office* (Chapmans, London 1992).

Dorril, Stephen, *MI6 – Fifty Years of Special Operations* (Fourth Estate, London 2000).

Downton, Eric, *Wars Without End* (Stoddart, Toronto 1987).

Dresch, Paul, *A History of Modern Yemen* (Cambridge University Press, Cambridge 2000).

Edwards, Frank, *The Gaysh: A History of the Protectorate Levies 1927–61, and the Federal Regular Army of South Arabia 1961–67* (Helion, Solihull 2003).

Fielding, Xan, *One Man in His Time* (Macmillan, London 1990).

Fiennes, Ranulph, *Living Dangerously* (Futura, London 1988).

Gat, Moshe, *Britain and the Conflict in the Middle East, 1964–1967* (Praeger, London 2003).

Gavin, R J, *Aden under British Rule 1839–1967* (Hurst & Co., London 1975).

Geraghty, Tony, *Who Dares Wins – The Story of the Special Air Service 1950–80* (Arms & Armour, London 1980).

Gorst, A (and W Lucas) (eds.), *Politics and the Limits of Policy* (Pinter, London 1991).

Gwynne-James, David, *Letters from Oman* (Blackwater Books, London 2002).

Halliday, Fred, *Arabia without Sultans* (Saqi Books, London 2002).

Harper, Stephen, *Last Sunset – What Happened in Aden* (Collins, London 1978).

Healey, Denis, *The Time of My Life* (Penguin, London 1990).

Hennessy, Peter, *Whitehall* (Secker & Warburg, London 1989).

_____*The Secret State – Whitehall and the Cold War* (Allen Lane Penguin Press, London 2002).

Hickinbotham, Sir Tom, *Aden* (Constable, London 1958).

Hoe, Alan, *David Stirling* (Little Brown, London 1992).

Holden, David, *Farewell to Arabia* (Faber, London 1966).

Hollingworth, Clare, *Front Line* (Jonathan Cape, London 1990).

Hosmer, Stephen, *The Fall of South Vietnam – Statements by Vietnamese Military and Civilian Leaders* (Crane Russak, New York 1980).

Ingrams, Harold, *Arabia and the Isles* (John Murray, London 1966).

_____*The Yemens – Imams, Rulers and Revolution* (John Murray, London 1963).

Ismael, Tareq, *The Arab Left* (Syracuse University Press, New York 1976).

_____ (and Jacqueline Ismael) *PDR Yemen: Politics, Economics and Society* (Frances Pinter, London 1986).

Jackson, Gen. Sir William (and Field Marshal Lord Bramall), *The Chiefs – The Story of the United Kingdom Chiefs of Staff* (Brassey's, London 1992).

_____ *Britain's Triumph & Decline in the Middle East – Military Campaigns 1919 to the Present Day* (Brassey's, London 1996).

_____ *Withdrawal from Empire* (Batsford, London 1986).

Johnston, Charles, *The View from Steamer Point* (Collins, London 1964).

Kahin, A & J, *Subversion as Foreign Policy: The Secret Eisenhower & Dulles Debacle in Indonesia* (New Press, New York 1995).

Kazziha, Walid, *Revolutionary Transformation in the Arab World* (Charles Knight, London 1975).

Kemp, Anthony, *The SAS – The Savage Wars of Peace* (John Murray, London 1994).

Kent, J (ed.), *British Documents on the End of Empire and the Defence of the Middle East, B4. Part III* (HMSO, London 1998).

King, Gillian, 'Imperial Outpost – Aden' in *Chatham House Essays:6* (OUP, London 1964).

Kitson, Brig. Frank, *Low Intensity Operations* (Faber & Faber, London 1971).

Kostiner, Joseph, *Yemen – The Tortuous Quest for Unity 1990–94* (Chatham House Papers, London 1996).

Kyle, Keith, *Suez* (Weidenfeld & Nicholson, London 1991).

Lackner, Helen, *PDR Yemen: Outpost of Socialist Development in Arabia* (Ithaca Press, London 1985).

Laqueur, Walter, *The Road to War* (Weidenfeld and Nicolson, London 1968).

Large, Lofty, *Soldier Against the Odds: From Infantry to SAS* (Mainstream, Edinburgh 1999).

Lashmar, Paul (and James Oliver), *Britain's Secret Propaganda War* (Sutton, Stroud 1998).

Ledger, David, *Shifting Sands – The British in South Arabia* (Peninsular, London 1983).

Little, Tom, *Modern Egypt* (Benn, London 1967).

_____ *South Arabia – Arena of Conflict* (Praeger, London 1968).

Longhurst, Henry, *Adventure in Oil – The Story of British Petroleum* (Sidgwick & Jackson, London 1959).

Lord, Cliff (and David Birtles), *The Armed Forces of Aden 1839–1967* (Helion, Solihull 2000).

Lunt, James, *The Barren Rocks of Aden* (Herbert Jenkins, London 1966).

Mackintosh-Smith, Tim, *Yemen – Travels in Dictionary Land* (John Murray, London 1997).

Macmillan, Harold, *At the End of the Day 1961–1963* (Macmillan, London 1973).

McCart, Neil, *HMS Centaur 1943–1972* (Fan Publications, Cheltenham 1997).

McGuffin, John, *The Guineapigs* (Penguin, London 1974).

McNamara, Robert, *Britain, Nasser and the Balance of Power in the Middle East 1952–67* (Frank Cass, London 2003).

Mitchell, Lt.-Col. Colin, *Having Been a Soldier* (Hamish Hamilton, London 1969).

Mockaitis, Thomas, *British Counterinsurgency in the Post-Imperial Era* (Manchester University Press, Manchester 1995).

Morris, James, *Farewell the Trumpets* (Faber & Faber, London 1978).

Mosley, Leonard, *Power Play – Oil in the Middle East* (Weidenfeld & Nicolson, London 1973).

Murphy, Philip, *Alan Lennox-Boyd* (IB Taurus, London 1999).

Newsinger, John, *Dangerous Men – The SAS and Popular Culture* (Pluto Press, London 1997).

_____*British Counterinsurgency from Palestine to Northern Ireland* (Palgrave, Basingstoke 2002).

Norris, John, *Anti-Tank Weapons* (Brassey's, London 1996).

O'Balance, Edgar, *The War in the Yemen* (Faber & Faber, London 1971).

O'Neill, Bard, *Insurgency & Terrorism: Inside Modern Revolutionary Warfare* (Brassey's, Washington 1990).

Oren, Michael, *Six Days of War – June 1967 and the Making of the Modern Middle East* (OUP, London 2002).

Osanka, Franklin (ed.), *Modern Guerrilla Warfare* (Free Press of Glencoe, New York, 1962.

Ovendale, Ritchie, *Britain, the United States and the Transfer of Power in the Middle East 1945–1962* (Leicester University Press, London 1996).

Page, Stephen, *The USSR and Arabia* (Central Asian Research Centre, London 1971).

Paget, Julian, *Last Post: Aden 1964–1967* (Faber & Faber, London 1969).

Pearce, Edward, *Denis Healey – A Life in Our Times* (Little Brown, London 2002).

Pieragostini, Karl, *Britain, Aden and South Arabia: Abandoning Empire* (Macmillan, London 1991).

Pridham, B (ed.), *Contemporary Yemen – Politics & Historical Background* (Croom Helm for Centre for Arab Gulf Studies, Exeter 1984).

_____*The Arab Gulf & the Arab World* (Croom Helm, London 1988).

Rahmy, Ali Abdel Rahman, *The Egyptian Policy in the Arab World: Intervention in Yemen 1962–1967* (University Press of America, Washington 1983).

Rathmell, Andrew, *The Secret War in the Middle East: The Covert Struggle for Syria 1949–1961* (IB Taurus, London 1995).

Rimington, Stella, *Open Secret: The Autobiography of the Former Director-General of MI5* (Hutchinson. London 2001).

Sadat, Anwar el, *In Search of Identity* (Collins, London 1978).

Sampson, Anthony, *The Arms Bazaar* (Hodder & Stoughton, London 1977).

Sayigh, Yezid (and Avi Shlaim) (eds), *The Cold War and the Middle East* (Clarendon Press, Oxford 1997).

Schmidt, Dana Adams, *Yemen, the Unknown War* (Bodley Head, London 1968).

Searight, Sarah, *Yemen – Land and People* (Pallas Athene, London 2002).

Smiley, David (with Peter Kemp) *Arabian Assignment* (Leo Cooper, London 1975).

_____*Irregular Regular* (Michael Russell, Norwich 1994).

Somerville-Large, Peter, *Tribes and Tribulations – A Journey in Republican Yemen* (Robert Hale, London 1967).

Starling, Joe, *Soldier On! The Testament of a Tom* (Spellmount, Tunbridge Wells 1992).

Stiff, Peter, *See You in November – The Story of an SAS Assassin* (Galago, Alberton RSA, 1985/2002).

Stookey, Robert, *South Yemen – A Marxist Republic in Arabia* (Croom Helm, London 1982).

Strawson, John, *A History of the S. A. S. Regiment* (Secker & Warburg, London 1984).

Stubbs, Richard, *Hearts & Minds in Guerrilla Warfare* (OUP, Singapore 1989).

Taylor, Maxwell, *The Terrorist* (Brassey's, London 1988).

Thompson, Sir Robert, *Defeating Communist Insurgency* (Chatto & Windus, London 1967).

Time-Life, *Life at War* (Time Life Books, 1977).

Trevaskis, Sir Kennedy, *Shades of Amber – A South Arabian Episode* (Hutchinson, London 1968).

Trevelyan, Humphrey, *Public and Private* (Hamish Hamilton, London1980).

_____*The Middle East in Revolution* (Macmillan, London 1970).

Tugwell, Maurice (ed.), *Armies in Low Intensity Conflict* (Brassey's, London 1989).

Verrier, Anthony, *Through the Looking Glass – British Foreign Policy in an Age of Illusions* (W W Norton, New York 1983).

Walker, Gen. Sir Walter, *Fighting On* (New Millennium, London 1997).

Waterfield, Gordon, *Sultans of Aden – With an Envoi by Stephen Day* (Stacey International, London 2002).

Weale, Adrian, *Secret Warfare* (Hodder & Stoughton, London 1997).

Wenner, Manfred, *The Yemen Arab Republic* (Westview Press, Oxford 1991).

West, Nigel, *GCHQ – The Secret Wireless War 1900–86* (Weidenfeld & Nicolson, London 1986).

_____*The Friends – Britain's Post-War Secret Intelligence Operations* (Weidenfeld & Nicholson, London 1988).

Wheen, Francis, *Tom Driberg – His Life and Indiscretions* (Chatto & Windus, London 1990).

Wilson, Keith (ed.), *Imperialism and Nationalism: The Anglo-Egyptian Experience 1882–1982* (Mansell, London 1983).

Yergin, Daniel, *The Prize – The Epic Quest for Oil, Money & Power* (Simon & Schuster, London 1991).

Index

(Ranks and titles shown are those held at the time of the insurgency. Regiments and Corps are in order of precedence.)

Abdullah, Fadhl, 73
Abyan, 27, 153, 287
Addali, Abdul, 11
Addaqa, Said, 205
Aden Airways, 210
Aden Association, 24
Aden Broadcasting Station (ABS), 120, 155, 209, 271, 273
Aden Commercial Institute, 266
Aden Intelligence Centre (AIC), 123, 142, 184
Aden Port Trust, 25–6, 205
Aden Protectorate Levies (APL), 6–7, 10, 26, 32–3
Aden Public Relations Department, 120–1
Aden State Legislature, 134, 147–50, 255, 266
Aden Trade Union Congress (ATUC), 25–6, 72, 78, 84, 121, 131, 176, 225
Aden Treasury, 266
Aden Veterans Association, 297
Aidrus Hill, 265
Aidrus Mosque, 268
Aircraft, British: Belvedere Helicopter, 81–2, 104; Blackburn Beverley, 97–8, 211; Buccaneer, 279; Canberra Bomber, 79, 175; Hawker Hunter FGA Mk 9, 31–2, 79, 81–4, 88, 97, 101, 104, 108–9, 174–5, 275; Meteor, 31–2; Sea

Vixen, 278; Shackleton Bomber, 32, 79, 81, 97; Sioux Helicopter, 211–12, 248; Twin Pioneer, 32, 98; Vickers Valetta, 98; Vulcan Bomber, 31, 79, 239; Wessex Helicopter, 81–2, 105, 108, 196, 223, 248; Westland Scout Helicopter, 99, 108, 212
al-Amri, General H, 127, 197
al-Asnag, Abdullah: rise to power, 25; character, 71–2; relationship with Nasser, 78; prison, 131; British Labour Party, 132, 224; thwarted by NLF, 148; on Colonel Gray's murder, 196; with Driberg, 225; torture allegations, 188; Nadia's story, 203; lack of tribal contacts, 275
al-Asqualani Mosque, 264
al-Baidani, Dr Abdurrahman, 49, 58–9
al-Beedh, Ali, 196
al-Hamad, Awad, 84–5
al-Ittihad, 26, 134, 242
al-Jiffri family, 24–5, 71
al Milah, 170
al Naqil, 104, 110, 203
al-Qadi, Lieutenant-General A, 86
al-Queda, 297–8
al-Said, Nuri, 15, 36
al-Sha'abi, Feisal: early rise, 72; detained in Cairo, 176; post 1967 events, 291
al-Sha'abi, Qatan: early flight to Yemen, 24; character, 71; in Taiz, 73; politics of, 74; distributing arms, 76; relationship with

Nasser, 78; detained in Cairo, 176; profile, 224; press conference, 273; refusal to negotiate, 274; at Geneva, 279; post 1967 events, 291
al-Shair, Abu, 297
al-Zaghir, H, 149
Alanbrooke, Lord, 9
Alexander, H, 240
Algerian War, 11, 13, 73, 110, 160, 188, 201, 232, 247, 298
Ali, Saif, 77
Ali, Salah, 250
Almarwani, Ahmed, 118
Amer, Major-General Abdul, 45, 59–60, 85, 167, 231
Amery, Rt Hon. Julian, 54–5, 158–9, 205, 277
Amery, Rt Hon. Leo, 54
Amnesty International, 186–7
Antar, Ali, 77, 210, 255, 296
Arab National Movement (ANM), 25, 72, 73, 85, 176
Arab News Agency (ANA), 54, 121
Arabian-American Oil Company (ARAMCO), 12–13
Ashworth, Tony, 119, 121–2, 155, 202, 209–10, 226, 271, 277
Atyia, Colonel Mahmud, 59
Audhali state, 22, 27, 130, 271, 273
Aushabi, Sub-Inspector Fadhl, 245

Baader-Meinhoff gang, 296
Baekeland, Susan de H, 146–7
Baharoon, Zein, 78, 147, 286
Bahrain, 275, 280, 291–2
Baidha, 110, 129–30
Bailey, Joan, 41
Bailey, Ronald, 41, 44, 49
Baines, Lieutenant-Colonel David, 157, 286, 296
Baker, Trooper P, 101–2
Bakri Ridge, 100–1, 107–8, 117
Balfour-Paul, Glencairn, 53, 154, 298
Banin Street, 266
Banks, Major M, 103
Barclay, C, 120
Barnett, Captain S, 156

Barrie, H, 141–2
Bartley, Gunner S, 193
Batterbury, P, 206
Baty, Lieutenant Brian, 261
Baxter, Sergeant, 104
Bayoumi, Hassan Ali, 36, 147–8, 209–10, 286
Bayoumi, Hussain (brother of Hassan), 270–1
Bayoumi Clinic, 269
Beard, 2nd Lieutenant, Nick, 241
Beeston, R, 201
Beetham, Group Captain M, 97
Beihan state, 22, 24, 54, 57, 63, 86–7, 128, 156, 272
Beihan, Sharif of, 52, 78, 86, 128, 135, 272
Beirut, 53, 154, 272, 275, 292
Belgian Congo, 203
Bell, Sir Gawain, 165–6
Bennenson, P, 187
Beswick, Lord, 165–6
Bidwell, R, 78, 152
bin-Laden, Osama, 297
Binns, Barbara, 206–7, 293
Binns, Charles, 206–7
Bir Fuqum, 239
Blacker, Brigadier Cecil, 106, 108
Blake, George, 122, 155
Blenkharn, Corporal J, 274
Blenkinsop, Lieutenant-Colonel R, 243–4, 249, 252, 260
Blindicide rocket launcher, 193, 228
Blunt, Sir Anthony, 53, 124
Blunt, Wilfred, 53
Bonfante, J, 203
Booth, M, 277
Borneo Campaign, 55, 99, 106, 145, 171, 261, 288
Boustead, Colonel Sir Hugh, 195
Bowen, R, 186
Boyle, Flight-Lieutenant A, 56
Bremridge, Captain M, 83
Brenchley, F, 87
Brennan, Major C, 106
Brezhnev, President Leonid, 86
Brierley, Major G, 229
Brind, Captain R, 109

British Army:
  Strategic Reserve, 14, 30–4, 292
  Middle East Command (MEC), 9,
    31, 34, 80, 105, 110–11, 117–18,
    121, 130, 156–7, 203, 227, 240,
    253–5, 259, 262–3, 268–70, 279,
    285, 287–9
  Middle East Land Forces (MELF),
    32, 80, 145, 171
  Brigades:
    Aden Brigade (formerly Aden
    Garrison), 134, 169, 192, 220, 232,
    241, 243, 249, 252, 260, 265
    24 Brigade, 31, 33, 80, 96, 132–4,
    156, 171, 184, 214, 239, 279
    39 Brigade, 106, 132
  Forces:
    Aden Garrison, 58–9, 80, 96, 134
    Radforce, 94, 106, 290
  Regiments and Corps:
    The Life Guards, 16, 170
    Royal Horse Artillery:
      1 RHA, 157, 193, Chestnut
      Troop, 212; 286
      3 RHA, 33, 80–1, 83–4, 96, 98,
      101, 103–4, 108, 156, 227
      7 PARA, 156
    1st The Queen's Dragoon
    Guards, 184, 189–90, 211, 222,
    242, 247–9, 265, 269, 271
    QDG Air Squadron, 189
    3rd Carabiniers, 34
    4/7th Royal Dragoon Guards,
    189
    5th Royal Inniskilling Dragoon
    Guards, 189
    9/12th Royal Lancers, 33
    10th Royal Hussars, 189
    11th Hussars, 34
    16/5th Queen's Royal Lancers,
    80, 189
    Royal Tank Regiment:
      1 RTR, 189
      4 RTR, 107, 109, 189
    Royal Regiment of Artillery:
      19 Field Regiment, 156–7
      47th Light Regiment, 265
    Corps of Royal Engineers:

    12 Field Squadron, 81–2, 96
    60 Squadron, 265
  Royal Corps of Signals, 16, 99,
    290
    15 Signals Regiment, 192
    Aden Signals Squadron, 192
    254/255 (Bahrain) Signals
    Squadron, 192
    603 Signals Troop, 192
  1 Coldstream Guards, 176–7, 204
  2 Coldstream Guards, 156
  1 Irish Guards, 196, 223, 261
  1 Welsh Guards, 170
  1 Royal Scots, 107, 130
  1 Royal Sussex Regiment, 157
  1 King's Own Royal Border
    Regiment (1 KOB), 241–2, 271
  1 Royal Northumberland
    Fusiliers (1 RNF), 222, 231,
    243–4, 247, 251–2, 254–5, 259,
    261, 264, 268, 293
  Royal Regiment of Fusiliers, 293
  1 East Anglian Regiment, 96, 103,
    105, 109
  1 Royal Anglian Regiment, 151,
    190, 211, 214, 222, 228
  1 Somerset & Cornwall Light
    Infantry, 184, 191
  1 Prince of Wales's Own
    Regiment of Yorkshire (1
    PWO), 171, 213, 268, 271
  South Wales Borderers:
    1/1st Brecknockshire, 5
  1 King's Own Scottish
    Borderers (1 KOSB), 130
  1 Lancashire Regiment, 214,
    224, 229–30, 240, 242, 265, 274,
    277
  Royal Green Jackets, 214
  1 Argyll and Sutherland
    Highlanders, 221, 231, 243,
    244, 247, 261, 264–6, 268, 270,
    294
  The Parachute Regiment:
    1 Bn (1 PARA), 212, 228, 241,
    274, 277, 280
    3 Bn (3 PARA), 96–7, 103–4,
    107–9, 118, 203

1 The Cameronians (Scottish
  Rifles), 190–2, 293
Special Air Service Regiment:
  22 SAS, 16, 55–7, 97–103, 107,
  117, 171, 190–1, 196, 223, 233,
  264–5, 290
Army Air Corps, 96, 104
Royal Corps of Transport:
  60 Squadron, 241–2
Royal Army Ordnance Corps,
  187
Royal Pioneer Corps:
  518 Company, 182
Royal Army Medical Corps, 188
Corps of Royal Electrical and
  Mechanical Engineers (REME),
  16
Intelligence Corps, 107
Army Special Branch Units, 184–5,
  191
Brigade structure, 293
Casualties, 285
Tactics: blue card, 182; stop and
  search, 183
British Government, 27, 35, 49, 54, 131;
  scandals, 56–7; MOD, 118–19, 159,
  202; failure to act, 166; Foreign
  Office, 122–3; British Petroleum,
  206; with Federation, 148;
  Defence White Paper, 165; United
  Nations, 224; June mutiny, 260;
  recognises NLF, 279; problems
  facing, 286; withdrawal from S.
  Arabia, 287–8; attitude to rulers,
  292; account of massacres, 295
British Labour Party, 25, 78, 118, 132,
  224–5
British Petroleum Ltd (BP), creation of
  refinery, 12, 205; Aden Port, 25–6;
  leasing to 45 Commando, 34;
  nationals, 48; terrorist incidents,
  135; security, 142–4; MECAS, 154;
  television, 155; Special Branch,
  185; accommodation and
  dependants, 206; murder of staff,
  206; strikes, 208; dependants
  evacuated, 265; last hopes, 277;
  post 1967 events, 297

British-Yemeni Society, 297
Brown, Rt Hon. George, 224, 226, 239,
  275, 288
Brown, N, 153
Buchanan, Trooper Jim, 106, 168, 173
Buchanan, Captain R, 266
Buraimi dispute, 12–13, 222
Bureiq, Colonel Nasser, 233–5
Burgess, Guy, 27, 119
Bushell, J, 87
Butler, A, 165
Butler, Staff Sergeant E, 241
Butler, Brigadier Hew, 214
Butler, RAB, 128

Caffery, J, 13
Cain, Gunner J, 212
Campbell, C, 14
Campbell-Baldwin, 2nd Lieutenant,
  243, 248–9
'Cap Badge', Operation, 93–106;
  lessons from, 168–9
Carrington, Lord, 134
Carroll, Lance Corporal Robert, 224
Central Intelligence Agency (CIA), 50,
  71, 222, 231
Champion Lines, 153, 240–5, 253–5
Charles, Sir Arthur, 149, 266
Chartered Bank, 248, 266, 270
Chauvel, P, 47
Cheek, Lance Corporal Terry, 184, 191
China, 10, 15, 44, 49, 160, 296
Christie, J, 126
Churchill, Randolph, 201
Civil Prison, 255
'Coca Cola', 103, 105
Cockerill, Harry, 34
Coleville-Stewart, H, 146
Collings, Corporal Mervyn, 134, 155–6
Collings, Mary, 155–6
Cooper, Major J, 56–7, 62, 127, 196
Cooper, Lieutenant-Colonel, 118
Copeland, Miles, 13, 50, 231
Cowper, Brigadier A, 130, 146, 187
Crater: history, 4; Jews attacked, 9,
  229–30; Freya Stark in, 119; SIS,
  124–5; surveillance, 181; Special
  Branch in, 141, 185; patrols in,

188, 232; SAS units in, 191; photo-journalism, 203; assassinations in, 219–20; rumours of attack, 243; decision not to enter, 253; wireless problems, 254; sealing off, 255; terrorists' control, 269; British snipers, 265; Davis's return to, 296
Crescent Hotel, 201, 277–8
Critchfield, J, 50
Crombie, Fusilier W, 249
Crook, Brigadier Paul, 166
Crossman, Rt Hon. R, 288
Crosthwaite, Sir Moore, 53
Crouch, Michael, 87, 154, 195, 201
Crowe, Major Nigel, 262, 266
Cubbon, Major-General John, 80, 94, 96, 117–18, 158
Cuthbert, Ann, 48, 99, 135, 142–4, 149, 208–9
Cuthbert, Charles, 149
Cuthbert, Derek, 48, 144
Cyprus emergency, xix, 4, 14, 31, 81, 106, 145–6, 166, 203, 261, 269, 288

Daintree, Davina, 207–8
Daintree, Dr J, 207–8
Daly, Ralph, 127, 152, 154
Dalyell, Tam, 295
Danaba Basin, 83, 97, 102–4, 111, 130
Dar Saad, 274, 278
Da Silva, John, 55, 79, 127
Dathina state, 22, 130, 271
Davey, P, 76
Davis, Brigadier Derek, 295–6
Davis, 2nd Lieutenant John, xvii, 243–50, 254, 259, 290, 295–6
Davis, Corporal, 93
Davis, Private M, 104
Davis, Pamela, 295–6
Day, Stephen, 27–8, 123, 152–3, 296
Dean, Sir Patrick, 88
Deffarge, M, 201
De la Billière, Major Peter, 55–6, 98–100, 154
Dhala, Amir of, 74, 77

Dhala state, 5, 22, 24, 63, 74, 76, 84, 93, 130–1, 152, 157, 191, 201, 255, 297; convoys through, 169–70
Denstone College, xvii
De St Jorre, J, 203
Detention Centre (al-Mansoura), 185–8, 202, 274
Dhofar Liberation Front (DLF), 196
Djibouti, 25, 54, 177
Douglas, Sergeant Robert, 208–9, 211
Downside School, xvii, 122
Downton, E, 47, 225
Downward, Lieutenant-Colonel Peter, 265
Driberg, Tom, 224–6
Duffy, Fusilier John, 248
Dulles, A, 13
Dulles, J F, 13–14
Dunbar, Brigadier Charles, 145, 188, 214, 253, 262, 265–6, 268, 278, 289
Dunkin, Marine, 109
Dunkley, Sergeant B, 193
Dutton, A, 134, 166, 219, 272
Dye, Brigadier Jack, 233–5, 254

Eales, Major D, 195
Eden, Rt Hon. Anthony, 13–14
Edwards, Bob, 25
Edwards, Captain Robin, 99–103, 117–18
Egypt: xviii; occupation of, 4; relations with US, 13, 222; aid to Yemen, 15, 50; Special Forces, 49; casualties in Yemen, 52, 57, 127; Air Force, 61–2, 227; rockets, 54, 58; comparison with YAR troops, 61; calibre of own troops, 85, 158; troop numbers, 59–60, 167; intelligence service, 11, 71, 76, 127, 176, 220; recognition of YAR, 63; Israeli border, 227; and Six-Day War, 230–2
Eichelberger, James, 13
Elliott, Nicholas, 47, 53, 55
Ellis, Jim, 152, 195, 228
Elworthy, Air Marshal Charles, 31, 80
Empty Quarter, 1, 8, 60

Fadhli state, 22, 271
Fadhli, Sultan of, 273
Fairholme, Superintendent Bill, 146
Falaise Camp, 160, 184, 297
Farid, Muhammed, 235
Farid, Sheikh, 166
Farrar-Hockley, Lieutenant-Colonel
    Anthony, 107–9
Federal National Guard 1 (FNG1), 10,
    26, 153, 233–4
Federal National Guard 2 (FNG2), 26,
    170, 234, 240
Federal Regular Army (FRA), 26, 33,
    58–9, 77, 80, 83–4, 96, 106, 118,
    169, 174, 214; 2nd Battalion, 80–2,
    109, 156; 3rd Battalion, 80; 4th
    Battalion, 80, 82; and Six-Day
    War, 231; converted to SAA, 233
Federation of South Arabia, merger
    with Aden Colony, 35–6;
    formation, 21–6; extraction of
    tolls, 74; threat of attack on, 58;
    public relations, 120–2; risk of
    collapse, 128; Greenwood pledge,
    132; rulers, 135; relations with
    HMG, 148; closes Yemen border,
    168; public relations, 202; officials
    assassinated, 219; suspension of
    Arab Colonels, 235; notice of
    unrest, 239; fears over SAA, 263;
    Crater re-entry, 266; poor
    intelligence, 270; collapse, 273–4,
    286; fate of rulers, 291
Fees, J, 52
Feisal, King (formerly Crown Prince),
    50, 58, 86, 128, 159, 167–8, 197,
    222, 231, 276
Ferguson, Major J, 156
Fincher, Terry, 203, 261
Finn, Acting Corporal Jim, 234–5, 280
Fleming, Captain John, 212
FLOSY, creation, 176; double agents,
    184; competes with NLF, 195,
    210; industrial unrest, 205;
    influence at BP, 208;
    broadcasting, 209; tactics, 219–20;
    fight with NLF, 222; and Labour
    Party, 224; with Driberg, 225–6;

strikes, 228–9; role in mutiny,
    260; future of, 262–3; attacks
    Argylls, 270; fall in support, 273;
    destruction of, 274–5; and HMG,
    287
Foley, Lance Corporal B, 171
Forde, Sergeant Pilot Martin, 211,
    247–8
Fort Morbut (Interrogation Centre),
    185–8, 210
Forward Observation Officers (FOO),
    105, 109
France, 2
Franks, Colonel B, 55
Free Yemeni Movement, 10

Gabriel, Guardsman, 188
Gandy, Christopher, 49, 53
GCHQ, 61, 79, 126–7
Ghizan, 62
Gibraltar, 166
Gibson, Lord, 54
'Gin Sling', 103–4
Girgirah, Abdul, 121
Glubb, General John, 15
Godwin, Captain P, 241
Golds, Flight Lieutenant Chris, 174–5
Gooch, Major P, 272
Goschen, Major Tim, 153
Government Guards, 8
Graham, Major-General F, 295
Gray, Edith, 196
Gray, Major Mike Wingate, 100, 223
Gray, Lieutenant-Colonel P, 196
Greenwood, Rt Hon. Anthony, 132,
    134, 142, 148–9
Gulf Sheikhdoms, 50, 128, 280, 290–3
Guthrie, Captain Charles, 223

Habash, G, 176
Habilayn camp, 100, 107, 168–9, 171,
    205, 223, 297
Hadhramaut, 8, 28, 30, 60, 196, 274
Hadhrami Bedouin League (HBL), 9,
    32, 195–6, 223, 275
Hadi, Sayed, 245, 250, 259, 262–3
Haines, Commander Stafford, 2, 4
Hamilton, R A B, 6–8, 151

Hamilton, Trooper B, 101
Hamilton-Meikle, Captain G, 103
Hancock, Tony, 208
Harbottle, Brigadier M, 80
Hardman, Sir Henry, 119
Hare, Alan, 54
Hargroves, Brigadier Louis, career, 94; 'Radforce', 96–7, 103, 106; Aden Brigade, 134; police liaison, 145–6; discovery of casualty, 150
Harib, 59–60, 87–8, 128, 158
Harington, Lieutenant-General Sir Charles, 74–5, 80, 98, 119, 201
Harney, D, 55
Hassan, Prince, 50, 52, 85, 167, 196
Hatton, Sergeant R, 187
Hauf, 196
Hawkins, 2nd Lieutenant W, 151
Healey, Rt Hon. Denis, 62, 118, 165, 226, 295
Heber Percy, Bill, 127, 154
Held, Colbert, 223
Henderson, George, 78
Herbert, Hon. Aubrey, 8
Hickinbotham, Sir Tom, 21
Higgins, Lieutenant, 271
High Commission, 25, 119, 122, 130, 146–7, 150, 195, 206, 222, 224–6, 262, 275, 277, 295
Hinchcliffe, Peter, 152
HMS Albion, 33
HMS Ashanti, 204
HMS Brighton, 228
HMS Bulwark, 33, 279
HMS Centaur, 104, 107
HMS Eagle, 279
HMS Fearless, 196
HMS Hermes 279
Hoare, CSM Peter, 244
Hobson, L, 121
Hodeidah, 42–7, 49, 197
Hoe, Alan, 55
Holden, David, 71, 86
Hollingworth, Clare, 202, 204
Hollis, Sir Roger, 124
Home, Lord (later Sir Alec), 49, 52–5, 79, 128, 132
Home, Charles Douglas, 295

Hone, Sir Ralph, 165
Hoult, Fusilier G, 244
Hudson, Captain Leslie, 279
Hughes, Gunner R, 193
Hughes, Sergeant B, 270
Humphrey, Air Vice Marshal A, 253
Hunter, Private J, 244
Hurd, Lord, xix
Husain, Niaz, 219
Hushein, Sheikh Husein, 29
Hussein, King, 16, 50, 52

Ibraham, Mohammed, 251, 259, 269
Imam Ahmed, assumes title, 10; and UAR, 15; and Federation, 24; relation with British, 41–2; and al-Badr, 44; and Soviet Union, 44; personality, 44; attempted assassination, 45; death, 45–6
Imam al-Badr: Soviet Bloc, 15; friendship with Sallal, 44–5; becomes Imam, 46; Yemen coup, 46; arrives in Hajjah, 50; and HMG, 55, 79; leadership, 159; language problems, 167; weaknesses, 276
Imam Yahya, 6, 9–10
India, 8, 9; Bombay Presidency, 2–4
Indian Army:
  Aden Moveable Column, 5–6
  29th Indian Brigade, 5
  Bombay Regiment, 2
  24th Regiment Bombay Native Infantry, 2
  Punjab Regiment, 9
  Hyderabad Lancers, 9
  Baluch Regiment, 195
Information Research Department (IRD): xvii, 277; formation, 119–21; Ashworth and Rose, 122; and AIC, 123; television and radio, 155, 209–10; and al-Asnag, 226
Ingledow, Anthony, 221
Ingledow, Monica, 221
Ingrams, Doreen, 8
Ingrams, Harold, 8, 151
Intelligence Services: xviii,

Security Service (MI5): release of
files, xix; in Aden, 46; satire on,
123; recruitment 124
Secret Intelligence Service (MI6):
release of files, xix;
representation, 46, 79; in Yemen,
47, 52, 57; and IRD, 120; and
ANA, 54, 121; composition, 125;
local agents, 126; scandals, 123;
and journalists, 204; successes in
S. Arabia, 287
International Red Cross, 60–1
Iran, 160
Iraq, 7, 10, 15–16, 32, 44, 160
Isa, Hadi, 197
Ismail, Abdul, 131, 141, 210, 263–4,
296
Israel: new state, 10; help to Yemeni
royalists, 53–4, Mossad, 227, Six-
Day War, 229–31
Italian forces, 6, 9, 42, 119

Jackson, D, 122
Jackson, Major, 108–9
Japanese Red Army, 296
Jawee, Hussein, 186
Jebel Akdar, 16, 56, 98
Jebel Bulaiq, 87
Jebel Huriyah, 108–10
Jebel Qara, 50
Jebel Radfan, 109
Jebel Shamsan, 2, 192, 222, 264
Jebel Widina, 109
Jefferies, Brigadier R, 260, 262, 265
Jefferson, Captain, 270
Jewkes, Captain E, 104
Johnson, Air Vice Marshal Johnny,
79
Johnson, Lieutenant-Colonel J, 55,
57–8
Johnson, President Lyndon, 86, 166
Johnston, Sir Charles, 36, 47, 56, 58, 62
Joint Intelligence Committee (JIC), xix,
32, 42
Jones, Acting Corporal G, 176
Jordan, 14–16, 50, 62, 160, 230
Journalists, 119, 122–3, 201–5, 260,
263–4, 270–1

Kathiri state, 30, 195, 274
Keeling, Lieutenant Andrew, 172
Keightley, Corporal J, 248
Kennedy, President J, 50, 52, 61, 63, 86
Kenya: Mau Mau rebellion, 11, 132,
147; independence, 14; expansion
of base, 15; and Strategic Reserve,
31, 34; Special Branch, 141, 146,
203
Khalifa, Fuad, 260, 264
Khalifa, Khalifa Abdullah, 148, 187,
225
Khalil, Inspector Fadhli, 141
Khormaksar, 1, 78, 106, 175, 191, 206,
208, 211, 251, 275, 279
Khrushchev, Premier Nikita, 48–9
Khuraybah Pass, 170
Knott, Lieutenant R, 212
Korean War, 261
Kuwait, 12, 32, 288, 292

Lahej state, 27, 130, 168, 254
Lahej, Sultan of: early Aden
settlement, 2; death of Sultan;
and Federation, 21–2; threatened
by Federation, 24–5; tribal
disputes, 29; exile, 72; as
Minister, 235; palace, 266
Lake Lines, 239–40
Lambe, Lieutenant Shaun, 169, 193
Lawson, Lieutenant-Colonel Richard,
233
Leckie, Major B, 121
Ledger, David, 185–6, 277
Le Fanu, Admiral Michael, 235, 243,
253, 270, 289
Le Gallais, Sir Richard, 263
Leng, Lieutenant-Colonel Peter, 211
Lennox, Corporal G, 187
Lennox-Boyd, Rt Hon. Alan, 22
Liddell, Lance Corporal T, 244
Limburg, 297
Linfoot, Major, 96
Lingham, Sergeant Reg, 100, 102
Little, Tom, 54, 122
Little Aden, 4, 8, 12, 134, 149, 157, 189,
206, 279
Littlewood, Rachel, 206–7

Lower Aulaqi state, 22, 275
Lower Yafa state, 22, 110, 130–1, 271
Luce, Sir William, 22
Lunn, Peter, 53
Lunt, Brigadier James, 27, 74, 80–1, 84
Lunt, 2nd Lieutenant R, 80

Ma'alla, 4, 125, 144, 185, 187, 189, 209,
    222, 261, 270, 280, 285
Mackawee, Abdul, 148–150, 182, 220,
    224–6, 286
Madram, Abdul, 264
Magdala, battle of, 4
Mahra state, 30, 195–6
Maidan Square, 250, 259, 264
Malaya Campaign: sultanates, 4–5;
    independence, 31; and SAS, 56,
    99; use of helicopters, 81; Maj-
    Gen. Cubbon, 94; and SIS, 120;
    local support, 129; Federation,
    132; and Special Branch, 141, 146;
    lessons, 173; 1 PWO, 213;
    comparisons, 288
Malcolm, Major Bryan, 244, 266
Malcolm, John, 127
Malin, Flight-Lieutenant David, 173–5
Malta, 166
Marib, 60, 85, 201
Marine Road, 243, 247, 255, 265
Marnham, J, 165–6
Martin, Flight-Lieutenant S, 251–2,
    254
McCarthy, Donal, 21, 35, 148, 235, 273,
    289
McCullin, Don, 203
MacDonald, A, 277
McGarel-Groves, Lieutenant-Colonel
    Robin, 157
McGregor, Robert, 44
McIntosh, Rifleman, 192
Mackay, Major I, 266
Maclean, Donald
McLean, Lieutenant-Colonel Billy, 52,
    54–5, 57, 62, 158–9, 196, 201, 277
MacMillan, General Sir Gordon, 294
MacMillan, Rt Hon. Harold:
    government, 15; formation of
    Fed., 22, 36; and Philby, 47;

Cuban crisis, 49; Yemen war, 61;
    use of journalists, 204
MacMillan, Maurice, 54
Maugham, R, 154
MECAS, 122, 154–5
Mechtel, W, 278
Meir, Golda, 54
Meynell, Godfrey, 76, 87, 152–3, 291,
    296–7
Meynell, Honor, 152
Mitchell, Lieutenant-Colonel Colin,
    background, 221; arrives in
    Aden, 231; relations with GOC,
    232; eve of mutiny, 240;
    identifying bodies, 260; IS duties,
    261; re-entry plan, 262, 265; re-
    entry Crater, 266; Armed Police,
    268–9; Part I Order, 269; with Le
    Fanu, 270; threat of disbandment,
    294; publications, 294–5
Mokha, 2
Mollet, Guy, 13
Monasir, Brigadier-General Kassim,
    167
Moncur, Major John, 244, 247, 250,
    254, 259, 268
Monk, Major John, 96
Monkhouse, Bob, 208
Monks Field Camp, 107, 193
Moores, Private J, 244
Morgan, Lieutenant-Colonel Dai, 34,
    280
Morocco, 160
Morris, J, 201
Mort, 2nd Lieutenant Simon, 33, 170,
    290–1
Mossman, James, 47
Mountbatten, Lord Louis, 76, 107, 225
Muflahi state, 271
Mukalla, 30, 192, 195–6, 228, 274
Mukeiras, 131, 156, 169, 224, 254
Musaymir, 212
Myrtle, Major A, 214

Naji, Mohammed, 219
Najran, 62
Napier, Sir Robert, 4
Nash, James, 152, 154

Nasir, Ali, 296
Nasr, Said, 72–3
Nasser, Gamel Abdel, takes power, 11; and US, 13; Suez, 15; intelligence, 45; destabilises Jordan, 50; Yemen war, xviii, 45, 59, 62, 158–9; cancels peace talks, 166–7; Harib Incident, 88; Radio Cairo, 120; journalists, 122; US relations, 231; and Israel, 197, 227, 231, 255; FLOSY, 210
Nasser, Naib, 273
National Liberation Front (NLF), formation, 72, 85; cell structure, 73, 84, 186; socialism, 74; Radfan, 76–7, 82, 84; tactics, 94, 170–1; recruitment, 93; sanctuaries, 110; propaganda, 121; 1964 operations, 130; PSP, 131; Aden Special Branch, 136, 141–2; 1st Congress, 148; 1965 operations, 151; assassination policy, 148, 153, 228, 278; OLOS, 176; agents, 184; Fort Morbut, 185; grenadiers, 192; night operations, 193; EAP, 195–6; industrial unrest, 205, 228–9; radical breakaway, 210; PORF killings, 220; bomb plot, 220–1; fight with FLOSY, 222; infiltrates police, 234; role in June mutiny, 240, 245, 247, 255, 262–4; success upcountry, 255, 271–3; attacks on Army and High Commission, 270–1; SAA infiltration, 273, 287; boards boats, 274; and HMG, 287; shift to Marxism, 291
National Security Agency (NSA), 127
National Service, 14
Nigerian Civil War, 292
Northern Ireland, 290, 295
'Nutcracker', Operation, 79–84, 93, 96
Nyerere, Julius, 132

Oates, Thomas, 270
O'Bryan Tear, Hubert, 46, 125
Observation Posts (OP), 192
Oman, actions 1958–9, 16; Sultan's forces, 56; rebellion, 98; terrorists, 196; air force, 292
Organisation for the Liberation of the Occupied South (OLOS), 148, 176
Ormerod, Major, 59
Ormsby-Gore, Katherine, 54
Ormsby-Gore, David, 49, 54, 86
Orr, Lance Corporal W, 269
Orwin, Lieutenant P, 171
Owen, Peter, 145, 251, 259, 262–3

Paddy's Field, 107
Paget, Lieutenant-Colonel Julian, xix, 254
Palestine, xix, 10, 13–14, 59, 141, 261, 264, 288
Pankhinia, S, 228
Pearman, Major M, 146
Pell, Sergeant F, 156
People's Democratic Republic of Yemen (PDRY), 296
People's Front for the Liberation of Palestine (PFLP), 296
People's Socialist Party (PSP), 26, 48, 72, 78, 131, 148
Philby, Kim, 47, 53, 155, 201, 225
Philby, St John, 8, 47
Poison gas, 62, 201
Police Forces,
   Aden Civil Police, 234
   Aden Special Branch, 141–6, 153, 184, 187, 293
   Armed Police, 144, 234, 243–5, 247, 250–2, 254–5, 259, 262–3, 265–6, 269
   South Arabian Police (SAP), 234, 240–2, 255
Political officers, 27, 151–3
Popular Organisation of Revolutionary Forces (PORF), 210, 220, 263–4, 271, 274, 277–8,
Prendergast, John, 146, 293
Price, Brigadier-General Charles, 5
Protectorates, history, 4, 7,
   WAP, 21–2, 30, 32, 78, 195
   EAP, 9, 13, 21–4, 30, 32, 166, 195–6, 223, 228, 275
Proudlock, Lieutenant M, 156

Pusineli, N, 150, 261

Qadhi, Abdullah, 228
Qadhi, Ali, 176
Qat, 25, 74, 181
Qataba, 74, 110, 117–18, 129
Qu'aiti state, 30, 195, 228, 274
Qudeishi, 108
Queen Arwa Road, 243–5, 247–8, 250–2, 255, 265
Quishn, 196

Radfan, terrain and camp, 74–7, 156, 202–3, 240
Radio Cairo, 11–12, 77–8, 84, 120, 126, 153, 195–6, 204, 231
Radio Sana'a, 58, 72, 77–8, 84, 88, 120, 126, 158
Radio Taiz, 117
Rais, F, 277
Ranft, Marine Peter, 34
Ras Marshag, 265–6
Rastgeldi, Dr, 186–7
Red Cross Clinic, 206
Reilly, Sir Bernard, 6, 9
Rennie, John, 120
'Rice Bowl', 97
Riddell-Webster, Lieutenant-Colonel D, 191–2
Riddick, Lieutenant, 248–9
Rimington, Stella, 149–50
Rippon, Angela, 205
Roberts, Jenny, 206
Robson, Pipe-Major K, 266
Roe, Rev Robin, 242
Rose, Bill, xvii
Rose, Derek, xvii, 122, 152–5, 277
Royal Air Force: British policy, xviii; air power, 6–7; proscription bombing, 7, 30, 58, 77; Central Reserve, 14; shell expenditure, 110; role of BASOs, 81; role of FACs, 105, 174; hospital, 259–60; threat to states, 272–5; Falklands War, 290
  Air Forces Middle East (AFME), 31 Squadrons,
    8 Sqn, 7, 10, 31, 79, 88

10 Sqn, 10
26 Sqn, 79, 81
37 Sqn, 31, 97
43(F) Sqn, 79, 88, 97, 101, 173–6, 275
78 Sqn, 31, 97–8
84 Sqn, 31, 98, 208–9, 211, 270, 275
208 Sqn, 31, 79, 84, 97, 101, 275
233 Sqn, 31, 98
621 Sqn, 9
RAF Police, 176, 234–5
Royal Marines:
  42 Commando, 33, 280
  45 Commando:
    Kuwait, 32–4; arrives S. Arabia, 32; composition, 34–5; Dhala convoy, 34; at little Aden, 48; on standby, 80; Africa, 96; Radforce, 96–7, 102–5; withdraws from Radfan, 109; Shab Tem, 118; accidents, 149; return to Radfan, 157; weapons and tactics, 171–2; in Tawahi, 183; street cordons, 189; Mahra operation, 196; journalists, 205; Ops around Crater, 259, 265; evacuation, 280; trickle drafts, 288
      X Coy, 97, 102–3, 108–9
      Y Coy, 97, 102–3
      Z Coy, 97, 102, 104
Royal Navy: FOME, 32; Navy Task Force, 278–80; after independence, 239
Royal Naval Air Service:
  815 Sqn, 81
  Search and Rescue, 96
Russell, Corporal Charles, 184, 190
'Rustrum', Operation, 83

Sackville-West, Vita, 8
Sada, 60
Sadat, Anwar, 48–9, 59
Said, Sultan, 196
Saleh, President Ali, 297–8
Saleh, Sultan, 166, 168, 273
Salih, Sultan, 228
Sallal, Colonel Abdullah, origins, 42–4;

coup, 46; character, 48; and recognition of YAR, 58; plot to kill Ahmed, 45; as President, 49; illness, 71; Moscow visit, 86; returns to Yemen, 197, leaves YAR, 276

Sana'a, 46, 61, 71, 73, 86, 197, 203, 219

'Sand Fly', 103–5

Sandys, Rt Hon. Duncan, 14, 35, 57, 63, 87, 131

Saud, Ibn, 12, 289

Saudi Arabia, geography, 8; Omani rebels, 16; and Nasser, 45; Kim Philby, 47; pressure on US, 50, 231; Yemen, 50–3, 59, 62; British aid, 128–9; Egypt, 290; air force, 61–2, 79, 174; takes in Sharif, 272

Schmidt, Dana Adams, 47, 201

Scrubber Line, 176–7

Secombe, Harry, 208

Seedaseer Lines, 253

Shab Tem, 100, 118

Shackleton, Lord, 224–6

Sha'ib state 130

Shamshir, Mohamed, 202

Sharpe, Major John, 212

Shaw, 2nd Lieutenant John, 244, 249–50

Sheba, Queen of, 1

Sheikh Othman, early settlement, 4, 8; Jews attacked, 10; Special Branch in, 141–4; 'Scrubber Line', 176; weapons cache, 182; patrols 189; SAS units, 191; assassinations in, 219; police station, 212–13; Paras in, 228–9, 274, 277

Shell, 154

Shewan, Major A, 265

Shipman, J, 195

Shu'aybi, 59

Sidey, Air Commodore E, 135

Sidey, Gillian, 135

Silent Valley Cemetery, 1, 160, 203, 260–1, 285, 295, 297

Singapore, 31, 35

Singapore Lines, 247

Sirah Island, 266

Six-Day War, 229–31, 264, 289–90

Slim, Lieutenant-Colonel J, 223

Smiley, Colonel David, 16; with SOE, 54; Sultan of Oman, 57; mercenaries, 58; royalists, 61; returns to London, 79; ambushes, 85; with Cooper, 127; Royalist caves, 159, 167; contract ends, 168; casualties, 276; returns to Yemen, 297

Smythe, Fusilier C, 249

Socotra, 30, 196

South Arabian Army (formerly FRA): Formation, 233; security, 234; colonels suspended, 235; NLF infiltrate, 239; upcountry threat, 253; mutiny, 254; tribal rivalries, 255; British re-entry into Crater, 263; hand-over, 271; fail to support Fed., 272–5; declares for NLF, 278

South Arabian League, 24, 36, 72, 220

Soviet Union, Cold War, xviii, 54; threat to Europe, 10; approaches al-Badr, 15; Cuban crisis, 48–9; CIA, 50; KGB, 47, 71; aid to Yemen, 42–4, 160, 227; Yemen War, 85–6, 232; world opinion, 119; and PDRY, 296

Sowrey, Air Commodore F, 253

Spencer, T, 203

Stagg, Major A, 83

Stark, Freya, 8, 119

Starling, Major Joe, 212

State of Emergency, 78

Steamer Point, 4, 9, 32, 123, 134, 147, 151, 185

Stephens, 2nd Lieutenant N, 249

Stevens, Lieutenant-Colonel P, 97, 102, 157

Stewart, Fusilier E, 249

Stewart-Richardson, Major P, 176

Stirling, Colonel David, 55–6

Stookey, Robert, 71

Storey, Fusilier John, 244–5, 247, 250–2

Straughan, Fusilier, 249

Stuart, S, 124, 221

Sudan, 2, 225

Suez, 4, 9, 11–14, 21, 31, 81, 120–1
Sukarno, President, 50
Supreme Court, 243–4
Sutton, Len, 145
Syria, and UAR, 15; against King Hussein, 16; and Egypt, 45; against Israel, 227; Six-Day War, 230

Taiz, 41–2, 47, 49, 59, 72–3, 110, 148, 224
Tanganyika, 14, 106, 132
Tasker, Sergeant, 102
Tawahi, 144, 177, 183, 185, 192, 209, 214, 224, 229, 271, 277
Taylor, Teddy, 295
Television International Enterprises, 56
Temple Cliffs, 244, 247
Theison, Captain J, 277
Thesiger, Wilfred, 8, 196
Thomas, Bertram, 8, 154
Thomas, Lance Corporal Ahmed, 185
Thomas, Lieutenant-Colonel Sandy, 22, 29, 32, 76
Thompson, Sir Robert, 129, 173
Thomson, Lieutenant David, 261, 266
Thomson, Rt Hon. George, 25, 225
Thorneycroft, Rt Hon. Peter, 158
Thumier, 77, 80, 83, 94, 96, 99–103, 117
Tillotson, Major Michael, 213–14
Tower, Major-General Philip, 227–8, 232, 240, 253, 261–2, 268–9, 295
Trevaskis, Sir Kennedy, formation of Fed., 21; and al-Asnag, 25; career, 62; Yemen War, 56; assassination attempt, 78, 131, 148, 225; Radfan Campaign, 77, 119; and Lunt, 80; Harib Incident, 87; Dhala Road, 94; press, 202; removal, 132; political officers, 151–2; last efforts, 277
Trevelyan, Sir Humphrey, Ambassador to Cairo, 13; at BP, 206; replaces Turnbull, 226; agrees not to re-enter Crater,

261–2; on RAF threats, 272–3; on al-Asnag, 275
Tribes, Tribal Guards, 8; and Fed., 21–6; character, 27–8; feuds, 29–30, 289; face, 28, 289; Qateibi tribe, 74–7, 84; Red Wolves, 82, 109; respect for, 193; Dathini tribe, 234; Aulaqi tribe, 235, 272; failure to support Fed., 272;
Troeller, G, 201
Trucial Omani Scouts, 16, 292
Turkish Army, 5–6
Turnbull, Sir Richard, 132, 142, 187, 224, 226

Uganda, 14, 146
United Arab Republic (UAR), formation, 15; tribal rulers, 21; Lahej to join, 24; collapses, 45, 59
United Nations, 36, 52, 62, 78, 88, 119, 186, 222–6
United States, and Middle East, 11; opposition to Britain, 13; intelligence, 46; mediation in Yemen, 62; in Taiz, 118; policy on Yemen, 160, 222; 'War on Terror', 297–8
Upper Aulaqi state, 22, 24
Upper Yafa state, 74
USS Cole, 297
Uthaiman family, 210

Verrier, Anthony, 128, 201
Vietnam War, 110, 166, 173, 204, 222, 288, 292, 298

Wade, Major P, 268
Wadi Boran, 97
Wadi Dhubsan, 107–10
Wadi Misrah, 77, 108–9
Wadi Rabwa, 77, 81–2, 97–8, 100–2, 130, 157
Wadi Taym, 77, 83–4, 97, 100, 104, 107, 111, 130
Wadi Tramare, 109
Waggit, Bob, 142
Wahad, Abdul, 46–7
Wahidi state, 22, 30, 210, 272, 275

Waldegrave, Lord, xix

Walsh, Lieutenant-Colonel M, 228, 274

Walters, Major Peter, 104

Warburton, Trooper N, 100–2, 117–18

Ward-Booth, Major A, 108

Waterloo Lines, 231, 244, 249

Watkins, Lieutenant-Colonel Bryan, 107

Watson, Lieutenant-Colonel Roy, 97

Watts, Major J, 171

Wazir, K, 206

White, Sir Dick, 55, 79, 126

Wigg, Rt Hon. George, 118

Wilkes, Ruth, 221

Willoughby, Major-General Sir John, 157–8, 227, 292

Wilson, Rt Hon. Harold, 132, 159, 187, 287

Wilson, Marine, 109

Wilton, John, 154, 228

Wiltshire, Arthur, 146

Womersley, Denis, 55

Woodhouse, Colonel John, 55, 99

Wyllie, Fusilier B, 244

Yafai, Abdullah, 259

Yafai, Sultan of, 291

Yemen: history and conflict with Britain, 1–16, 30, 41–2; defections to, 24; Federation, 24; immigrants from, 25; Soviet Union, 42; Nasser destabilises, 44–5; geography, 42, 60; army, 45; coup, xviii, 46–52, 63; McLean and Smiley, 53–5, 127–8, 167–8, 196–7, 276–7; 'picnic disaster', 59; YAR troops, 61; NLF, 73; relations with US, 86, 222, 231; and Six-Day War, 231–2; British intelligence, 46–7, 53, 55, 78–9, 125–6; Harib incident, 87–8; sanctuaries, 72–3, 110; 'heads incident, 117–19; radio range, 120; casualties, 127; Prime Minister, 127–8; Civil War, 57–63, 85–8, 158–60, 196–7, 296–7; journalists in, 201, 204; executions, 219; against Egypt, 275–6; and 'War on Terror', 298

Young, 2nd Lieutenant A, 240–1

Young, Robin, 87, 152, 154

Younghusband, General Sir George, 6

Zaydi sect, 2, 24